The FBI and Religion

The FBI and Religion

Faith and National Security before and after 9/11

EDITED BY
Sylvester A. Johnson and Steven Weitzman

UNIVERSITY OF CALIFORNIA PRESS

University of California Press, one of the most distinguished university presses in the United States, enriches lives around the world by advancing scholarship in the humanities, social sciences, and natural sciences. Its activities are supported by the UC Press Foundation and by philanthropic contributions from individuals and institutions. For more information, visit www.ucpress.edu.

University of California Press
Oakland, California

Library of Congress Cataloging-in-Publication Data

Names: Johnson, Sylvester A., editor, author. | Weitzman, Steven, editor, author.
Title: The FBI and religion : faith and national security before and after 9/11 / edited by Sylvester A. Johnson and Steven Weitzman.
Description: Oakland, California : University of California Press, [2016] | Includes index.
Identifiers: LCCN 2016025507| ISBN 9780520287273 (cloth : alk. paper) | ISBN 9780520287280 (pbk.) | ISBN 9780520962422 (ebook)
Subjects: LCSH: United States. Federal Bureau of Investigation. | Law enforcement—United States—Religious aspects. | Religion and law—United States.
Classification: LCC HV8144.F43 F264 2016 | DDC 363.250973—dc23
LC record available at https://lccn.loc.gov/2016025507

Manufactured in the United States of America

25 24 23 22 21 20 19 18 17 16
10 9 8 7 6 5 4 3 2 1

Contents

Illustrations

Acknowledgments

This book shares something in common with both the FBI and the religious communities that it has encountered over the decades: it is a collaborative effort, a project that has involved many people. Our goal was to produce a book much more cohesive than a typical edited volume, and to tell a fairly continuous story from the beginning of the FBI to the present. This required more patience and flexibility from our contributors than is typical. We want to express our gratitude to the scholars who have contributed to this volume, both for their essays and for their continued commitment as we worked to create an integrated whole. They responded quickly to deadlines, honored every request for revision, and never complained despite the pesky queries we kept sending their way. It has been a rewarding pleasure to coauthor with them.

Each of us also has separate debts that we want to acknowledge. The FBI, American religion, security studies—all these topics represent a very significant departure from the sort of research Weitzman normally pursues (ancient Jewish Studies), and his first foray into the subject was only a few years ago, an essay published in the *Journal of the American Academy of Religion* ("Religious Studies and the FBI: Adventures in Academic Interventionism," *JAAR* 81 [2013]: 959–95, which forms the basis of his contribution in this volume). As he made his way into a new topic, he benefited immensely from conversations with several people, including Gregory Saathoff, Jean Rosenfeld, Eugene Gallagher, Nike Carstarphan, Steve Herrick, Bruce Lawrence, Kathryn Lofton, Shazhad

Bashir, Holly Folk, Michael Barkun, Catherine Wessinger, and Kathryn Gin-Lum (the latter three represented in this volume). For the colleagues who suppressed laughter when he told them that he was working on this project, he will not name names, but he is grateful to them too.

As our introduction makes clear, Weitzman also learned a lot from one of his students at Stanford, Sharia Mayfield. He is grateful to her for sharing her own experience, not to mention that she was a terrific student, and he hopes this book makes some small contribution to overcoming the problems that created such turmoil for her family. As in everything he does, Weitzman is also indebted to his wife, Mira Wasserman, and his four children, Yosef, Hillel, Lev, and Na'or.

Sylvester Johnson's gratitude extends to numerous colleagues and supporters as well. The faculty and graduate students in the Department of African American Studies, the Department of Religious Studies, and the Center for African American History at Northwestern University provided generous feedback on an early version of the chapter on the Moorish Science Temple of America during a campus colloquium. Johnson is especially grateful for the written feedback and extended conversations provided by Martha Biondi, Nitasha Sharma, Robert Orsi, William Caldwell, Jeffrey Wheatley, Matthew Smith, and Aram Sarkisian. In addition, Edward Curtis IV has been a longtime friend and intellectual colleague who has enriched Johnson's work on this subject in many ways. Johnson also extends warm gratitude to the Weinberg College of Arts and Sciences for helping to fund assistance with research, editing, and indexing. Thanks are due as well to the Religious Studies Department of Stanford University for hosting a colloquium to discuss the book project.

Countless friends and colleagues have encouraged us to pursue this project upon hearing about it. Thinking about the relationship between religion and the FBI is not exactly second nature to most scholars of religion, and we were initially uncertain of just what the reception to this project might be. So it has been especially gratifying to see this book come to fruition and to intersect with a broad range of interests. Most of all, the unmatched support of Heather Nicholson, Ayanna Efiom, and Rainah Johnson have buoyed Johnson's work on this project since its inception, and he remains forever grateful.

No undertaking like this can succeed without efficient and skilled assistance. Jeremy Rehwaldt's attentive editing and careful fact-checking of the manuscript has been essential. The assistance provided by Niomi Patel and Aanchal Saxena was also important in communicating with contributing authors and preparing the manuscript for production.

We feel privileged to have worked with our editor at the University of California Press, Eric Schmidt: his enthusiasm and supportiveness were outstanding, and we can only hope we get an opportunity to work with him again. His assistant, Maeve Cornell-Taylor, was the consummate professional—diligent, patient, and always helpful. We are deeply thankful to them both. We are also both grateful to the anonymous reviewers of the book for their encouragement and excellent recommendations for improving the manuscript. Finally, as every author knows, no manuscript becomes a book without the skilled work of the production team, and we express to them our deep thanks as well for helping to bring this project to completion, especially Jessica Ling and Cindy Fulton for overseeing the production process; Steven Baker for his expert copyediting; Lia Tjandra for designing the cover; and Jen Burton for producing the index, to mention those we know by name.

INTRODUCTION

"True Faith and Allegiance"—Religion and the FBI

SYLVESTER A. JOHNSON AND STEVEN WEITZMAN

> I do solemnly swear that I will support and defend the Constitution of the United States against all enemies, foreign and domestic; that I will bear true faith and allegiance to the same, that I take this obligation freely, without any mental reservation or purpose of evasion; and that I will well and faithfully discharge the duties of the office on which I am about to enter. So help me God.
>
> —FBI oath of office

In September 2011, just days following the tenth anniversary of 9/11, U.S. news agencies published recently used FBI training documents meant to prepare field agents to surveil Muslims as part of the FBI's counterterrorism program. The documents included instructional presentations that cast Muhammad, the prophetic founder of Islam, as a "cult leader," described the Islamic practice of giving charity as a "funding mechanism for combat," and featured a graph that charted how, over the centuries, followers of the Jewish and Christian Bible had grown less violent while followers of the Qur'an did not (overlooking events like the Crusades and the Holocaust).[1] For defenders of religious and civil liberties in the United States, the material was shocking in its claim that even mainstream American Muslims were prone to be terrorists or terrorist sympathizers.

The FBI itself was quick to disavow this material when it became public, stating on its website that the material "does not reflect the views of the FBI and is not consistent with the overall instruction provided to

FBI personnel," and in 2012, it purged its antiterrorism training curricula of elements determined by an undisclosed group of "Subject Matter Experts" to be offensive to Muslims. This kind of hostile mischaracterization of a whole religious community was not a blip on an otherwise clean record, however, and it did not come out of nowhere. Rather, it developed from the FBI's long, often tortuous relationship not just with Islam but with religion in general.

As early as 1917, in fact, the bureau began to target religious communities during wartime in an effort to unearth internal enemies, though in this earlier era the focus was not Muslims but members of a Christian community: certain congregations of the Church of God in Christ suspected by the FBI of fostering anti-Americanism. In the 1930s, the FBI became suspicious of an African American Muslim community known as the Moorish Science Temple of America (MSTA), eventually recruiting operatives to infiltrate the group by posing as prospective converts. This strategy proved a harbinger of the bureau's relationship in the 1950s with the Nation of Islam, which it also sought to penetrate and disrupt from within. In more recent decades, the FBI has found itself investigating or in conflict with religious communities that cover the gamut of American religious life, from White supremacist churches to the Southern Christian Leadership Conference (SCLC) under the leadership of Martin Luther King Jr., and from pacifist Catholic priests opposed to the Vietnam War to the Branch Davidians, who believed their conflict with the FBI was prophesied in the Book of Revelation. Muslims are not the first religious community to find themselves under suspicion, nor the first to have their religious claims interpreted as a cover for criminal behavior or terrorism.

The FBI's engagement with religion is worthy of investigation because it bears directly on important questions about state security, the separation of church and state, civil liberties, the history of race relations and racialization, and the treatment of political dissent. The experience of 9/11 and its aftermath gave some of these questions new force, but the nation has been struggling with them for practically the entire history of the FBI, and certainly during the tenure of its most famous director, J. Edgar Hoover, who led the bureau from 1924 to 1972 and who, in his effort to combat communism and other alleged threats, targeted a number of religious leaders and organizations for investigation and in some cases harassment or arrest. This book is an effort to think in a more comprehensive way about the FBI's century-long engagement with religion and to understand the history of its interactions and conflicts with specific communities and leaders.

Beyond its impact on governance, law enforcement, and civil liberties, the FBI's interaction with various religious communities is also fascinating for what it reveals about the history of religion in the United States. Although it acts on behalf of a secular state and is legally restricted by the First Amendment, the FBI has proven itself to be a significant religious actor, and sometimes intentionally so. At times it treats religious leaders or communities as criminals and enemies, but at other times the FBI has sought to align itself with religion, to protect religious communities, and to recruit them as allies in its war against those identified as a threat to the public order or to democracy.

There is no better example of the FBI's role in American religion than the religious interventions of Hoover himself. A former Sunday school teacher, Hoover (or perhaps we should say those who authored the works published under his name) had a lot to say about religion: he cast his war against communism not just as an effort to preserve the American way of life but as a crusade to defend religion itself against a godless atheism bent on religion's destruction. In *Masters of Deceit,* a best-selling work published under Hoover's name that was once required reading in some schools, Hoover argued that despite their tolerance and respect for dissent and the constitutional separation of church and state, Americans should not lose sight of the fact that Western civilization was rooted in religious values and that belief in a supreme being was the source of democracy and its faith in humanity. Communism, by contrast, was supposedly rooted in an atheistic materialism inexorably opposed to religion. Communism claimed to be secular and scientific, but, in reality, it was its own kind of religion, according to Hoover, a false religion driven by a perverse messianic zeal. This threat was difficult to recognize, he claimed, because communism dissembled under the guise of religion, infiltrating churches in order to gain respectability, reach the youth, and enlist clergy as a front for communist objectives. Hoover used his influence to promulgate a particular conception of religion, one that not only rendered progressive and pacifist Christians highly suspect but also distinguished left-leaning Jews from Judaism, and differentiated between authentic and mongrelized forms of Islam. Under his direction, the FBI at once defended the United States and policed the borders between true and false religion.

As may be seen over the course of this book, Hoover's efforts had a significant effect. His FBI invested a lot of time, resources, and energy defending the country from subversives whose religious motives he questioned. His targets included "holy outlaws," such as the priest Daniel

Berrigan, pursued by the FBI during the Vietnam War era for his antidraft activities, and also religious leaders never accused of crimes, such as Father Robert F. Drinan, SJ, the first priest elected to Congress, and Rabbi Abraham Joshua Heschel, investigated by the FBI because of his connections to the civil rights movement. As Dianne Kirby argues in chapter 4, the effort to discredit antiwar and other religious activists helped to fragment mainstream Protestantism and to set the stage for the emergence of the religious right (though it too was targeted by the FBI). As Douglas Charles suggests, the FBI's activities, shaped by Hoover's religious and moral views, also recast homosexuality as a national security issue that required federal intervention. We are not suggesting that Hoover's FBI is singularly responsible for the religious-moral-political landscape of American society in the final decades of the twentieth century, but we would argue that it was one of the forces that shaped that landscape.

The era that followed Hoover's death in 1972 brought many organizational and cultural changes to the FBI, but the bureau has continued to play an influential role in American religious life at both the individual and the collective level. The current FBI does not play the same highly visible moralizing role that Hoover assumed for himself, but it still comes into conflict with religious communities now and then, as tragically illustrated by the standoff with the Branch Davidians in 1993 and by more recent tensions with the American Muslim community. Some of these conflicts have had much broader repercussions. For example, the Oklahoma City bombing in 1995, which killed 168 people, occurred on the second anniversary of the fire that destroyed the Branch Davidian compound and may have been motivated by the perception that the federal government was unfairly targeting unpopular religious groups.[2] The belief that the federal government was engaging in the persecution of religious communities reflected paranoid conspiracy thinking limited to a specific subset of people, but, especially since 9/11, reports of the profiling and surveillance of Muslims by the FBI do give one reason to worry about the bureau unjustly profiling religious individuals when their faith is associated with a security threat.

An ordeal suffered by Sharia Mayfield, a student Weitzman taught when he was at Stanford, brought this subject home to us. Sharia's father, Brandon Mayfield, is an attorney, and he and his family are Muslim. In March 2004, terrorists launched coordinated bombings against the Madrid train system, an act that killed 191 people. Mayfield lived in far-off Oregon, but the FBI connected him to the bombing through an apparent match with fingerprints found on a plastic bag used to cover the detonator for one of the bombs. Seeking more evidence but not wanting to tip Mayfield off, the FBI sought authorization from the secret Foreign Intelligence Surveillance Court, which allowed agents to place listening devices in the Mayfield home and in Brandon's law office; to search through drawers, closets, and computers; and even to take DNA samples from his wife's cigarettes. Sharia recalls a period of acute anxiety and confusion as her family began to suspect, while being unable to figure out what was going on, that someone was sneaking into their house and tampering with things.[3]

When the media began to inquire about a possible suspect, the FBI became concerned that its investigation was about to become public and thus moved quickly to secure a warrant in order to detain Mayfield as a material witness. Its affidavits, it is now clear, included misleading and false information, even mentioning Sharia's Spanish homework as evidence of a connection to Spain. On May 6, 2004, her father was arrested and imprisoned, and things seemed headed toward a trial in which he would have to defend himself against what seemed incontestable scientific evidence. What saved him was the intervention of the Spanish police, who had contested the FBI's fingerprint match from the very beginning and then finally undercut the FBI's case by announcing that the prints pointed to an Algerian named Ouhnane Daoud. The errors were so egregious that the FBI admitted that its identification of Mayfield had been mistaken, and it acknowledged for the first time that it had used a secret search warrant to copy and seize material, including DNA. Seeking to avoid a lawsuit that could undercut the constitutionality of its actions, the government agreed to pay $2 million in restitution to the Mayfields and issued a (rare) public apology. For his part, Mayfield, having refused to give up his right to challenge the constitutionality of the law that had expanded the government's power to investigate suspected terrorists, secured a court ruling that recognized two provisions of the USA Patriot Act as unconstitutional (though an appellate court later nullified that ruling, effectively restoring the constitutionality of these provisions).[4]

Aside from the lessons this story holds about the unreliability of fingerprint evidence and about the proper legal response to terrorism, it also reveals how, decades after Hoover's persecution of clergy he deemed subversive, the FBI can still be led astray by religious bias. "Not only does my detention as a material witness to the Madrid bombing underscore the fallacy that fingerprint identification is reliable," Mayfield observed in a news release after reaching his settlement with the government; "I hope the public remembers that the U.S. government targeted me and my family because of our Muslim religion." Mayfield's suspicion that he was targeted for being Muslim was at least partially supported by a Department of Justice inspector general's report in 2006 which found that while Mayfield's religion was not known to the fingerprint examiners at the time they made the match, it may have been a factor in the FBI's failure to revisit the identification or to recognize its mistake after questions about the match were raised.[5]

Apart from the problem of continued religious profiling, the contemporary FBI has acted in other ways that raise questions about its approach to religion. The FBI today may not exert the broader cultural influence that it did in Hoover's heyday, but it continues outreach and educational efforts that can influence how the public perceives and interacts with religious people, and some of those efforts can perpetuate bias.

In November 2015, for example, the *New York Times* reported that the FBI was launching a new educational tool, an interactive computer program meant to train teachers and students to prevent young people from being drawn into violent extremism. The program, called "Don't Be a Puppet," features a sequence of games and tips meant to help the viewer identify someone being recruited to an extremist ideology. While the FBI sought advice from religious and community leaders, the program has raised strong objections from Muslim and other religious and civil rights leaders who note that it focuses mostly on Islamic extremism and exaggerates the threat that such extremism poses to schools (especially in comparison to gun violence). "The program is based on flawed theories of radicalization," noted counterterrorism expert Arjun Sethi, who was invited to give feedback on the program; "[it assumes] that individuals radicalize in the exact same way and it's entirely discernible. But it's not, and the FBI is basically asking teachers and students to suss these things out."[6] In the wake of this and other public criticisms, the FBI suspended the program for several months, but it was not to be deterred and has recently relaunched a new version of the website (see https://cve.fbi.gov/home.html), which while careful to emphasize the FBI's respect for religious liberty, operates according to the same theory of radicalization that alarmed critics such as Sethi and might still encourage teens to profile their Muslim peers.

This kind of initiative is not unprecedented in the history of the FBI, as it echoes earlier educational efforts during the Hoover era to counter the threat of communism. Hoover's FBI also sought to enlist the public in its effort to counter enemy indoctrination: it too released educational materials to thwart communist recruitment, and it also used a new technology—

the film industry—to shape public opinion. Whether we are dealing here with an ingrained institutional habit is unclear, but the "Don't be a Puppet" episode shows that, decades after the Cold War, the FBI continues to see it as part of its role to counter the indoctrination efforts of a dangerous but hard-to-recognize enemy (and this despite a 9/11 Commission recommendation in March 2015 asserting that the FBI is not an appropriate vehicle for producing prevention programs to oppose violent extremism), which means in turn that there is continued risk that such efforts will perpetuate discrimination against religious minorities, just as Hoover's educational efforts led to the targeting of Jews, Catholic dissidents, and others deemed puppets of an insidious foe.[7]

The persistence of these issues is reason enough to look more carefully into the FBI's relationship with religion—how officials and agents learn about religious communities, what preconceptions they bring to their interactions with religious individuals and communities, how the bureau balances its investigatory and enforcement goals with the obligation to respect civil liberties, and what can be learned from past mistakes and misdeeds. We come to this subject, however, not as experts in law enforcement but as scholars of religion, and our goal in this volume is to understand the FBI as part of the history of religion. What do past interactions between the FBI and various religious communities tell us about the relationship between church and state—not just in a legal sense but as that relation actually unfolds in moments of crisis? How has the influence of religious ideas, values, and biases inflected the government's treatment of African Americans, Jews, Muslims, Mormons, gay men, and other groups? In what ways has religion influenced government discourse, ideas, and practices, and, conversely, in what ways have religious discourses, ideas, and practices been influenced by the government? We address all of these questions in the following chapters.

At an even broader level, by focusing on the relationship between religion and the FBI, this book seeks to contribute to an understanding of how secularism and religion have shaped each other. In recent decades, scholars of religion have come to rethink the categories of secularity and religion, attending to how their relationship to each other in American culture is constantly being traversed, contested, and revised. The FBI is such an illuminating case study from the perspective of this larger interest because its duties require it to move back and forth between the two realms, to operate outside religion yet also to negotiate with it, investigate it, infiltrate it, combat it, defend it, co-opt it, emulate it, and treat it as an ally.[8] We would by no means collapse the distinction between the FBI and religion—this book is born of our respect for the First Amendment and its separation of church and state—but the history recounted here shows that they cannot be neatly distinguished from each other, that the government in the form of the FBI has infiltrated religious life in the United States (both literally and metaphorically), and that American religion has likewise infiltrated the culture of government.

This book is the first sustained attempt to investigate the religious dimensions of the FBI's history, but we hasten to note important precedents to which we are indebted for information and guidance. A monograph by Steve Rosswurm investigates the FBI's relationship to the Catholic Church. There are many important studies of the FBI's treatment of Martin Luther King Jr., as well as its standoff with Branch Davidians and other fateful episodes. In addition, voluminous and important scholarship explores the history of the FBI in general, its treatment of African Americans and other minorities, the biography of Hoover, the role of the FBI in the Cold War, and other topics directly germane to the subject. The chapters in this book uncover facts and insights that go beyond this previous scholarship, however, and this book as a whole is an effort to draw the threads together by framing specific episodes and conflicts within a larger historical and cultural context, probing the intersections of race and religion in the FBI's relationship to African Americans and other groups, and recasting what is usually treated as security studies as a part of the history of American religion.

Because our own scholarly abilities by themselves did not suffice for such an undertaking, we enlisted a range of scholars from a variety of subfields—specialists in FBI and U.S. history, but also experts in African American religion, the Cold War, new religious movements, American Jewish culture, Islam, and other topics. The essays ask different questions, are written in different styles, and employ different approaches, but we have endeavored to integrate their contributions into a narrative that takes the story from the beginning of the FBI to the present moment, from the Civil War and the Gilded Age to the Waco standoff, 9/11, and its aftermath.

A survey of histories of the FBI—works such as Rhodri Jeffreys-Jones's *The FBI: A History* and Tim Weiner's *Enemies: A History of the FBI*—reveals that there are many ways to recount the history of the FBI and many ways to partition that history into discrete periods.[9] The following chapters are organized in roughly chronological order and fall loosely into three major periods: (1) the decades leading up to the moment when the FBI was first established and began to develop practices and objectives that would shape its interaction with religious communities; (2) the era of the Cold War and the civil rights movement, the era of Hoover and Martin Luther King Jr., wherein religion played a central role in the war against communism and in efforts to quell dissent against U.S. government policy; and (3) the era since the end of the Cold War, a period shaped by Watergate and increased cynicism toward the federal government, by the Jonestown massacre and other events that fueled the public's fear of "cults," by the Reagan era and the rise of the religious right, and most recently, by 9/11 and the War against Terror.

The book begins with chapters by Kathryn Gin Lum, Lerone Martin, Theodore Kornweibel Jr., and Sylvester Johnson (1–3), meant to illumine the situation prior to World War II, the period when the FBI itself came into being and when some of the patterns in its interaction with religious communities began to take shape. Already in this period the bureau was suspicious of religious pacifism, developing an antagonistic relationship not just with communists but with groups that challenged the economic status quo by defending the interests of the poor and working class. During this time, the White middle-class background of agents was conditioning their interaction with African Americans and other minorities. The bureau was even conducting social-moral campaigns inherited from still-earlier religiously motivated reform movements.

Moving into the period after World War II (chapters 4–8), the book delves into the most legendary, and infamous, period of the FBI's history—the age of Hoover, the Cold War, McCarthyism, and the civil rights movement. The Cold War, as Dianne Kirby, Jonathan Herzog, and other scholars have recently shown, had an important religious dimension.[10] Kirby, in fact, describes the Cold War as one of history's great religious wars. Not only was communism associated with godlessness and the persecution of religion, after all, but Christianity played a central role in anticommunist propaganda and church leaders were in the front ranks of Cold Warriors. The chapters in this section of the book—by Kirby, Michael McVicar, Regin Schmidt, and Sarah Imhoff—bear out this thesis by investigating the FBI's role in the religious dimensions of the Cold War, including the religious rhetoric of Hoover himself, the FBI's efforts to stigmatize religious leaders it deemed subversive, its alliances with various religious leaders, and its complex and ambivalent relationship to Jews. Kirby's overview of the period is followed by studies that focus on specific religious communities: McVicar's essay focuses on the FBI's efforts to infiltrate fundamentalist and evangelical religious groups, and how those groups in turn emulated some of the practices of the FBI. Schmidt's contribution shifts the focus from Protestantism to Catholicism, tracing the development of an alliance between the FBI and the institutionalized Catholic Church over the course of World War II and the early Cold War. Imhoff's essay brings Jews into the picture by trying to account for the seeming contradiction between the FBI's treatment of Jews as likely communists and its representation of Judaism as a natural ally in democracy's war against communism.

Together, these studies confirm the thesis that the Cold War represents a major transformative moment in the history of American religion and that the FBI played an important role as a catalyst for some of the changes. The FBI's persecution of religious leaders it thought of as subversive was one factor that reshaped the organization and internal dynamics of both Protestant and Catholic groups. Another factor was the rhetoric produced by the FBI, often published under Hoover's name, which had a major impact on how Americans defined the difference between authentic and inauthentic religion, on the relationship between religion and the left, and on the public's attitude toward sexual behavior. Douglas Charles's contribution rounds out the section on the Cold War by focusing on the FBI's public relations and educational arm. Charles illustrates the FBI's influence on the public's conception of morality by exploring how Hoover's FBI framed its persecution of homosexuality as part of an effort to preserve the moral character of the nation, an effort that treated gay men as a public enemy and that deployed against them some of the same tactics used against communism.

Another major development during the Hoover era was the rise of the civil rights and Black Power movements. Rooted in organized social activism, both movements challenged fundamental structures of anti-Black racism that ranged from legal apartheid to the state murder of unarmed Blacks that typically occurred through policing of African American neighborhoods. The political aims and strategies of Black liberationists also extended to U.S. foreign policy, including critiques of U.S. colonialist practice in the Third World, and revealed connections between structural poverty within the United States and the expansion of the nation's global military infrastructure. The FBI viewed these developments as constituting a massive "Negro rebellion," and Hoover identified Martin Luther King Jr. in particular as its de facto leader, placing the organization that he led, the Southern Christian Leadership Conference (SCLC), in the bureau's sites as a domestic security threat. By 1967, in fact, the agency concluded that King was the single most dangerous Black person in the United States, though that did not stop it from also seeing other Black religious leaders, particularly el-Hajj Malik el-Shabazz (Malcolm X) and Elijah Muhammad of the Nation of Islam, as major threats as well.

These issues are taken up in the chapters 9 and 10, by Karl Evanzz and Sylvester Johnson. Johnson explains how the bureau succeeded in disrupting the SCLC's efforts to transform racial power during the final years of King's life, culminating in the increasing criminalization of civil rights activists and causing King to wonder whether the SCLC should abandon its Poor People's Campaign given the violence erupting during protests as a result of the FBI's counterintelligence practices. Focusing on the FBI's relationship with the Nation of Islam, Evanzz describes the circumstances under which the FBI infiltrated this Muslim group to counter the aims of its leader Elijah Muhammad and the influence of its chief minister, Malcolm X, whose charismatic sermons and speeches targeted the role of racial Whiteness in fatal violence against non-Whites in the United States and in poor, non-Western countries. Both chapters elucidate how a growing relationship between the bureau and local police departments was integral to criminalizing these religious movements and the public activism they inspired.

It would be a mistake to infer from these chapters that the bureau's relationship with America's religious groups has been consistently hostile. The relationship between the FBI and Mormonism is a fascinating example in that regard. Although in the nineteenth century Mormons found themselves at odds with the federal government, over the twentieth century that relationship changed as Mormons sought integration into American culture and aligned themselves with civic virtues like patriotism, treating it not just as a political duty but as a religious act. Mormon efforts to align the church with the government proved so successful that, by the 1980s, a federal organization like the CIA could look to the Mormon community as a natural recruiting ground for agents.

In chapter 11, Matthew Bowman follows the developing relationship between the FBI and Mormons during the latter half of the twentieth century, and he notes an interesting turn in this relationship during the 1980s. By this period, the Reagan era, Mormons were seen not only as exemplary Americans but also as exceptionally loyal and morally disciplined and thus uniquely fit for intelligence service. Over the course of the 1970s and 1980s, however—as the public's perception of the federal government changed—Mormon association with the government backfired, contributing to a reemerging suspicion of Mormons in popular culture. The public image of the federal government and Mormons developed in parallel ways, both becoming objects of conspiracy thinking and cynicism, and Bowman's analysis suggest the two developments are not unrelated, reflecting the very association between Mormonism and the government that Mormons themselves had worked to foster. Focusing on the FBI, Bowman's analysis traces this shift in ways that help to explain the end of the religious alliance that Hoover had worked so hard to cultivate during the Cold War.

Chapters 12–15 focus on the FBI's history since the end of the Hoover era, and especially since the 1990s. The FBI's institutional culture was greatly affected by the fallout from the Watergate scandal and by subsequent institutional and cultural changes—including the Senate investigations led by Frank Church in 1975, which exposed problematic intelligence-gathering efforts by the FBI, including Hoover's decade-long effort to discredit Martin Luther King Jr.; the issuance of new guidelines that have since been revised several times; the growth of drug trafficking; spying scandals like that associated with Robert Hanson; advances in digital and information technology and the concomitant rise of cybercrime, and other changes—but it was also affected by developments in the larger religious culture. During the 1970s and 1980s, especially after the Jonestown massacre in 1978 (which involved the death of more than nine hundred members of a utopian religious community known as the People's Temple), many Americans felt menaced by a new threat, the "cult"—a term used to describe religious groups seen to be deviant or sinister—and they associated such organizations with kidnapping and brainwashing (a concept inherited from Cold War fears of communist mind control). More recently, the 9/11 attacks carried out by Al-Qaeda, the terrorist organization founded by Osama bin Laden in the late 1980s, refocused the government's attention on militant Islam as a major threat to national security. The FBI was called to defend against both threats, and that effort is the focus of the book's final chapters.

Two events in particular loom large in this section: the standoff with the Branch Davidians in 1993 and, of course, 9/11 and its aftermath. The first event involved a fifty-one-day siege of the Branch Davidians' compound, the Mount Carmel Center Ranch near Waco, Texas, that culminated on April 19, 1993, with an FBI assault that left seventy-six people dead, including twenty children, two pregnant women, and the group's leader, David Koresh. The Branch Davidians split from the Seventh-day Adventist Church in 1955, but in popular imagination, the media, and the minds of some of those offering advice to the FBI during the siege, they were a cult. What happened during that conflict, including the FBI's role, has always been controversial, and the chapter by Catherine Wessinger offers a revisionist interpretation of the standoff in light of evidence not taken into account in official reviews of the FBI's conduct, which mostly exonerated the bureau.

The 9/11 attack is perhaps too familiar to many readers to require recounting since we are still living in its shadow. Its impact on the FBI's mission and organization—and its implications for the FBI's interactions with the American Muslim community—are recounted by Michael Barkun, a political scientist who has written extensively on religion and violence and whose contacts with the FBI go back to the period of the Waco siege. As he notes, 9/11 forced the FBI to change its mission: beyond investigating crimes and apprehending criminals, it was now charged with preventing terrorist attacks, a preemptive role that required it to intensify its intelligence-gathering efforts. This was the period in which the FBI conducted its surveillance of the Mayfields, and Barkun's essay helps to fill in the context in which such actions happened.

Barkun also rounds out a series of chapters devoted to the Islamic community. In addition to being organized chronologically, the book also focuses on different religious communities—Protestants, Catholics, and other Christian groups, but also smaller or more marginalized groups such as Mormons and Jews.[11] In part because Muslim Americans have been the focus of so much attention since 9/11, however, we have included several chapters on Islam, which, collectively, tell a story that goes back to the very beginnings of the FBI and is continuing into the present.

In e-mail correspondence with us, Michal Barkun recalled a meeting he had in 2006 with two dozen or so terrorism analysts. What struck him about the experience was that the analysts admitted knowing little about Islam. What makes their ignorance all the more surprising is that the FBI has such a long history with Muslims, going back to the 1930s and its effort to surveil and infiltrate the Moorish Science Temple of America, an African American Muslim organization formally organized by Timothy Drew in 1926. Sylvester Johnson tells the story of this effort, showing how the FBI's repression of the Moorish Science Temple intensified during enforcement of the Selective Service Act in the Second World War and extended to harassment as the bureau deepened its response to the group's antiracist theology and its creation of collective farms to enable Black entrepreneurship and economic independence. Evanzz's chapter, drawing on his research into Elijah Muhammad, continues this history through the Nation of Islam. More recent dimensions of the FBI's relationship to American Muslims emerge in Junaid Rana's chapter on the FBI's attempts to prosecute an American Muslim who had immigrated from Pakistan to the United States—a history which suggests that a century-long pattern of Islamophobia and the racialization of Islam continues into the Obama era.

This brings us to the present moment and the future of the FBI's interaction with religious communities. We intend this book for a broad readership—for general readers as well as for fellow scholars—and one of the audiences we hope to reach is the FBI itself, which in recent decades has shown a disposition to learn from academia, to the point of reaching out for expertise to the American Academy of Religion, the nation's largest organization devoted to the academic study of religion. We hope to encourage such engagement, but we must acknowledge that it has had limited impact so far, and we think that calls for some self-reflection, not just from the FBI but from scholars of religion who think they have something to teach the FBI. Has the expertise of scholars of religion been as helpful as they expected or would like it to be, and if not, why not?

The effort to develop communication between the FBI and scholars of religion raises other questions as well. In the past decade, scholars have found themselves in difficult situations that expose the ethical challenges of working with the government. In recent years, for example, there have been sharp and important debates about whether it is appropriate for anthropologists to work with the military in Afghanistan and Iraq or for psychiatrists to abet the government in its efforts to coerce information from detainees. Part of the problem is that the government does not always use scholarly expertise in intellectually sound or ethical ways, but there is another side to this issue as well: sometimes the FBI has gone astray by relying too much on questionable sources and pseudo-experts—cult deprogrammers or antiterrorism experts—who can perpetuate misinformation about the religious communities they claim to know so much about. Undertaking a book like this has compelled us to think not just about the FBI but also about the roles and responsibilities of scholarship itself as part of the interaction between the government and religion, an issue we address in the final chapter.

Investigating the FBI's history is fraught with challenge. By its very nature, the FBI is a secretive organization. It is also extremely complex and multilayered, and it is difficult to penetrate into thinking and decisions that are not part of the public record. It is also very difficult to maintain an objective stance about the FBI's behavior: one should not naively accept its self-representation, but, on the other hand, suspicion of the FBI—mirroring a broader suspicion of the federal government that has taken root under the influence of the Vietnam War, Watergate, and the war against terror—can also skew interpretation. Factoring in religion, an always-elusive subject that scholars are still struggling to define and understand, only magnifies the complexity of the subject. And yet, as we think the following chapters demonstrate, one cannot understand the FBI without factoring in religion. Religion has shaped the attitude, rhetoric, and behavior of its leaders and agents, and religious bias has intersected with racism and economic disparity in shaping the FBI's role as a defender of the public order. We cannot claim to have treated the subject in a definitive way, but we hope this volume opens up new lines of research and new discussions about how the FBI relates to religious communities, treats issues of religious liberty, and approaches religiously motivated dissent.

We begin this introduction by quoting the oath taken by new agent trainees in the FBI on their first day of instruction at the FBI academy and repeated during their graduation ceremony. We did so for two reasons. First, the oath makes clear that the primary responsibility of the FBI is to defend the Constitution of the United States against all enemies foreign and domestic. What is at stake in the history of the FBI's interaction with religious communities is, of course, the First Amendment, its protection of religious liberty and freedom of protest, and if we focus on how the government has transgressed this boundary, that is because we hope, in our way, to also defend it.

But that brings us to the second reason we begin with the oath. As the reader is likely to have discerned, the oath itself is suffused with religious language: "I will bear *true faith* and allegiance. . . . I will well and *faithfully* discharge the duties of the office . . . *so help me God.*" The FBI is woven into the history of American religion, and religion, as the oath illustrates, is woven into the culture of the FBI, though sometimes in ways that those who administer and take this oath do not intend or recognize. While we are unsettled by the dark side of the FBI's treatment of religious communities—the attempts at delegitimization and co-optation, the periods of persecution and moments of conflict—we think it a simplification to treat the FBI and religion as inherent antagonists or even as clearly distinguishable actors: the FBI is suffused by religious influence, enters into relationships with religious actors and has aligned itself with religious values. The First Amendment establishes a boundary that we honor and certainly want to sustain, but religious life as it actually plays out does not always stay within the boundaries we would impose on it. Sometimes, it is not so easy to distinguish the religious from the secular. Sometimes, like it or not, a government meant to be distinct from religion can become a part of religion. We find the blurring of that boundary threatening, but we also find it fascinating, and we are grateful to the contributors to this volume for helping us tell the story of how the FBI's transgression of it has helped to shape American religious history.

1

American Religion and the Rise of Internal Security

A Prologue

KATHRYN GIN LUM AND LERONE A. MARTIN

THE OFFICIAL ORIGIN STORY

The sanctioned history of the birth of the Bureau of Investigation (renamed the Federal Bureau of Investigation in 1935) is tightly tied to the Progressive Era. The bureau was officially created in 1908 as the brainchild of Attorney General (AG) Charles Bonaparte and President Theodore Roosevelt. The president and his AG appointee, the bureau's official history notes, "were 'Progressives.' They shared the conviction that efficiency and expertise, not political connections, should determine who could best serve in government." Their "progressive" notions posited that "government intervention was necessary to produce justice in an industrial society," and thus they "looked to 'experts' in all phases of industry and government to produce that just society."[1]

When Roosevelt and Bonaparte took their respective offices, the investigation of federal crimes did not reflect a wholesale and permanent commitment to proficiency and professionalism. From its creation on July 1, 1870, the U.S. Department of Justice (DOJ) did not have its own detectives or investigative force. Rather, U.S. attorneys—when not laden with court proceedings—investigated crimes, interviewed witnesses, and collected evidence themselves. When the work of an "expert" investigator seemed warranted, the DOJ utilized two strategies. First, the AG had a small team of special-assignment agents as well as accountants. Second, the DOJ possessed a small discretionary fund for hiring detectives from private agencies (usually the Pinkerton Detective Agency) and skilled operatives from other agencies, namely the Treasury Department's Secret Service.[2]

Congress put a stop to both policies. In 1892, in response to the use of Pinkerton agents as strikebreakers, the legislature outlawed the DOJ and other federal agencies from hiring persons employed in the private sector. Contracting with the Secret Service came to an end on May 27, 1908, when it was discovered that the DOJ hired Secret Service agents to investigate and later convict two U.S. congressmen. Congress believed that such activities not only posed a threat to American democracy but also reeked of totalitarianism. An alarmed legislative branch warned that the executive branch must be stopped from "employing secret service men to dig up the private scandals of men."[3]

A seemingly powerless and exasperated Bonaparte petitioned Congress twice for funding to employ his own investigative force. True to his Progressivism, he argued that it was "absolutely necessary" for the DOJ to have a "continuous" team of professional detectives hired by and dedicated to the DOJ. Hiring investigators on short-term contracts was inefficient at best, haphazard at worst. He testified before Congress, "You must remember that the class of men who do not work as a profession is one you have to employ with a good deal of caution." Nevertheless, Congress denied his request both times.[4]

A savvy Bonaparte, however, went beyond Congress. On June 29, 1908, during the summer congressional recess, the AG used the DOJ's "miscellaneous expense fund" to hire ten former Secret Service agents as DOJ employees. The following month, on July 26, 1908, Bonaparte increased the number of agents to thirty-four and appointed Stanley Finch the chief examiner of the squadron. Finch was charged with leading the modern investigative force. "This action," the bureau's official history marks, "is celebrated as the beginning of the FBI."[5]

In January 1909, the president and AG convinced Congress that the AG's actions during the recess had been justified. As both elected officials prepared to leave office in March of that year, they pleaded that a fixed detective force at the DOJ was an absolute necessity for the efficient and professional enforcement of federal laws. Congress accepted the recommendation and adopted the caveat that the DOJ's skilled agents would not carry guns or be empowered to make arrests. Rather, they would be limited to the mission of the DOJ: "the detection and prosecution of crimes against the United States." On March 16, 1909, AG George Wickersham, Bonaparte's successor, dubbed the DOJ's detective squad the Bureau of Investigation, and changed the title of chief examiner to chief of the Bureau of Investigation. The bureau was officially born.[6]

This origin story suggests that the Federal Bureau of Investigation's roots extend back only as far as the Progressive Era. The story of the FBI typically continues with the influence of J. Edgar Hoover, the bureau's longest-serving director, whose fingerprints on the bureau remain to this day. Under Hoover's twentieth-century leadership, which began in 1924 during the "return to normalcy era," the bureau engaged in its most notorious activities. Hoover's leadership yielded the voracious pursuit of alleged subversives during the Cold War—surveillance and counterintelligence aimed at socialist and communist political organizations, civil rights reformers, student activists, and Vietnam War protesters, among many others. Such activities have forever shaded the history of the FBI. Indeed, the name of the FBI headquarters is the J. Edgar Hoover FBI Building. The shadow of the twentieth century thus looms large over the FBI.

However, the FBI was also shaped by and took deeper root in the religious landscape of the nineteenth-century United States. To be sure, twentieth-century developments gave way to the "official" birth and expansion of the FBI. Nevertheless, detailing how the DOJ hired Secret Service agents to investigate the competing civil religions of the postbellum era offers much-needed perspective on the bureau's origins. Moreover, examining the cultural milieu of the broader nineteenth century—particularly the themes of the aftermath of emancipation, industrialization, and immigration, in addition to Progressive reform—gives further context for the storied and enduring relationship between religion in America and the FBI.

COMPETING CIVIL RELIGIONS

The competing civil religions that emerged following the Civil War threatened the internal security of the nation and spurred the initial steps that would ultimately lead to the establishment of the Federal Bureau of Investigation. The massive bloodshed of the Civil War, in the words of historian Harry Stout, "taught Americans that they really were a Union." He continues: "Something mystical and religious was taking place through the sheer blood sacrifice generated by the battles."[7] Stout and others have pointed to the Civil War as a watershed moment in the creation of an American civil religion, when the state became a unifying object of worship for a bitterly divided citizenry. A nation arose from the "altar of sacrifice," and Americans ceased to refer to the nation as *these* United States—a loosely bound federation of largely independent regions—and began referring to the country as *the* United States—a singular, unitary entity. In the years after the Civil War, this sacralized nation-state greatly expanded its borders, bureaucratized its government, consolidated its security measures, and broadened its ambitions overseas.

But alongside all these developments came another, an alternative civic religion that competed with the federal government for the allegiance of Americans: the religion of the Lost Cause. The religion of the Lost Cause grew from the antebellum South's sense of itself as distinct from the North—as a chivalric society based on the assumption that hierarchy was the natural order of things and that Southerners were the true keepers of Puritan piety. It flourished after the war, as Southerners, including ministers, lionized Confederate soldiers as crusading Christians fighting against infidel Yankees. Just as Christian tradition posits God's eventual triumph after an initial age of trials and tribulations, so the religion of the Lost Cause held that Southern victory would eventually come to pass despite the defeat and humiliation imposed by the Civil War. The Confederates might have lost the battle, but by staying faithful through the trials of the subsequent age, they would ultimately prevail and reassert themselves. As Charles Reagan Wilson puts it, "The idea that Confederate defeat was a form of discipline from God, preparing Southerners for the future, was fundamental to the belief in ultimate vindication."[8]

But Lost Cause devotees were not content simply to sit back and wait for "ultimate vindication": they also threw themselves into the defense of White supremacy after the war's end. Another component of the Lost Cause was the juxtaposition of supposedly familial and gracious Southern planter paternalism against grasping, unscrupulous northern Yankees, who after the Civil War were not content to leave the defeated South alone. Of course that was a fiction—the South was every bit as capitalistic as the North, if not more so—but the Lost Cause religion spun an image of the Yankee as an alien of questionable White identity or foreign origin because of the North's association with immigration, and maliciously motivated. Both sides had of course demonized each other during the war, and their mutual vilification laid the groundwork for the competing civil religions that emerged in its aftermath.[9] Defenders of the Lost Cause fought tooth and nail against Radical Reconstructionists, who would allow them back into the fold only when satisfied that they were submitting to the Republicans' demand for racial justice.

The Ku Klux Klan emerged as one of the most visible signs of the religion of the Lost Cause. In 1866, in Pulaski, Tennessee, six Confederate-veteran college students organized in order to "play 'pranks' on the residents of Pulaski and uplift the spirits of the war-torn region."[10] Their "pranks" understandably intimidated the region's newly freed slaves and Northern "carpetbaggers." Emboldened, the group soon organized more "clubs" to spread this climate of terror, adopting a costume meant to invoke "the ghosts of the Confederate dead"—"tall conical witches' hats of white cloth over cardboard" that "exaggerated the height of the wearer, adding anywhere from eighteen inches to two feet to his stature." By the spring of 1867, this group of Ku Klux Klansmen, as they became known, had morphed from a prankster club to a "paramilitary movement" bent on defending White supremacy by any means.[11] By 1868, the same year as the ratification of the Fourteenth Amendment, the Klan had spread to nine Southern states. The religion of the Lost Cause had its Knights Templar in the crusade against Reconstruction.

The federal government responded to this internal security crisis by creating agencies to secure and defend the newly reconstituted nation. In 1870, the Department of Justice (DOJ) was established to assist the attorney general in "the detection and prosecution of crimes against the United States."[12] Among its most important duties was to ensure compliance with the three Enforcement Acts passed by Congress in 1870 and 1871. These laws were aimed at stopping the Klan's racial and sexual violence against African Americans and their White allies by ensuring the safety and the vote of the largely Republican freedmen. The laws made it a federal crime to interfere with or infringe on the right to vote, established a procedure for federal supervision of registration and voting, and authorized the military to enforce such laws. Under the Enforcement Acts, White terrorism was deemed an insurrectionary act, and the DOJ designated the leader of the KKK as the greatest internal security threat to the nation.[13]

The newly established Justice Department, lacking its own bureaucracy, relied on U.S. Marshals and borrowed Secret Service agents from the Treasury Department—both versed in undercover work—to investigate and provide intelligence. The crew of federal investigators focused on uncovering plans and actions that violated the Enforcement Acts, but in a broader sense their role was to enforce fidelity to the civil religion of the union. To this end, the assembled team constituted the nation's first federal antiterrorist intelligence program. Its directives against the Klan and White terror yielded one of the largest investigations in American history, leading to hearings that lasted for several months and produced thirteen volumes of firsthand testimony from both White and Black citizens. Federal grand juries, in turn, issued more than three thousand indictments. The results of its efforts were mixed, however. An underfunded DOJ, a ballooning case volume, and a wavering commitment to racial equality led the Grant administration to implement a policy of leniency against racial terrorists. Nearly two thousand cases were dropped, and in the summer of 1873 a newly reelected President Grant released from jail all those who had been convicted of White terrorism. In all, the large-scale investigation netted about six hundred convictions, with only sixty-five receiving federal prison sentences of up to five years.[14]

Despite the outcome of their extensive investigation of the KKK, the DOJ and its host of "borrowed" investigators learned a lesson that would also be taken to heart by the Federal Bureau of Investigation many decades later—that religion, in this case the religion of the Lost Cause, could be dangerously subversive, a motive for the commission of "crimes against the United States."

EMERGING AFRICAN AMERICAN AUTONOMY

The bureau's approach to religion was influenced not only by the religion of the Lost Cause but also by another trend that took shape in the final decades of the nineteenth century—an ethos of self-determinism and institution building among African Americans.

In the midst of the reign of White terrorism, the Supreme Court's decision in *Plessy v. Ferguson* in 1896 made "separate but equal" the law of the land. Clergy, race leaders, teachers, business owners, and Black citizens alike debated what the future of their race would and should be in a legally segregated America, and how Blacks should relate to a White American culture. One position in this debate called for greater Black autonomy. Two years after the *Plessy v. Ferguson* decision, W. E. B. Du Bois advocated that, to achieve their "destiny," Blacks should not aspire to "absorption" by White America or to the "servile imitation of Anglo-Saxon culture." Rather, Du Bois maintained, the future of African Americans rested on a "stalwart" commitment to "Negro ideals." African Americans, he argued, had a "duty" to conserve their gifts and "spiritual ideals" and to dedicate them to the establishment of race unity and race organizations inspired by "the Divine faith of our black mothers." The creation of a Black parallel society, Du Bois proffered, was not a capitulation to race prejudice and segregation. Rather, Black organizations would provide African Americans the opportunity and means for racial progress, even as they provided shelter from and criticism of White supremacist thinking.[15] Du Bois, it turns out, was articulating a religiously inflected aspiration to achieve self-determination embraced by many other African Americans.

To be sure, Whites who felt threatened by emerging Black autonomy were forceful in defending themselves. Almost 2,000 African Americans were lynched between 1877 and 1899, with 104 meeting this fate in 1898 alone. But African Americans made great strides in creating independent organizations for themselves, and religion played a seminal role in this process. Dating back to colonial America, independent African American churches were among the earliest Black organizations to be established, and this form of self-organization exploded following the Civil War, giving birth to the two kinds of Black institutions that would go on to transform Black life and the relationship of African Americans to the nation-state: independent religious denominations and schools, the latter often initiated by churches. These institutions not only offered Black citizens a measure of autonomy but also constituted the foundation of Black civic life.[16]

The Colored Methodist Episcopal Church in America (CME) was the first independent Black denomination founded following the Civil War. The CME was founded in 1870 in Jackson, Tennessee (in 1954 it was renamed the Christian Methodist Episcopal Church in America). Born out of the desire for self-determination among African Americans in the Methodist Episcopal Church South, the denomination was a response to that church's desire to separate from its formerly enslaved members. Thus, for example, in South Carolina, Black membership in Southern Methodist churches declined from 42,469 in 1860 to 653 in 1873, while, conversely, the nascent Colored Methodist Episcopal Church had a membership exceeding 100,000 by 1890. Similarly, Black Baptists also expressed a strong desire for autonomy following the Civil War. In 1858, South Carolina's Southern Baptist Black membership numbered some 29,000. In 1874 there were fewer than 2,000 members. In a related trend, Black Baptist clergy grew nationally from slightly more than 5,000 in 1890 to more than 17,000 in 1906. The explosion of independent Black Baptists across the country organized into state conventions and eventually came together to form the National Baptist Convention USA in 1895 (incorporated in 1915), which remains the largest organization of African Americans.

Several Black-sanctified churches were also established around the turn of the century. The most notable of these is the Church of God in

Christ (COGIC), the focus of chapter 2, by Theodore Kornweibel Jr. Incorporated in Memphis in 1897, the COGIC remains the largest body of Black Pentecostals in America. The two independent Black denominations founded during the antebellum period also grew exponentially following the Civil War. The African Methodist Episcopal Church (AME) boasted a membership of almost half a million by 1880, while membership in the African Methodist Episcopal Zion Church (AMEZ) grew from 27,000 in 1860 to 200,000 in 1870. Both continued to flourish well into the twentieth century.[17] Of the 8.3 million African Americans in the country by 1890, 2.7 million, or about 33 percent, were church members. Fewer than forty years after emancipation, in other words, the independent Black church movement had managed to encompass a critical mass of the Black population. Black America, it seemed, was uniting and consolidating its resources under the banner of Christianity.[18]

The reach of Black denominations extended beyond church membership. For Black faith communities, Black destiny and self-determination were nothing without education. Thus, in addition to the host of Black schools founded by White missionary societies, such as Morehouse and Spelman, Black faith communities also started their own schools following the Civil War. The AMEZ Church, for example, founded Livingstone College in Salisbury, North Carolina, in 1879, while the AME Church established several schools, including Morris Brown in Atlanta in 1885. Black Baptists also established schools such as Arkansas Baptist College in Little Rock in 1884, and the CME Church founded Lane College in Jackson, Tennessee, in 1882. By 1930 the total number of Black college graduates produced in the twentieth century, largely from Black colleges, was four times greater than the number produced in the entire previous century.[19] Black America was increasingly formally educated, and this transformation was largely initiated by faith communities.

While these newly formed Black institutions were shrines of autonomy for some, for others this trend was deeply troubling, suggesting a Black race no longer content to accept second-class status and increasingly willing to challenge or break free from the status quo. Thus, in the very period when the bureau was being established, the emergence of autonomous Black religious communities came to be seen as a threat to the nation's internal security. The federal government was contending with the Klan and the insurgent civic religion of the Lost Cause, even as the South was being shaped by independent Black churches, clergy, and their respective offspring institutions. Collectively, this Black Protestant establishment amounted to the largest and most influential force in a segregated Black America, as it set the discourses, practices, morals, and ideals that governed Black political, cultural, and religious life well into the twentieth century.[20] Taking shape in the same period as the Black Protestant establishment, the nascent Bureau of Investigation would soon learn that it needed to engage Black America through its faith communities.

INDUSTRIALIZATION AND IMMIGRATION

The intersection of religion with the processes of industrialization and immigration that would reshape America in the late nineteenth and early twentieth centuries also influenced the bureau's approach to religion. The sequence of events that marked the transition from the age of Reconstruction to the age of big business—the depression of 1873, the breakdown of Radical Reconstruction, and the corrupt compromise that ushered Rutherford B. Hayes into office in 1877—turned the focus of the federal government away from enforcing civil rights toward protecting business and free enterprise. The growing conflict between labor and capital and rapid immigration from Europe threatened—or were seen to threaten—the nation's domestic security and economic well-being. The changes also had a major impact on religious life as the nation's White Protestant establishment, already feeling menaced by more autonomous African Americans, also felt threatened by Catholic immigrants. The bureau emerged in an age of economic conflict that also had a sectarian dimension, and its role was to protect a certain conception of the social-economic-religious order.

This was the so-called Gilded Age of American history, during which a veneer of prosperity masked profound social inequality and unrest. Advantaged by the support or at least the blind eye of the government, the new captains of industry—railroad magnates, steel and oil barons, real estate and retail titans—amassed capital with abandon, while the laboring classes saw no such gains. Journalists and authors armed with new flash photography brought the disparity to the broader public. Jacob Riis's articles, which later culminated in the publication of *How the Other Half Lives: Studies among the Tenements of New York* (1890), vividly described the wretched conditions of tenement housing, the lack of sewage and garbage collection that plagued workers' surroundings, and the sweatshop conditions and paltry wages of workers and laboring children.[21] The disparities between the haves and have-nots reached unprecedented levels.

As overwhelming poverty and blatant disparity pushed some to the brink of violence, the struggle between labor and capital was fought in the streets, but it also played out in debates within the church. As violent confrontations between striking workers, law enforcement, and armed militias became more common, Catholics and Protestants alike wrestled with what their faith had to say about the blessings and ravages of industrial capitalism, and advocates of both labor and capital sought religious support for their respective stances.

Thus, for example, reformers such as Nannie Helen Burroughs, Reverdy Ransom, Jane Edna Hunter, Henry Hugh Proctor, Walter Rauschenbusch, and Washington Gladden called on the church to respond to the needs of the working classes. Faith communities, they contended, needed to aggressively engage labor and the poor even as secular society needed to be Christianized. To put Christianity into practice, they argued, was to support labor unions and their collective demands (such as the eight-hour workday and child labor laws). Opponents, however, such as the Reverend David Swing, vehemently disagreed with these Social Gospellers, as they become known. "The conflict between classes in the cities of our country is not a conflict between labor and capital," Swing argued in an 1874 editorial, "but between successful and unsuccessful lives." In other words, poverty and the social unrest that threatened to tear society apart were the result of individual moral failure, not industrial capitalism. Other opponents went further, seeing the Social Gospel and its advocacy for workers and labor reform as a radical socialist-inspired takeover of the church and the nation under the guise of social Christianity. Collective bargaining, they argued, was unchristian at best, socialism and anarchy at worst.[22]

The influx of immigrants from Europe and Asia only compounded concerns about the growing chasm between the classes, and it also added another religious dimension to the extent that many of these immigrants were not Protestant. Immigrants not only threatened the economic security of those already in America but also brought with them Catholicism, atheism, and other creeds antithetical to the belief system of Protestants.

One person who held this attitude was Josiah Strong, a Protestant minister and Social Gospel proponent who cast immigration and its religious effects as a "crisis" for American identity and security. He famously warned about the perils threatening "our country" in his 1885 book of the same name: immigration, Roman Catholicism (which he saw as connected to the immigration issue), Catholic and secular influences in the public schools, Mormonism, intemperance (which he also largely blamed on immigrants), socialism, materialism, and rapid urbanization (again traceable to immigration). Strong articulated an anxiety and sense of siege felt by many Americans who identified as Anglo-Saxons. "Immigration is detrimental to popular morals," he warned, and "has a like influence upon popular intelligence. . . . [I]mmigration complicates our moral and political problems by swelling our dangerous classes."[23] Strong also articulated the backlash that such anxiety triggered. The White Anglo-Saxon was the chief representative of a "pure, spiritual Christianity," a racial-religious class with a special role in history decreed by God.[24] This class had the power to shape its own destiny and was destined to survive: "Men of this generation, from the pyramid top of opportunity on which God has set us, *we look down on forty centuries!* We stretch our hand into the future with power to mold the destinies of unborn millions. . . . Notwithstanding the great perils which threaten it, I cannot think our civilization will perish."[25] Strong sought to reassure his White Protestant readership that "its present crisis" could be reversed, but only if it seized its God-given destiny. That meant resisting the influence of Roman Catholic immigrants and others and working to imprint the Anglo-Saxon Protestant stamp on the American West and the rest of the world. For Strong, protecting the nation's Anglo-Saxon population and the integrity of its faith was the key to its domestic security. This kind of nativism developed in tandem with growing anxieties about other social problems associated with immigration. Worries about organized crime networks, for example, raised questions about who would investigate a criminal force that had overseas connections.

Charged with the role of safeguarding the nation, the Bureau of Investigation had to pursue its mission in an increasingly industrialized, economically divided, urbanized, and heterogeneous society, and the position of the DOJ and the bureau in the resulting conflicts was solidified when anarchists declared war on capitalists, sending a bomb to the tycoon John D. Rockefeller and successfully bombing the home of U.S. attorney general A. Mitchell Palmer in 1919. It was at this time, in August 1919, that a young J. Edgar Hoover, then only twenty-six, was appointed head of the bureau's General Intelligence Division, which set the stage for a massive roundup of presumed radical labor union members and anarchists, the Palmer Raids. From the perspective of the DOJ and the bureau, advocates of the labor movement and immigration, and religious leaders sympathetic to the same, were security threats, and it fell to officials like Hoover to defend against them.

PROGRESSIVE REFORM

In its role as a defender of American society, the bureau, as we have seen, also drew on the legacy of Progressive Era moral reform, influential between the 1890s and 1920s. Progressives, often motivated by strong religious beliefs, responded to the pressures of modernity and industrialization by trying to assert some control over society through self-discipline, vigorous activity, efficiency, and social and political interventions. In this they were following the example of antebellum reformers.[26] Indeed, antebellum reformers targeted many of the same issues that the reformers of the Progressive Era would address, including temperance and prostitution. While the latter reformers exhibited similar moral concerns, however, the experience of the Civil War imposed a change of tactics.[27]

The primary tactic of antebellum reformers was moral suasion, trying to convince fellow Americans that their immoral behaviors would imperil not only their own individual souls but also the welfare of the nation. They also stressed the importance of self-discipline, as when Catharine Beecher urged readers of her *Treatise on Domestic Economy* to pursue "a habit of system and order" in order to have enough time to devote to religious reflection, and minister John Todd explained to readers of his *Student's Manual* how to eat, exercise, and brush their teeth as a preparatory step in the disciplining of their hearts.[28]

After the Civil War, reformers began to back up their calls for moral self-improvement by seeking legislation—"tough purity laws," as political scientist James Morone puts it—driven by the aspiration to enforce proper moral behavior or protect against immoral behavior deemed a threat to society. For example, the politician Anthony Comstock, who founded the New York Society for the Suppression of Vice in 1873 to supervise the public's morals, induced Congress to pass the Comstock Law in the same year, which outlawed the transport and delivery of any "obscene lewd or lascivious . . . print or other publication of an indecent character or any article or thing designed . . . for the prevention of conception or procuring of abortion, nor any article or thing intended or adopted for any indecent immoral use or nature."[29] Another example is the Woman's Christian Temperance Union (WCTU), founded soon after passage of the Comstock Law. The WCTU enlisted women in fighting impurity and intemperance because "liquor turned men brutish" while "mother love" had the power to triumph over it, and it too sought legal changes in order to advance its moral agenda.[30] Frances Willard, president of the WCTU from 1879 to her death in 1898, was a supporter of women's suffrage, for instance, because she believed that women's votes would help protect the virtue of society and the sobriety of men.

Moral reformers in the late nineteenth century also tended to treat urbanization as a major threat to individual and collective well-being. This led another Social Gospeller and supporter of woman suffrage, Jane Addams, to found Hull House, a settlement house in Chicago, in 1889. The house was conceived as an "experimental effort to aid in the solution of the social and industrial problems which are engendered by the modern conditions of life in a great city."[31] Life in the big city lacked outlets for one's active impulses, and Hull House was designed as a solution to this problem. Young people "hear constantly of the great social maladjustment," she wrote, "but no way is provided for them to change it, and their uselessness hangs about them heavily. . . . These young people have had advantages of college, of European travel, and of economic study, but they are sustaining this shock of inaction."[32] Other late-nineteenth-century outlets for the malaise of White middle-class youth included the YMCA and YWCA, the muscular Christian vogue for exercise and gymnasiums, and the trend of seeking adventures in the West to prove one's mettle and manliness. Theodore Roosevelt, the president under whom the bureau was founded, embodied the ideal, a man mocked for his effete background who achieved a manly character through exercise and adventure (working as a rancher in the Dakota Territory, killing a buffalo, and so on).[33]

This era of Progressive reform, coupled with the idealization of muscular activity as a form of salvation, forms part of the background from which the Bureau of Investigation emerged and from which it developed its vaunted culture of virility, excitement, morality, purity, and discipline. Consider as an example the role of discipline in the bureau's culture. From its very inception, the bureau was supposed to be composed of highly disciplined men—and by discipline, we mean a moral discipline. In a letter to President Roosevelt half a year after the July 1908 inauguration of the bureau, AG Bonaparte acknowledged that it was difficult "recruiting a trustworthy and efficient detective force." Detectives "must have some acquaintance with the haunts and habits of criminals," Bonaparte stressed, "and its members are obliged to frequently associate with and use in their work persons of extremely low moral standards."[34] While detectives had to be conversant in immorality in order to police it, however, it was equally crucial that they have the character to avoid falling into it themselves.

To prevent his force from degenerating into "the evils which have caused, and in some measure, justified, the dislike and suspicion entertained for the profession," Bonaparte proposed that the bureau provide compensation and prestige sufficient to "render the service attractive to intelligent and courageous men of good character and adequate education." He also flagged the importance of "extremely strict discipline" in the ranks, "so that they may understand that any exhibition of insubordination or other form of official misconduct, or any serious delinquency in morals or decent behavior, will result in immediate separation of the guilty person from the force."[35] Bonaparte's concept of the ideal detective echoes the role of discipline in Progressive reform as the key to protecting the boundary between morality and immorality.

The bureau did not simply emulate the ethos of moral reform; it also continued the mission of reform. Because such moral reforms now had a legislative dimension, the newly formed bureau also addressed some of the same social ills. It was the bureau's responsibility, for example, to enforce the Comstock Law, along with the 1910 Mann Act, which outlawed the interstate transportation of women "for the purpose of prostitution or debauchery, or for any other immoral purpose." (For more on how the later FBI sought to combat sex crimes and obscenity, see chapter 8, by Douglas M. Charles.) The Mann Act, incidentally, illustrates the intersection of moral zeal, concern for the welfare of women, anxiety about the effects of urbanization, and the racism fused into some versions of Progressive reform: this law (also known as the White Slave Traffic Act) was motivated in part by a desire to protect susceptible young, single, White women who had moved to find work in cities where, among other perils, they ran the risk of entering into interracial relationships. This is how the bureau came to use the Mann Act to pursue and eventually convict Jack Johnson, the famous African American boxer, for having relationships with White women—a tragic example of how the bureau's activities advanced both the moral objectives of White Progressive reform and its biases as well.[36]

CONCLUSION

We have sketched the fraught religio-racial landscape in which the Bureau of Investigation was founded at the beginning of the twentieth century, a context that would condition its approach to religion and religious communities in later periods. In geopolitical terms, the nation was perhaps stronger than it had ever been, not only unified after vanquishing the

Confederacy but now also an international colonial power in the wake of war in Cuba and the Philippines. Still, American culture was also riven by racial, economic, and religious differences. Indeed, as the bureau's very own *The FBI: A Centennial History, 1908–2008* argues, "by 1908, the time was right for a new kind of agency to protect America."[37]

In this charged atmosphere, the bureau arose as a major effort by the federal government to establish racial, ethnic, economic, and social order. That mission led to encounters with religion: conflicts with the Klan, pro-union Social Gospellers, Black Protestant congregations, and others it deemed a threat, and alliances with those who would defend the social order or who sought to curb the moral ills of modern life. In this early period, the bureau was a tiny operation—in 1908 it had only twenty-three agents and a limited jurisdiction, and its first major field office was created only when the bureau began to enforce the Mann Act—but it was arguably already on the path that would later shape its interaction with various religious actors during the interwar period, the Cold War, the civil rights era, the Branch Davidian standoff, and the age of 9/11.

2

"If God be for you, who can be against you?"

Persecution and Vindication of the Church of God in Christ during World War I

THEODORE KORNWEIBEL, JR.

Alarms about "enemy aliens," anticapitalist labor agitators, fifth columnists, and legions of unpatriotic "slackers" stirred the anxieties and prejudices of the American public during World War I.[1] It is remarkable, then, that the arrests of southern Black clergy on charges of obstructing the war effort elicited few headlines. Although grand juries ultimately exonerated leaders of the Church of God in Christ (COGIC), before that vindication they faced vigilante mobs and government officials intent on compelling patriotism and military service. COGIC elders, like others advocating biblical convictions against war, fell victim to a serious wartime curtailment of religious expression and free speech.

The agency tasked with enforcing the draft was the Bureau of Investigation, established in 1908 and renamed the Federal Bureau of Investigation in 1935. Its earliest mission centered on enforcement of federal antitrust, land fraud, banking, naturalization, bankruptcy, and peonage laws and, in 1910, the Mann ("White Slave Traffic") Act. Aside from a Mann Act vendetta against Black boxing champion Jack Johnson, who flaunted both his superiority over White pugilists and his coterie of beautiful White women, the bureau first took notice of the Black population in 1915. Blacks were beginning to stream out of the South seeking good-paying industrial jobs, better schools, less segregation, and the right to vote. This Great Migration—involving one and a half million Blacks who fled the South between 1915 and 1929—triggered a broad bureau inquiry when congressional Democrats claimed that Republicans were plotting to entice massive numbers of pliable Blacks into northern ghettos, where they could be marched to the polls. After a nationwide investigation several months long, the allegations proved groundless. The bureau then refocused on customary matters unrelated to the Black population, until the United States entered World War I. It had neither Black agents nor insight into Black life, including its religious diversity. The agents of this era were few in number and were typically middle-class White males with some legal experience who were assigned to the regions from which they came and with which they were presumably familiar. They were thus ill-prepared by race and class to fairly or accurately understand the distinctiveness of the Church of God in Christ.

The COGIC story has a rare ironic twist, though. Despite federal persecution of the group, the legal system resisted both inflamed fears and superpatriotic passions, thus ultimately permitting, if not guaranteeing, the exercise of religious expression. This is also one of the most striking examples of a more assertive mood—fueled largely by the migration's raised expectations—growing within Black America. African Americans, acting on their religious convictions, defied the federal government by refusing to perform military service, despite broad public disapproval and the likelihood of prosecution. Unsurprisingly, some southern Whites fell back on an ancient default: for them, "outside agitators" were stirring up an otherwise happy (enslaved) population. Shades of Nat Turner.

The Church of God in Christ, scarcely two decades old, had no established pacifist doctrine at the onset of World War I. In fact, its Pentecostal theology was still in flux as it expanded beyond its Baptist origins. Its founder, Elder Charles Harrison Mason, was born in the shadow of slavery (various sources list his birth year as 1864 and 1866). His parents toiled as agricultural laborers on a succession of farms and plantations in Tennessee and Arkansas. Although Mason attended school only to the fourth grade, he did not lack for scriptural training, being well taught by his Missionary Baptist parents. Even as a child he was said to have displayed unusual spiritual understanding. In 1893, while still in his twenties, he led a revival in Preston, Arkansas, where many repented of their sins. Later that year, hoping that formal education would make him a better preacher, he enrolled in Arkansas Baptist College in Little Rock, only to leave after three months. "The Lord showed me that there was no salvation in schools and colleges."

Returning to life as an itinerant preacher, Mason's Pentecostal theology developed in stages. Salvation would come through the preaching of a twofold blessing. The first blessing was conversion—a saving knowledge of Jesus Christ through a personal relationship with Jesus. The second was sanctification—the believer's purification from all sin. To these would later be added a third blessing—baptism by the Holy Spirit—which first occurred on the Day of Pentecost as narrated in Acts 2. At that time the Spirit promised by Jesus appeared in three "supernatural extraordinary manifestations." It first materialized as a sound like a wind, even though no wind was blowing. The second manifestation was tongues of fire descending on the believers. Finally, the believers were enabled to speak intelligibly in previously unlearned languages.[2] This postconversion, experiential "third blessing" would become important as the Church of God in Christ's Pentecostal distinctiveness was refined in its first two decades.

Capitalizing on this added blessing, Mason and three like-minded preachers planted the seeds of a new Pentecostal movement while conducting a revival in Jackson, Mississippi, in 1896. Great numbers were "converted, sanctified, and healed by the power of faith," but the theophanic aspects—particularly speaking in tongues and healing—were too demonstrative for most Baptists, whose doors subsequently closed to the evangelists. The owner of an unused cotton gin in Lexington, sixty-three miles north of Jackson, made it available for further revival meetings, and here in 1897 the first Church of God in Christ congregation was born.[3] Spiritual warfare quickly ensued. "The Devil" prompted persons unknown to fire a pistol and shotgun during a "miracle deliverance revival . . . [right] into the midst of the saints while they were shouting and praying." While some were wounded, there were no fatalities.[4]

During the early years of the twentieth century, holiness embers burst into flame in widespread corners of the world. A particularly dramatic manifestation was the interracial Azusa Street Revival in Los Angeles, led by Black evangelist Elder William J. Seymour beginning in 1906. This revival was the turning point in Mason's life. Seymour began "preaching the new doctrine of a third blessing—baptism by the Holy Ghost and fire—which empowered saints to cast out devils, heal the sick, and speak in other tongues." Soon, hundreds of Blacks and Whites, including Mason, made pilgrimages to Seymour's renovated livery stable on Azusa Street seeking the anointing of the Spirit.[5] The doctrine of a third blessing provided Mason with the missing theological piece of a Pentecostal order. Now based in Memphis, he went to Los Angeles, received the gift of tongues, and returned to spread the fire of revival. All-night meetings stretching over five weeks aroused dramatic interest in the new Pentecostal worship and belief.[6]

A leadership rift soon occurred when some elders opposed the "delusion" of speaking in tongues. Mason was disfellowshipped by several of them, but other elders kept faith with him. Charles Harrison Mason was named general overseer and chief apostle of the Church of God in Christ at its first general assembly in Memphis in 1907. Rapid growth took place in Mississippi, Tennessee, and Arkansas among rural sharecroppers and urban mill hands.[7] Expansion into Texas soon followed. Then, as Black Texans migrated to the West Coast in the 1910s, the church established itself in Southern California under the leadership of Elder E.R. Driver. It also spread eastward, with churches planted in Norfolk, Pittsburgh, Philadelphia, Detroit, and New York (in Harlem and Brooklyn). Expansion up the Mississippi Valley led to outposts in Saint Louis, Kansas City, and Chicago. Although the majority of COGIC members were still concentrated in Arkansas, Florida, Louisiana, Mississippi, Oklahoma, Tennessee, and Texas, by 1917 the burgeoning church had congregations in all the major midwestern and eastern cities that attracted Blacks during the Great Migration.[8] Despite its rapid growth, the church would have remained invisible to Whites, who likely would not have noticed new urban storefront and rural southern sanctified congregations had it not been for World War I. The war brought unanticipated challenges and attention from public authorities as well as superpatriotic vigilantes. It was the time of testing for the Church of God in Christ.

In the supercharged wartime atmosphere, patriotic organizations and public officials alike exacerbated prejudices against conscientious objectors, who were frequently accused of being enemy sympathizers. All but the most single-minded devotees of unpopular causes found it prudent to fall silent and comply with patriotic demands. Religious objectors to participation in war suffered at times draconian persecution. Neither the government nor the public was tolerant of those who believed God forbade them from rendering military service unto Caesar. Nonreligious objectors, including some Blacks, faced even greater hostility. Those who were jailed suffered worst: "The treatment of the imprisoned World War I resisters was barbaric," one historian concludes.[9] Given such an intolerant popular mood, the Church of God in Christ's leaders were fortunate to escape severe punishment. After months of intense investigation, mainly by agents of the Justice Department, two grand juries in Texas ultimately exercised unusual good sense in rejecting the arguments of federal prosecutors and ended an ill-conceived attack on an inoffensive religious sect. Little did FBI agents foresee the power of faith and prayer they would encounter in their pursuit of the COGIC.[10]

America's modern domestic intelligence bureaucracy was birthed during World War I. The Secret Service, which historically had handled such security investigations, was muscled aside by a fractious network of agencies that included the rapidly growing Bureau of Investigation, the Military Intelligence Division (MID) of the War Department, and the investigative arms of the Post Office and State Departments. In tracking down alleged German spies, draft dodgers, and other species of subversives, the bureau and the MID were assisted by more than 200,000 American Protective League "secret service" volunteers. Although these agencies deployed their operatives unevenly, they cast a broad net. Some of their actions, like apprehending draft evaders, were clearly mandated by law. But the business of catching spies, hunting subversives, and silencing dissenters rested on less certain foundations. Such pursuits were often motivated less by national security considerations and more by exaggerated fears of subversion and public demands for enthusiastic patriotism. Bureau agents and their civilian assistants were armed with presidential executive orders and the Espionage, Sedition, and Trading with the Enemy Acts. These acts' vagueness permitted federal prosecutors, who were often responding to political pressure, to define disloyalty and sedition very broadly. The civil liberties of Blacks and Whites, noncitizens and citizens, took a beating, all with the approval of the federal courts. First Amendment guarantees of protected speech and press freedoms were not yet anchored in a substantial body of case law and legal doctrine. According to constitutional historian Paul L. Murphy, "The story of civil liberties during World War I is a dreary, disturbing, and in some respects, shocking chapter out of the nation's past. Americans . . . stood by on the domestic scene and saw liberty and justice prostituted in ways more extreme and extensive than at any other time in American history."[11]

World War I generated widespread fears, at times approaching the level of hysteria, that German agents were poised to sabotage the United States, either by their own acts or by sowing dissension among the population. There were enough isolated instances of German intrigue—for example, the Black Tom explosion—to give credence to the belief that enemy agents lurked everywhere.[12] Many Whites, particularly in the South, believed that such plotters were taking deliberate pains to propagandize African Americans. Blacks, it was imagined, were easy targets for manipulation, and their grievances readily exploited. Given such a climate of alarm in the South, any unfamiliar White person living, working, or trading among Blacks, any diminution in accommodating behavior, or simply any nighttime gatherings were seen as evidence of enemy influence or disloyal intentions. Bureau agents investigated hundreds of such rumors. Actual German plots to incite Blacks to acts of treason were nonexistent, but not a few Blacks wished for German success as punishment for White racism. Some may actually have believed that a German victory would bring them economic and social equality. In the end, these phenomena produced new victims. Blacks suspected of harboring such sentiments were often arrested at the behest of bureau agents and harshly interrogated or jailed. Few Whites, and certainly only a handful in federal or local law enforcement, possessed the insight to understand that migration and war had exponentially raised Blacks' aspirations and dissatisfaction with the racial status quo. It was simpler and more comforting to believe that a diabolical enemy was subverting an otherwise contented race.

Leaders and members of COGIC drew the scrutiny of the federal government because church doctrine forbade the shedding of blood, a belief that compelled their noncompliance with the draft. The Department of Justice was responsible for enforcement of selective service regulations. U.S. attorneys prepared legal cases while the rapidly expanding Bureau of Investigation gathered evidence and apprehended nonregistrants and refusers. Constitutional liberties were often trampled, the most notorious example being the 1918 "slacker raids." Although caught in the crossfire of public intolerance and zealous enforcement of conscription, COGIC members and other religious objectors refused to disobey the scriptures. Although Elder Mason and other church members did not articulate political or racial opposition to the war or raise challenges to the racial status quo, their willingness to stand up to the government and its (White) symbols of authority is evidence of a larger willingness to abandon Bookerite accommodation and more assertively seek racial progress.[13]

By the time the United States entered the war in April 1917, millions had already died on the battlefields of Europe. Soldiers had to be conscripted quickly if the United States was to have a decisive combat role. Congress, in creating the draft, provided that only conscientious objectors who were members of religious bodies opposed to participation in war would be granted exemptions. President Wilson declared that members of "a well recognized religious sect or organization" that had a creed prohibiting military service were eligible for exemption from combat, but they still had to perform noncombatant duty. (That is, there was no provision for complete exemption or for alternative service under civilian direction.) Applicants had to convince local draft boards of the sincerity of their beliefs. In practice, the Mennonites, Quakers, Church of the Brethren, and a few smaller longtime pacifist sects were the only denominations whose pacifism was recognized without extreme difficulty. And the government demanded that even they don military uniforms and work under military discipline.[14] Hundreds who refused to cooperate were court-martialed and sentenced to long, abusive terms at maximum-security prisons such as Alcatraz and Leavenworth. Seventeen men received death sentences, though their sentences were commuted after the war. Public opinion associated conscientious objection with anticapitalist radicals and pro-German sympathizers. An assistant secretary of war admitted the public's "dislike and distrust of this small minority of Americans professing conscientious objections to warfare."[15] The public often made little distinction between conscientious objection and disloyalty: a refusal to bear arms was tantamount to treason.

The administration of the draft was compromised not only by hostile public opinion but also by bias and inconsistency on the part of draft boards. Southern boards, staffed typically by local middle- and upper-class White patriots, were ill-equipped to assess evenhandedly the claims of members of the Church of God in Christ for exemption on the basis of conscience. In general, Blacks were much more likely to be declared fit and eligible for induction than were Whites, and they were less likely to receive deferments for agricultural necessity or family support. Not surprisingly, the proportion of Black to White draft "delinquents" was more than two to one.[16]

Given such attitudes and policies, Elder Mason and members of the Church of God in Christ were guaranteed tribulation in 1917 and 1918. Despite COGIC professions of patriotism and love for country, the public misunderstood the church's stand against participation in war. Church doctrine, refined during World War I, included an unambiguous prohibition on combatant military service. Jesus Christ's teaching on the virtue of brotherly love and the sinfulness of hating others called for obedience. "We believe the shedding of human blood or taking of human life to be contrary to the teaching of our Lord and Saviour, and as a body, we are adverse to war in all its various forms." This was not the same as being sympathetic to Germany. Addressing a large baptismal gathering on June 23, 1918, Mason preached a sermon entitled

"The Kaiser in the Light of the Scriptures." The German ruler was said to be the "Beast" or Antichrist depicted in Revelation 13. Mason found scriptural approval, in Matthew 5:42, for the purchase of Liberty Bonds, and he would later claim to have raised more than $3,000 for that cause. His sermon ended in prayer not only that all peoples would beat their swords into plowshares and study war no more, but also that the "German hordes" would be driven back behind their borders.[17] But while offering such patriotic assurances, Mason still encouraged male parishioners to seek conscientious objector status.

Elder Mason first drew federal scrutiny in September 1917 when an alarmed chancery court clerk in Lexington, Mississippi, warned authorities that the Black preacher "openly advised against registration and made treasonable and seditious remarks against the United States government."[18] The Church of God in Christ had many members in Holmes County, in Mississippi's Delta region, where Blacks constituted nearly 80 percent of the population, and local Whites worried not only about meeting draft quotas but about maintaining White racial dominance and privilege.

Bureau of Investigation agent M. M. Schaumburger, whose jurisdiction included rural Mississippi and Louisiana, was assigned to verify these allegations. Interviewing indignant Whites who attended Mason's assemblies, he learned that the "negro revivalist preacher" had conducted nightly meetings during the first two weeks in August with overflow crowds of two or three thousand. Mason was said to exert as much influence over his race as did Billy Sunday among Whites, and to have amassed considerable personal wealth, including a $60,000 mansion in Memphis. Informants charged that he taught opposition to war and bloodshed while informing his members they need not register for the draft. Worse, Schaumburger learned that Mason had allegedly labeled the present conflict a rich man's war and a poor man's fight in which Blacks had no grudge against the Germans, a good people who treated Blacks better than did other Whites. Mason was said to have praised Germany so profusely that one of his fellow preachers threatened to quit the church. Schaumburger believed all this was sufficient to convict Mason of committing treason, obstructing the draft, and giving aid and comfort to the enemy, particularly since two church members had not reported for induction.[19]

Confident of prosecution, Schaumburger obtained sworn statements from members of both races. The affidavits of four members of the

(Black) Mississippi Cavalry who had attended Mason's meetings were couched, however, in such racially guarded language that they proved to be useless. Schaumburger noted ruefully, "While all the men know by reputation that Mason is a menace to the country, they are unable to furnish direct testimony."[20] Hence, on its first attempt to prosecute Mason, the government was stymied, possessing only hearsay evidence. Of course, this failure did nothing to allay the racial anxieties of local Whites or federal authorities.

The next individual to come under government suspicion was Elder E.R. Driver, overseer of COGIC churches in California and one of the denomination's founders. He was summoned to the bureau office in Los Angeles in February 1918 and accused of being "pro-German and bitter toward the Government." Driver insisted on his loyalty while defending the church's opposition to taking life, but Agent George T. Holman was skeptical of Driver's patriotism: "This colored minister is supposed to have considerable influence among a number of people of his race and his attitude is very aggressive with reference to this country's entrance into the war. . . . It would be possible for him to be of considerable menace to the country." The agent vowed to keep Driver under observation and halt his activities should they become "pronounced."[21] Such a confrontation was typical. Bureau conscription case files are replete with records of inquisitional interviews in which agents argued with suspects, assailed them with patriotic bombast, and threatened them to gain compliance with the draft.

Many southern Whites suspected that Blacks' loyalty had been subverted by "German gold." Beliefs about such dastardly deeds were seemingly confirmed by an April 1, 1917, headline in the *Vicksburg Post*: "Draft Evasion in Holmes County Due to Pro-German Teachings among Blacks." The paper reported that the state adjutant general's office, which commanded the Mississippi National Guard, had found it "virtually impossible" to persuade Lexington Blacks to comply because of Mason's allegedly pro-German sermons and advice to "resist" conscription. Investigators accepted as factual the rumor that three weeks earlier a mysterious foreigner, Dimitrius Giannokulion, had conducted a meeting at Mason's church during which he received a message in code. To anxious Whites there was no coincidence between this "information" and the allegation that Mason was "suddenly wealthy," enjoying a new brick-and-stone residence in Memphis. The situation seemed all the more sinister because in the preceding two months only a small proportion of several hundred Black registrants had reported for induction. In desperation the adjutant general published the names of seventy alleged Holmes County draft dodgers, offering a fifty-dollar reward for each one delivered to the nearest military post. The story linking Mason, Giannokulion, and draft resistance was picked up by the national wire services, which spread this fantastic tale of German intrigue across the country. Only Black newspapers, such as the *New York Age*, debunked the idea of enemy subversion through Mason's church. It called instead for an investigation of southern draft boards said to be inducting all Black registrants regardless of fitness while exempting many eligible Whites.[22]

These "revelations" prompted the Bureau of Investigation to open a new case on Elder Mason. At the same time, thanks to the patriotic tip of a local U.S. Food Administration official, the military intelligence section of the War Department was alerted to this perceived threat to preparedness. Henceforth the bureau and army officers would share information on Mason and the Church of God in Christ.[23]

Agent Harry D. Gulley found matters to be somewhat different from the reports in the excited press. Local officials in Lexington told him that the number of Black draft respondents was indeed alarmingly low but that part of the blame lay with the draft board's inefficiency and poor record keeping. Nothing was learned about Giannokulion, though Gulley heard new rumors of five suspicious foreigners—three Germans, an Englishman, and a Frenchman—who were believed to have some connection with Mason. Gulley interviewed alleged draft delinquents held in the local jail, but only one had been to Mason's church, and he denied hearing any antidraft propaganda. Hearsay that charged Mason with supporting Germany and holding secret antidraft meetings at three o'clock in the morning also surfaced. Although Gulley could substantiate nothing, he nonetheless concluded that Blacks "had evidently been admonished not to talk 'war talk.'"[24]

One church member did agree to speak with Gulley. But James Lee, one of five ordained COGIC preachers in Holmes County, insisted that neither he nor Mason had preached antidraft or antiwar messages. Gulley's only success was in obtaining several church documents, including a doctrinal statement drawn up the previous August by Mason and elders W.B. Holt (White) and E.R. Driver. This piece affirmed loyalty to all God-given institutions, including magistrates, civil laws, the Constitution, the president, and the flag, while also stating that taking life or shedding blood was contrary to the teachings of Jesus. Church members were allowed to perform any other service that did not conflict with the no-bloodshed principle. Of subsequent intense interest to the bureau was a blank petition, signed by Mason and addressed to draft boards, to be used by registrants seeking exemption based on church doctrine. Another document was an earlier doctrinal statement, written by Holt as long before as 1895, forbidding members to shed blood or bear arms.[25]

Despite the absence of specific evidence, Gulley was convinced that church leaders had induced Blacks to disobey the draft law and that doctrinal statements against war had only recently been adopted, supposedly to increase membership. Disregarding Holt's 1895 document, Gulley also warned that COGIC's recent association with White churches in the West could well be the result of German antidraft activities. Lacking even a shred of concrete evidence of such activity, Gulley urged the U.S. attorney in Jackson and bureau agents in Memphis and Los Angeles to further investigate Mason, Holt, and Driver.[26]

Ironically, by assuring townsfolk that the "menace" was being taken seriously, Gulley's investigation gave Mason temporary protection from outraged White Lexingtonians. Events elsewhere had demonstrated that when worried patriots felt no government action was forthcoming, vigilantism could easily occur. One victim of such action was Rev. Jesse Payne, a COGIC pastor in Blytheville, Arkansas, sixty miles upriver from West Memphis, who was fortunate to escape with his life on April 18, 1918. Under the headline "Negro Preacher Tarred," the *Memphis Commercial Appeal* reported that this

> pastor of the colored holly [*sic*] roller church in the southeast suburbs of this city, was given a coat of tar and feathers last night as a result of alleged seditious remarks for some months concerning the president, the war, and a white man's war.
>
> Earlier in the evening the preacher is alleged to have said something about the kaiser being as good a man as the president, and that the kaiser did not require his people to buy bonds and some one landed a solar plexus on him sending him into the ditch, from which he got up running. . . . [After being tarred and feathered, Payne] repeated the soldier's oath, and promised to talk Liberty Bonds and Red Cross to the end of his life and the end of the war.
>
> It is said his flock has shown no interest in the war work, while the negroes of other churches have been most liberal, $2,000 having been subscribed by the Methodist and Baptist churches Sunday night. This church is circulating literature which he says was sent to him by a brother preacher in Memphis, showing from Bible quotations that it is not right for Christians to fight. The literature is scattered broadcast over the country.

The newspaper concluded by editorializing that the pastor's punishment "will result in great good to demonstrate to not only blacks but some whites that it is time to get into the war work and quit talking such rot as is attributed to Payne."[27]

Bureau of Investigation personnel continued COGIC inquiries in the South and West. Mason agreed to an interview with Memphis special agent in charge W.E. McElveen, in which he claimed to have advised those who became church members after passage of the draft act to register but also to claim conscientious objector exemptions, recommending that church members should respect and obey current laws. Mason also said he sent a telegram to President Woodrow Wilson after passage of the draft act explaining the church's doctrines and offering to meet with him. Regulations concerning conscientious objection had been sent to Mason, which he claimed to have followed. Proclaiming his patriotism, Mason avowed support for Liberty Bond, war stamp, and Red Cross drives. Despite these statements and even though Mason denied any outside funding or pro-German preaching in COGIC pulpits, McElveen remained convinced of German influence in the church. Finding nothing concrete to confirm suspicions of subversion, McElveen concluded that Mason was less extreme than other religious objectors such as the Seventh-day Adventists.[28]

In light of McElveen's concerns, Mason remained under surveillance. After Mason conducted a camp meeting in late May at E.R. Driver's Los Angeles church, local "agents" of the American Protective League, the organization of more than 200,000 "secret service" volunteers, supplied the bureau with an excited report of dramatic increases in COGIC membership due, it was alleged, to members thereby receiving noncombatant status. The web of suspicion went further, with the APL reporting that several members of Driver's church were German and that other wealthy "Teutons" gave generous donations. "Fine autos quite frequently stop at the above church and their occupants are of a strong German type." And White neighbors who did not appreciate the late-night revivals reported receiving threats.[29]

By now, Bureau of Investigation headquarters in Washington was keenly monitoring the case. In the opinion of Chief A. Bruce Bielaski, enough evidence had been amassed from Mississippi, Tennessee, and California by the late spring of 1918 to warrant Mason's prosecution. Believing that "there is some special basis for complaint of pro-German activities in these sections of the country," he directed that "a strong case should be prepared in order to make a striking example of some of the alleged agitators."[30]

At this point events overtook the bureau, forcing it to guard the life of the man it suspected. Elder Mason returned to Lexington in early

June 1918, unaware of the seriousness of the antipathies of local Whites, who blamed him for an alarming decline in draft compliance. Many Black registrants had failed to appear for induction. When apprehended, they produced COGIC petitions containing religious objections to war. White residents claimed Mason had told would-be converts that "if you want to stay out of this war you must get right with God, and join my church. There is no occasion for the negroes to go to war; the Germans are the best friends the negroes have. Germany is going to whip the United States for the mistreatment accorded the negroes, if for no other reason. This is a rich man's war anyway." A lynching appeared likely, prompting the sheriff to protect Mason by arresting him for obstructing the draft. This action, plus news of imminent intervention by federal authorities, momentarily quelled the mob spirit. But when Agent Eugene Palmer arrived in Lexington, he discovered local Whites were not pacified by the arrest. Fearing the worst, Palmer borrowed the sheriff's car, got Mason out of jail, and drove him the thirteen miles to Durant, where they caught a southbound Illinois Central Railroad train, arriving safely in Jackson. Arraigned there on draft obstruction charges, Mason pleaded not guilty, waived a preliminary hearing, and posted $2,000 bond guaranteeing his appearance in federal court in November. Meanwhile, back in Lexington, a "large number" of Black men said to have been influenced by Mason were summarily rounded up and sent to Camp Pike, Arkansas, for induction.[31]

In numerous instances during the war, alarmed southern Whites found it difficult to believe that Blacks could hold genuine antiwar beliefs or have persuasive reasons for being disenchanted with the war. It was much more comforting to believe their disaffection was the result of enemy agents manipulating gullible Blacks. The hoary southern myth of "outside agitators" stirring up an otherwise contented Black population had clearly not died with slavery. The *Jackson Daily News* hailed Mason's arrest as "an important step in countering German propaganda," holding the preacher responsible not only for the large number of Holmes County Blacks who allegedly evaded the draft but also for "making false statements for the purpose of promoting the cause of Germany, and detrimental to the military welfare of the United States." When Palmer examined Mason's suitcase, however, he found nothing to establish an enemy connection other than several pieces of "anointed cloth" and a bottle of German cologne with which to perform the consecration.[32]

Meanwhile, the Military Intelligence Division, which conducted unhindered and widespread investigations of civilians during the war, was mustering its own evidence against Mason. Like the Bureau of Investigation, MID developed a focus on alleged Black subversives as well as any activity threatening to deter enlistment. Colonel Marlborough Churchill, the current head of MID, instructed intelligence officers in Los Angeles and St. Louis to investigate elders E. R. Driver, W. B. Holt, and Randolph R. Booker to determine whether there was German influence behind the church's conscientious objection stand. He addressed a similar letter to bureau chief Bielaski recommending further investigation of COGIC leaders and its "propaganda," and urging that "the inquiry concerning William B. Holt should be especially rigid." Churchill explained that Holt "is a white man, very insulting and overbearing in manner, and [that he had] traveled all the way from Los Angles to Jackson to arrange bail for Mason, putting up $2,000 in cash."[33]

Soon thereafter the bureau opened a case on Henry Kirvin, pastor of a COGIC congregation in Paris, Texas. Although it believed that Kirvin was undermining military preparedness, Mason was the real target of the case. Agent DeWitt S. Winn, a former Burns Detective Agency sleuth, unearthed information that, if provable, would have damned the entire church leadership. Kirvin was reported as saying the Red Cross was the "blood of the Beast" described in the book of Revelation and warning his flock not to contribute to that charity. Winn also learned that Kirvin's congregation contributed $125 so that he could accompany Mason to Washington to gain draft deferments from Woodrow Wilson personally. Not surprisingly, the two did not see the president but did meet with a selective service official, who supposedly arranged members' immunity from the draft and from Red Cross, Liberty Bond, and war thrift-stamp contributions. Henceforth, each member of Kirvin's congregation—adult and child—was assessed twenty-five cents monthly, allegedly on the authority of the president, to ensure congregants' exemptions.[34]

Learning that Mason, Holt, and Kirvin were in Austin raising funds for Mason's legal defense, Winn telephoned Agent Claude McCaleb to urge investigation, though not a hasty arrest. McCaleb covered Mason's meeting but heard nothing incriminating. Undeterred, McCaleb, Winn, and U.S. Attorney Clarence Merritt continued to prepare a case for prosecution. Records of Kirvin's church were examined. Holt, whom McCaleb fancied was German, was already jailed in Paris on charges of possessing a gun, which suggests that federal and state authorities and perhaps local officials were all cooperating on the case. But no provable charges had yet been leveled against Mason and Kirvin. When grilled by

McCaleb, Kirvin described how, on orders from Mason, all church members had been enrolled the previous January and assessed twenty-five cents monthly for legal representation of men who might be drafted. But he denied discouraging Red Cross participation and said, "I am now teaching that nations ought to chastise one another."[35]

Mason was interviewed once again, and in that interview he maintained that although the part of the COGIC doctrinal statement detailing opposition to military service was first printed in 1917, after the draft law was passed, it had long been an article of faith. There had simply been no need to publish it earlier. Denying unpatriotic motives, Mason avowed that he was "just trying to teach the scriptures." Answering questions about Holt, he declared that the White elder had joined the church in May 1917 as superintendent of Spanish missions. Here Mason was less than candid. Elder Holt had been appointed national field secretary at the COGIC's founding back in 1897. Concerning Holt's arrest for weapons possession, Mason explained that he was authorized to carry a badge and gun as a deputy sheriff in California.[36]

Henry Kirvin and Charles H. Mason were arrested on July 16, 1918, and charged, along with William B. Holt, with impersonating federal officers and conspiring to commit offenses against the government. The former infraction carried a maximum three-year sentence and $1,000 fine, the latter permitting a $10,000 penalty and two years' incarceration. These were federal offenses. Regarding the first charge, Mason was said to have told church members he was an emissary of President Wilson with authority to collect twenty-five cents monthly to ensure their exemption from military service. The *Paris Morning News* coarsely simplified the issue, headlining that Mason was "charged with working holy roller negroes." Holt remained in jail, unable to raise $5,000 bond, an extraordinarily high amount. The others were released on their own recognizance. Given a climate in which White outsiders were often suspected of being enemy agents, Holt was clearly deemed the more dangerous. A trial date was set for late October, which suited federal prosecutors who would have to work hard to present a credible conspiracy case.[37] But these were no ordinary times. By July, American troops were finally engaged in combat on the Western Front. Back in Mississippi, the entire National Guard, including infantry, field artillery, cavalry, and engineers, was pressed into active duty.[38]

Meanwhile in Los Angeles, Agent V.W. Killick gathered additional evidence against the defendants, interviewing Elder Driver, overseer of COGIC churches in California. He denied being a "Negro," claiming his father was an East Indian who married a Black woman after the son's birth. That bit of irrelevancy aside, Driver described Mason as devoted heart and soul to his ministry, adding that Mason was sometimes misunderstood because of his lack of formal education. Driver claimed never to have heard Mason criticize the government or encourage evasion of military duty. Rather, Mason had instructed COGIC members who were drafted to seek positions "that did not necessitate their engaging in the actual taking of human life." Killick tried to bait Driver, arguing that noncombatant soldiers were also culpable since they helped those actually fighting. In response, Driver maintained that noncombatants were absolved before God of any wrongdoing. Convinced of neither the church's nor Driver's sincerity, Killick concluded, with a partiality not uncommon to bureau agents of that era, that

> his attitude was very commanding and dictatorial, and his general personality very repugnant. I could easily imagine that this man, if crossed and aggravated, might become wildly fanatical on any issue which might confront him. In my opinion, I do not believe that the principle of opposition to warfare was ever established as a fundamental of this church prior to the entrance of the United States into the war. . . . I believe that the members of this church were anxiously desirous of evading military service in every respect.[39]

But could conspiratorial intent be proven in a court of law? A jury—an impartial one at least—was unlikely to be convinced by the bureau's evidence to this point.

Meanwhile, the fear of German subversion still preoccupied army intelligence officials. Upon receipt of Agent Winn's reports, MID requested still more surveillance to determine if enemy aliens were promoting obstruction of the draft. MID operatives tapped Driver's telephone in a futile attempt to prove German associations.[40] Colonel Churchill's office waited impatiently for the trial of Mason, Holt, and Kirvin, stressing to John Lord O'Brian, the special assistant to the attorney general responsible for overseeing Espionage Act cases, that prosecution was "fairly important for our counter-propaganda work, as there are outcroppings of this negro religious agitation in other parts of the country with which we have to deal." This was a reference to the Pentecostal Assemblies of the World, Churches of the Living God, Church of God and Saints in Christ, and Black Church of Christ congregations, all of which similarly opposed participation in the war.[41]

If the Department of Justice was to succeed in prosecuting Mason and his associates, though, hearsay evidence was insufficient. Credible firsthand testimony by church members was essential. The most promising witness appeared to be Rev. W.C. Thompson, who had left the church in disagreement over performing military service. Interviewed by bureau agents in Chicago, Thompson alleged that COGIC members were discouraged from buying Liberty Bonds because Mason wanted them to give him money for a new house. He charged further that Kirvin's antiwar stance was simply for personal gain. To the bureau's chagrin, however, Thompson defended Mason and Kirvin as basically patriotic, even if mistaken. This was hardly the "smoking gun" that the Justice Department needed in order to convict the COGIC leaders.[42]

The government suffered another setback when the sudden death of DeWitt Winn in the influenza epidemic left the bureau without its most informed, diligent, and professional operative on the case.[43] Winn's replacement, Lewie H. Henry, continued assisting U.S. Attorney Merritt in preparing the case for a federal grand jury. Using the Paris church registry, Henry took statements from thirteen members, including two lay preachers, gaining much new information but no solid evidence that federal crimes had been committed. The members related how, after his trip to Washington with Mason, Pastor Kirvin instructed the congregation to pay twenty-five cents to register so that the president would "know" who the saints of the church were. All those paying and so enrolled would not have to go to war, but those who did not would be cut off from the church and afforded no protection from military service. Women were urged to register too, so as to avoid forced Red Cross work. Members were also required to purchase, for fifteen cents, a document entitled "Doctrinal Statement and Rules for Government of the Church of God in Christ," which stated that "we believe the shedding of human blood or the taking of human life to be contrary to the teachings of our Lord and Savior, and as a body we are adverse to war in all its various forms." If men were inducted, Kirvin said, they could use the pamphlet to plead for mercy and not be sent to the front lines. Members were admonished to "live the life" if they expected the church to stand behind them. Church finances were also investigated, but nothing useful for the prosecution came to light. What most shocked Agent Henry was learning that Holt hugged and kissed Mason. The culturally unsophisticated bureau agent interpreted this as a shocking display of interracial intimacy, rather than as what it was: the "holy kiss," a scriptural form of Christian greeting.[44]

On October 29, 1918, even as newspaper headlines predicted the imminent collapse of Germany and its allies, a federal grand jury convened in Paris, Texas, to weigh evidence against Mason, Kirvin, and Holt. A large number of church members attended the hearing, presided over by Judge DuVal West of San Antonio, no stranger to cases of alleged Black disloyalty. Surprisingly, despite local prejudices and passions, the grand jury declined to indict the three on the charge of conspiring to hinder the draft, finding that the preachers' activities "were not conducted in a way that was covered by any federal statute." It found no more merit in the charge of impersonating government officials. Disappointed but unwilling to admit defeat, the assistant U.S. attorney prosecuting the case suggested that the defendants next be tried in Lamar County Court for swindling, in connection with the monthly assessments. Agent Henry persuaded county attorney Grady Sturgeon to prosecute, promising access to all evidence gathered by the bureau. So on November 1 the defendants were back in custody.[45]

Local prosecution, in which Whites' racial fears might easily be exploited, was potentially dangerous. The press focused particularly on Holt, reported to have eaten and lodged with Blacks and to have hugged and kissed Black preachers. Kirvin and Mason made bond, but again Holt's bond was set higher and he could not raise the sum. The *Paris Morning News,* in language common to the southern White press, reported, "The white man who was arrested with the negro holy roller preachers on the charge of swindling is still in jail. None of the brethren have so far made bond for him, although the darkies have been released."[46]

This final attempt to prosecute the Church of God in Christ leadership must have ended in futility. The *Paris Morning News* did not mention the trio after November 5. The minutes indexes for both the federal district and Lamar County courts contain no information, and the county grand jury did not keep minutes in this era. Apparently only William B. Holt was convicted. He pleaded guilty to vagrancy on December 6 and was fined $1. This was the last recorded harassment of the COGIC's White elder.[47]

Elder Mason saw his legal ordeals in Mississippi and Texas as nothing less than persecution, and the evidence supports his interpretation. The church's antiwar doctrine in all likelihood antedated the declaration of war in April and the introduction of the draft in May 1917. The fact that it was not published earlier is inconsequential. There simply was no need before the war to delve into a tangential subject like conscientious objection. What was important was possession by the Spirit as evidenced by speaking in tongues or miraculous healing.

Clearly, neither Mason nor other COGIC pastors were pro-German. Mason's sermon "The Kaiser in the Light of the Scriptures" expressed clear opposition to German policy and a willingness to support Liberty Bond drives. It is equally clear that there was never a conspiracy to obstruct the draft. But ordinary citizens and public officials alike were disinclined to differentiate between religious objection to all wars and opposition to the present conflict. Part of the reason was that other Blacks did express unmistakable political dissent. African American socialists such as A. Philip Randolph and Chandler Owen, editors of the *Messenger,* viewed the war as the inevitable product of exploitive capitalism. And many other Blacks, including ex-southerners trapped in northern urban ghettos where the Promised Land seemed as remote as ever, saw no reason to fight a "white man's war."[48] By contrast, COGIC doctrine was apolitical. The church should have excited no more interest or disfavor than did the Quakers.

Regarding the allegation that Mason impersonated a government official, the evidence is no stronger. It is clear that the twenty-five-cent assessments were to pay for the legal costs incurred by Mason, other arrested leaders, and those seeking draft exemptions.[49] This was probably the easiest way to raise a defense fund, and the money collected seems to have been used appropriately. Mason may have naively assumed from his talks with draft officials in Washington that the government approved his church's antiwar doctrines and that this approval was sufficient to ensure exemption from conscription, at least for those men who were COGIC members before passage of the selective service law. Inexperienced in dealing with the wider world, Mason relied less on the nuances of the law than on the strength of a sovereign God whom he knew far better.

But the mood in 1917 and 1918 was intolerant of any nonconformity. Even recognized peace churches such as the Mennonites and Quakers had difficulties. Newer denominations without venerable traditions, not to mention sects about which the government had no reliable information, were regarded even less sympathetically. Given this hostile climate and the racially biased operation of many southern draft boards, it was almost inevitable that Black religious objectors and their leaders would be perceived not as devout adherents to their faith but as pawns of the German enemy or other traitors. Neither was tolerated. Southern responses to the Church of God in Christ reflected a vocal majority of the country that had no patience for anyone, whether religious sectarian, political dissident, or slacker, who refused to demonstrate unalloyed patriotism. Wartime passions inevitably led to wartime excesses. Bureau of Investigation agents, who were White, male, middle-class, and patriotic, were not immune to intolerance. Agents assigned to southern offices were likely to hold conventional White supremacist views and grave suspicions of any Black nonconformity.

Years later, Elder Mason recalled his tribulations during World War I. Time had blurred the accuracy of his chronology, but not the details of his ordeals:

> In 1918 I was called to appear before the judge of the Kangaroo Court in Paris, Tex. The presiding officers [*sic*] looked at me and laid down his books, and said, "You all may try him; I will not have anything to do with him."
>
> In 1918, at Lexington, Miss., I took a scriptural stand against the ungodly deeds of the various races, about how many souls were being hurled into eternity without chance of seeking God for their soul's salvation, knowing that without the hand of the Almighty there could be no remedy for the same.
>
> The Holy Ghost through me was teaching men to look to God, for he is their only help. I told them not to trust in the power of the United States, England, France or Germany, but trust in God. The enemy (the devil) tried to hinder me from preaching the unadulterated word of God. He plotted against me and had the white people to arrest me and put me in jail for several days. I thank my God for the persecution. "For all that live godly must suffer persecution." 2 Tim. 3:12.
>
> Later in the same year I was called to Jackson, Miss., to answer to the charge that the devil had made against me. The presiding officers talked with me, after which they told me that I was backed up by the Scripture, and would not be hurt by them. . . . If God be for you, who can be against you![50]

Reasons for the federal government's inability to prosecute Mason remain speculative. Perhaps the proceedings were simply dropped after the armistice on November 11, 1918, though the Justice Department continued to pursue other wartime cases for many months after the end of hostilities. It is plausible that a grand jury indeed indicted Mason—such bodies rarely failed to bring indictments in this period—but federal attorneys, distinguishing winning from losing cases, dropped Mason's case before it came to trial. Such actions were usually not recorded, and thus the absence of information in the minutes and dockets of the district court is mute evidence in support of that conclusion.[51] In any case, Mason, Driver, Kirvin, and Holt were fortunate to escape having to defend themselves in the midst of a White populace ready to believe even the most ludicrous rumors.

• • •

Many federal officials and ordinary citizens during World War I genuinely believed that enemies within the gates imperiled the country. The notion that a sinister adversary was manipulating gullible Blacks' loyalties was widely held. Considering the experiences of others who opposed the war on political or religious grounds, Elder Mason and most of his associates were fortunate to find legal vindication and, with the exception of Elder Holt, only brief incarceration.

The Justice Department, tasked with enforcement of selective service regulations, had a legitimate interest in investigating the church and its leadership. The tragedy in this case is not the fact of federal scrutiny but the degree to which an overenergized Bureau of Investigation, urged on by military intelligence, compromised objectivity by succumbing to popular fears and prejudices. Some agents, such as the unfortunate DeWitt Winn, conducted themselves professionally, but in this and other cases many others imbibed the anxieties of an overwrought White populace.

The relentless pursuit of COGIC leaders and their arrests on flimsy conspiracy and impersonation charges lend credence to Elder Mason's claim to persecution, his ultimate exoneration notwithstanding. But there is likely also a veiled story of resistance. Although reliable COGIC membership figures for the World War I era are lacking, it is likely that hundreds, if not thousands, of members were drafted. An unknown number probably never appeared for induction. Some may have hidden out, while others sought the anonymity of a big city, particularly in the North. Yet others undoubtedly submitted to induction even while bearing copies of the church's doctrinal statement. Given the absence of COGIC members in lists of those who became absolutist war resisters—who refused to put on the uniform and were court-martialed and imprisoned—it may reasonably be assumed that COGIC objectors, once under the army's authority, were browbeaten or frightened into complying with military orders and shouldering a rifle. Extant records, unfortunately, do not mention such individuals.[52]

The Church of God in Christ's opposition to participating in war was both religious and political. It began from a religious conviction. Church doctrine held that Jesus taught the substitution of brotherly love for the sin of hatred. "The shedding of human blood or taking of human life" was unequivocally wrong. On another level, however, the COGIC stance was solidly political. The federal government never recognized the church's antiwar convictions as legitimate or sincere. No surprise, then, that it refused to grant conscientious objector status to church members. Given such opposition, it is remarkable that Black men, for the most part poorly educated sharecroppers and urban laborers, challenged government authority in such numbers and with a persistence not seen since the

Civil War and Reconstruction. Although most of them likely submitted to military orders upon induction, their assertions of conscientious objection were politically charged challenges to White authority. These assertions could not go unheeded by those in government who appointed themselves guarantors of White supremacy and Black submission. Persecution of church members emerged from legitimate concerns about draft evasion, but also from war-generated paranoid racism. The American public during World War I generally condoned wholesale abridgements of constitutional rights such as freedom of speech. An authority on early Pentecostal pacifism concludes that COGIC members suffered from "collusion between local intolerance and war support and the federal government's unyielding prosecution." Ironically, Elder Charles H. Mason's reputation would be enhanced by his travails. For decades thereafter, he was characterized as a church leader who preserved faith and character intact in the face of persecution and prosecution.[53]

Pacifism faded in the Church of God in Christ after World War I. Anecdotal evidence suggests that during World War II, at least some men whose membership antedated 1941 did not fight, but how many gained recognition as conscientious objectors is unknown. Only twelve members worked in Civilian Public Service (CPS) camps, so very likely their total number was small. As COGIC membership grew rapidly during the 1950s and 1960s, its pacifist heritage receded from view. A new generation of members performed combat duty in Vietnam. Today, church doctrine still states, in the exact language of World War I–era documents, that "the shedding of human blood or the taking of human life is contrary to the teachings of our Lord and Saviour, Jesus Christ, and as a body, we are adverse to war in all its forms." This official statement instructs members, should they be drafted, to submit to induction as conscientious objectors, to undergo only basic training while refusing instruction in "advanced weapons," and to seek noncombat roles. But few members today seem to know of, much less follow, that noncombatant doctrine. The early restorationist Church of God in Christ nurtured pacifism. But as happened in other sects that grew in membership and sought to enter the denominational mainstream, conscientious opposition to war became a forgotten tradition.[54]

Strangely, this entire historical chapter is missing from the official publications of the COGIC. The church's website is entirely silent on the World War I trials and tribulations of Charles H. Mason. It serves no useful purpose to bury these events. Mason provided strong inspirational leadership under considerable duress and at times real danger.

For an infant denomination, Mason's conduct and example—"I thank my God for the persecution"—was precisely what was needed.

As for the Bureau of Investigation and the Military Intelligence Division, they were ill-prepared and ill-equipped to understand, much less appreciate, a new mood beginning to blossom in Black America. The Great Migration offered not just the hope of new, better-paying employment but new race relations and a freer social environment. World War I further politicized Blacks who questioned whether a "white man's war" was their cause too. The Black population, despite widespread White prejudices, was neither gullible nor stupid. Many Blacks clearly knew where their self-interest lay. But government agents remained almost totally oblivious to these developments, acting instead on presuppositions and stereotypes born in the era of Nat Turner and the abolitionists. This was clearly not their finest hour.

3

The FBI and the Moorish Science Temple of America, 1926–1960

SYLVESTER A. JOHNSON

This chapter briefly examines the history of the Moorish Science Temple of America (MSTA) and its interactions with the FBI as a way of introducing the FBI's now eighty-year history with American Islam. Remarkably, already in the 1930s and 1940s, long before Al-Qaeda and even before the Nation of Islam, the FBI was engaged in surveilling Muslims, and its approach was marked by a suspiciousness that anticipated its later response to certain Muslim groups in the twenty-first century. In the case of the MSTA, this response was certainly conditioned by the racism endemic to American society, but it was also inflected by the FBI's religious preconceptions and biases, by what it understood as authentic religion, and by how it constructed the relationship between race and religion. By tracing this history, we can see that the FBI's recent approach to the threat of Islamic terrorism did not develop in a vacuum after 9/11 but reflects a more deeply rooted and institutionalized pattern of behavior that has its origins in the racial-religious politics of the early twentieth century.

The first American Muslims to be engaged by the bureau were members of the MSTA, an African American Muslim sect. The MSTA first emerged in the American Midwest as a small group under the leadership of the self-proclaimed prophet Noble Drew Ali (born Timothy Drew), and it was formally organized in 1926. With its center in Chicago, the MSTA quickly grew to operate dozens of branches throughout the United States, reaching a membership in the tens of thousands during the 1930s. In the wake of Drew Ali's untimely death (he died mysteriously after being released from police custody), the MSTA split into multiple factions while maintaining a mainstream center that easily outnumbered the others. Official membership numbers are not available, but at its height the movement had upward of thirty thousand registered members with an undetermined number of informal adherents.

ORIGINS OF THE MOORISH SCIENCE TEMPLE

The MSTA's emergence as an Islamic revivalist movement resulted from a complex history of Muslim transnationalism vigorously abetted by efforts to critique and resist Western imperialism in predominantly Muslim geographies. Prominent among these was the rise of Egyptian nationalism and the deliberate efforts to preserve Islamic education in West Africa (for example, in present-day Nigeria) amid sustained efforts by Western Christian missionaries to make Christian conversion an essential qualification for civic and institutional participation.[1]

Islamic Africa was not the only source of the ideas that shaped the MSTA. Of special importance as well was the Ahmadiyya mission, which emerged in South Asia during the 1880s under the leadership of Mirza Ghulam Ahmad. Ahmad created a revivalist movement among Muslims by preaching that a promised messenger (the Mahdi) would appear to restore faithful adherence to the divine message of Islam. Ahmadi Muslims drew on a tradition of Mahdi theology that dated back to the tenth century, if not before, and that inspired hope in a special, divinely appointed messenger. Not surprisingly, Ahmadis also reflected the influence of South Asia's *convivencia* of multiple religions, shaped by many centuries of relative harmony among Muslims and Hindus and a growing Christian presence. Ahmadi missionaries rooted their theology in Quranic scripture but also drew on the scriptures of Hindus and Christians. What held all these influences together was the belief that the Mahdi fulfilled the expectations and essential message of the world's many religions.[2]

Shortly following the end of World War I, Ahmadis opened a mission site in Chicago, where they quickly attracted a following among Blacks who admired the movement's critique of racism and its emphasis on interracial harmony, which the Ahmadis foregrounded. Although there exists no clear evidence that Drew Ali was tied to the Ahmadis, he and his followers were likely influenced by the movement's efforts to promote Islam as a harbinger of racial harmony in a world marked by strident disparity and injustice.

As is evident from the Moorish Science Temple's "science" of spiritual knowledge, numerology, and esotericism, Freemasonry also influenced the MSTA's belief system and ethos. (Since taking shape in Europe during the eighteenth century, Freemasonry has long made science central to its self-representation.) As Michael Gomez has emphasized, however, this does not diminish the significance of the Islamic heritage of African American Muslims, which is richly attested throughout slavery and up to the early twentieth century. While its intellectual genealogy goes back to many sources, the Moorish Science Temple is appropriately situated as part of this larger history of Black Islam.[3]

The Moorish Science Temple officially dates its beginnings to 1913 when Noble Drew Ali putatively founded a "Canaanite Temple" in Newark, New Jersey. Little hard evidence illumines the life of this organization at this point in its history. What is certain is that by the mid-1920s, Drew Ali's movement had developed enough of a following for a process of institutionalization to occur, with founding members registering the new religious group on November 29, 1926, as the "Moorish Temple of Science." Not until May 21, 1928, however, did they officially change the name to the Moorish Science Temple of America. The initial moniker more clearly emphasized that scientific knowledge (a science of spirituality, numerology, and the like) was integral to the theology and ethos of this Islamic community. The second, permanent name retained the reference to spiritual science but also signaled the group's efforts to identify with U.S. nationalism, efforts that in turn sought to promote the rights of citizenship for Blacks.[4]

The larger context in which the MSTA thrived was marked by numerous Black political movements that criticized White racism while promoting reforms to achieve racial equality and Black political empowerment. Among these were the Universal Negro Improvement Association (founded by the married couple Amy Garvey and Marcus Garvey), the Peace Movement of Ethiopia, the Ethiopian World Federation Council, and the Pacific Movement of the Eastern World.[5] It was not uncommon for members of the Moorish Science Temple to affiliate with these other organizations, particularly the Garvey movement, and the Garveys' distinct view of race and politics is mirrored in the MSTA's theology. Diaspora identity, for instance, was central to the MSTA's claim of Moorish identity. By conceptualizing the Moorish religion as encompassing a range of non-White races united by the experience of racism and colonialism, converts to Moorish Science developed a sense of national identity marked by political membership in a diasporic community—for them, Islam was not so much a confession of faith as a kind of citizenship in a racially defined civilization that spanned the globe. This political community of Asiatic peoples, as conceived through religious formations of Moorish networks, is emblematic of what J. Lorand Matory has theorized as a nonterritorial formation of the nation.[6]

What the Moorish Science Temple added to this critique of colonialism and racism was an embrace of U.S. nationalism, the belief that African Americans should seek and enjoy membership in the political body of the United States. From the very beginning of Drew Ali's leadership and continuing through a steady tradition of teaching, the MSTA enjoined obedience to government authorities and insisted that converts exhibit loyalty to both their religious community and the United States.

BEGINNINGS OF FEDERAL REPRESSION

J. Edgar Hoover was first alerted to the Moorish Science Temple's status as a threat by a report from the Philadelphia FBI field office, which presented findings from its covert observations of the group. Thus, from the beginning, Hoover associated these African American Muslims with racial insurgence. In 1931, during the early phase of the FBI's covert surveillance, a field agent interviewed (under false pretenses) J. T. Bey, an African American barber who led the MSTA membership in Reading, Pennsylvania. The agent had already questioned Bey's landlord, a woman who rented to African American boarders. Bey, innocently enough, informed the undercover agent of the movement's proper name (the FBI had referred to it as the Moorish "Shrine" Temple) and explained the fundamental aim of members' faith—recovering their Moorish heritage. As Bey made clear, the MSTA—from its membership cards to its organizational practices—rejected the ideology of White supremacism and taught instead that "Moorish" peoples merited treatment on the basis of racial equality. Accordingly, converts were told that displaying their membership cards at local restaurants would ensure they received "every courtesy and equal privileges with other races." Upon learning this, the FBI concluded that Bey was "a fanatic on the subject of equality for all races." Strikingly, the FBI dismissed the belief system of the group as the result of mental imbalance and delusion: bureau officials were quick to note that "reliable Negroes" not affiliated with the MSTA regarded the Moorish group to be "crazy" and "more or less of a joke."[7]

The FBI's response to the antiracist theology of the MSTA exposes the assertive commitment to anti-Black racism that the Department of Justice manifested in this period. Inasmuch as the MSTA opposed White supremacy and opposed the legal practices of apartheid throughout American society, the FBI was technically correct in identifying the group as opposed to the nation's standard practices of political order. In this sense the movement was literally subversive of the social order that the FBI was seeking to defend.[8] The FBI's racist presumptions that Whites were inherently superior to Blacks led them to dismiss the MSTA's self-understanding as Moors. For the FBI, their true identity was racial—they were Black, defined "by the appearance and characteristics of a full blooded negro." Their claim to be Muslim was a ruse, a fake identity, that used religion to perpetrate a fraud.[9] The MSTA's assertion of ethnic heritage thus functioned as evidence for the FBI that these Moorish Americans were engaged in religious deception.

In accord with this understanding of the MSTA, the FBI coordinated with state and local law enforcement to harass and intimidate MSTA leaders, notwithstanding the fact that they were engaged in legal and constitutionally protected activities. By 1941 the FBI's infiltration of the MSTA in Springfield, Illinois, for instance, led the bureau to focus on Robert Washington, who headed a local branch of the group. Washington claimed that a Japanese victory against the United States would bring an end to U.S. racism because the Japanese were an Afro-Asiatic people (recall that the MSTA espoused the idea of global unity among peoples of color in opposition to Western colonialism and racism). The bureau lacked any legal justification for prosecuting Washington, who had no connections with Japan and received no foreign material support. The FBI's own investigation confirmed that he derived his income from selling badges and robes to new converts in the MSTA, yet the bureau coordinated with the Illinois state attorney general's office to intimidate Washington into silence by telling him he would be prosecuted by the U.S. government for "obtaining money under false pretenses." Unnerved by the threat, Washington agreed to stop seeking converts in exchange for avoiding imprisonment.[10]

SELF-SUFFICIENCY AND RACIAL SUSPICION

The MSTA's efforts to create a reliable independent system of financial self-support culminated in 1939 with its acquisition of 138 acres of land in Prince George County, Virginia. There, members of the group created what they called a "national home" that provided an economic base for crop production and commerce (they later created similar settlements in Becket, Massachusetts, and Woodstock, Connecticut). The Virginia property also functioned as a resting place or resort for MSTA members, who initially envisioned it as a retirement facility for elderly Moorish Americans. At first, several dozen residents moved to the farm. Their numbers increased to approximately seventy-five men and women by 1942, and the national network of temples provided regular donations to support the Virginia property. Fred Nelson-Bey was the initial leader of the home. Born in North Carolina in 1890, Nelson-Bey was a seasoned devotee of the MSTA and proved to be a visionary and judicious administrator. He oversaw the construction of the first buildings—one major temple and three or four other concrete-block buildings. In addition to these, residents built a few log cabins insulated with mud. In the early years of the national home, however, simple tents were the most common shelters.[11]

Central to the Moorish Science Temple's broader sense of connection was the national home's production of the *Moorish Voice,* edited by Nelson-Bey's wife. She produced a monthly issue and mailed five hundred copies of the periodical to the various branches of the MSTA throughout the country. The publication was essential to the movement's unity and dissemination.

By 1942, FBI surveillance and infiltration of Moorish Americans had increased sharply. Field office agents in cities such as Detroit and Chicago displayed a stridently suspicious disposition toward the MSTA. By contrast, law enforcement officials in Virginia initially took a less suspicious approach to MSTA members of the national home. Much of this was due to the disarmingly forthcoming methods that Nelson-Bey used to engage with local police and the FBI agents who visited the farm. Upon their arrival, residents of the national home had been treated by local law enforcement as criminal suspects. In fact, the Prince George County sheriff's office claimed a spate of robberies had occurred in the region and arrived on location in 1942 to question Nelson-Bey as soon as the compound was established, suggesting residents must have been involved because the robberies had begun at the time of their arrival. Nelson-Bey informed the sheriff that they were a religious community whose only concern was justice and ethics, and he further assured the sheriff by declaring that he should feel free to inspect their homes and other buildings at any time with no warrant necessary. An initial inspection, not surprisingly, showed that the group had not stolen any property and that members were committed to maintaining a rugged and honest existence through their own labor with financial assistance from the MSTA's national headquarters.[12] Nelson-Bey also reassured local authorities by taking in an individual placed on probation by the local court system. By the account of circuit court judge Frank Binford, Nelson-Bey not only kept the judge informed of the individual's behavior but eventually reported that the man was violating probation, turning him over to court authorities who returned him to jail.[13] By cooperating with local White political officials in these ways, the MSTA community leader won a measure of trust essential to mitigating the police harassment, abuse, and social control to which Blacks were routinely subject.

Subsequent leaders of the MSTA's national home included Mary Clift Bey, who held extensive experience as the grand sheikess (temple leader) of Louisville, Kentucky. For several years, she skillfully led the Prince George County group and ensured its stability while parrying suspicions of and harassment by FBI and police officials. It so happens that Clift Bey's original encounters with the FBI began long before she assumed leadership of the MSTA's national home. Born in Tennessee, she had eventually moved to Chicago, where she first joined the Moorish Science Temple. Around 1941, she moved to Louisville, Kentucky, where she worked as a teacher. Upon her arrival in Louisville, Clift Bey opened a new temple that soon grew to at least fifty members. As the temple's grand sheikess, she communicated directly with Charles Kirkman Bey, the MSTA's national leader, and she coordinated with other temple leaders to promote Black conversion to Islam.[14]

The Louisville field office of the FBI began investigating Clift Bey as soon as it learned of her activities. Bureau agents initially suspected that she and her followers were affiliated with the neighboring St. Mary's Church. In fact, the FBI initially suspected that the church was merely a front for the Moorish Science Temple, following reports by casual observers who took notice of elaborate, Moorish "costumes" the church's parishioners wore during their meetings. They quickly surmised, however, that Clifton Bey was operating a temple under her own leadership. As was routinely the case with MSTA members, the FBI was immediately alarmed that the Louisville followers of Moorish Science identified themselves as Asiatics, refused to use what they called "slave names," and insisted that their actual Moorish names be indicated with the suffix "Bey" or "El" when registering to vote or when registering under the Selective Service Act. City officials eventually forced the MSTA members to register using the objectionable names that White slave owners had forced on their ancestors, though this happened only after some legal and political wrangling.[15]

Whereas the FBI's earlier investigation of the MSTA was limited to its members, the bureau's Louisville field office escalated its scrutiny of the city's African American Muslims by conducting a massive survey of Louisville's predominantly Black neighborhoods. Understanding that MSTA members consistently employed the use of Moorish names for conducting business and acquiring housing, the FBI arranged for the local air raid warden to conduct a house-by-house search and census of African American residences to produce a list of every single Black Muslim living in the area.

NATIONAL SECURITY AND THE MILITARY DRAFT

The most severe FBI repression of the Moorish Science Temple emerged during World War II as a consequence of the Selective Service Act. As early as the summer of 1942, the Military Intelligence Division of the U.S. War Department became interested in the MSTA when members of the religious community protested being classified as "Negroes" or "Blacks" during their interviews with local Selective Service registration officials. The army's Military Intelligence Division, in fact, communicated directly with J. Edgar Hoover to inform him of these encounters with Black Muslims.[16]

Given the racism evident in the FBI's earlier response to the MSTA, it should be noted that FBI field offices went on record confirming that various branches of the MSTA conformed to the Selective Service Act (SSA) and showed no evidence of being a national security threat. A critical mass of MSTA members did refuse to register with the selective service, as federal investigators found in Kansas, for instance, during 1942. But when FBI director J. Edgar Hoover instructed agents throughout the country to investigate and infiltrate a number of MSTA branches, the bureau's field offices repeatedly found that members of the movement were largely conforming to the SSA's mandate. The Newark, New Jersey, office reported in December 1942 that members of the Moorish Science Temple in that city showed "no indication of failure to register" for the draft. Likewise, during the same month, other FBI agents judged the fledgling group of approximately twelve Moorish Americans in Anderson, Indiana, to be free of any pro-Japanese tendencies. Even the much larger MSTA membership in Louisville, Kentucky, eventually passed muster under FBI infiltration and surveillance. The only irregularity the agents found, in fact, was the failure of some members to update changes of address with their local draft board registration office.[17]

FBI officials in other regions, however, often came to less benign conclusions, wreaking havoc on local MSTA temples. During 1942, several Moorish Americans in Mississippi were prosecuted and convicted for violating the southern state's antisedition legislation. Among these was one individual who had joined the MSTA in February 1942 after paying a registration fee of $1.25 and monthly dues of $0.75. This conferred rights of membership as well as a $60 burial insurance policy ($900 in today's dollars). One prospective convert reported that MSTA members claimed that those converting to the Moorish Science Temple would be exempt from the military draft. In the eyes of Mississippi's FBI field agents, however, these MSTA members were not a religious community but a rebel group of racial enemies threatening the ability of the White race to control the government of Mississippi and that of the nation. Once convicted, the MSTA members (all men) were sentenced to jail time, an example to any other Blacks who might be inspired to challenge the brutal hegemony that Whites waged over the lives of Black people.[18]

Even the Black Muslims of Anderson, Indiana—a group later shown by the FBI's own investigation to have no pro-Japanese sympathies—were subject to punitive measures. Before reaching its conclusion that the MSTA branch evidenced no threat to national security, the bureau raided the Anderson MSTA temple, seized its possessions, and closed its operations. What had been a small but thriving branch of sixty to seventy members eventually reopened, but with only about a dozen members, who were understandably traumatized by the brazen counterintelligence methods that treated them as presumptive criminals.[19]

THE MSTA DURING THE CIVIL RIGHTS ERA

The 1950s and 1960s witnessed the emergence of a wide spectrum of activist movements and organizations that achieved major changes in the racial status quo. Veteran organizations such as the National Association for the Advancement of Colored People (NAACP, founded in 1909) and the Congress of Racial Equality (CORE, founded in 1942) found new company with the Southern Christian Leadership Conference (SCLC, founded in 1955) and the Student Nonviolent Coordinating Committee (SNCC, founded in 1960). Of these, only SCLC was an explicitly religious organization. With SCLC's entry, however, Black churches began an unprecedented level of activism in concert with the NAACP, CORE, SNCC, and other organizations.

By 1960, moreover, the Nation of Islam (NOI) had risen to public visibility, especially as the press began to focus attention on NOI chief minister el-Hajj Malik el-Shabazz (better known as Malcolm X) and his criticism of global White supremacism, colonialism, and the criminalization of self-defense among victims of anti-Black violence. Although there were important differences of philosophy and practice, the NOI shared with the MSTA a theological critique of White supremacism and a central emphasis on diasporic identity as part of the Asiatic races. Both also promoted conversion to Islam as a way to ameliorate the racial subjugation of Blacks in the United States.

The convergence of secular and religious Black organizations produced an array of Black liberationist projects unprecedented and profound in their resonance and impact, and this broader context injected a new sense of urgency into the FBI's engagement with the MSTA. One Moorish American leader in particular, Turner-El, captured the attention of the FBI during the 1950s by expressing an interest in civil rights activism. In the spring of 1956, Turner-El resolved to host a conference in Norfolk, Connecticut, to address the desperate conditions of Black migrants from the South, people who had been driven to resettle in northern cities to escape the dire poverty of sharecropping and the willful denial of employment opportunities by Whites. Drawing on the MSTA's longtime identification with Morocco as a paradigmatic Islamic state, the Moorish devotee publicized a meeting sponsored by the "Moroccan Executive Congress," which was intended to serve as one element of a larger "Moroccan United Organizations Federation, Inc." (MUOF). Since at least 1950, the U.S. Army's military intelligence unit had been made aware that a smaller offshoot of the MSTA, the Moorish Science Temple Divine and National Movement of America, had organized the MUOF with Turner-El at the helm. Because Turner-El claimed that he would meet with the DOJ's chief of civil rights (Arthur Caldwell at the time) during the planned conference, it appeared to the FBI that the Moorish organization might instigate political unrest and trouble, and at a highly volatile time: just after the U.S. Supreme Court's *Brown v. Board of Education* decision (1954) had ruled against legal segregation in public schools and in the midst of an ongoing boycott of Montgomery's public transit system and a related legal suit being appealed to the Supreme Court.[20]

The MUOF had made clear its conviction that the U.S. government needed to "protect and defend the human rights" of all African Americans and that refusal to do so would require the MUOF to "repatriate all Afro-Americans who are suffering as slaves under Southern tyrannical rule." The FBI responded to the MSTA's efforts to advance civil rights with a campaign of infiltration, intimidation, and racial panic-mongering. Despite MSTA officials' ample justification for opposing state-based racism and for demanding an ethical, just response from the U.S. government, the FBI interpreted their efforts to advance racial equality as a threat to the domestic order and moved against the MSTA as if it were a danger to national security.[21]

CONCLUSION

Accounting for the FBI's repression of the Moorish Science Temple raises the perplexing question of why state authorities persisted decade after decade in disrupting a religious movement that explicitly embraced and promoted U.S. nationalism. The group claimed to possess an Islamic ethnic heritage while teaching that members' Moorish nationality (that is, their membership in a Muslim diaspora) would garner respect from Whites and facilitate their inclusion in the body politic of the United States. In retrospect, it is evident that the vast majority of these African American Muslims adhered to the mandates of U.S. draft laws; we know this because FBI officials repeatedly found—and reported—that they were abiding by the law. It is also clear that, contrary to initial conjecture by federal agents, the Moorish Science Temple was never a front for foreign entities and never received funding from international enemies of the United States. Again, the FBI's own records firmly establish this.

Even the fact that MSTA members were Black does not by itself account for the FBI's response. Anti-Black racism was certainly endemic to FBI culture in this period, but the bureau lacked the resources to infiltrate and repress every Black movement on an ongoing basis. Why, then, did the FBI focus so much attention on the MSTA and single it out for surveillance and persecution over such a long period, cultivating confidential informants, planting undercover spies within the movement, coordinating extensive alliances with municipal law enforcement agencies, and deploying debilitating tactics of intimidation and prosecution in an effort to disrupt and cripple the group's institutional life?

A more precise explanation for the repression must begin with the intersection between the national security paradigm and the tactics of identifying racial enemies in wartime. The FBI's formation during the early twentieth century anchored a larger process of establishing counterintelligence as a central mechanism of governance. Counterintelligence, furthermore, was concerned with identifying and disrupting not criminals per se, but political enemies of the state. Because this was not a criminal status, it should come as no surprise that the African American Muslims who were victims of state repression were typically innocent of crimes. In a political sense, they were racial enemies and not criminals. The Islamic, Asiatic nature of the diaspora that Moorish Americans signified was inevitably in conflict with the imperatives of racial Whiteness. Under these conditions, Moorish Americans were asserting an ethnic heritage that conflicted sharply with the symbolic and material realities of the United States as a racial state.

4

J. Edgar Hoover, the FBI, and the Religious Cold War

DIANNE KIRBY

Although the Cold War has long been remembered as a secular conflict, a number of scholars since 2000 have argued that religion played an important role in how it unfolded, shaping its nature, its conduct, and the rhetoric used to frame and justify it.[1] Understanding the role of religion in this conflict provides critical insights into the domestic repercussions of a struggle in which each side proclaimed universal values, sought religious legitimation, and privileged those religious groups and institutions that supported the state over those that criticized it.

A striking characteristic of East-West Cold War rivalry was that it was fought on two fronts, not just abroad but also at home. On the domestic front in each of the two blocs, as Fred Halliday has observed, there was "repression of those suspected of sympathies for the other side (persecution of Titoists in Eastern Europe, McCarthyism in the USA)."[2] The effort to suppress internal dissent took different forms in each bloc, and in the West, it was particularly evident in the United States, the leader of the "free world," with the FBI playing a central role.[3] Hoover's FBI was well armed to confront any hint of radicalism or dissent from the domestic discipline and Cold War conformity that the bureau was enlisted to impose. By 1946 the FBI employed more than three thousand agents, was endowed with presidential sanction to engage in wiretapping and other forms of surveillance, and enjoyed a seemingly unlimited budget along with widespread public support, including that of most American clergy.[4] This chapter surveys the role of religion in the FBI's efforts to prevail in the Cold War, its recruitment of religious allies, and its use of religious rhetoric to justify its war against internal dissent, and also touches on the FBI's impact on the development of organized American religious life during and in the wake of the Cold War.

RELIGION AND THE COLD WAR

Well before the Cold War, Marxist atheism justified an "absolutist" brand of anticommunism that, by claiming to be a defender of religion, recruited a range of powerful potential allies among religious institutions and organizations. Hoover was a leading promoter of this strain of absolutist anticommunism, using his influence to advance the perception of communism as a supreme and unqualified evil seeking world domination.[5] He was helped by key church leaders, particularly from within the U.S. Roman Catholic Church, as has been well documented.[6] The Cold War facilitated the widespread acceptance of absolutist anticommunism, which invoked religion as a way of imposing political, social, and moral conformity.

The emergence of the Soviet Union as a major power in the postwar world posed a serious challenge to both the capitalist powers and organized religion, and that threat was seen as an insidious one, coming from within as well as from without. From its earliest days, the FBI identified internal dissent, whether from revolutionary radicals or from advocates of reform, with the Soviet Union. The emergence of the Cold War meant that a range of "dissenters" could be identified as traitors, subversives who were unpatriotic, immoral, and godless, allies if not agents of an enemy committed to the destruction both of the American way of life and of religion.

The "religious cold war" took a variety of forms and was not unique to the United States, either in deploying security forces to monitor religious critics of the status quo or in seeking religious allies to help maintain it. In Nazi propaganda against the Allies, Hitler, who had proclaimed his invasion of the Soviet Union a crusade against the atheist Bolsheviks, fully exploited the Soviet record on religion. Allied with the Soviet Union during World War II, however, Britain and the United States had reason to avoid dwelling on the anti-religious character of Marxism, and in fact Christianity served as a bridge between the West and the Communist East.[7] The postwar effort to cast the Soviets as the enemy of religion was not simply a return to a well-established interwar tradition but also a means of signaling to the American people, and those elsewhere, that the wartime alliance was over.

The United States had emerged from the war divided not simply over what its global role should be but also over whether it should even have a global role.[8] Those who championed an active global role were inclined to emphasize the Soviet threat to the world in an effort to persuade the American people to support the interventionism required for their country's continued economic well-being. This included President Truman, who called on a righteous-nation narrative to engender national unity. Drawing on the notion of divine chosenness that has been a part of American self-representation since its colonial beginnings, the president's rhetoric was infused with religious language that reinforced the image of a righteous nation with a God-given mission.[9] This rhetoric was part of what allowed the Truman administration to justify a costly policy of military, political, and economic intervention on a worldwide scale. David Caute, the distinguished historian of America's postwar Red Scare, remarked that through the carefully constructed Truman Doctrine, the president "inflamed the natural missionary piety of Americans." Bernard Baruch, Caute noted, likewise described it as "tantamount to a declaration of an ideological or religious war."[10] This effort to develop a religious mission for postwar America was echoed by Hoover, who, like one of the era's most notorious figures, Senator Joseph McCarthy, cast himself as a defender of Christianity against communist atheism.[11]

Fears that the nation might slip back into depression, which had tested and threatened American capitalism, permeated the thinking of U.S. leaders in a variety of key institutions. The economic crisis had demonstrated the need to remain engaged with the world and to spread free-market ideology. However, the latter was not necessarily the most appealing model to colonial peoples throughout the Global South, who aspired to higher standards of living free from the shackles of Western imperialism and foreign exploitation of their natural resources. The demise and discrediting of fascism meant even Europeans were inclining more toward social democracy than toward America's capitalist model. In addition, the Red Army's courage, the immense Soviet wartime losses, and the significant shift in the position of religion had helped transform Soviet standing on the world stage.

Threatened by the ascendancy of a rival to capitalism, many leaders from American industries, businesses, media, churches, and government "concluded that religious faith was one of the most potent arrows in the quiver of domestic security."[12] Together they constructed what Jonathan Herzog has termed the "spiritual-industrial complex," which he defines as "the deliberate and managed use of societal resources to stimulate a religious revival in the late 1940s and 1950s." Herzog places Hoover at the heart of this complex, contending that "fewer Americans brooded more about the dangers of domestic communism, and fewer benefitted more from the fears they helped create."[13] A prolific writer and speaker who enjoyed a reputation as "America's most respected authority on Communism," Hoover turned the FBI into an effective anticommunist propaganda tool: "The Bureau trained its field agents to cultivate a nation-wide anti-Communist consensus by working with local media groups. It leaked intelligence estimates to anti-Communist allies like HUAC (the House Un-American Activities Committee) and established liaisons with Hollywood studios."[14]

As is well known, the bureau abetted the rise of McCarthyism and the reign of domestic political repression that it represented. Hoover fully supported Senator Joe McCarthy, notorious for his use of smears and innuendo against suspected subversives; indeed, many names and allegations derived directly from FBI files. In the view of FBI agent Robert Lamphere, McCarthy "harmed the counterintelligence effort against the Soviet threat because of the revulsion it caused." Yet, he observed, "all along, Hoover was helping him."[15] Hoover also sought to cultivate and influence the White House, seeking to ingratiate himself and the bureau with the president by supplying him with information about critics of the administration. Beyond providing intelligence, in fact, Hoover sought to smear specific groups and individuals he associated with radicalism, including labor movement activists and Christian leaders advocating for equality and justice for those at the bottom of the socioeconomic scale. Thus, for example, in an effort to forestall a "flood of propaganda from Leftist and so-called Liberal sources," an FBI proposal of February 27, 1946, recommended the publication of "educational materials" to influence public opinion against labor unions, persons prominent in religious circles, and liberal elements.[16] (For more on the FBI's efforts to "educate" the public in this period, see chapter 8, by Douglas M. Charles.)

In assigning religion a prominent place in his battle against American radicals, Hoover used a tactic also deployed by other American leaders in the period, including Truman, who helped to create a Cold War civil religion by marshaling religious vocabulary on behalf of the United States. On assuming the presidency in 1945, for example, Truman declared: "I believe—I repeat, I believe honestly—that Almighty God intends us to assume the leadership which he intended us to assume in 1920, and which we refused. And I believe if we do that, our problems would almost solve themselves."[17]

In their effort to align America with religion, both Truman and Hoover cultivated a working alliance with the Roman Catholic Church that included benefiting from its intelligence networks. Truman openly moved toward the Vatican, the postwar locus of ideological opposition to communism in Western Europe, when he instructed Myron C. Taylor, formerly Roosevelt's wartime representative to Pius XII, to return to Rome as his personal representative on April 20, 1946.[18] In the same year, Hoover and Cardinal Francis Spellman, a friend of Pius XII, coauthored a pamphlet that warned of the dangers of communism.[19] Subsequently, in 1947, Truman and Pius XII effected a highly publicized letter exchange that implicitly indicted the Soviet Union as evil and insisted that a lasting peace could be built only on Christian principles.[20]

The letter exchange can be seen as a spiritual counterpart to the country's political and economic efforts to counter communism—the Truman Doctrine in March 1947 and the Marshall Plan in June 1947. Truman was particularly anxious at this time about isolationist sentiments in Congress and public opinion. A State Department survey had concluded that two years after American GIs embraced Red Army troops on the banks of the Elbe, 70 percent of Americans opposed a hard-line anti-Soviet policy.[21] Hoover's activities on the home front, albeit presented by some scholars as a challenge to the president, can also be seen as an extension of the same policy to the extent that it emphasized communism as an internal domestic threat.[22] Shortly after the enunciation of the Truman Doctrine, Hoover delivered an address to Congress that highlighted communism's insidious and conspiratorial nature, depicting it as a psychic and spiritual disease that destroyed from within.[23]

In the same week in June that George Marshall proposed what became the European Recovery Program, Hoover appeared on the cover of an issue of *Newsweek* that included an article he wrote entitled "How to Fight Communism." The article is relevant to our subject because of the way it links democracy and individualism with Christianity.[24] Hoover's binary representation of reality—his effort to align democracy with religion on one side against godless communism on the other—suggests "an ideological world view that explains everything in terms of conspiracy; that reduces complex issues to a struggle between good and evil, and that exaggerates the evil to the point of paranoia; that prompts a self-righteousness on the part of the faithful; and that ultimately rests on a blind faith."[25] In line with Truman's rhetoric, in other words, Hoover cast the struggle against communism not just as a conflict between two political or economic systems but as a battle between religion and anti-religion—a framing that, among other profound domestic consequences, endowed the FBI with a missionlike quality that gave it an exceedingly wide scope.

MASTERS OF DECEIT

Hoover would develop this position in his 1958 book, *Masters of Deceit.* Its arguments demonstrate the rhetorical tactics by which he allied himself with religion. *Masters of Deceit* was written at the suggestion of Assistant Director William Sullivan and was actually composed by bureau agents, though it fully reflected Hoover's sentiments and objectives. Touted as a manual on "Communism in America and How to Fight It," the book, with Hoover's imprimatur, was a best seller: 250,000 copies in hardcover and 2,000,000 in paperback. It was also required reading in many schools.[26] Written in an authoritative, scholarly tone lightened by anecdotes, *Masters of Deceit* reinforced Hoover's reputation as a leading expert on communism and had a major impact on how it was perceived by the American public.

Following Francois Houtart, one can see that *Masters of Deceit* adopts the Roman Catholic Church's practice of caricaturing Marxist positions in order to criticize them more easily.[27] The book is certainly marked by strong religious themes, though by this point Hoover's references to religion were less explicitly centered on Christianity and more inclusive of other faiths, reflecting a broader shift in the religious discourse of America's political elite during the Cold War era. Dwight D. Eisenhower, who became president in 1953, also allied America with religion, but his conception of religion was more relativistic and inclusive, making room for Jews, for example. As he put it in 1955, "Recognition of the Supreme Being is the first, the most basic, expression of Americanism. Without God, there could be no American form of government, nor an American way of life."[28] The vagueness of Eisenhower's religiosity disturbed some Christian leaders who by now recognized the political motives at play, and Christianity remained central to the anticommunism of many Americans, as when the National Council of Churches, established in 1950 to confront communism, materialism, and secularism, embraced the slogan, "the building of a Christian America in a Christian world."[29] But this kind of Christian missionizing language was unacceptable in a Cold

War contest for the allegiance of the world's peoples, many of whom would perceive it as Western imperialism. In *Masters of Deceit,* Hoover seems to have taken his lead from the administration, referring, like Eisenhower, to a more generic "Supreme Being" rather than God or Christ, and explicitly expanding his critique beyond Christianity by including a chapter titled "The Communist Attack on Judaism." (For more on Hoover and the Jews, see Sarah's Imhoff's contribution to this volume, chapter 7.)

Masters of Deceit asserts key religious cold war themes, in particular that communism was a false religion, that it was intent on world domination and the eradication of all religion, and that Marxism and Christianity were incompatible. These themes come through especially clearly in the chapter titled "Communism: A False Religion," in which Hoover develops the contrast between Soviet false religion, an ersatz and duplicitous imitation of religion's qualities, and the authentic religiosity of America. In America the individual was endowed with dignity and worth, but to the Soviets the individual was simply a "pawn of the state." The Soviets treated the needy with calculated ruthlessness, unlike the United States, where "belief in mutual responsibility, of our obligation to 'feed the hungry, clothe the naked, and care for the less fortunate,'" prevailed. Hoover celebrated America's resistance to communist objectives even as he emphasized America's commitment to the idea that love is the greatest force on earth. This conviction "forbids our accepting the communist division of mankind that by arbitrary standards singles out those fit only for liquidation."[30]

In Hoover's view, far too many churchmen were far too sympathetic to causes that had communist support, and he was keen to impress on the American people the incompatibility between religion and communism, another important tenet of the religious cold war. Hoover proclaimed that no Marxist could adhere to religion (either Christianity or Judaism) because the "utter elimination of all religion" was communism's "final goal." Americans had to remain vigilant in defense of faith and nation, Hoover argued, because communism recognized religion as its "most potent foe" and believed that it "must first sap religion's spiritual strength and then destroy it."[31]

Published in 1958, *Masters of Deceit* illustrates how important the idea of the "godless Soviet bogey" was to the Eisenhower administration and its effort to build an anticommunist consensus at home and abroad.[32] Eisenhower, elected president by an American populace in the throes of a religious resurgence, developed the religious interpretation of

America's destiny that Truman had initiated. Rather than simply allying the state with organized religion, political rhetoric in this era identified the nation as a kind of religion in its own right, identifying faith with proper patriotic commitment. Hoover internalized this conception of patriotism, repeating it in *Masters of Deceit*: "No hesitant, indifferent, half-apologetic acts on our own part can suffice. Out of the deep roots of religion flows something warm and good, the affirmation of love and justice; here is the source of strength for our land if we are to remain free. It is ours to defend and to nourish."[33] For Hoover, what mandated the struggle against communism—and by extension what justified the role of the FBI as a part of that fight—was the need to defend the core values that were the source of America and of religion, freedom, and faith.

HOOVER AND THE CHURCHES

The onset of the Cold War was accompanied by a "you are either with us or against us" attitude, by the insistence that a position be taken for or against communism. This presented a dilemma for ecumenically minded American churchmen committed to the World Council of Churches, which not only sought the participation of churches under communist rule but had also put "peace" and "colonialism" on its agenda. The FBI targeted key ecumenists, most notably Bishop G. Bromley Oxnam. In the early Cold War period, Oxnam was one of the Methodist Church's most powerful bishops, a force first in the Federal Council of Churches and then in the subsequently formed National Council of Churches, and a massive presence in the liberal Protestant establishment. Attacking him was an effort to undermine that establishment. The FBI's targeting of clergy and denominations that involved themselves in political, economic, and social matters also contributed to divisions among the churches, with war and racism proving particularly polarizing.

While the Cold War environment promoted by the FBI weakened and divided the mainstream liberal churches, it also facilitated the rise of the Christian right. Conservative evangelicals were able to move from a tangential to a more central cultural position owing to the emergence of a new patriotic evangelicalism and the way in which religious cold war discourse intensified strands of premillennialism. Although it was not Hoover's intent, his Manichaean rhetoric fostered a worldview that allowed for evangelical perspectives to merge into the civil discourse of American politics. Despite the considerable disparities between different groupings of evangelicals, the religious cold war allowed evangelicals of all stripes to develop a closer relational identity with the rest of the United States than had previously been the case, which helped them assimilate into mainstream culture and facilitated their participation in the political system.[34]

Radicals of the Christian right were not, however, embraced by the FBI. In the Eisenhower years, Hoover sent intelligence reports on the Christian right along with other organizations that were critical of the administration—another example of the extent to which FBI surveillance was responsive to White House requests and interests. Ironically enough, Hoover even submitted a report on Christian fundamentalist pundit Carl McIntire, whose views in many ways mirrored those of the FBI director when it came to liberalism in the churches. McIntire was the founder of the International Council of Christian Churches, set up as a counter to the liberal World Council of Churches, and later a supporter of pro–Vietnam War demonstrations, but he too was a subject of FBI scrutiny. While particular right-wing Christian leaders and organizations were the object of FBI suspicion, however, Hoover's promulgation of evangelical patriotism was one factor that led to the rise of the religious right in the 1970s and early 1980s.

During the Eisenhower era, the FBI "refined and extended [its] earlier efforts to influence official policy and public opinion."[35] The outcome was COMINFIL (Communist Infiltration), the code name for a broad program to collect information on dissident activities that was undertaken even though these years also witnessed the decline of communist influence and membership (which were never a significant force in American life to begin with). Hoover, despite the furor that followed McCarthy's attack on America's Protestant churches, was determined that the American public remain vigilant against communist infiltration of their churches. Liberal churchmen had been subjected to suspicion and smears prior to the Cold War, but COMINFIL marked a new era of particularly zealous witch-hunting within churches. The House Committee on Un-American Activities (HUAC), a recipient of FBI "intelligence," led the way, publishing the pamphlet *100 Things You Should Know about Communism and Religion*.

A cacophony of charges against churchmen also emerged from informers from within the Communist Party USA (CPUSA), the largest communist party in America. The best known was Herbert Philbrick.[36] Philbrick, an undercover agent for the FBI for nine years, first came to public attention as a witness in the Smith Act trial of communist leaders in 1949. Following their successful prosecution, Philbrick joined the circuit of professional communist traducers. He wrote a memoir of his underground ventures, which became a televised series. He also wrote a syndicated column for the *New York Herald*.[37] From his elevated position in the public domain he warned, "The communists are after your church."[38] Notably, Philbrick subsequently became involved with the Christian Anti-Communist Crusade headed by Baptist preacher Dr. Fred C. Schwarz.

FBI files reveal the number of people who believed that there was a communist campaign to subvert America's churches. Parishioners throughout the country mailed their suspicions to the bureau. Some simply sought clarification, but even those queries show the extent to which Hoover's criteria for measuring potential subversives had instilled doubt and suspicion of innocuous and conscientious clergymen. Liberals and former New Dealers usually ranked among those who needed to be watched. Hoover set in motion a disturbing trend of Christians spying on other Christians that remained discernible throughout the Cold War, and the phenomenon was not confined to the Christian right questioning the credentials of their liberal counterparts. Those within other religious orders, even within the Catholic Church, could also suspect one another, as illustrated by the case of Father Robert F. Drinan (1920–2007), a pacifist Jesuit priest and the first priest elected to Congress.

Drinan's FBI file reveals that in 1971 a nun wrote to Hoover doubting that a real Catholic priest could hold his "un-American" views and suggesting that he was an infiltrator planted to harm the church. As it happens, Drinan was later subject to a full FBI investigation when he was being considered for an appointment by the Clinton White House. That investigation showed him to be a man broadly admired for his integrity, but that reputation had not prevented the FBI from having already amassed a considerable file—something Drinan only accidentally discovered to his outrage during a congressional tour of FBI headquarters. There he learned of the file, which included the letter from the nun accusing him of being a communist plant.[39]

Hoover knew from experience that churchmen could be severe critics of American policies at home and abroad, which in his eyes made them valid subjects for surveillance. The FBI practice of linking dissent with disloyalty was most obvious with regard to Christian concerns over peace and war, which in this era translated into reservations about U.S. foreign policy and the nuclear arms buildup. Peace activists, especially opponents of nuclear weapons, were identified with the "Soviet-inspired" peace movement, which in the era of McCarthyism automatically implied that the activists were "fellow travelers" or communist stooges. FBI surveillance itself usually demonstrated that most were not seeking to serve Soviet interests; nonetheless, as one former FBI agent cogently remarked, "investigations of hundreds of perfectly harmless people continued on through the years."[40]

Those supporting racial justice and the civil rights movement were also perceived by Hoover as tools of a communist agenda. Soviet propaganda highlighted the abysmal treatment accorded Black Americans, which was particularly damaging to America's image in the developing world, and those who fought for equal rights within the United States were linked to the communist effort to discredit the country. Martin Luther King Jr.'s Southern Christian Leadership Conference deliberately inserted "Christian" into its name to deflect charges of subversion, but to no avail.[41] Christian dissent was considered even worse than secular dissent because, as Hoover put it in *Masters of Deceit,* every communist success in infiltrating, subverting, and bending religion to the party's aims made "the comrades diabolically happy."[42]

In line with his understanding of religion as the polar opposite of communism, Hoover believed that "a dedicated clergyman, being a man of God, is a mortal enemy of communism." Whatever the intentions, however, such a person could nonetheless inadvertently lend prestige and support to the communist cause by as simple an act as signing a petition for a seemingly worthy cause.[43] Hoover acknowledged a difference between those who knowingly supported the communists and those who did so unwittingly. Despite acknowledging the sincerity of the latter, Hoover derogated them as "dupes" and made it clear that, while they might have no disloyal inclinations, they were as useful to the communists as the more willing variety of fellow traveler, if not more so. Hoover found within the Senate a receptive audience for his suspicions of dissident clergy, supplying senators with information that included a list of Christian ministers.[44]

What these clergy had in common was that all were campaigners in areas the FBI regarded as subversive and were linked to groups identified by the FBI as communist fronts. Named and subsequently imprisoned was the Reverend Dr. Willard Uphaus—a Methodist lay preacher, a pacifist opposed to the Korean War, and a civil rights activist who not only supported precisely the sort of radical causes identified with communist front activities but compounded his sins by visiting Moscow and attending the 1950 World Peace Conference in Warsaw. In 1953, Benjamin Gitlow, a former CPUSA helmsman who by 1939 had turned against the party, identified Uphaus as one of the "principal individuals involved in the Communist conspiracy," a charge Uphaus categorically rejected.[45] Gitlow subsequently became involved with the evangelical leader Billy James Hargis, known for founding a variety of Christian anticommunist organizations before a sex scandal forced him to resign from his role as president of American Christian College.

Uphaus faced an indeterminate period in prison, which he knew, at age sixty-nine, could well become a life sentence, because he refused to name names to the New Hampshire attorney general, who had been empowered by the state legislature to investigate whether there were any subversive persons within the state.[46] In 1955 the attorney general, Louis Wyman, demanded that Uphaus reveal those who in 1954 and 1955 had visited the interfaith, interracial world fellowship center of which Uphaus was executive director, but he refused to disclose this information. The investigation found no evidence of wrongdoing on the part of Uphaus, who had fully cooperated with every other aspect of it, but the open-ended sentence was nonetheless upheld by the U.S. Supreme Court in June 1959, albeit with four justices dissenting.[47] Despite the widespread protest sparked by the case, Uphaus was jailed for one year.

Another Christian leader subject to FBI surveillance was British-born Harry F. Ward, an influential Methodist leader, professor of Christian ethics at the prestigious Union Theological Seminary, chair of the American Civil Liberties Union for two decades, and a prolific writer and speaker. Active during both of the United States's two postwar Red Scares, Ward was subjected to FBI surveillance from the First World War through the Vietnam War. He was a radical Social Gospeller, and all the evidence shows that his activities derived from his Christian convictions. From the perspective of the FBI, however, his causes and associations, defense of the Soviet Union, peace activism, and pursuit of civil liberties and racial equality—even his "foreign" birth—all placed him firmly in the security risk category.[48]

As early as 1922, Ward drew the ire of William J. Burns, director of the Justice Department's Bureau of Investigation (forerunner of the FBI), who indicted him as an "alien . . . who like so many of them . . . while our guest, reviles our sanctuary, pollutes the temple, and spreads from the very sanctum itself the seeds of discord, envy, and strife." It seems to have been Ward's denunciation of the Justice Department in 1924 as "functioning to destroy civil liberty" that brought him to the attention of Hoover shortly before Hoover assumed the directorship after Burns's departure.

Ward persistently criticized what he regarded as the damage done to America by political repression, and in his oratory during the 1950s he identified "four cornerstones" at the base of the police state that had emerged during the Cold War—"the FBI lists, HUAC's inquisition, the US attorney general's list of subversive organisations as a test of employee loyalty, and paid informers"—criticism that did nothing to endear him to the government. Indeed, for years one of his sons was unable to secure government employment and was told quite categorically it was because of his father's activities. Nonetheless, despite smears, surveillance, HUAC hearings, and marginalization within his church, Ward was never deterred from his quest for social justice, and the FBI's final assessment of Ward when it deactivated his file two years before his death in December 1966 revealed that, even from its perspective, he was never much of a threat: "Subject's file has been reviewed at the Bureau. He is a white male, 90 years of age, who is a retired minister. He studied in Russia between 1924 and 1932 and was reportedly a Communist Party member between 1943 and 1945. Since 1945 he has supported various Communist party front organizations."[49]

Even ardent anticommunists who supported the Cold War consensus, indicted the Soviet Union, and were declared patriots could find themselves subject to FBI scrutiny if they happened to have an association with what the FBI deemed radicalism. As a young man, the Methodist bishop G. Bromley Oxnam had been committed to social justice and civil liberties, and was also mentored by and defended Harry Ward. Between 1922 and 1924, Special Agent A. A. Hopkins wrongly smeared Oxnam as a radical activist and advocate of the Soviet system, a charge that became the foundation of a dossier that would grow to more than four hundred pages. Not only was Oxnam unaware of the file or the surveillance to which he was subjected, but "to the day of his death he praised the Bureau and its leader, J. Edgar Hoover."[50] Indeed, Oxnam even wrote an article published in June 1953, "How to Uncover Communists," in which he endorsed the FBI, "its thorough work, its loyalty to American traditions, and its spiritual leader, J. Edgar Hoover."[51] When, at his own request, he appeared before HUAC less than a month later, he in effect "named names."[52]

In the end, however, it did not matter that Oxnam criticized Stalin and the Soviet regime or that he was a committed Cold War warrior and anticommunist to the core (indeed, he was friendly with John Foster Dulles, the famous anticommunist secretary of state). The HUAC was predisposed to see any supporter of liberal causes as a communist sympathizer and, accordingly, attacked the bishop.[53] For his part, Hoover denied Oxnam's requests to meet him and declined Oxnam's invitations to address the Methodist General Conference and its bishops or groups, though the director was always cordial to Oxnam, who had the strength of the Methodist Church behind him, as well as the support of Secretary Dulles.

Hoover was careful in his dealings with the churches to justify FBI activities as intended for their benefit. His strategy consisted of claiming that American communists were plotting to subvert the churches and turn them into allies of the very people who sought the churches' destruction. FBI surveillance was therefore presented as a means of protecting churches from communist infiltration and of preventing churchmen from supporting causes that would ultimately prove detrimental to country and church. Christian criticism of the status quo or dissent from the Cold War consensus was attributed to external communist influence, however tenuous that accusation and regardless of whatever concerns might really have prompted the dissent.

Masters of Deceit warned that communists sought to exploit the churches and "to neutralize religion as an effective counter weapon" by appearing to align themselves with religion, while the CPUSA made sure to avoid appearing anti-religious. According to Hoover, when it was tactically expedient, CPUSA members even likened themselves to the early Christian martyrs suffering persecution for attempting to aid humankind. Hoover insisted that the CPUSA focus on peace, democracy, and, of course, civil rights was a ruse, part of a communist strategy to weaken and eventually destroy America by attacking the source of its strength, its faith. Hoover derided the way in which "the anti-religious Communist Party is now to be found in close united front cooperation with dozens of churches and other religious organizations on questions of immediate economic and political interest to the toiling masses." For Hoover, Christian preoccupation with inequality and poverty offered communists an ideal opportunity to critique the American way of life and promote their ideological alternative. As Hoover explained, the "church's legitimate interest in better housing and the elimination of social injustices" allowed communists to exploit "immediate economic and political problems."[54]

Hoover asserted that the communist movement was reaching out to the churches in open fellowship and encouraging members to infiltrate religious organizations in order to recruit them for the communist cause. He explained that "Comrades" who infiltrated church circles would find respectability and a wider audience for their views. Presenting themselves as having their roots in Christianity rather than communism facilitated the implantation of Marxist-Leninist thought among idealists, particularly the young. Hoover explained that churches offered communists a means of identifying their programs, intended to promote Soviet interests, with "genuine religious values" such as peace, brotherhood, and justice. The churches, however inadvertently, provided conduits by which communists could most effectively exploit the natural yearning for peace: "Every possible deceptive device is being used to link the Party's 'peace' program with the church." Indeed, Hoover claimed that Communist Party members were advised to join small churches "so that one can more easily work himself into a position of leadership."[55]

While he cast his efforts as a defense of religion, Hoover was in fact seeking to undermine the churches' authority and influence in areas of potential conflict with the administration. He accused communism of cynically exploiting religion, using it to legitimize the communist agenda while seeking to undermine religion from within. The irony is that Hoover's FBI was deploying some of the very tactics that he identified with the communist enemy. The FBI aligned itself with religion to legitimize its agenda and, in the process, sewed the division and distrust among the religious that Hoover claimed the communists wanted.[56]

THE BREAKDOWN OF CONSENSUS

At the end of the Eisenhower administration Reinhold Niebuhr, America's leading theologian, declared that the West had been successfully inoculated against communism "by the historical dynamism of the Judeo-Christian tradition."[57] The religious triumphalism concealed a more complex reality that would become apparent over the course of the 1960s. American policies and practices were coming under increasing scrutiny and criticism, and the depiction of the East-West confrontation as one between good and evil, a crucial element for Hoover's exercise of power and influence, was becoming less and less tenable. More and more mainstream churchmen worried about a military Cold War confrontation and potential nuclear holocaust and were receptive to some sort of accommodation between the United States and the Soviet Union.[58] Within the United States the impact of the civil rights movement and then the Vietnam War eroded the political culture based on the Manichaean anticommunism of the early Cold War. Vietnam caused Niebuhr himself to question whether the two superpowers were radically different and to wonder whether they had each revealed "similar imperialist impulses."[59]

Niebuhr would go on to become a founding member of Clergy and Laymen Concerned about Vietnam (CALCAV), and the history of this antiwar group illustrates what became of the FBI's tactics during the 1960s and 1970s as more and more people became disenchanted with the religious cold war ideology promulgated by Hoover. Formed in the autumn of 1965 to support the right to protest the government's conduct of the Vietnam War, CALCAV proclaimed dissent as a Christian tradition and declared: "To characterize every act of protest as communist-inspired or traitorous is to subvert the very democracy which loyal Americans seek to protect."[60] The FBI displayed little interest in CALCAV until the 1968 Spring Mobilization made opposition to the war impossible to ignore. Despite the fact that its own surveillance revealed no evidence of communist affiliation or violent tendencies on the part of CALCAV, the FBI placed the organization under Internal Security and Selective Service Act investigations in the latter part of 1968 on the familiar pretext that the movement was part of a communist conspiracy.

Despite efforts by various intelligence agencies to weaken the peace movement, CALCAV continued to grow. FBI interest in the organization intensified as well, though its views did not reflect the attitude of the majority of the churchgoing population. CALCAV leaders assumed that their phones were tapped and that they were being watched. Assistance provided by CALCAV to "underground" deserters violated federal laws, and Hoover ordered an investigation for sedition. Although the inquiry found no evidence and Hoover conceded CALCAV's nonviolent nature, the internal security and sedition investigations continued.

The FBI's surveillance of what were deemed "radical" Christians was intended to intimidate and deter. Those still prepared to adopt the tactics of civil disobedience, break the law, and accept the consequences in order to dramatize and publicize the issues faced the full brunt of the law, including imprisonment. They included the Berrigan brothers, priests Phil and Dan (a cofounder of CALCAV). Along with other Christians involved in their protest, they became fugitives to maximize the political symbolism of their cause. A massive FBI operation was implemented that involved surveilling and searching religious buildings and personnel, but the FBI's manhunt for the Berrigans ended as a public relations debacle for the bureau.

Dan Berrigan proved not only elusive but openly defiant, giving interviews and appearing on protest platforms, which prompted William F. Buckley, the conservative commentator, to mock the FBI for its ineptitude: "If you needed an extra speaker at your peace rally, an extra interviewee on your talk show, or an extra drummer at your rock festival, you could find Father Berrigan without any trouble; but for some reason the FBI could not find him at all."[61] Hoover, always highly sensitive about adverse publicity and embarrassment, doubled already-extensive efforts. Helped by paid informants and the naiveté of Phil Berrigan, the FBI eventually got their priests, and agents also recovered letters discussing a plan to make a citizen's arrest of a prominent public official who had contributed to the war effort. The discovery became a pretext for outlandish claims by Hoover before a Senate subcommittee in November 1970, when he sought millions of dollars in additional funding to combat a supposed anarchist group, led by the Berrigans, who, he said, were planning to kidnap a highly placed government official. As Hoover offered no substantive evidence to support his allegations, however, he was pilloried in the press, exacerbating the adverse publicity he was usually so careful to avoid.

The history of CALCAV shows that FBI practices and views did not change in this period, but it also reveals Hoover's declining ability to control public opinion, along with growing division and discontent within churches regarding their relationship with the state. The resulting shift on the part of mainstream churches opened the door to the Christian right, which had far fewer qualms about U.S. foreign and domestic policies. However, that very split reveals the cracks in the religious cold war alliance that Hoover had worked so hard to foster. As Heather Warren has cogently observed: "By the late 1960s ecumenical Protestantism's consistent opposition to racism and war ironically made it a contributor to the dissolution of the national consensus that it had helped hold together for many years."[62]

CONCLUSION

In times past, the alliance between religion and state was the most effective means of social and political control of national populations. The two global wars in the first half of the twentieth century demonstrated how in wartime very different and ostensibly secular regimes still invoked religion to support their causes. In the latter part of the twentieth century, the Cold War also had a significant religious dimension because of the Western propaganda claim that the Soviet Union was bent on the eradication of all religion. It was a claim that caused concern among the leadership of the newly formed World Council of Churches, the institutional expression of the ecumenical movement, despite its impeccable anticommunist credentials. As the Cold War and American religious rhetoric both escalated, the general secretary of the WCC, W. A. Visser 't Hooft, felt compelled in March 1949 to circulate a secret memorandum to key ecumenical Christians, including Geoffrey Fisher, the archbishop of Canterbury and a WCC president, with the stipulation that it not be quoted. The memorandum stressed that communist policy, contrary to the claims of Western propaganda, was not the eradication of churches, but their domestication.[63] Communist regimes wanted not to get rid of their churches, but, like their predecessors and their western counterparts, if not to control, then at the very least to strongly influence them.

All religious groups in the Soviet bloc confronted difficulties that included imprisonment, surveillance, censorship, and other means of oppression and control. In the United States only *some religious organizations and individuals* were subject to such measures, but the American political system similarly used state power to monitor, control, and repress religiously motivated dissent. This process was one in which J. Edgar Hoover and the FBI played a crucial role, and it has had lasting effects, contributing to the declining influence of America's liberal mainstream churches and the rise of the Christian right.

5

Apostles of Deceit

Ecumenism, Fundamentalism, Surveillance, and the Contested Loyalties of Protestant Clergy during the Cold War

MICHAEL J. MCVICAR

On March 26, 1947, FBI director J. Edgar Hoover testified before the House Committee on Un-American Activities (HUAC) about proposed legislation to outlaw the Communist Party of the United States of America (CPUSA). Hoover, then fifty-two years old, had overseen the FBI and its predecessor organization, the Bureau of Investigation, for nearly twenty-three years. He came before the committee as a widely respected public figure. His bureau had battled organized crime during the Prohibition era and the Great Depression, protected the nation from sabotage and foreign spies in World War II, and vigilantly guarded the nation against communism and foreign subversion since the First World War. As an anticommunist and guardian of the American way of life, Hoover stood beyond reproach in the popular imagination. He came to lecture the committee—and therefore the nation—about the threat the CPUSA posed to the United States.

Hoover's testimony before HUAC had all of the drama and pomp of a medieval court processional. As one commentator recounted, "Hoover came before the Committee like the archbishop paying a call on a group of lay brothers. He patronized them; they fussed over him."[1] Hoover had, in the words of historian Stephen J. Whitfield, a "flair for sermonizing."[2] The director delivered a fire-and-brimstone exhortation on communism's threat to the United States. Hoover's testimony painted a stark picture of the battle between the United States and an international, Soviet-led communist conspiracy. The implications were theological in nature and cosmic in scale: "The great god of the American Communists, Comrade Lenin—whose writings are their Bible—in various speeches and writings urged the use of deceit and trickery and his converts live by his injunction," Hoover warned.[3] "Communism," he told the committee, "in reality, is not a political party. It is a way of life—an evil and malignant way of life."[4] Average Americans—good-natured, trusting, and marked by Christian charitableness to all—hardly grasped the conspiratorial treachery they faced:

> I do fear for the liberal and progressive who has been hoodwinked and duped into joining hands with the Communists. I confess to a real apprehension so long as Communists are able to secure ministers of the Gospel to promote their evil work and espouse a cause that is alien to the religion of Christ and Judaism. I do fear so long as school boards and parents tolerate conditions whereby Communists and fellow travelers, under the guise of academic freedom, can teach our youth a way of life that eventually will destroy the sanctity of the home, that undermines faith in God, that causes them to scorn respect for constituted authority and sabotage our revered Constitution.[5]

The Communist Party threatened to infiltrate America's great institutions—especially its churches—and chip away at Americans' faith in "Judaic-Christianity" and slowly replace it with the new gods of Lenin and the state.[6]

This chapter explores the interconnections between the FBI's concern for the communist infiltration of the nation's churches and the development of a network of conservative fundamentalist groups whose leaders modeled their activities on the secret file collecting and investigative activities of the FBI to attack their foes in mainline Protestant denominations. Dismissed as cranks, rank opportunists, and fringe demagogues by their contemporary critics and many modern historians alike, these figures and the organizations they built must be viewed within the context of Hoover's warnings regarding the infiltration of churches by foreign communist agents.[7] Hoover's calls for vigilance against foreign agents resonated with socially and theologically conservative evangelicals and fundamentalists who saw "modernizing" or "liberalizing" theological trends in ecumenical American Protestantism as extensions of philosophical materialism and atheistic humanism. No Protestant body reflected these ecumenical trends more clearly than the National Council of the Churches of Christ in the USA, informally known as the National Council of Churches (NCC). As the largest Protestant ecumenical body in the nation, the NCC comprised more than 140,000 churches—including African American, Orthodox, Methodist, Presbyterian, and Lutheran congregations—with a membership of nearly 40 million Americans pastored by 107,000 ministers.[8] Popular anticommunist sentiment led the FBI and average citizens to suspect that the NCC's ecumenism had "red" origins. At the height of the controversy in the 1950s and early 1960s, the FBI's concern about communist infiltration of the NCC helped shape the development of a tiny network of fundamentalist churches and ministers who attacked the NCC Goliath. This chapter shows how these fundamentalists appropriated the intelligence-gathering activities of the FBI to create massive file systems designed to track domestic religious actors in the United States and link the activities of theological liberals with agents of foreign subversion.

Hoover's March 1947 testimony is now widely recognized as a turning point both in his career as a public figure and in the cultural history of the United States during the Cold War. He built relationships with key members of HUAC—including freshman California representative Richard M. Nixon—and established a liaison with the committee to leak secret FBI information to congressional investigators.[9] The director's testimony and subsequent relationship with the committee helped shape the Cold War at home by baptizing HUAC and numerous state investigative legislative committees with the authority of the FBI's vast domestic and international surveillance operations.[10] Hoover brazenly challenged the Truman administration's reluctance to endorse publicly the work of the committee and to confirm Hoover's narrative of a vast, Soviet-directed conspiracy to infiltrate America's civil and voluntary institutions. The director's testimony framed the struggle between the United States and the international communist conspiracy in cosmological terms: communists were engaged in an apocalyptic battle to overthrow Christian civilization and enslave human beings to the state. And yet, for all of Hoover's rhetorical flourishes, hyperbolic warnings, and unflinching support of HUAC, he also struck an ostensibly balanced position by denouncing the proposed legislation to outlaw the CPUSA and condemning the excesses of red-baiters. These moves doomed the bill and solidified the perception that the bureau—and not elected officials—should protect America from foreign communist threats. The director's testimony helped frame the way Americans—from elected officials and elite bureaucrats to average citizens—would think about the political, philosophical, and moral threat posed by communism.

Besides these important cultural and political contributions, Hoover's testimony also had a profound effect on mid-century religion. His fleeting reference to communist efforts to "secure ministers of the Gospel" to "espouse a cause that is alien to the religion of Christ and Judaism" rang out as a clarion tocsin to thousands, perhaps millions, of Americans. Since the beginning of the twentieth century, socially and theologically conservative White evangelical Protestants had worried about the influence of communism and socialism on American churches. With the development of fundamentalism as a social and theological project in the 1910s and 1920s, these concerns intensified until they reached a fever pitch following World War II. Hoover's testimony, wittingly or otherwise, further catalyzed an intense debate within American Protestantism about the loyalties of clergy, the power of the laity, and the place of the church in Cold War culture. A network of socially and theologically conservative evangelicals and fundamentalists mobilized to attack mainline Protestant churches. They argued that major ecumenical bodies, such as the NCC, represented an un-American and foreign form of religion.

ALIEN FORCES

Hoover's warnings to HUAC regarding the infiltration of churches and the dangers of naive clergy duped by sophisticated foreign agents prompted an FBI public relations blitz to America's churches. From the late 1940s through the 1960s, Hoover and his agents delivered a consistent message that America's clergy—whether Protestant, Catholic, Jewish, or even "Mohammedan"—must play a vital role in resisting communism by guarding against the infiltration of churches, seminaries, and Sunday schools by foreign ideologies.[11] This public outreach coincided with a broader push by the bureau to link its public image with popular concerns about educating children, policing adults, and maintaining the sanctity of the American family. In this cultural environment, clergy became simultaneously a check against communist sedition and figures of intense suspicion and even outright hostility.

The bureau's shift in public outreach coincided with what historian and Hoover biographer Richard Gid Powers has identified as an important turning point in FBI public relations from the late 1940s through the early 1960s.[12] According to Powers, the bureau shed its reliance on the G-man persona of its special agents. Agents transformed from sleuthing gumshoes into moral paragons of family values, Christian virtue, and 100 percent Americanism. While these themes were already standard fare in the popular mythology about the FBI, by the 1950s they took on deeper significance as the bureau sought to burnish its public identity through films, books, and journalism as concerns about the threat of international communism mingled uneasily with domestic anxieties related to race, crime, and the breakdown of the nuclear family.[13] The FBI stood as a guardian of domestic social order, and the special agent—memorably portrayed by humble everyman Jimmy Stewart in Warner Brothers' *The FBI Story* (1959)—became a family man and an empathetic "social worker" who, according to Powers, "radiate[d] kindness and understanding," rather than the noir cop brawler of the 1930s or the Nazi-chasing superspy of the 1940s.[14]

In *Masters of Deceit,* the best-selling 1958 study of communism in the United States, Hoover illustrated these concerns with the tale of "Jack," a young midwesterner who left his family for college and lost his faith in "God and religion."[15] Hoover recounted how Jack, as a naive college student, "found himself with an exceedingly curious mind but one uncontrolled by any spiritual faith." Jack eventually read *The Communist Manifesto* and found his way into the CPUSA. "In many instances we know," Hoover counseled readers, "joining the Communist Party comes from a loss of faith, so to speak, in our Judaic-Christian heritage and earnest, though perverted, seeking for a new faith. The individual is trying to find solutions to problems, real or fancied, that disturb his life."[16] Hoover publicly proclaimed that he believed all forms of criminality and aberrant social behavior had their roots in the kind of crisis of faith experienced by Jack, who had unwittingly come under the foreign influence of "secularism."[17]

Years before he recounted Jack's descent into communism, Hoover told a body of Methodist ministers, "Sin and crime are matters of degree, but they stem from a common source—godlessness or . . . Secularism."[18] Since the country "started with God and flourished with God's help," the rise in crime and godlessness in the United States must therefore be explained, Hoover argued, by the importation of some foreign philosophy. Here the FBI director saw the work of communists: "The danger of Communism in America lies not in the fact that it is a political philosophy but in the awesome fact that it is a materialistic religion, inflaming in its adherents a destructive fanaticism. *Communism is secularism on the march. It is the mortal foe of Christianity.* Either it will survive, or Christianity will triumph, because in this land of ours the two cannot live side by side."[19] Hoover's lesson to the Methodist clergymen was simple: America and Christianity stand united in a cosmic struggle against the lawless secular religion of communism.

Clergy play a critical role in the religious education of Americans and are, therefore, on the front lines of the nation's parallel struggles against crime and communism.

To drive home this point, the director and many of his agents promoted the conviction that Americans were uniquely religious people who had through their civic and voluntary institutions cultivated the "spiritual side" of the "human creature."[20] As literary historian Jason W. Stevens has pointed out, Hoover's emphasis on the essential spirituality of Americans assumed "that the human being is structured so that he cannot rest without belief in something that will forgive his guilt, give him hope of continuity despite his finitude, and restore meaning to a reality that appears fragmented to him."[21] Hoover's conceptualization of the relationship between religion and communism echoed traditional Christian theological themes related to guilt and the need for salvation. His spiritual view of the "human creature" placed him squarely in the company of many of his mid-century peers, ranging from elite theologians such as Reinhold Niebuhr to such popular evangelists as Billy Graham.[22]

Hoover's deputies at the FBI publicized their boss's view of the inherently spiritual nature of the average American. For example, FBI assistant director William C. Sullivan couched his advice about resisting communism in the vernacular of the religious self-help rhetoric of the era. He advised Americans battling communism to "start with oneself. Engage regularly in self-examination as a means of better understanding, developing, and applying daily the moral and religious values of our Judeo-Christian heritage."[23] Sullivan assumed that god-fearing, Christian Americans were naturally resistant to communism. But the social values of Christianity, such as charity and social justice, were especially vulnerable to communist subversion. Similarly, Hoover wrote that the danger of communism came from its "chicanery and deceit" and in the failure of Americans to understand its "machinations."[24] Bighearted but unreflective American Christians might inadvertently support communist ideas and groups because they failed to take "the time to examine what the group's true objectives were."[25] Education by vigilant church leaders was essential to the "self-examination" prescribed by Sullivan and Hoover.

Hoover most clearly explained the important role clergy played in battling communism in a series of articles published in the early 1960s in *Christianity Today,* the "flagship" intellectual journal of American conservative evangelicalism. Hoover had a cordial relationship with Southern Baptist minister Billy Graham—undoubtedly the most influential and respected White evangelist of the era—who founded *Christianity Today* to serve as a voice for conservative evangelicals who rejected the social separatism of fundamentalism for a more socially engaged brand of "Neo-evangelicalism."[26] The editors of *Christianity Today* gave Hoover a prominent place to hold forth on the theological implications of communism, laud clergy and laypeople alike for their efforts to resist communism, and chide the naive and foolish who failed to recognize the threat of communism.[27]

In a 1960 *Christianity Today* article, Hoover used militaristic imagery drawn from modern warfare to describe communism. In a metaphor carried throughout the piece, Hoover warned readers of "communist gunners" who were "sighting in" American clergy so they could launch "atheistic missiles" to "mangle, cut, and obliterate the spiritual tendons of life—belief in God, faith in Judaic-Christian values, love of the Church."[28] With echoes of Martin Luther, Hoover warned that communists attacked the "mighty fortress of God" to undermine the "spiritual firepower of the Christian Church."[29] Nodding to the nuclear fears of the period, Hoover argued that communists' "ultimate weapon" was atheism, which could destroy the Christian church.[30]

Behind all of the metaphorical bombast, the director developed his basic theme that American clergy were—mostly—loyal Americans who served as "America's most formidable barriers against communism."[31] As a consequence, any major communist infiltration in American churches must be explained as a product of foreign influences upon the clergy. To achieve this subtle subversion of the clergy, communists encouraged "churchmen to endorse, support, and even participate in Communist front groups; to sign Communist-sponsored petitions; to neutralize clerical opposition to communism."[32] These tactics allowed communists to exploit Christian "brotherliness" by encouraging hoodwinked members of the clergy to inadvertently support causes detrimental to their flocks and to the country. Well-informed clergy served the important political and social function of reinforcing citizens' natural resistance to communism. If smart clergy avoided unwittingly and naively supporting communist fronts because of their high-minded ideals, then they could teach Americans the spiritual values necessary to combating the subterranean psychic influences of communism.

Hoover's warnings to clergy reading *Christianity Today* and many other religious journals for which he and his agents wrote in the middle of the century illustrate the FBI's two basic assumptions regarding the relationship between religion and communism in the United States.

First, the FBI viewed clergy as naive about the dangers of communism, though mostly loyal to the United States. Second, communist subversion of churches, despite the director's public rhetoric, was largely nonexistent. In fact, even by the bureau's promiscuous standards of evidence, investigators found few indications of systematic communist infiltration of church groups or religious organizations. In a March 1960 review of investigations "into the overall picture of the efforts of the Communist Party . . . USA, to infiltrate religious organizations in the United States," the authors concluded that "the CPUSA has not been able to infiltrate our religious institutions to the extent it exerts any control over their policies on a national scale."[33] The report concluded that the CPUSA was successful "in persuading ministers to lend their names to issues of interest to the party and by signing petitions." The careful wording on this point is significant. As the bulk of the accumulated evidence showed, some ministers addressed issues "of interest to the party." But the issues—mostly related to social justice, economic equality, civil rights, and the end of blacklisting and legislative investigations of un-American activities—were not communist issues per se, but issues that the ministers and the party supported for independent reasons.[34] The bureau concluded there "is no indication the CPUSA is dictating the national policy of the NCC" or other groups, even if some ministers had signed petitions the party supported.[35]

Since Hoover understood the CPUSA to be little more than a domestic organ of Soviet Russia, any self-conscious communist rhetoric in U.S. churches had to be of foreign origin. As historian Rhodri Jeffreys-Jones has noted, this fit into Hoover's basic "operating assumption" that any form of political radicalism in the United States "was alien and that aliens were behind radicalism."[36] As Hoover wrote in the pages of *Christianity Today*:

> Here at home, alien forces strive to destroy the faith which forms the foundation of individual freedom. The sickness of secularism permeates large areas of our society. The Ten Commandments are ignored; the teachings of Christ dismissed. To many people, the word principle—fixed, immutable, unchanging—is simply a word and nothing else. Scores of pseudo-sophisticates today imply that it is not possible to adhere to a creed and remain intellectually free. These fervent worshipers of unbelief apparently are unable to comprehend man as a spiritual creature.[37]

As spiritual creatures crying out for individual regeneration, Americans who lost religion might experience a profound sense of meaninglessness and adopt foreign philosophies meant to fill the void. The clergy could guard against such anguish, but only if they comprehended how communists used Christianity to undo itself.

A ONE-WORLD CHURCH

By endorsing the position that foreign communists were trying to infiltrate America's churches and sway its clergy in subtle, anti-American ways, the FBI waded into a long-simmering feud in American Protestantism. Since the end of the nineteenth century, American evangelicals had disagreed over the use of the church as an agent of social reform. In the late nineteenth century, "modernist" or "liberal" theologians argued that Christianity must come to terms with recent advances in science, including Darwin's theory of evolution, and developments in biblical scholarship that undermined faith in the strict facticity of Christian scripture. Further, theologically liberal clergy such as Washington Gladden and Walter Rauschenbusch offered a pragmatic philosophy of social reform that insisted the truth of the Christian project came in the form of Progressive social activism. This philosophy came to be known as the Social Gospel. It downplayed evangelical revival in favor of collective social action—including church outreach, missionary activities, government regulation, and legislative reform—that could further God's kingdom on earth by Christianizing the nation's social environment.

In contrast to theological modernists, fundamentalists not only insisted on the "fundamentals" of Christian orthodoxy—the inerrancy of scripture, the divinity of Christ, Jesus's virgin birth, and the reality of the miracles recounted in scripture—but they also grew increasingly skeptical of Progressive social reform. Over the first two decades of the twentieth century, fundamentalists came to equate theological liberalism with social liberalism. In the eyes of fundamentalists, both positions seemed to downplay Jesus in favor of a collectivist, human-centered philosophy. Fundamentalists cast a skeptical glance toward any teaching that portrayed sin as a social problem. Instead, fundamentalists insisted that political solutions to social problems must be subservient to individual religious regeneration. By the 1930s many evangelicals and fundamentalists equated the Social Gospel with socialism—or worse, communism—and insisted on direct theological and philosophical links between social progressivism, materialism, and atheism. Although many Christians remained loyal to their traditional denominations, the controversy led some laypeople to view the clergy and bureaucrats who ran their churches with increasing suspicion.

J. Edgar Hoover's public warnings about communist infiltration of churches confirmed the deepest suspicions and cultural biases of many conservative evangelical and fundamentalist Protestants: foreign agents and domestic ignoramuses were undoing America's traditional Christian civilization. First, fundamentalists and evangelicals found much to admire in Hoover's simplistic associations of theological liberalism with atheism, materialism, and, ultimately, communism. These themes had become commonplace assumptions in many conservative churches by the 1950s, and Hoover found ready allies in many Protestant pulpits preaching a similar message.[38] Next, as a conservative Presbyterian, Hoover linked traditional religion with the preservation of Christian civilization. Many Protestants influenced by Calvinism shared Hoover's worldview that anchored American civilization in its Christian foundation.[39] Finally, Hoover's appeal to individual education and the primacy of individual spirituality resonated with deeply ingrained pietistic traditions that emphasized personal salvation and deemphasized the power of centralized religious institutions in the lives of rank-and-file Christians.

Hoover's religious approach to fighting communism unleashed the restless energies of the critics of liberal, mainline Protestantism. Over the course of the early twentieth century, theologically and socially conservative evangelicals had condemned the willingness of mainline denominations to set aside theological and doctrinal differences in order to cooperate on issues ranging from social reform to political lobbying. Most prominently, fundamentalists increasingly coupled theological conservatism with political conservatism as they came to identify the Social Gospel and Protestant ecumenical cooperation as political expressions of modernist theology.[40] By the 1920s, fundamentalists criticized efforts by other American Protestants to build ecumenical church organizations designed to highlight Christian unity and respond to modern social and cultural problems. They were especially critical of the Federal Council of Churches of the Churches of Christ in the USA (FCC), an ecumenical body formed in 1908 to represent the unity and social reform efforts of several denominations. By the end of World War I, the FCC had become nearly synonymous with the Social Gospel, modernist theology, and global Christian ecumenism.[41] In the middle of the twentieth century, the FCC evolved into the complementary bodies of the NCC and the World Council of Churches (WCC). The NCC claimed to represent the "common faith in Jesus Christ" of nearly 40 million Americans. It did so by working, "in spite of the diversity of

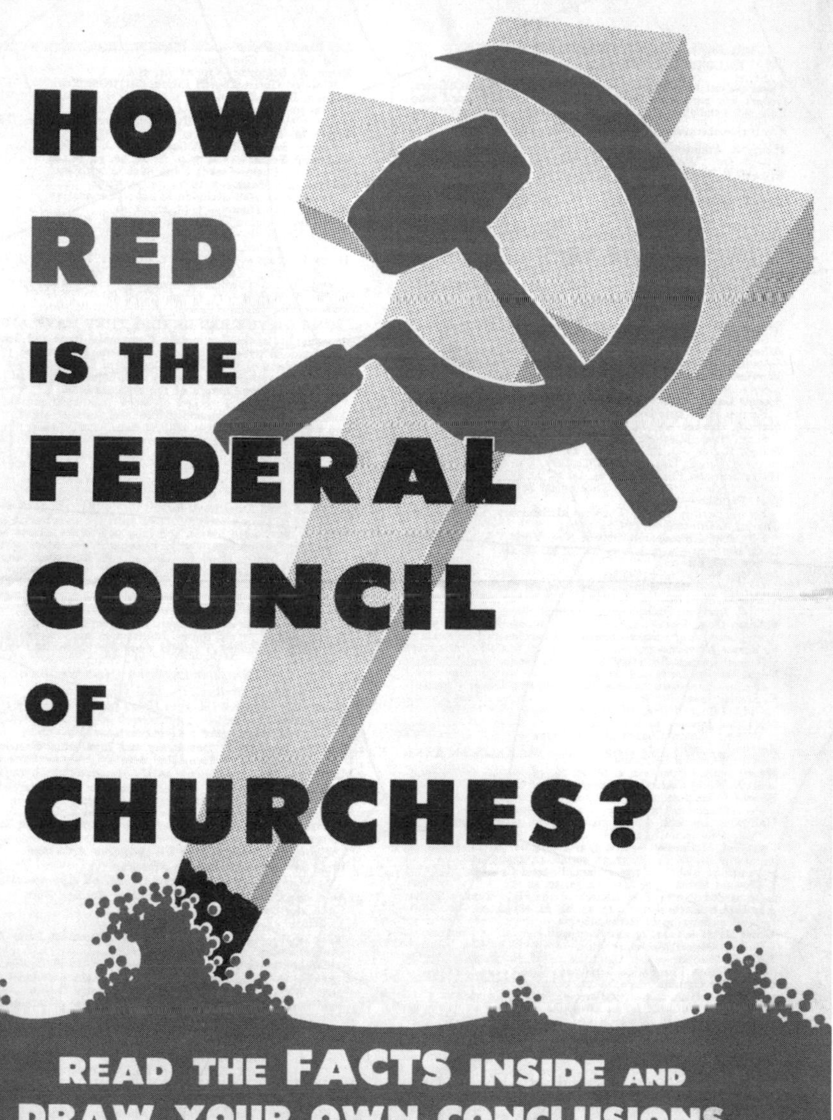

FIGURE 5.1. Pamphlets such as this Council of Christian Laymen's 1948 broadside, titled "How Red is the Federal Council of Churches?" provided midcentury critics of the FCC with ample "evidence" of the communistic leanings of liberal Protestants and prompted many Americans to write the FBI regarding the council. Courtesy of Special Collections, University of Arkansas Libraries, Fayetteville (Billy James Hargis Papers MC#1412, box 72, folder 17).

FIGURE 5.2. Reverend Carl McIntire, founder of the American Council of Christian Churches, huddles with Major Edgar C. Bundy of the Church League of America during a September 29, 1970, news conference in Washington, D.C. AP Wire photo by Bob Daugherty, courtesy of AP Images.

form and doctrine," to make Christians in member denominations "more aware of the central unity of their faith."[42]

Following World War II, fundamentalists and evangelicals renewed their attacks on ecumenical Protestant bodies. They took issue with the NCC's claim to represent different denominations in spite of their diversity. Instead of unity, fundamentalists insisted that the NCC's goal was bland religious homogeneity. Fundamentalists criticized the FCC, NCC, and WCC for glossing over theological differences and attempting to build a Babel-like "Superchurch" that would impose theological and social ideas on American Protestants.[43] On one end of the conservative spectrum stood the Presbyterian firebrand and radio broadcaster Reverend Carl McIntire.[44] McIntire condemned the NCC as envisioning "a one-world church, a one-world government, and one-world race."[45] This program, in McIntire's mind, was identical to the mission of communists and thus indicated that, on some level, the NCC and the CPUSA shared the same agenda. At the other end of the spectrum, more temperate Protestants associated with Billy Graham's Neo-evangelicalism and the National Association of Evangelicals similarly condemned the NCC but also saw it as an important model for how conservative Christians could cooperate to have their voices heard in Washington, D.C., and elsewhere.[46]

The NCC's commitment to ecumenical outreach, social justice, and racial and economic equality, along with its willingness to seek common ground between denominations on controversial theological issues such as evolutionary theory and scriptural criticism, created tensions between the professional clergy who administered NCC-affiliated churches and the laity who composed its constituent bodies. Professional clergy often pushed issues and encouraged social reforms out of step with many of their parishioners. This was especially true regarding desegregation and civil rights activism in the American South, matters on which the clergy were far more progressive than their flocks. Within NCC denominations, laypeople formed committees designed to monitor clergy, observe the bureaucratic work of the NCC, and generally push for more recognition of laypeople's concerns.[47]

DEAR MR. HOOVER . . .

In this environment of heightened religious suspicion, Americans by the hundreds and thousands wrote Hoover and the FBI requesting information about this or that clergy member, organization, or petition. Hoover's numerous written statements and appearances before various congressional committees teased citizens with vague information drawn from the bureau's seemingly boundless intelligence-gathering apparatus. Many citizens assumed that the FBI had information on their neighbors, clergy, and community leaders. Not only did many of the FBI's most patriotic correspondents view this intrusion of government surveillance into their daily lives as acceptable, but they also hoped that the bureau would publicly reveal the most intimate secrets of their pastors and priests.

Although perennial nativist concerns related to the influence of Jews and Catholics made up a significant portion of the inquiries about the communist infiltration of religion, by far the largest single set of letters dealt with Protestant institutions. In fact, correspondents aimed a significant amount of their requests at the NCC. While the correspondent's religious background is not evident in most of the letters, many of the writers seeking information about the loyalties of NCC clergy made it clear that they accepted many aspects of evangelical and fundamentalist criticisms of ecumenical Protestantism and the Social Gospel. They associated both movements with communism and the threat of foreign influences.

Letter after letter—most beginning "Dear Mr. Hoover"—poured into the FBI's Washington, D.C., headquarters and into field offices across the country. The inquirers took Hoover at his word. They accepted the director's binary opposition between Judaic-Christianity and communism. They also enthusiastically embraced his call to guard vigilantly their local churches and voluntary societies. The result was an explosion of letters, informal inquires, investigative paperwork, and follow-up letters authored by bureau scriveners. The file systems of the bureau metastasized to manage the surge in inquiries driven by Hoover and his surrogates' ceaseless warnings about the threat of communist infiltration of local churches and the CPUSA's covert manipulation of Christians' humanitarian impulses.

Letters came from Americans of all social positions, classes, and regions. An enlisted man stationed at a U.S. Air Force base in California wrote Mr. Hoover about his "big problem in regard to the translation of the Revised Standard Version (RSV) of the Bible."[48] The NCC oversaw the revision of the American Standard Version of the Bible, with a complete translation of the New and Old Testaments appearing in 1952. The RSV sold more than 26 million copies in its first year, but, as Hoover's correspondent illustrates, it also sparked concerns about the political loyalties of the panel of translators involved in the project.[49] "What I would like to know sir," the airman wrote, "is whether or not there is any truth to a very strong 'rumor' that a number of these people on the committee were ever or now communist, communist sympathizers, or on communist front organizations."[50] An organizer of the Minnesota United Church Women heard a radio news broadcast claiming "the *Council of Churches* was infiltrated with communism." "Kindly inform me," she requested, "if this statement came from your department and to what extent the communists are working in this organization."[51] A Methodist in Colorado whose church belonged to the NCC explained, "I have heard several times of late that the National Council of Churches, or at least the head men in this organization, are pro-communist." This prompted the writer to wonder "just how much truth there is in the rumors."[52] In another case, a correspondent informed Mr. Hoover, "It has been brought to my attention that your Department classified the Federal Council of Churches, the predecessor of the

National Council of Churches, . . . as subversive. I am writing to see if you will verify that accusation."[53] Regardless of the exact content of the letters or the nature of the information sought, most of the writers shared a clear sense of concern for the loyalties of NCC leaders and betrayed a deep unease regarding the authority of clergy.

Officially, the FBI responded to citizens' concerns about the communist infiltration of religious groups with a mixture of tepid endorsement and benevolent condescension. Hoover disdained form letters, so the FBI offered a range of replies to citizens' queries that all delivered the same basic message: the FBI has noted your concern and appreciates your vigilance, but please understand that the FBI's files are for its official, internal use only.[54] Over Hoover's signature, agents authored thousands of letters to citizens addressing concerns about communist infiltration of America's civic institutions. In one representative letter to a citizen concerned about communist infiltration of the NCC, the bureau responded:

> I have received your letter . . . and appreciate your interest in writing. While I would like to be of assistance to you, I must advise that the jurisdiction and responsibility of the FBI do not extend to furnishing evaluations or comments concerning the character or integrity of individuals, publications or organizations. Please do not infer in this connection either that we do or do not have in our files the specific information you desire. I am, however, enclosing some material on the subject of communism which may be of interest to you.[55]

The correspondent received a reprint of Hoover's speech "Communist Illusion and Democratic Reality."

Unofficially and concealed from the correspondent, the bureau's vast investigatory machinery meticulously processed every incoming piece of mail. Many correspondents would likely have been surprised to discover that the FBI's first action was to investigate the letter writer, not the alleged communist sympathizers.[56] For all incoming letters, agents searched bureau files for any reference to the correspondent. In the case of the previously cited letter seeking information about the NCC, research showed that bureau files made "no reference" to the correspondent. Agents then indexed the correspondent's name and cross-referenced it against the bureau's extensive NCC files. If the writer had already contacted the bureau, researchers would then have typed notes summarizing any previous correspondence. Regarding the correspondent's concern about the NCC, the agent placed a note in the file reporting, "The National Council of Churches is currently a controversial organization and has been for some years."[57] Given the "specific information" the correspondent desired regarding the NCC, it is unlikely that the short note regarding the confidentiality of the FBI's files and the reprint of Hoover's vague comments regarding communist infiltration of local voluntary societies satisfied the questioner.

THE CHURCH LEAGUE OF AMERICA

The bureau's cryptic and frequent admonition that correspondents should assume nothing about the content of its files undoubtedly encouraged many readers to conclude that the FBI did indeed possess the information in question and implied the director's wise discretion and capable handling of such sensitive information. Hoover recognized that much of the bureau's public allure hinged on its ability to walk a tightrope between exposing too many of its secrets and revealing too few. Hoover embraced HUAC as the primary channel for releasing the information he thought Americans needed. He argued that the committee served its "greatest contribution" when it "publicly reveals the diabolic machinations of sinister figures engaged in un-American activities."[58] Shortly after his March 1947 testimony before HUAC, when he first made this point, Hoover reiterated it in *Newsweek*: "As this committee fulfills its obligation of public disclosure of facts it is worthy of the support of loyal, patriotic Americans. This committee has for its purpose the exposure of un-American forces and as such its files contain voluminous information which, when used with discretion, provide an excellent source of information. The FBI, unlike this committee, must of necessity keep the contents of its files confidential."[59] As usual, Hoover kept his own pronouncements about communist activities in the United States vague. When it came to religion, Hoover told *Newsweek* readers, "Ministers of the Gospel desecrate their faith when they describe themselves as 'Christian Communists,' and call for the overthrow of the 'Economic Oligarchy,'" but he revealed no specifics about communist efforts to infiltrate the NCC or other groups.

Federal law prevented the FBI from disclosing its files to average citizens seeking information about subversive activities. This prohibition, which Hoover aggressively defended, opened a space for enterprising individuals to fill the vacuum. The mid-century period saw an explosion of antisubversive groups seeking to bridge the information gap between the FBI's secret files and the clamor for information regarding communist infiltration of American institutions. Hoover's warnings about communism were not the sole factor driving the development of such groups. Most prominently, business interests, with their deep pockets and friendly relationships with local, state, and federal law enforcement agencies, built their own intelligence-gathering networks and developed their own subversive lists—which they happily shared with clients for a price. Hearkening back to the nineteenth-century union-busting, anti-communist, and anti-anarchist ethos of the Pinkerton National Detective Agency, organizations such as the American Security Council, American Business Consultants, and Western Research Foundation operated private detective agencies that supplied subscribers with background information about potential employees who might have subversive leanings. These agencies often maintained ties with local police departments and federal law enforcement agencies, employed former law enforcement officials, and sold their files to nervous employers. Likewise, private voluntary associations maintained similar file systems. Some, like the American Legion and Daughters of the American Revolution, maintained close connections to the FBI by sharing information and personnel with the bureau. Other organizations, such as the ultraconservative John Birch Society, attempted to burnish their reputations by recruiting former FBI agents and supporting the speaking and writing careers of former FBI informants.[60]

Operating at the fringes of these business and private groups, a network of religious organizations maintained their own subversive lists. Many of these groups were one-person operations run by ministers or laypeople seeking to police this or that denomination. Some ran tiny organizations out of garages or dens. Others had a national scope; their leaders had direct connections to military intelligence and law enforcement, or they were former employees of the American Legion or similar organizations. Four of the largest religiously affiliated antisubversive operations—M. G. Lowman's Circuit Riders Inc., Billy James Hargis's Christian Crusade, Major Edgar C. Bundy's Church League of America, and Verne Kaub's Council of Christian Laymen—emerged from fundamentalist organizations supported by business, law enforcement, and religious interests in the wake of World War II. These groups fused the intelligence-gathering, secrecy-obsessed culture of the FBI with the populist anti-elitism and anti-intellectualism of twentieth-century fundamentalism into a potent attack on mid-century mainline, ecumenical Protestantism.

Of the four prominent organizations mentioned above, the Church League of America (CLA) represented perhaps the most concentrated mid-century effort to collect and disseminate information about "liberal" religious organizations and their alleged connections to the international communist menace. Founded in 1937 by a group of Chicago-area business and religious leaders, the CLA focused on exposing the threats of socialism and communism in American culture.[61] In its earliest incarnation under the leadership of advertising executive George Washington Robnett, the organization took on several right-wing issues including public education, Franklin D. Roosevelt's Supreme Court "packing" scheme, New Deal labor policies, and interventionist foreign policy. As the CLA grew in national recognition, it focused on exposing the perceived theological and political liberalism of America's clergy. The NCC bore the brunt of its wrath.

To gain authority in the already-crowded field of mid-century anti-communist watchdog groups focusing on religious issues, the Church League pursued an aggressive policy of information collection and dissemination. When Robnett passed most of the control of the CLA to Major Edgar C. Bundy, a former U.S. Air Force intelligence officer and ordained Baptist minister, the organization reimagined itself as a private intelligence-gathering operation.[62] To gain public support for the CLA's reinvigorated mission, Bundy leveraged his own personal history as an intelligence officer and appealed to the widespread respect for the FBI's domestic intelligence operations. In *Apostles of Deceit,* a scathing attack on the NCC and liberal clergy, Bundy informed his readers, "A citizen . . . cannot go to a local FBI office or to Mr. Hoover's headquarters, and ask for the names of all clergymen or church groups which have aided the cause of Communism, and expect to get them. They are not available. However, this does not mean that they do not exist."[63] He then proudly proclaimed that the CLA's dossiers on private American citizens and organizations were second only to the FBI's. He told audiences that the CLA's Wheaton, Illinois, headquarters housed in its research library "the largest and most comprehensive files on subversive activity."[64] In countless books, newsletters, and public lectures Bundy deftly exploited the secrecy surrounding the FBI's files to encourage laypeople and business leaders to hire the league's staff to research specific individuals or organizations in its massive index. For ten dollars, a supporter could hire the "services of our research staff, stenographers, etc." to run background checks on up to four individuals. Individuals above this four-person cap were priced at five dollars apiece.[65]

With over ten tons of documents on hand by 1967, the CLA operated a massive library of meticulously indexed private intelligence dos-

FIGURE 5.3. This undated promotional image of the Wheaton, Illinois–based headquarters of Major Edgar C. Bundy's Church League of America was intended to highlight the vastness and orderliness of the operation's research library. Courtesy of Special Collections, University of Arkansas Libraries, Fayetteville (Billy James Hargis Papers MC#1412, box 75, folder 26).

siers that subscribers could use for a fee.[66] The vast bulk of the CLA's data came from public sources—bookstores, newspapers, public government documents, HUAC hearings, the letterheads of subversive organizations, and so on. More dramatically, however, Bundy told supporters that some files "were smuggled out of the Soviet Union, the Satellite states and Red China."[67] Bundy claimed that the league also operated a network of "undercover operatives" in the United States who "sat in on Communist and leftist meetings and brought out not only miniature tape recordings of the proceedings but armloads of their literature." Armed with "tiny cameras," his agents photographed rallies, secret meetings, and student groups. His "agents" "ingratiated themselves with leftists that accepted their volunteer help to work in various headquarters."[68] In short, Bundy claimed that he oversaw a vast, secret network of spies and that he ran a multimillion-dollar private espionage firm out of a converted ranch house in suburban Illinois.

Within the context of the era's paranoia, Bundy's aspirations were breathtakingly ambitious and totalitarian. In one pamphlet to donors, he outlined the CLA's research and hinted at his organization's aspirations toward total information control:

> The uniqueness of the Church League files is that every name of every person, organization, movement, publication or subject of significance has been put on a reference card with one incident per card, each referring back to the original document in the files. Full page ads in newspapers, such as the *New York Times,* calling for the abolition of Congressional investigating committees, or attacking our security laws, have sometimes carried names running into the thousands. Each one of these names has been carded and indexed with the reason for it appearing in the ad put on the card. Likewise, if an individual made a speech or wrote an article or book attacking and ridiculing a major doctrine of the Christian Faith or the American way of life, that individual's name and the article or book were each carded.[69]

With more than 3 million cards indexing thousands of individuals, organizations, and publications, the CLA could reveal connections between any number of subversives, clergy, and foreign agents. Through *News and Views, The National Layman's Digest,* and numerous special reports, bulletins, and urgent fund-raising letters, the CLA kept supporters supplied with a steady stream of material documenting communist infiltration of schools, governmental bodies, and churches.

Although the organization's financial records make it difficult to determine how many CLA supporters used its research services, anecdotal evidence indicates that some individuals and organizations hired the CLA to look up suspected communists in its indexing system.[70] Some of the most prominent figures to solicit CLA research services included fundamentalist church leaders from across the United States. Most notable, perhaps, was Bundy's collaboration with Billy James Hargis and Carl McIntire. Hargis, a radio preacher whose *Christian Crusade* program once aired on 150 stations, relied on the Church League's exposés for his broadcasts. He and his staff subscribed to *News and Views* and the *Digest*. Surviving copies of these publications in Christian Crusade's archives indicate that Hargis's researchers relied on the CLA's material as an important source for the preacher's radio broadsides condemning the NCC and other "liberal" Protestant organizations.[71]

The circulation of information from Bundy to Carl McIntire was even more extensive. In fact, McIntire relied on a network of anticommunist research organizations to build his own theological and political case against the NCC.[72] McIntire's popular *Twentieth Century Reformation Hour* radio program aired on more than five hundred stations. He also worked with a network of small fundamentalist churches through his American Council of Christian Churches (ACCC). McIntire was a former minister in the Presbyterian Church USA who left that mainline denomination for a fundamentalist sect. In 1941 McIntire formed the ACCC as a small "cross-denominational" body—as opposed to an "ecumenical" council—committed to the principles of separatist fundamentalism and resistance to the ecumenical project of the FCC and its successor organization, the NCC. By the mid-1950s, McIntire's ACCC had become one of the loudest voices attacking the NCC. McIntire relied on the public disclosures of Bundy's CLA to expose the alleged subversion of its leaders and generated considerable suspicion about the loyalties of its clergy.

CONCLUSION

The interlocking media output of the ministries of Bundy, Hargis, and McIntire drove a significant amount of the FBI's vast correspondence regarding the communist infiltration of the NCC and other mainline Protestant denominations. As early as the mid-1950s, internal FBI documents conceded that nearly all of the "derogatory information" about the NCC "comes from rival church groups."[73] The bureau specifically cited the work of the three men and investigated their ministries because of the numerous allegations they generated. The intense suspicion provoked by these and other groups eventually forced the bureau to respond. In 1961, Hoover tried to tamp down the controversy by telling readers of a popular Baptist publication that the vast majority of America's Protestant religious leaders

> are today doing a magnificent job. They are helping to preserve the dignity of man as the image of God and to mold the individual to be a worthy citizen in a democracy. Over the years, as could be expected, churches and religious

> organizations have been—and will so remain—targets for communist infiltration. In the past, some clergymen, unfortunately, have been drawn into the communist movement. But the overwhelming majority of our clergymen are today wholly loyal to our nation and are working valiantly to protect our freedoms.[74]

The director asked Americans to avoid "name calling" and to resist the tendency to issue "unfounded accusations or publicity-seeking charges designed to confuse, divide and weaken."[75]

To further clarify matters, Assistant Director William C. Sullivan drew the thankless chore of addressing many of the wild charges circulating in the media among "professional anti-Communists." Sullivan, a Catholic, was the head of the bureau's intelligence division and had long been engaged in monitoring communist activities in the "religion field." He was a master at public relations who spoke widely across the United States during the late 1950s and 1960s on a number of issues, including the communist infiltration of domestic institutions. On a series of speaking tours, Sullivan, under Hoover's authorization, insisted that the vast majority of America's clergy were loyal and that communists had not infiltrated organizations such as the NCC. As he explained to a group of Methodist ministers in Dallas, Texas, in 1962, "It can be stated factually and without equivocation that any allegation is false which holds that there has been and is, on a national scale, an extensive or substantial communist infiltration of the American clergy, in particular the Protestant clergy. This statement applies with equal force to the Methodist as it does to other religious denominations."[76] Sullivan spent much of 1962 defending clergy and condemning the extremism of the "far right" in an effort to rein in the rhetorical excesses of the previous decade.[77] Not surprisingly, Sullivan's comments caused an uproar among the Bundys, Hargises, and McIntires of the world. But it also did much to dispel public concerns about communist infiltration of the mainline organizations. Embattled clergy across the United States embraced the FBI's new endorsement of their loyalty. Simultaneously, the bureau shifted its attention away from religion toward new homegrown issues related to the rise of the New Left, the student movement, and the radicalization of the civil rights movement in the 1960s and 1970s.

In this new era, much of the public obsession with the NCC likewise dissipated. Hoover's death in 1972 wrought a sea change in the FBI's interests as its leaders shifted their focus toward reforming a broken institution plagued by serious personnel issues, allegations of mismanagement of internal files, and evidence of widespread disregard for civil liberties and constitutional limits on the power of federal law enforcement agencies. In terms of religion, by the mid-1970s, the FBI's new administrators largely abandoned the dated anticommunist obsessions of the former director and turned their attention to other religious threats: cults, the influx of foreign religions, and radical White supremacist groups that rationalized their hate with theology. Meanwhile, the rise of the so-called new religious right in the late 1970s deflated the anticommunist fervor that had powered the ministries of Bundy, Hargis, and McIntire. The formation of the Moral Majority and similar organizations siphoned funding and support away from the faltering CLA and like-minded anticommunist relics of the mid-century period. Resources flowed to new organizations focused on social issues such as the breakdown of the American family, controversies over abortion, and campaigns to defeat the Equal Rights Amendment. In short, the religious right of the 1970s abandoned the FBI as its bureaucratic model and turned toward the mechanisms of modern political parties. Political action committees and voters' guides replaced dossiers and subversive indexes in the fundamentalist war against liberal religion.

6

The FBI and the Catholic Church

REGIN SCHMIDT

In early October 1945, shortly after the surrender of the last remaining Axis power, the Japanese Empire, and before the outbreak of the Cold War, a thirty-seven-year-old Catholic priest, professor of economics, and fierce anticommunist, John F. Cronin, sat down to write a worried letter to the general secretary of the National Catholic Welfare Conference, the administrative staff of the U.S. bishops. Cronin was completing a study for the bishops, and he had received some alarming and highly sensitive information from confidential sources that he was unable to reveal. As he noted in the letter, "My informants tell me that a disclosure of what I know would imperil national security and hinder current counterespionage."[1] This is the classic dilemma for intelligence agencies: how to use sensitive information without revealing their sources and methods. But what kind of confidential information had a staff member of the American Catholic Church gained access to and which intelligence or security agency did his "informants" belong to? And what was the nature of the secretive study, referred to in church correspondence as the "Special Research Project"?

The relationship between the Federal Bureau of Investigation and the Catholic Church was complex and changed over time. It is well known that the bureau and the hierarchy of the church cooperated and supported each other during the early part of the Cold War.[2] However, there is more to the story. During the bureau's first three decades—from its founding in 1908 to the late 1930s—there was little contact between the two institutions, and, in fact, they held opposing views on such an important topic as the problem of communism. For a number of reasons, that situation changed during the late 1930s and World War II, and a mutually beneficial relationship was established during the following decades. At the same time, the Catholic Church was never a monolithic entity, and the bureau maintained surveillance of progressive and radical Catholics who questioned the Cold War consensus. This chapter focuses on a little-known event at the end of World War II when the bureau played an important role in influencing the hierarchy of the Catholic Church to abandon its traditional liberal (or positive) anticommunism for a conservative (or negative) anticommunism.

A CRIME-BUSTING BUREAU AND AN IMMIGRANT CHURCH

Following the bureau's founding in 1908, contact between the FBI and the Catholic Church seems to have been limited. The bureau was initially tasked with investigating federal crimes such as antitrust cases, but it became involved in the surveillance of radical, pacifist, and leftist activities during World War I and the Red Scare (a fear of revolution triggered by the Bolsheviks' 1917 seizure of power in Russia and postwar domestic turmoil). However, in 1924, following a number of scandals during the administration of President Warren G. Harding, the attorney general limited the bureau to investigating violations of federal law.[3] During the following years, the bureau and its newly appointed director, J. Edgar Hoover, focused on reorganizing the bureau, introducing scientific law enforcement methods, and pursuing John Dillinger and other gangsters of the Depression era.[4] In 1936, the bureau's mission was again expanded when President Franklin Roosevelt directed Hoover to monitor fascist, Nazi, and communist activities within the United States. Hoover used the instructions to establish a wide-ranging surveillance operation directed particularly against communist, radical, and leftist organizations and individuals, an operation that continued unabated until his death in 1972.[5] At the same time, Hoover and the bureau initiated a campaign to promote its image and to influence public opinion by cooperating with sympathetic contacts in the media.[6] These two decisions—to reinstitute political surveillance and to influence public opinion—put the bureau on a path that would soon intersect with that of the Catholic Church.

The national voice of the Catholic Church in the United States was the National Catholic Welfare Conference (NCWC), originally established during World War I by a number of dioceses, Catholic organizations, and the Catholic press to coordinate the Catholic war effort and then made permanent following the war. The NCWC's staff, directed by a committee of seven bishops, was tasked with carrying out the general policies of the hierarchy, which were decided at the annual meeting of the bishops. The bishops' social policies were executed by the Social Action Department (SAD), directed from 1920 to 1945 by Father John A. Ryan, who was strongly influenced by the Church's teachings about social justice.[7] As set forth in the encyclical *Rerum Novarum* by Pope Leo XIII in 1893, Catholic social justice was seen as an alternative both to the greed and inhumanity of capitalism and to the autocratic state of socialism. In the tradition of the Catholic corporatist system of the Middle Ages, the Church argued that private property should be guaranteed and the rights of labor to a "just wage" and to join Catholic-led unions should be protected. This thinking influenced the NCWC's stand on communism in the interwar years and gave it a decisively liberal bent. The NCWC's study on communism, *Bolshevism in Russia and America,* published in 1920, concluded that the fundamental causes of communism were the unequal distribution of wealth and the injustices of capitalism. "As long as capitalism stands, we are not safe from revolution," the study warned.[8]

As the voice of the bishops, the NCWC continued to espouse a liberal line during the 1920s and 1930s. The Catholic population was overwhelmingly composed of working-class immigrants, who were among the most enthusiastic supporters of President Franklin Roosevelt's New Deal reforms during the Great Depression.[9] However, the American Catholic Church was a part of a transnational and worldwide church, and the persecution of its members in other parts of the world affected its American brethren. Three developments overseas convinced American Catholics that the Church was threatened by the forces of communism and persuaded them to see communism as a political-military threat rather than a social ill. First, the Church followed with growing anxiety the religious persecution in Soviet Russia following the revolution. The NCWC decided to educate the public about the conditions in Russia, and in 1923 the organization protested to the Soviet commissar for foreign affairs against the jailing and execution of Russian clergy.[10] Although the bishops took no official stand, the NCWC lobbied the U.S. government in 1933 not to recognize the Soviet government, but without success.[11] Second, the American Catholic hierarchy reacted with horror against the killing of priests and nuns and the destruction of churches by Loyalist forces during the Spanish Civil War, which broke out in 1936, and they condemned Loyalist supporters in the United States.[12] Third, the American Church worried as the Soviet Red Army, having repulsed the Nazi invaders from the Soviet Union, in late 1944 began liberating Eastern Europe from the German occupiers. The bishops warned President Roosevelt, expressing their concern that the Soviet leader Stalin sought to dominate Eastern Europe. They advised him that Catholics in the United States would punish him if they felt that he was sacrificing the freedom of Eastern Europe to appease the Soviet Union.[13] Seeing communism as a threat to the Catholic Church and its members, the American hierarchy and its staff began to abandon social justice in favor of a more conservative and repressive form of anticommunism.

SHARED VALUES

During the mid-1930s, as the FBI began to play a public role, promoting its image and influencing opinion, it established links with members of the Catholic hierarchy. As director, J. Edgar Hoover exercised absolute control over the ideology and values of the bureau, and his worldview was traditional and conservative. He saw crime and subversion as a moral, as opposed to a social, problem, caused by lack of character, and in countless speeches and articles he called for a return to traditional values—discipline, hierarchy, hard work, family, faith, and country.[14] This conservative ideology aligned Hoover and the bureau with like-minded conservative Catholic prelates. During the 1930s and 1940s Hoover established friendly relations with a number of bishops based on shared antimodernist, anticommunist, and patriarchal values. These were mutually beneficial friendships in which the bureau disseminated information and services and the bishops provided intelligence and public support for the FBI.[15]

Such relationships can be illustrated with the cases of two Catholic leaders. Francis J. Spellman, archbishop of New York and the leader of the American hierarchy, was described in internal bureau correspondence as a friend who had expressed his admiration for Hoover and who was ready to support the bureau at all times.[16] Spellman and Hoover agreed on the moral causes of social problems; in 1942 Hoover commended the archbishop for stating that the nation's victory in World War II depended as much on "our morality at home" as on the progress on the war fronts.[17] The two men also shared a concern about juvenile delinquency, the need to protect children from child molesters, and the threat of communism.[18] The bureau provided the archbishop with certain services: he was put on the Special Correspondents List and given copies of the director's speeches and articles, invited to give the graduation address at the FBI National Academy, provided information on communist infiltration of youth groups, and given the results of a bureau investigation into a book critical of the archbishop.[19] In exchange, Archbishop Spellman expressed his support and admiration for Hoover and the bureau, gave information on Church matters, aided the bureau's operations in Latin America during World War II and the Cold War, and invited the director to make Spellman's views known in speeches and articles. In 1954 his relationship with the bureau was institutionalized when he was named a SAC (special agent in charge) contact.[20]

Reverend (later Bishop) Fulton J. Sheen was the public face of American Catholicism, having hosted popular radio and television shows, authored numerous books, and directed the Society for the Propagation of the Faith.[21] Like Spellman, Sheen agreed with Hoover's moral philosophy and believed that the nation's survival depended on its inner character, and he praised Hoover and his men for having established "a tradition toward Divine justice."[22] The bureau maintained friendly relations with Sheen by placing him on the director's mailing list and inviting him to speak at the graduation ceremony of the FBI National Academy and at the FBI Communion Breakfast.[23] For his part, Sheen was an enthusiastic supporter of the bureau and its mission; according to a bureau memorandum from 1967, Sheen had consistently exhibited "an active interest" in the bureau, had always been "of assistance," and had willingly met with bureau officials.[24] However, the priest played a particularly valuable role in the Church: he was famous for aiding prominent Americans to convert to Catholicism. Some of the converts were communists, such as the editor of the party's paper the *Daily Worker*, Louis Budenz, and the Soviet intelligence courier Elizabeth Bentley. In these cases the bureau assisted Sheen, providing him with background information on the prospective converts and, in return, gaining intelligence about the defectors.[25]

JOHN F. CRONIN AND THE FBI

John F. Cronin was a Catholic priest and professor of economics at St. Mary's Seminary in Baltimore, Maryland. Experiencing the poverty and deprivations of the Great Depression following the stock market crash on Wall Street in 1929, he became interested in economics and John A. Ryan's thinking about social justice. This led him to join in the activities of Catholic labor schools and the campaign by the Congress of Industrial Organizations (CIO) to establish unions for the nation's large number of industrial workers. During the war, he became involved in the struggle between anticommunists and communists in the unions in the shipyards of Baltimore, and he came to believe that communists threatened social harmony and cooperation on the home front. Consequently, he aligned himself with conservative anticommunists within organized labor and, more important, established links with special agents of the FBI's Baltimore field office. The field office, with the approval of bureau headquarters, provided Cronin with confidential information from its files on Baltimore communists, which the priest used in the struggle for power within the unions.[26]

In October 1942, when he was a thirty-four-year-old, battle-hardened warrior of the often merciless fight against the communists, Cronin had become so concerned about the threat to the nation that he wrote Archbishop Edward Mooney of Detroit, who served on the administrative board of the NCWC. In describing his experience in Baltimore, Cronin referred to "reliable information" (possibly from the FBI) indicating that it was part of a national plan, adding, "It seems that Joe Stalin has a different idea of the second front than most military commentators."[27] Cronin urged the archbishop to raise the problem during the bishops' next board meeting, stressing that "I am particularly concerned with the resurgence of communist activity."[28] Cronin's description of the situation in Baltimore must have disturbed Archbishop Mooney, who requested that he prepare a report on the problem. When he submitted the report a few days later, Cronin called on the NCWC to commission further national-level studies of this "really menacing" threat.[29] The Baltimore report detailed the "notable and alarming resurgence of Communist activity," particularly among workers and Blacks, which Cronin attributed to the popularity of the Soviet Union because of its resistance to Nazi aggression, apathy among the population, and the "sheer unscrupulousness" of the communists. Cronin warned that the communists planned to capture the unions in strategic areas of the economy, which would give them "a dominant position" throughout industry and among Blacks after the war. Cronin advocated a strategy of "intelligent opposition" to communism by working for social justice and training workers to resist the communists' advances.[30] Thus, Cronin still believed in Catholic social justice as the antidote to communism.[31]

The bishops and the NCWC did not act immediately against the alleged threat. Two years later, however, the American hierarchy, as noted above, became notably alarmed about the advancing Red Army and the threat it posed to the Church and its members in Eastern Europe. Consequently, in November 1944 the bishops requested the NCWC to undertake a study of the "nature, extent, causes, and remedies" of communism. The NCWC's administrative board placed Bishop Karl J. Alter, who served as chairman of the Social Action Department, in charge of the study, and he appointed Cronin to undertake it and report his findings to the bishops. Cronin was directed to report monthly on his work to Bishop Alter and to two officers of the NCWC, Michael J. Ready and Raymond McGowan.[32] Cronin, then, had succeeded in lobbying the hierarchy and gaining a position as the Church's official investigator of communism, thereby enabling him to influence the views of the hierarchy on the major problem of the time.

Cronin was able to use the Catholic Church's considerable resources and widespread network in the United States. The NCWC appropriated an initial $5,000 to cover the study's expenses for a period of five months (in the end, it took a year to complete the project). This sum was to cover the salaries of Cronin and a small staff (consisting of an assistant director, research assistants, and secretaries) as well as sundry other expenses such as travel and mimeographing.[33] During the initial phase, Cronin consulted with priests, government investigators, and labor officials familiar with communism, and he was given access to the files Archbishop Spellman had received from the bureau. Next, he built up an "extensive file" on communist organizations, individuals, and activities based on information from "reliable outside investigators" and reports from forty priests. At the same time, he directed two researchers to analyze communist activities and influence within organized labor. Cronin also sought to involve the hierarchy in the study. He sent out questionnaires to all bishops and three hundred selected priests to gauge the extent of communist activity nationwide and to invite the opinions of the clergy involved in social action.[34]

More important, Cronin established links with the intelligence community and official investigators, who were able to provide him with confidential information on communism. No doubt, Cronin's status as an official representative of the Catholic Church, widely acknowledged as a staunch defender of the United States and its traditional values, aided him in gaining access to intelligence officials. Among those who assisted Cronin were Raymond E. Murphy, an official in the State

Department; J.B. Matthews, an anticommunist expert on the staff of the House Committee on Un-American Activities (the Dies Committee); the intelligence divisions (so-called Red Squads) of the police departments of New York and Chicago; and the Office of Naval Intelligence.[35]

The FBI nevertheless played a pivotal role in the compilation of the Cronin report. As one of his first actions, Cronin reestablished his contact with the FBI field office in Baltimore, requesting information relevant to the study. After the hierarchy had vouched for Cronin's credentials, he met with an official of the FBI headquarters in Washington, D.C., who provided Cronin with promising leads. Later during the study, the priest also received assistance from the Chicago and Baltimore field offices as well as from FBI contacts in New York. During the study's final phase, the Washington, D.C., headquarters provided vital information from its files and reviewed and rewrote a draft of the report.[36]

The sensitivity and accuracy of the information Cronin received from his intelligence contacts is indicated by a communication from the priest to one of his superiors, NCWC general secretary Howard J. Carroll. In this letter from early October 1945, Cronin advised Carroll that he had received information that State Department official Alger Hiss was a secret communist and that the Soviets had obtained "a formula, nearly complete, but *not everything*," on the atomic bomb that had been developed during the top-secret Manhattan Project at Los Alamos, New Mexico.[37] The case against Alger Hiss, as well as the conviction and execution of Ethel and Julius Rosenberg, for aiding Soviet intelligence in stealing the atomic bomb design excited controversy during the Cold War.[38] But we now know, after the opening of intelligence archives in Washington, D.C., and Moscow following the end of the Cold War, that Hiss was indeed a spy for Soviet military intelligence and that Julius Rosenberg worked for a Soviet intelligence network that stole information about the atomic bomb.[39] Only a select few intelligence officials and policy makers at the highest levels knew about Hiss and Rosenberg, which indicates the high value of Cronin's intelligence. Cronin and his superiors went to great lengths to protect their sources. References to the most sensitive sources were omitted from the report, and in some instances public sources were used as a cover. Since the report named names and made the NCWC (and the Church) vulnerable to libel suits, the report's distribution was limited to the bishops with the understanding that it would be kept confidential and not quoted publicly. An abstract would later be provided to priests.[40] Despite these precautions, the report apparently circulated within conservative anticommunist circles.[41]

THE CRONIN REPORT

On November 12, 1945, Cronin submitted his final report, titled *The Problem of American Communism in 1945*, to the NCWC administrative board.[42] FBI officials could be pleased with the 166-page report, which closely mirrored the views and opinions of the bureau and the intelligence community. Their assistance played no insignificant role in convincing the hierarchy of the Catholic Church in America to shift its position on communism to the right, in the process abandoning the idea of social justice as the solution to the problem.

Thus, bureau officials and other intelligence sources used the Cronin study to formulate and disseminate the basic assumptions of U.S. Cold War thinking. In doing so, the intelligence community acted ahead of the official foreign policy line of the Truman administration, which, despite its growing concerns over Soviet behavior, was still pursuing a policy of cooperation and negotiation in late 1945. While bureau officials from Director J. Edgar Hoover on down clearly saw the Soviet Union as pursuing the goal of world domination and domestic communists as a fifth column, the Truman administration would not settle on a policy of containment until early 1947. The Cronin report might be seen as an attempt by the FBI and the intelligence community to influence the Catholic Church as well as the U.S. government toward taking a clear anticommunist stand, domestically as well as internationally.

The Cronin report was based on the assumption—and this had been the bureau's view since the Red Scare in 1919—that the activities of the Communist Party of the United States of America (CPUSA) should be seen in the context of Soviet foreign policy. According to the report, the Soviet Union was an expansive power that sought the imposition of world communism by "encirclement and aggression." The report described the advances of Soviet power during the war and alleged that the Soviet dictator, Stalin, had designs on Africa, the Turkish straits, and Asia. Based on information that must have originated from intelligence sources, Cronin even hinted at Soviet plans for an invasion of France and Spain in the spring of 1946.[43] Seen in this context, the role of the CPUSA was to act as "a potential fifth column," defending Soviet actions and thereby confusing the public and paralyzing U.S. foreign policy.[44]

The bulk of the report was devoted to a detailed account of how the CPUSA exercised its influence through phony organizations (so-called front organizations) and infiltration of the labor movement.[45] At least some of this information must have come from bureau files, and it seems to have made quite an impact on Cronin; as he noted, "The extent of infiltration and control was greater than this writer had previously realized."[46] The bureau, too, was most likely the source of some of the report's most explosive allegations concerning communist infiltration of the government. According to Cronin, the communists had targeted the State Department in order to undermine U.S. efforts to counter the Soviets, and he singled out Alger Hiss as "the most influential Communist" within the department.[47] Cronin reflected the opinion of bureau officials and many conservative anticommunists in accusing the Democratic administrations of Presidents Roosevelt and Truman of being naive and soft on communism, enabling the communists to infiltrate government agencies during the New Deal era of the 1930s and the wartime alliance.[48] This would later be the core of Senator Joseph McCarthy and fellow Republicans' charges against the Democrats for having "lost China" because of treason in high places. One of the sources of McCarthy's information was the FBI.

Cronin's report, influenced by the bureau, concluded by abandoning the Catholic Church's traditional line of social justice. Since the communist threat was caused by Soviet expansionism and fifth column activity, social reforms were irrelevant to neutralizing it. As Cronin noted in a key section, "It is hard to see how social reform in the United States will restore liberty to Poland or free Hungary and Czechoslovakia from Soviet economic domination."[49] Consequently, communism should be combated by the Catholic Church with a combination of education, training in social action, and aid to anticommunist labor activists, which Cronin believed would undermine communism and in addition strengthen the Church's position in America.[50]

The report's strengths and weaknesses were, not surprisingly, the result of the influence of the bureau and fellow intelligence agencies. On the one hand, the information on Soviet espionage against the Manhattan Project and the activities of Alger Hiss was accurate. On the other hand, Cronin exaggerated the threat posed by the Soviet Union, which in 1945 was devastated and weakened by the war; he also exaggerated the influence of the domestic communist movement, which had been compromised by the Hitler-Stalin Nonaggression Pact from 1939 to 1941. Finally, he exaggerated the communists' influence on U.S. foreign policy and ignored the Truman administration's tough stand against Soviet actions. The weakened position of communism in the United States became apparent three years later when the communist-supported Henry Wallace and the Progressive Party polled only about 2 percent of the vote in the 1948 presidential election.

FBI, CRONIN, AND THE RIGHTWARD SHIFT OF THE CATHOLIC CHURCH

The bureau's aid to Cronin played a part in the American Church's increasing conservatism after the war. In September 1945, as Cronin was putting the finishing touches on his report, John A. Ryan, the long-serving director of the NCWC's Social Action Department, died. Ryan had been the guarantor of the NCWC's liberal line, but his death provided new opportunities for more conservatively inclined church officials. Cronin, who had become the bishops' expert on communism partly as a result of the bureau's assistance, was a strong candidate for Ryan's former position. On November 12, 1945, Cronin was made one of two assistant directors of the SAD.[51] This appointment had far-reaching implications for the political line of the hierarchy and its administrative apparatus. Cronin by now openly criticized Ryan's social thinking and his emphasis on the need for a "living wage," warned of the power of the centralized state, and expressed acceptance of the capitalist system.[52] With persistent prodding from Cronin, the NCWC moved to the right during the early Cold War, abandoned advocacy of social reform, and embraced a version of conservative anticommunism. Whereas Ryan had been an enthusiastic supporter of Roosevelt, Cronin became an aide and speechwriter for the rising star of the Republican Party, Richard M. Nixon.[53]

Cronin's status as an anticommunist authority was much in demand during the early years of the Cold War. He published *Communism: A World Menace* in 1947, participated in the launching of the anticommunist magazine *Plain Truth,* and instructed newly elected congressman Nixon about Soviet espionage and Alger Hiss.[54] However, his friendly relations with the FBI did not last long. In 1946, he publicly revealed that there were some two thousand secret communists on the government payroll who worked for Soviet intelligence. Hoover reacted with anger, since the bureau did not want this information in the public domain, and he cut links to the priest.[55] As the fear of communism ebbed somewhat after the death of Stalin and the end of the Korean War in 1953, Cronin's attention shifted back to social reforms, and during the 1960s he participated in the civil rights movement.[56]

EPILOGUE: FROM COOPERATION TO SURVEILLANCE

The relationship between the FBI and the Catholic Church as it developed after World War II must be seen in a transnational context; after all, the American Church was a part of a universal church, and the FBI was a part of the executive branch of a government pursuing global interests. During the early Cold War, a convergence of interests led to a close alliance, as the United States needed religion as a bulwark against communism and the Vatican saw the United States as the only counterweight to Soviet expansionism. During the 1960s and 1970s, however, Pope John XXIII and his successor, Paul VI, positioned the Vatican as a neutral player in the Cold War, stressing peace in Vietnam, negotiations with the East, and social justice. Although the pope who followed Paul VI, John Paul II (who succeeded John Paul I, who died thirty three days after his election in 1978), was of Polish descent and an outspoken anticommunist, and while the Reagan administration established diplomatic relations with the Vatican in 1984, the parties did not always see eye to eye on international issues. The pope pressed for aid to the Third World, and the American bishops denounced nuclear deterrence as immoral.[57]

The FBI's attitude toward the Catholic Church followed these developments. At the height of the Cold War, the FBI perceived the Catholic Church and its members as dependable allies in the struggle against communism. For example, Joseph P. Kennedy, the father of the first Catholic president, was one of the bureau's contacts, and FBI officials secretly leaked information to the Catholic Senator McCarthy in his crusade against communist infiltration of government.[58] However, as anticommunism was replaced by civil rights, poverty, and the war in Vietnam as the nation's main concerns, some Catholic activists became engaged in social reform and protest movements. In doing so, they became the targets of FBI suspicion and surveillance. One longtime target was Dorothy Day and her Catholic Worker movement. Day, who has been proposed for sainthood in the church, was a pacifist, an advocate of distributism, and a social activist. Hoover described her as "an erratic and irresponsible person" who was "consciously or unconsciously being used by communist groups," and the bureau placed her on the list of potential subversives to be interned in case of war.[59] Another was César Chávez, the hardworking, idealistic, and devout leader of the National Farm Workers Association (NFWA) who strove to organize some of the poorest and most exploited migrant workers of Hispanic and Filipino origin. From 1965 to Hoover's death in 1972, the FBI maintained Chávez under surveillance, trying in vain to find evidence of communist infiltration of the NFWA.[60]

The story of the alliance between the FBI and the Catholic Church, then, is quite complex and dynamic. The framework was conditioned by the transnational context—the Cold War, U.S. policies toward the Communist bloc, and the views of the Vatican. Since the Catholic Church and its American members were as varied as the population at large, the bureau cooperated with conservative members of the hierarchy (and conservative politicians) while keeping liberal and radical Catholics activists under surveillance. As the case of the bureau's assistance to Cronin illustrates, the FBI was able to influence the Church's position during the early Cold War. There were limits to the bureau's power, however, and the Catholic Church always pursued its own agenda, such as its moral condemnation of nuclear weapons during the rearmament of the Reagan administration.

7

Hoover's Judeo-Christians

Jews, Religion, and Communism in the Cold War

SARAH IMHOFF

In 1960, a Milwaukee dentist told his longtime patient that "the Zionist party in this country makes up more than 90% of the communist party." The dentist claimed to have come by this "information" while serving in the "Intelligence department of the Navy" during the war. His patient, a housewife who identified herself as "a second generation American citizen [of] the Jewish faith," was so concerned by what he told her that she wrote to FBI director J. Edgar Hoover to ask if this could possibly be true.[1]

She was not alone in her concern. When the Cold War began in 1947, the murder of Jews under Nazi rule had ceased, and the Nazis' antisemitic ideology had been discredited. Yet some American Jews found themselves targets of a subtler form of prejudice. Hoover's FBI and other government agencies called on Americans to help them find and root out the communists in their midst. Not all were as openly anti-Jewish as the Milwaukee dentist, but many harbored a suspicion that Jews in the United States were communists.

The FBI's approach to Jews and Judaism during the Hoover era was shaped not only by a suspicion of Jews as potential communists but also by the image of America as a land of equality and religious tolerance. In the years after World War II, the link between Jews, Judaism, and communism was fraught. On the one hand, being Jewish was prima facie evidence that one may be communist; on the other hand, Judaism played an essential role in the concept of a religious America. In this period, as Dianne Kirby shows in chapter 4, Americans used religion as a way to differentiate themselves from the communist USSR. "Communists have been, still are, and always will be a menace to freedom, to democratic ideals, to the worship of God and to the American way of life," Hoover told the House Committee on Un-American Activities (HUAC) in 1947.[2] Unlike the "godless communists" in the USSR, Hoover argued, Americans lived in a religious nation. President Eisenhower famously asserted: "Our form of government has no sense unless it is founded in a deeply felt religious faith, and I don't care what it is. With us of course it is the Judeo-Christian concept but it must be a religion that all men are created equal."[3] Eisenhower, like Hoover, assumed that the category of religion in general—as well as the religiosity of the United States—included Judaism. Eisenhower's identification of American governmental ideals as "Judeo-Christian" points to a role that Judaism would play in the Cold War: the inclusion of Judaism allowed Americans to claim that the United States was both generically religious and accepting of religious diversity.

For anticommunist crusaders in general, and for Hoover and the FBI in particular, these two dimensions—the association of Jews with communism and the embrace of Judaism as a defining component of American religiosity—posed a conundrum: how could Jews be un-American while Judaism formed a foundational part of American values? On the one hand, midcentury antisemitism and Cold War ideologies combined to create suspicion of Jewish leftists, as the antagonistic relationship between the FBI and Hollywood demonstrated. On the other hand, "Judeo-Christian" rhetoric and the embrace of a "Judeo-Christian" mythology became an essential part of what differentiated America from the "godless" USSR, with its Marxism and persecution of religious groups.

This chapter charts the FBI's engagement with these two approaches to Jews and Judaism. The first part begins with a brief history of Jews and the FBI, focusing on the years from 1947 to the early 1960s, and explores the cultural assumptions about Jews as communists. While the first part is about Jews, the second part is about Judaism (or the "Jewish faith," as the Milwaukee housewife put it) and its role in the FBI's representation of a religious America's struggles against communism. Building on this foundation, the third section turns to the question that drives this chapter: how could Hoover and the FBI's embrace of Judaism as essential to American culture coexist with their proclivity to see Jews as communists?

JEWS AND COMMUNISM

Well before the end of World War II, many Jews associated with the political left. Some who emigrated from Eastern Europe before 1924 participated in the Bolshevik Revolution. Among those investigated by the Bureau of Investigation, for example, was the famous Jewish anarchist Emma Goldman. After Goldman served a two-year sentence for conspiring against the draft, Hoover re-arrested her and persuaded the courts to deport her as a foreign-born radical. Few American Jews were as politically radical as Goldman, but many others were committed leftists. Some had, before they left Eastern Europe, been members of the Bund, the secular Jewish labor party. In the United States, many continued or joined that tradition and joined labor unions. Leftist politics were even evident in the first decades of the twentieth century in the three major New York Jewish newspapers: the socialist *Forverts,* the anarchist *Freie Arbeiter,* and the communist *Morgen Freiheit.*

But by the postwar period, the close association between Jews and the Communist Party had waned. The Hitler-Stalin Pact of 1939 dealt the party a heavy blow. Most Jews were still politically left, but there were far more socialists than communists. And though Jews were demographically overrepresented in Communist Party membership, the party was neither exclusively nor even overwhelmingly Jewish. In the 1950s, the American Jewish population exceeded four million, and the Communist Party peaked at around fifty thousand members.[4] Just as only a small percentage of American Communists were Jews, only a small percentage of American Jews were communists. Indeed, a number of Jewish organizations actively combatted communism: the American Jewish League Against Communism was founded in 1948, and larger organizations, such as the Jewish Federation, the American Jewish Committee, and the Anti-Defamation League, created their own anticommunist committees.[5] These national Jewish organizations aided the FBI and even conducted their own purges of known communists from their ranks.[6]

While most Jews were not communists, many did identify with the political left, and some began to fear that they would be targeted as communists, whether they were or not. This fear was not unfounded. A significant number of Americans continued to associate Jews and communism, and formed judgments as to who was a good American based on race or national origin. A 1951 *New York Times* article illustrates such judgments: it reported that government officials declared that an East

Tennessee atomic plant was not a likely target for saboteurs because of the "lack of Communists" there. The officials justified this conclusion by citing "the prominence of pure Anglo-Saxon stock" in the nearby population.[7] (Ironically, in 2012, three White Christian pacifists, including an eighty-two-year-old nun, broke into the facility to protest nuclear weapons.[8]) Jews and African Americans bore the brunt of such assumptions about communism. A 1948 survey by the American Jewish Committee found that 21 percent of Americans believed that "most Jews are Communists."[9] Another survey found that 19 percent of people answered "Jews" when asked which "nationalities, religious, or racial groups" were communistic.[10]

Throughout the Cold War, the FBI suspected and pursued many individual Jews, as well as Jewish and Zionist groups suspected of colluding with communists, though the FBI rarely claimed that it had pursued someone *because* the person was Jewish. Of the late 1940s investigations into Post Office employees for "disloyalty," 90 percent of the cases were against African Americans or Jews.[11] An American Jewish Committee document from the late 1940s reported that the FBI estimated that 50 to 60 percent of communists were Jews.[12] The FBI kept tabs on dozens of Jewish organizations, from the Zionist Organization of America to the politically progressive Emma Lazarus Federation of Jewish Women's Clubs.[13] It even tried to police representations of Jews and antisemitism on the radio, on television, and in movies.

A 1949 American Council for Education (ACE) publication found that rhetorical combinations such as "Jews and atheists" and "Jews and communists" appeared frequently in a variety of publications, especially student textbooks.[14] The tendency to conflate communism and Jewishness is also detectable in FBI files. For instance, Charlie Chaplin's file includes information from an informant "who claims to have a number of confidential sources concerning Communist and Jewish activities operating in Los Angeles."[15] Beyond the walls of the FBI, this slippage between Jewish and communist did not go unchallenged. The ACE study, which had been funded by a grant from the National Council of Christians and Jews, denounced assumptions that all Jews were communists and declared that "equally disturbing is the combining of Jewish with other groups which lack prestige with many Americans." That the ACE deemed such a study necessary, however, suggests that the tendency to identify Jews as communists was recognized at the time.

Because of such associations, as well as social and professional prejudice, the bureau itself was an institution from which Jews were largely excluded. Almost all FBI agents in this period were White Protestants or Catholics. Before 1960, the bureau as a whole employed only five African American agents. Similarly, the Jewish FBI agent Al "Wallpaper" Wolff, one of Elliot Ness's Untouchables, recalled his long and varied FBI career "working in all those departments as the only Jew."[16] Until the time of Hoover's death, fewer than 2 percent of agents came from racial or religious minority groups.[17]

However pervasive antisemitism may have been within the FBI in this era, Hoover certainly did not want the FBI to seem antisemitic. If the bureau, its agents, or even its informants seemed prejudiced against Jews, FBI projects would be open to critique. The FBI's solution was not to denounce antisemitism or to avoid association with those who professed anti-Jewish bias, however, but rather to keep overt declarations of antisemitism out of the record. Agent Jack Levine recalled that when one informant told him that all Jews were communists, he was not allowed to include the comment in his written report because the bureau worried that bias would discredit the report.[18] Since the FBI nevertheless used the report and the information it contained, it is clear that the antisemitic bias of the informant did not discredit the informant's testimony in the bureau's view. What was important was that the FBI not seem to be endorsing such an attitude.

Not only did the FBI try to keep antisemitism from being recorded in its own documents, but in some cases it also tried to keep it from being depicted in popular media. The FBI justified its objection to portraying American culture as antisemitic on the grounds that such a representation would give the enemy fodder for anti-Americanism. For instance, it concluded that the highly acclaimed 1947 film noir classic *Crossfire* bordered on aiding the communist enemy in plainly depicting and denouncing antisemitism in America. *Crossfire* did not lack for critical success—it was nominated for an Academy Award for best picture. The FBI, however, pronounced that the whodunit, a story about a Jewish man murdered by an American soldier, "was near treasonable in its implications and seeming effects to arouse race and religious hatred, through misleading accusations [including] the use of a drunken, maladjusted soldier to typify our courageous service men and the use of minority groups to arouse suspicion and sympathy." To highlight "the racial angle" was "decidedly the wrong approach to overcome racial hatred," and it played into the enemy's hands.[19] This effort to render the problem of American antisemitism invisible extended beyond the bureau's taste in films to its own internal policies. In 1949, Hoover wrote to Jacob Javits, the Jewish congressman from New York: "We do not use the word 'Jew' or 'Jewish' in describing the race or nationality of criminals in connection with the issuance of our identification orders furnishing details on individuals wanted by the F.B.I. Several years ago the F.B.I. adopted the rule of prohibiting the use of words descriptive of religion to describe a race or nationality."[20]

Hoover's effort to distance the FBI from antisemitism was in line with the growing marginalization of antisemitic anticommunism after World War II. This was in part due to greater tolerance of Jews in American culture, but also due in part to a desire to distance American culture from Nazism. As the sociologists Aaron Beim and Gary Allen Fine demonstrate, spouting the kind of antisemitic anticommunist rhetoric that had been popular in the 1930s was no longer considered appropriate and could prove a significant public relations liability.[21]

Although its public and overt manifestations had become gauche, antisemitism remained an unspoken undercurrent in many social and political circles. Thus, for example, government agencies disproportionately pursued Jews as potential communists. McCarthy's Senate Committee on Homeland Security and Government Affairs was one highly visible instance. Of the 124 people questioned by the committee in 1952, 79 were Jews.[22] The most famous communist-hunting arm of the American government, HUAC, pursued Jews specifically. HUAC also worked closely with Hoover. Although Hoover tried to keep the bureau's role quiet, the FBI consistently leaked information, witnesses, and even charges to HUAC.[23] Hoover himself occasionally made an appearance at HUAC hearings, and when he did, committee members praised him and fawned over him. Over its years of operation, HUAC compelled the testimony of hundreds of Jews as suspects and as witnesses; in many cases Jews made up the overwhelming majority of those called before the committee. Thirteen of the first nineteen people brought before HUAC were Jewish.[24] Ten of them refused to cooperate and instead denounced HUAC, quickly becoming the first to be blacklisted and jailed. Of the blacklisted "Hollywood Ten," six were Jews. As Joseph Litvak shows, "antisemitism, and the systematic recruitment and display of Jewish collaborators, were very much on HUAC's" agenda.[25]

The targeting of Jews suspected of communism had tragic consequences. The popular radio and television actor Philip Loeb, for instance, committed suicide after he was blacklisted. Loeb played the lovable patriarch on *The Goldbergs,* an immensely popular radio show from 1926 to 1946, and then moved to television in 1950. Likely because of his union work with the Actors' Equity Association and the Television Authority, Loeb was listed in a 1950 pamphlet titled *Red Channels: The Report of Communist Influence in Radio and Television.*[26] Although in most cases it offered no concrete evidence of entertainers' communist involvement, *Red Channels* listed 151 entertainers (about a third of whom were Jewish) who were effectively blacklisted from then on.[27] Philip Loeb was on the list. Although his costar and *Goldbergs* owner, Gertrude Berg, did not want to fire him, when General Foods dropped its sponsorship and CBS dropped the show, she acquiesced.[28] His wife had died years earlier, and he was the only means of support for his mentally ill son; after *Red Channels,* he struggled to find work. Only days after he overdosed on barbiturates in a New York hotel room, the FBI cleared Loeb of membership in the Communist Party.

Most Jews were not communists, but the fact that two of the most famous communists were Jews reinforced the popular association. Julius and Ethel Rosenberg, both American-born Jews, were convicted of what Hoover called "the crime of the century," giving nuclear secrets to the Soviets in order to help them build a bomb.[29] The FBI played a crucial role in gathering evidence against the Rosenbergs, a story that has been told many times.[30] The Justice Department, bolstered by the bureau's information, argued that Julius had headed an espionage operation during the war and subsequently stole nuclear secrets, with the help of his wife, Ethel. The Rosenbergs and their supporters claimed that the government had fabricated evidence against them because of their communist beliefs and even their Jewishness, but such arguments were made to no avail. The Rosenbergs faced a sensational trial, and were convicted and then executed in 1953.

The FBI also followed American Jewish groups with Zionist goals. In the late 1940s, the FBI kept close tabs on several Jewish organizations working to bring about a Jewish state in Palestine. The FBI admitted it had put the Zionist Organization of America (ZOA) under "limited investigations in 1949, 1954, and 1970" to determine whether it qualified as a foreign agent.[31] But it had clearly been keeping tabs on the organization for years before 1949: documents from 1947 refer to "the concern recently expressed by the Director" about "the present situation in Palestine."[32] Although the FBI was concerned about weapons being supplied to Jews in Palestine (a legal gray area), it spent much of its time trying to get the ZOA on charges that it had not properly registered itself as a foreign aid organization. Although some Americans, such as the dentist mentioned in the opening anecdote, assumed Zionism and communism went hand in hand, the bureau rarely linked its investigations of Zionist organizations explicitly to communism (though it did reply to one woman's letter asking about the Zionist movement not with information about Zionism, but with enclosures of "What You Can Do to Fight Communism" and "The Communist Menace: Red Goals and Christian Ideas").[33] Most of the time, the FBI justified its surveillance of Zionist organizations by citing their support for a foreign political project, not on the grounds of a perceived connection to communism. In *Masters of Deceit,* Hoover's best-selling work, it is the communists who are anti-Zionist; thus instead of attacking the Zionist movement openly, Hoover sought to discredit its leadership as a way of undermining it without alienating its rank and file.[34]

But there were times when Hoover and his FBI seemed to suspect a connection between Zionist organizations and communism. The bureau also kept a detailed file on the Irgun, an underground paramilitary Jewish organization committed to building a Jewish state in Palestine. Hoover himself took an interest in the underground organization as it tried to garner American support.[35] To create a Jewish state, the Irgun claimed, Jews would have to fight the British and the Arabs, and it was willing to break the law to do so. The FBI, in its response, also skirted the spirit of the law, if not the letter: instead of wiretapping Americans directly, it told British intelligence whom to wiretap and then used the information from the British wiretaps in its investigations. The bureau also occasionally assumed a connection between Zionist groups and communism. Hoover approvingly cited an American Jewish Congress remark about the prominent Irgun activist Peter Bergson (a pseudonym for Hillel Kook) that described him and his Irgun associates as "disreputable Communist Zionists."[36]

JUDAISM AS PART OF A JUDEO-CHRISTIAN AMERICA

> And this is how they [the Founding Fathers in 1776] explained those: "we hold that all men are endowed by their Creator . . ." not by the accident of their birth, not by the color of their skins or by anything else, but "all men are endowed by their Creator." In other words, our form of government has no sense unless it is founded in a deeply-felt religious faith, and I don't care what it is. With us of course it is the Judeo-Christian concept, but it must be a religion with all men are created equal.

Eisenhower's famous remarks, given as part of a speech to the Freedoms Foundation in 1952, captures the mix of attitudes toward Judaism and the civic religion that emerged in the United States during the Cold War: (1) "Our form of government" must be based on religious faith. (2) America was not theocratic or sectarian, however: it did not matter what the content of that faith was, provided that it recognized that "all men are created equal." (3) While America was religiously pluralistic, there was nonetheless a sense of a religious "us" and "them," and the "us" was to be identified with "the Judeo-Christian concept," a concept that seems to identify Judaism as a source of the religious values with which the president identified.[37] But the Judaism that helped constitute the Judeo-Christian tradition had little to do with Judaism as such. It was scarcely ascribed a distinctive theology or practice and was valued only for the ways its users imagined it to coincide with Christianity.

That Eisenhower was giving voice to widespread views is suggested by the popularity of the phrase "Judeo-Christian" in the Cold War era. The term appears in print only a handful of times before the 1940s, but it had proliferated by the 1950s.[38] Newspapers, books, and casual exchanges all adopted the term, and Hoover himself used it in his writing.[39] What exactly "Judeo-Christian" meant in this context is not as clear-cut as it might seem. It did not serve a descriptive historical or sociological function, since no individuals described themselves as Judeo-Christians and no religious community called its creed Judeo-Christianity. In combining two broad religious groups, the term skirts deep theological differences, sociological separations, and historical conflict. But the elisions inherent in the term allowed many Americans to ally Judaism and Christianity in the fight against a third enemy—godless communism. Adding "Judeo-" as part of America's religious heritage provided a way to assert the religiosity that supposedly distinguished American culture from communism while also reaffirming a commitment to tolerance and inclusiveness.

The trend of referring to Protestantism, Catholicism, and Judaism as the three American faiths also reached its heyday in the early Cold War period. This tripartite vision sometimes even had the imprimatur of the U.S. government itself, as when it allowed the National Council of Christians and Jews to send teams composed of a rabbi, a Catholic priest, and a Protestant minister to present popular public "trialogues," first to enlisted men and women and then, after the war, to cities throughout the United States.[40] Even those sharply critical of the shallowness of this American religiosity recognized the ascendance of this tripartite vision of religious pluralism. Will Herberg's 1955 classic, *Protestant, Catholic, Jew,* included all three within the "American way of life," despite his critique of that way of life as theologically vacuous.

When Herberg described the national imagination, he argued that religion formed a central part of American culture and identity, and by "religion" he meant that practiced by Protestants, Catholics, and Jews.

Hoover also used the language of "Judeo-Christian," and by doing so, he signaled his participation in this particular brand of Cold War American religious pluralism. As noted elsewhere in this volume, Hoover cast communism as the enemy of religion, by which he meant both Christianity (including Catholicism) and Judaism. As he explained in his prepared remarks for HUAC in 1947, for example, communism was "evil work" and "a cause so alien to the religion of Christ and Judaism."[41] In the 1958 *Masters of Deceit,* in which he developed his thesis that communism was a false religion, Hoover made sure to include a chapter on its efforts to destroy Judaism. As this work makes clear, Hoover distinguished between Jews who were drawn to communism and Judaism as a religion. Many communist leaders called themselves Jews or claimed a Jewish origin, and the Soviets reached out to Jews. The apparent sympathy was duplicitous, however, and the persecution of Jews in the Soviet Union, especially the government's targeting of rabbinic schools, revealed that its true intention was to destroy Judaism, a goal that reflected its broader antipathy toward all those who worship God, "regardless of their faith."

Although this conflation of Judaism and Christianity made some Jews wary of the language of "Judeo-Christian," others adopted it to emphasize their own American belonging and anticommunist stance. This was how the American Jewish League Against Communism used it, for example, when it referred to communism as "a conspiracy aimed at God, the Ten Commandments and Judeo-Christian morality."[42] For some Jews, aligning themselves with "Judeo-Christian tradition" served as a way to distance themselves from the communist ideology with which Jews were often identified.

The effort to position Judaism as part of "Judeo-Christian" America helps to explain why, even while the FBI pursued countless American Jews on suspicion of communism, the bureau also leapt into action to defend Judaism. A dramatic instance occurred in 1958 when a late-night caller told the United Press International: "We bombed a Temple in Atlanta. . . . We are going to blow up all Communist organizations. Negroes and Jews are hereby declared aliens."[43] No one was killed, but the explosion caused at least $100,000's worth of damage. President Eisenhower told Hoover to send the FBI to Atlanta to investigate the bombing, even though it was not exactly a matter under FBI jurisdiction, and Hoover quickly complied, committing the FBI to "offer assistance" and sending reports to the president updating him on the investigation's progress. Although Hoover's FBI was targeting many individual Jews as potential enemies of the state, it saw an attack against a synagogue as an attack against the American ideals of tolerance and religiosity. The rabbi of the synagogue expressed a similar sentiment to the press when he claimed that the bombing exposed "the contrast between the ideals of religious faith and the practices of Godless men."[44] Many Jews and non-Jews alike saw the bombing as a godless attack against religion and, by extension, America itself, an attempt to destroy "the religious and democratic foundations of our country."

DEFENDING JUDAISM, DEFENDING AGAINST JEWS

Hoover saw the "Judeo-Christian concept" as quintessentially American. It was the major feature that differentiated the United States from the USSR. And Judaism formed a critical part of American God-fearing democracy. Individual Jews might ally themselves with communism, but Judaism's presence in the United States affirmed the country's moral stature and commitment to tolerance. How could Hoover's FBI see Jews as potential communist enemies but simultaneously treat Judaism as an integral part of the religious-democratic American order that the bureau was established to defend?

There are two related possibilities that allowed for the apparent contradiction. The first is a Christian theological view of Judaism that renders present-day Jews invisible. The Christian concept of supersessionism—that Christianity is the fulfillment of biblical Judaism—has long allowed many devout Christians to overlook or disparage their Jewish contemporaries while embracing the biblical legacy as their own, as if Judaism were a religious tradition that ended after the coming of Jesus. This position associated Judaism with ancient biblical Jews rather than contemporary American Jews. In other words, Judaism was a thing of the past, part of the religious legacy to which Christians themselves, rather than present-day Jews, were heir. The American Council for Education survey suggested that this view was widespread: across the 315 textbooks from the era, three-quarters of the space dedicated to Jews and Judaism consisted of references to events prior to the year 79 CE, fewer than 12 percent of the books mentioned modern Judaism at all, and discussion of Jews in America was "conspicuously absent."[45] For many Americans in this period, Jews were the chosen people of the Bible, the spiritual forebears of Christians, and contemporary Jews were simply overlooked.

Another possibility for making sense of this dissonance involves a different claim about the relationship of Jews and Judaism: the only real Jewishness is religious, an assertion which denies that ethnic Jewishness is possible. Hoover, for instance, does not articulate supersessionist theology in its classical form, but in *Masters of Deceit* he develops a definition of Jews that is exclusively religious. There he defines Jews as "the people who gave the world the concept of our monotheistic God and the Ten Commandments," and claims they "cannot remain Jews and follow the atheism of Karl Marx and the deceit of the communist movement."[46] For Hoover, this passage suggests, Judaism was a religious creed associated with the past and with the Bible, the source of "our" monotheistic God and the Ten Commandments, and it was impossible to be Jewish without adhering to that religious legacy. "Persons of the Jewish faith and communists" share nothing in common, he argued. Hoover's book told about one party member who explained to "our agents" that when he joined the Communist Party, he renounced God, became an atheist, and began trying to convert others to atheism. His fellow Communist Party members, he went on, did not attend synagogue, observe holidays, or otherwise associate with Judaism.[47] "It is a matter of record that numerous Communist Party leaders call themselves Jews and claim a Jewish origin."[48] Jews who allied themselves with communism might claim to be Jews, but by adopting its ideology they could only "claim" a Jewish origin, because they were no longer true Jews.

Hoover and those who shared his views may have never consciously considered the relationship between American antisemitism and certain forms of theology, or between their suspicion of Jews as communists and their embrace of Judaism as an American religion. We do know, however, that Hoover was proud of the Judaism chapter in *Masters of Deceit,* in which he sought to demonstrate the incompatibility of Judaism and communism, and we can glimpse how it helped him both to stigmatize Jewish communists and also to position himself in the role of Judaism's defender. When he received the letter from the concerned Milwaukee housewife whose dentist was "quite a fanatic on the subject of communism and what groups of people make up the party in this country," he replied personally (or at least he appeared to, though the letter might have been written by bureaucratic underlings). In his letter, Hoover told her that he could not be sure about the number of Zionists in the Communist Party, but he referred her to *Masters of Deceit*—a highly telling response, for if she happened to read that book, she would have been presented with evidence that there were Jews in the communist leadership. But as an American citizen of "Jewish faith," perhaps she would also have been reassured by the book's claim that such Jews were not really Jews and that Hoover and his FBI were resolved to defend Judaism against them.

8

Policing Public Morality

Hoover's FBI, Obscenity, and Homosexuality

DOUGLAS M. CHARLES

J. Edgar Hoover served as director of the Federal Bureau of Investigation for forty-eight years, an unusually long period, during which he routinely espoused the centrality of religiously based morality in curbing crime and mitigating social disorder. Central to this extended effort was Hoover's creation in 1935 of the bureau's Crime Records Section (in 1938 it became a division), the arm of the FBI charged with handling the bureau's public relations. This arm not only propagated the vaunted, self-serving image of FBI agents as upstanding, scientific investigators who always captured their targets, but it also worked under Hoover's direction to educate the public on a host of issues of interest to him. Topping Hoover's list, of course, was the ever present threat of communism to American life, but the list also included the perceived threats of obscenity and homosexuality. FBI educational campaigns, which used publications produced by Crime Records and written under Hoover's byline, were a central focus of the bureau's mission. These efforts, which reflected Hoover's sense of morality, helped to shape the way Americans perceived public morality in the areas of sexuality and obscenity. While not an exhaustive exploration, this chapter surveys several prominent examples of FBI educational efforts with respect to obscenity and homosexuality, and explores the FBI's efforts to shape the moral consciousness of the American public.[1]

In December 1971, just five months prior to his death, Hoover granted an interview to the columnist Trude Feldman in which he discussed his religious values and their impact on his career and work. Hoover's comments shed some light on religion's influence on his directorship or, perhaps more accurately, how he chose to frame his sense of religiously based morality for public consumption. The interview, therefore, is worth exploring.

Feldman first asked Hoover how the Bible influenced his life, career, and work. Hoover responded that he had read the Bible throughout his entire life and found time each day "to meditate and pray," and that the Bible's teachings "have been the guide to my daily life." He then expanded on this assertion to describe how his religious morality underpinned his administration of the FBI, taking care in his comments to adhere to the long-propagated official FBI image: "I have administered the FBI on the principles of honesty, integrity, and fair play." While he claimed to prioritize protecting individual rights, he asserted that "religion, if it is to be meaningful, must be an integral part of everyday life."[2]

Hoover then connected respect for law and order (and by extension his FBI) with religious values: "The man who is motivated by religious ideas realizes the vital significance of obedience to law." While casting law as the force that holds society together, Hoover added, "Take away the law—thru disrespect or actual disobedience—and the whole keystone of society crumbles and with it the dignity of man as a child of God."[3]

Asked whether youth were turning away from religious values and religion, Hoover offered his diagnosis: "A great tragedy is that some young people have turned away from religion and attendance at religious services." He believed there were many reasons for this, but singled out "failure of the home and the church and the synagog [*sic*] to enlist the enthusiasm and sincere support of youth." Hoover was not without hope for the future, however, suggesting that young people were gravitating more toward religion, and he invoked the biblical book of Proverbs as support for how to educate them: "Train up a child in the way he should go, and when he is old he will not depart from it." The FBI director added, "This is as true today as when it was first uttered."[4]

Religion and church, Hoover always claimed, were central foci of his life. While his parents were not regular churchgoers during Hoover's Washington, D.C., childhood in the early twentieth century, his brother Dickerson developed a serious and enthusiastic religious orientation, and Edgar, as he was known, joined his brother's Sunday school and accompanied him on religious missions and lectures. As a youth, in fact, Edgar regularly attended both Presbyterian and Lutheran churches before permanently deciding on Presbyterianism, and he became a dedicated Sunday school teacher.[5]

While Hoover remained a lifelong member of the National Presbyterian Church, close to Judiciary Square, and although the official FBI line had it that he regularly attended church, it appears his formal church attendance dropped off as he became a skilled career bureaucrat. Nevertheless, as if to continue his former role as a Sunday school teacher, Hoover never hesitated in his use of FBI resources to influence and educate Americans on morality, especially in the areas of sexuality and obscenity.[6]

Hoover's FBI treated homosexuality and obscenity as similar moral threats that imperiled the American public, and its responses in both cases were similar as well. Both threats surfaced during periods of social and cultural upheaval and were cast as major moral crises tied to a larger moral decline in society. In both cases, the FBI cast its response as an attempt to defend America's children. And in both cases, the FBI responded to the threats both by enforcing the law and through educational efforts that extended into the realm of communal, family, and even religious norms.

THE CAMPAIGN AGAINST "SEX DEVIATES"

The FBI's first foray into educating the public about homosexuality and its perceived threat was in 1937, and that effort needs to be understood against the backdrop of the Great Depression. Prior to this era, during the 1920s, gay people were not understood as a threat that necessitated a federal response. Before the Great Depression, homosexuality was regarded as a moral issue but not a moral threat to society or its youth. Thus, we see no systematic federal targeting of gays on a national scale before the 1930s; even with the Newport Navy Base scandal of 1919 (an antigay witch hunt in the navy initiated by then–assistant secretary of the navy Franklin D. Roosevelt), the response was limited to that geographic area, and the FBI had no interest in lending assistance. By 1930, however, when the Great Depression was setting in, Americans' perception of gender roles and masculinity underwent a significant shift. The American male suddenly found himself struggling to fulfill his assigned roles as husband and father. He lost his job; he failed in supporting his family; he lost his home; he sent his children away to be cared for by relatives; and sometimes he even became homeless. As this conception of American masculinity was becoming imperiled, the perception of men who were sexually attracted to other men also underwent significant redefinition. Gay men were suddenly regarded not merely as bizarre people engaged in curious immoral acts; now they were seen as significant threats to children and family. They were recast as dangerous predators and criminals who, during a time of crisis, were considered threatening enough to warrant a federal response.[7]

For the FBI, the perception of gay men as a threat to the family crystallized in early 1937. Two days after Christmas in 1936, ten-year-old Charles Mattson—the small, blond-haired son of a prominent surgeon—was kidnapped. The abductor demanded a $28,000 ransom, and the case quickly became a national cause célèbre reported in newspapers from coast to coast, especially after the boy was found brutalized, raped, and murdered. One reason the case became a national issue was FBI director Hoover's claim in 1935 that child kidnappings were no longer a threat. Child kidnappings had been a popular phenomenon in the early Depression, but with a new federal law allowing the FBI to investigate them after the infamous Lindbergh kidnapping case of 1932, Hoover proclaimed the problem eradicated. The Mattson kidnapping made his comments appear foolish, and President Roosevelt's decision to comment publicly on the Mattson kidnapping drew even more attention to the case. The president promised that the FBI would use its resources to find the kidnapper and would never stop until he was caught. Roosevelt's intention was to promote a new role for the federal government in law enforcement, and his public declaration on the case compelled a significant response from J. Edgar Hoover.

Hoover held a unique position in the federal government. He was the only significant conservative bureaucrat retained from the Coolidge and Hoover administrations when FDR took office in 1933. While FDR's nominee for attorney general had initially planned to replace Hoover, his untimely death and replacement by a New Dealer who thought retaining Hoover was the easiest action salvaged Hoover's career. Still, as a conservative among liberal New Dealers, Hoover worked hard to ingratiate himself with Roosevelt, both to preserve his job and to expand the power and influence of his FBI. Thus, he catered to FDR's every whim, including submitting political intelligence reports on the president's critics and even going so far as to offer FBI resources to help the secretary of the interior, Harold Ickes, determine who had been stealing chicken eggs from his farm. Thus when the president publicly commented that the FBI would never stop until the Mattson kidnapper had been found, Hoover had no choice but to respond in force.

The question was where to look to find the kidnapper. Given popular stereotypes about gay men and the recent reassessment of their threat, it was not surprising that the FBI targeted them. FBI agents scoured local mental institutions, checked on ex-convicts, and targeted hobos. (While hobos were the most visible and iconic sign of the Great Depression, it is forgotten today that, at the time, they were popularly believed to include many sexual perverts who traded in sexual favors and targeted youth.) For all the FBI's efforts, it never did solve the Mattson case (which was not officially closed until the 1980s). However, the search for the culprit marked a watershed moment in the history of the FBI, prompting systematic efforts to collect information about "sex offenders," including many gay men, and to target them for suspicion and investigation.[8]

The bureau's public relations arm, the Crime Records Section, was part of this effort, used by the FBI to help educate the public about the threat posed by sexual predators. In late September 1937, for example, under Hoover's byline, the Crime Records Section simultaneously published in the *New York Herald Tribune* and *Los Angeles Times* an article titled "War on the Sex Criminal!" which outlined the danger of sex offenders. From the article's first sentence, Hoover warned: "The sex fiend, most loathsome of all the vast army of crime, has become a sinister threat to the safety of American childhood and womanhood." Hoover then singled out "women and little girls" being murdered coast to coast "by this beast." Although gay men were not overtly singled out for suspicion here—the article referred to the victimization of women and girls—it was widely believed at the time that gays targeted all children, an assumption made explicit by one reputed expert in the 1950s when he wrote that "the homosexual" was "an inveterate seducer of the young of both sexes."[9] Even if Hoover's agents had failed to solve the Mattson case, this kind of public educational effort allowed Hoover to argue that he was on top of an issue the president had made a priority.

Hoover appealed to Americans to see sex criminals (and, by implication, homosexuals) for what they really were. A sex deviate was not "some fabled monster," he wrote. "He is a definite and a serious result of apathy and indifference" in the way society dealt with "out-of-the-ordinary offenders." The FBI director called for more in-depth examination into the background of these criminals, and he claimed that the FBI had discovered what converted an "ordinary offender" into "a dangerous predatory animal." The causes included "parental indifference, parole abuses, political protection and other factors," including the fact that offenders were "taught" that they "can get away with it."[10] Hoover also detected a pattern in how such offenders developed. Their criminal destiny, he warned, could be ascertained in "their every action," which was "a blazing signpost pointing to a future of torture, rape, mutilation and murder." The FBI director continued, "The sex fiend is a progressive criminal" who "begins with annoyances . . . progresses to the sending of obscene letters," "exhibitionism," "annoying children," and finally murder.[11]

The reason for the dramatic escalation of sex criminals, Hoover argued, was the public's apathy, which led to "a condition whereby such potential murderers are merely slapped on the wrist." The only effective response was an aggressive, multifaceted approach that included studying patterns of drug use, the pathology of perversion, and the psychology behind this affliction. Hoover called for the social segregation of all suspected sex offenders and treatment of them with constant "suspicious scrutiny." He was so wary of them that he even called for witnesses against sex offenders at trial to be protected from "shameless buzzards of the law who defend these wretches" and willfully "defame honorable people in an effort to obtain freedom for their miserable clients." Sex offenders could threaten anyone, Hoover warned, but the threat could be mitigated though "public vigilance and indignation."[12]

Ten years later, another crisis erupted that again prompted Hoover to warn that gays were a threat to society: the advent of the Cold War and the fears of domestic subversion it sparked. During the start of the Cold War, another sex crime panic ensued following a succession of highly publicized murders of children, and yet again, the public, spurred on by Hoover's FBI, focused on sex offenders, not distinguishing between gay men and true predators. Repeating what it had done in 1937, the bureau's Crime Records Division published another article in Hoover's name repeating many of the old themes. In "How Safe Is Your Daughter?" appearing in *American Magazine,* Hoover cited the recent progress in stemming venereal disease made possible by Americans overcoming the taboo against talking about the subject and by their focusing on facts, and he called for a similar effort when it came to "degeneracy." He likened the situation to wild animals escaping a circus—that is, sexual predators were a threat that required public authorities to react with all due force—and he repeated his warning that too many were ignoring this threat. Again his focus was on the victimization of young girls and women, but, even so, it is clear that he included gays in the category of sex criminals, especially in the targeting of children.[13]

The FBI director called for protecting the identities of sex crime victims (as was the policy of most newspapers at the time) "while proclaiming to the world the identities of the wrongdoers." It was common at the time for gay men arrested for soliciting sex to post and forfeit collateral and automatically receive a disorderly conduct violation, while avoiding an appearance in court. Hoover criticized communities for allowing sex offenders who were arrested to take the "routine and innocuous" charge of disorderly conduct rather than committing the offender after a trial to "medical observation." Hoover called for an end to such leniency; for him, the only acceptable options were either curing the deviant or "depriving the offender of his freedom to continue such activity."[14]

In 1957, a decade after "How Safe Is Your Daughter?" appeared and in the midst of the intense midcentury Lavender Scare—another witch hunt targeting gay men and lesbians—Hoover published another article on the dangers of "the sexually psychopathic criminal." Admitting from the outset that his recommendation at this time was "radical," Hoover called for quarantining sex offenders. In "Needed: A Quarantine to Prevent Crime," the FBI director argued that, in the same way the physically ill, such as those afflicted with smallpox or typhoid, were quarantined, sex offenders should be isolated so as to receive "the medical and psychiatric treatment they so desperately need." Even those who might otherwise spend only a short time in jail might need to be "quarantined for several years while treatment progresses" and perhaps never released.[15] Hoover concluded: "Compulsory quarantine is the only way in which we can really protect ourselves and our children and still do our conscientious duty toward these pitiable men—and women—who are criminals in spite of themselves."

The public's cooperation was essential to this effort, precisely because it was in part a medical issue. The FBI director assured his readers that his admittedly radical solution was workable if law enforcement, medical authorities, and religious groups came together to make it possible. The public's assistance could help ensure that legal and medical authorities had "the opportunity to bring sex deviates—and other mentally and physically ill people—into treatment at the earliest possible moment." At the time the Mattachine Society, the earliest successful gay rights group, applauded Hoover in its newsletter, which is surprising given that Hoover included gay men in the category of potential sexual offenders. Mattachine's approval suggests that it was trying to remove the gay men that it represented from that suspect category.[16]

THE CAMPAIGN AGAINST SMUT

Hoover's educational campaign in the area of obscenity was similar to his "sex offender" effort. Both sex crime panics and anti-obscenity movements were functions of traumatic times. Concern over dangerous gays targeting children developed during the Great Depression and the advent of the Cold War; concerns over the dangerous influences of obscenity (often construed as a threat to children) likewise surfaced during periods of traumatic social dislocation when values and notions of morality seemed under attack. The FBI's battle against obscenity began during the Progressive Era, a period of rapid industrialization when, after passage of the White Slave Traffic Act (aka the Mann Act) in 1910, bureau agents began pursuing prostitution rings commonly believed to be run by immigrants who targeted naive young girls. In the course of those investigations, FBI agents began collecting large amounts of obscene literature, which they came to believe went hand in glove with prostitution. By the mid-1920s, in an age shaped by concern over out-of-control youth and the collapse of Victorian morality, Hoover's FBI developed a procedure for filing and mailing obscene items to headquarters (they were sealed in plain envelopes with "OBSCENE" written on them). It was no accident that this FBI procedure was created during the height of the so-called Clean Books Crusade, a reactionary and moralistic censorship drive that developed after the First World War. Yet again, during the Second World War, amid rising public concern about protecting young, naive draftees from negative influences, the FBI dedicated a special Obscene File to combat the problem.[17]

By 1957, American jurisprudence in the field of obscenity law began to evolve rapidly. In its decision in *Roth v. United States,* the Supreme Court ruled that obscenity was not protected by the First Amendment, though it also made a legal distinction between sex and obscenity. The Court formulated a uniquely American definition of obscenity that included evaluating an entire work (rather than selected passages) and factoring in community standards when judging whether a work appealed to prurient interests. These developments, especially that of distinguishing sex from obscenity, had the unintended consequence of creating a boom in the American pornography industry, with books, magazines, and films suddenly proliferating. Despite its efforts to combat obscenity, by July 1959 the FBI had come to realize that it was collecting "an ever increasing amount of material on pornography."[18]

These developments prompted FBI officials to create a special research file (separate from its Obscene File) on pornographic material that "would be of benefit to the Director, in the event he would like to inform the American people on this subject, as he had in the past." This research file—located in the Crime Records Division—would be similar to FBI educational efforts in the areas of "Parole and Probation and Sex Offender[s]." It would be valuable to the extent that the collected material would reveal "many informative facets," including the social effects of obscenity, how law enforcement might effectively target obscenity, and, paraphrasing moral crusader Anthony Comstock, "various side lights on this many-sided monster."[19]

Two FBI publications in 1964 illustrate this effort. Again through the FBI's Crime Records Division, Hoover published two pieces on the moral threat of obscenity, each directed at a different audience. In the spring, Hoover sought to educate professionals in the legal community—lawyers, judges, and legal scholars—by publishing an article in the *University of Pittsburgh Law Review* outlining the FBI's work in anti-obscenity cases. In December, in the national Catholic newspaper *Our Sunday Visitor*, a periodical he often enlisted as a vehicle for his educational efforts, Hoover aimed to engage a religious audience topping one million.[20]

The first of these essays, "Combating Merchants of Filth: The Role of the FBI," was published in March 1964 in order to outline for legal professionals the seriousness of obscenity in American life, the sophisticated nature of smut peddlers, and the various legal issues surrounding the topic. Hoover began the article by highlighting several examples of obscenity's negative effects on Americans, particularly children. He cited a teenager who became a prostitute "after reading a number of cheap novels" and explained that the rapists of one young man were found to possess "a virtual storehouse of obscene photographs, literature and other pornographic materials." He wrote of "depraved sex offenders" who targeted children using alcohol and pornography to induce them into "wild orgies," cited a case in which peephole magazines helped to identify "a vicious sex offender" who was subsequently convicted for kidnapping and murder, and concluded by recounting how two young New York "terrorists" were led to assault victims by "reading lurid books."[21] Such examples illustrated "why law enforcement officials, educators, civic leaders, and other informed citizens" were so concerned with obscenity and how it "pollutes the atmosphere of virtually every community across the United States." By obscenity, he meant not just hard-core pornography but various efforts to glorify sex, the representation of vice and sadism on television, and contemporary literature he considered lurid—all part of a "pornography racket" that was "so scurrilously vulgar" in Hoover's judgment that some of it defied description. As scientific support for his position, Hoover cited a psychiatrist who had concluded that pornography was "an instrument for delinquency" as well as "an insidious threat to moral, mental and physical health."[22]

Hoover then outlined the challenges with which law enforcement groups had to contend as they sought to combat obscenity. The Post Office Department, Hoover wrote, was "often hampered and thwarted" by smut peddlers who knew how to exploit the shortcomings of the legal system. The Customs Bureau was focused on foreign importation, while the FBI handled interstate transport and, at the time, the broadcast of obscene language. The FBI's limited jurisdiction made it difficult for it to halt the distribution of obscene material. Because smut peddlers were well versed in local, state, and federal anti-obscenity statutes, they knew how to sidestep them.[23] One major issue for the FBI, for example, was a law that made it illegal to transport obscenity across state lines using a commercial carrier but did not cover such transport in a private vehicle.

This particular loophole, Hoover noted, was rectified only when Congress amended the law in June 1955 to include the private transportation of multiple items of obscenity in a quantity that could be considered intended for commercial sale. He cited this law as the factor that enabled the FBI to achieve seventy-eight federal convictions for violation of the anti-obscenity statutes. Despite such progress, Hoover argued, serious challenges remained. For instance, real data about smut peddlers and their work was sorely lacking because when one dealer was stopped, others quickly took his place and even began to produce their own obscene products. With just one "initial sale [of obscenity], a chain of corruption begins—a chain in which the lives of countless children invariably become ensnared."[24]

Hoover concluded with an anecdote about a clergyman who asked the FBI whether smut peddlers could actually be tracked down and stopped. Hoover responded to the question by outlining the Supreme Court's *Roth* decision and explaining that, even within this legal framework, obscenity prosecutions, especially involving pornography, were complex. Hoover called on the public to play a role in the war against obscenity, just as he had in the battle against sexual offenders: success required not only effective, sound, and enforceable laws but also "zealously maintained" standards of decency. "To lower the barriers of good taste and moral acceptability in *any* area—and in the highly vulnerable fields of entertainment, literature and art, in particular—is to invite an eventual floodtide of moral corruption and spiritual decay."[25]

Hoover took a different tack in the second article, published in December 1964, "Poison for Our Youth: FBI Chief Calls for Nationwide Effort to Curb Obscenity." As he did in his law review piece, the FBI director began with an example of the impact of obscenity, a story about a concerned mother who wrote to him about how her twelve-year-old son had come across obscene photos torn from a lurid magazine while walking down the street. Together, the mother and son burned the material, but the incident revealed how difficult it was to prevent children from being exposed to pornography. Saying he understood this mother's concern and "anxiety," Hoover blamed the incident on "the vicious racket of pornographic literature" that was a "grave concern to all responsible citizens." Peddlers of such obscenity, he warned, preyed on children's "natural curiosity and often immature judgement" in ways that led to "grave damage to the mental, moral, and physical health of our youth." "Sampling this deadly merchandise," according to Hoover, often led children into the depths of "antisocial" behavior.[26]

As evidence, the FBI director then cited an increase in crime rates, including sex offenses, among juveniles. While conceding it was not "possible, of course, to estimate the number of these crimes committed because of the influence of obscene materials," Hoover nevertheless suggested a causal connection. Writing that "we are all aware" of the influences on juvenile delinquents, he offered the opinions of public authorities as proof of the "link between many crimes of sex and violence and smut literature." As it happens, three years later President Lyndon Johnson would form the Commission on Obscenity and Pornography, which, by 1970, would conclude that obscenity and pornography had no measurable impact on social problems. Hoover argued, however, that "there must be a cause" for the recent increases in youth crime, and he pointed to obscenity as "one of the largest causes."[27]

One of the authorities that Hoover cited in his argument was Francis Cardinal Spellman, with whom Hoover had maintained a close relationship since 1942 in their common quest to curb juvenile delinquency and obscenity. So close was their relationship that Hoover placed Cardinal Spellman on the FBI's Special Correspondents List—Hoover's list of trusted individuals to whom his bureau provided information in an effort to influence public opinion. In the *Our Sunday Visitor* essay, Hoover quoted Spellman's claim that "pornography encourages brutality, violence, injustice, irreverence, disrespect for authority, illicit pleasure seeking abnormality, degeneracy, and other signs of mental maladjustment."[28] Then, as further evidence for this connection, Hoover enumerated examples of youth assaulting, raping, or murdering others, and he speculated about how obscene literature and other materials led them to such pernicious crimes.

According to Hoover, smut peddlers argued that their products were intended only for "sophisticated adult readers," but "the facts belie their claims." To discredit the idea that such products were being distributed only to adults, he noted that pornographers targeted children when distributing "unsolicited mailings of advertisements for obscene pamphlets and pictures." Smut peddlers "also lurk around schoolyards and campuses," going so far, Hoover claimed, as to recruit school dropouts to infiltrate "locker rooms and playgrounds" to push the smut peddlers' wares. Before they could be caught in these nefarious activities, Hoover warned, smut peddlers typically moved on to a new school.[29] At stake in the battle against obscenity was the welfare of the nation's children.

Hoover concluded the article with suggestions for reducing the impact that obscenity was having "on the morality and well-being of our young people." He was encouraged that "church and civic groups" had already taken some action in this arena, and he singled out a group of high school students for taking the initiative and influencing their elders to act against obscenity. As he did in his campaign against sexual offenders, Hoover stressed that community involvement and cooperation were "essential" to the campaign. The public needed to alert authorities about smut, understand the laws concerning it, and "promote more effective safeguards against the smut dealer."[30]

The most important bulwark against obscenity, Hoover stressed, were parents. He declared that it was their duty "through their example and counsel to provide their children with a solid foundation of spiritual and moral values." Note here the use of the word *spiritual*: in Hoover's view, "a Christian home is mighty armor against the attempts of those who seek to corrupt our young people." Hoover also had advice about parenting. Instead of "threatening" children "with dire consequences" for their curiosity about obscene literature, he recommended as the best approach to "appeal to [children's] intelligence and sense of decency to rebuff the smut merchant." Through this approach, and by inculcating high moral standards, America could protect its youth from corruption.

Hoover and his FBI were focused not only on communism and its threat to the American way of life. Homosexuality and obscenity were also seen as major threats, and education was one of the weapons the FBI used in the battle against them. In 1937, having failed to solve the Mattson kidnapping and murder, Hoover drew on the information his FBI had collected about "sex offenders" to initiate an educational campaign that helped to foster a sex crime panic. By the early 1950s, this effort had evolved into Hoover's Sex Deviates Program and File, which was used to harass gays and lesbians and purge them from federal employment and other contexts. By this point, the American public's anxiety about sex crimes was compounded by its anxieties about the Cold War and subversion from within. In the midst of this troubled period, in 1947, Hoover escalated his campaign against sex offenders (and by extension gay men) by recommending the detention and isolation of such people on the grounds that they were a moral, medical, and legal threat.

In the field of obscenity, the FBI's interest evolved over many decades dating from the 1910s. This chapter traces this concern through a variety of actions: the FBI's discovery of obscene material as it targeted prostitution rings via the Mann Act; the development of a filing and mailing procedure for obscenity in 1925 during a popular censorship drive; the opening of a dedicated Obscene File by 1942 as the public was growing concerned about the influence of obscenity on draftees and children; Hoover's creation of another research file on obscenity and pornography in 1959 in an effort to educate the nation about the dangers of obscenity; and the FBI's efforts to shape the view of obscenity within both the legal community and the general public through publications and outreach efforts. Essential to this battle against both sex offenders and smut peddlers was Hoover's public relations arm, the Crime Records Division, which in Hoover's name undertook a sophisticated educational operation to influence the public's moral views, enlist the public in its law enforcement efforts, and even shape parenting practices.

Hoover's educational efforts with homosexuality and obscenity had an impact. With regard to gay people, Hoover's educational campaigns not only helped to sustain the intensity of homophobia appearing with the advent of the Great Depression but also inflamed the sex crime panics of the 1930s and 1940s, culminating in the so-called Lavender Scare during the 1950s, a period of antigay fear and persecution that parallels the Red Scare. The impact of Hoover's anti-obscenity efforts was more limited. While Hoover was active in his campaign against obscenity into the 1960s, American culture and social mores were developing in a different direction, as is evident from the 1970 presidential commission's report that obscenity and pornography had no significant negative social impact. When Richard Nixon subsequently became president, Hoover had an opportunity to reassert his anti-obscenity efforts, but those ended with Hoover's death and the political demise of Nixon in 1974. Although Hoover's efforts against obscenity did not prevent the process of liberalization, he arguably succeeded in limiting a more extensive liberalization process.[31] Somewhere in the background of these campaigns against homosexuality and obscenity, perhaps going back to Hoover's experience as a Sunday school teacher, was the director's concept of religion and morality, which shaped his willingness to use bureau resources not only to enforce the law but also to instill his values among members of the public.

9

The FBI and the Nation of Islam

KARL EVANZZ

What had begun in the early 1940s as a legitimate pursuit by the FBI to deter subversive activities conducted by revolutionary African American organizations devolved twenty years later into a scorched-earth policy on the First Amendment for nearly every radical group in the United States. Contrary to a widely held assumption, however, the Federal Bureau of Investigation never had the founder of the Nation of Islam under surveillance. While there is a declassified FBI file on Wallace D. Fard, all of the documents are dated after 1942, nearly a decade after he was last seen in this country. The FBI discovered Fard and the Nation of Islam, the sect he founded in 1930, incidental to an investigation of African American support of Japan following the bombing of Pearl Harbor on December 7, 1941.

On September 27, 1940, Japan, Germany, and Italy created an alliance called the Axis Powers. President Franklin D. Roosevelt, Joseph Stalin, and Winston Churchill responded by forming the Allied Forces. The first peacetime draft was enacted by Congress that same month, and by October the first able-bodied American men began registering. In Chicago, Detroit, and several other large cities, Selective Service registrars noted that some African Americans were refusing to register. The majority of those resisting the draft in this way shared three factors in common: (1) they cited religious grounds; (2) they described themselves as Muslims; and (3) they did not seek an exemption as a "conscientious objector," because they would not comply with its requirements.

At the same time, the FBI began receiving reports that agents of the Japanese government were financing radical African American groups yearning for a racial revolution. In April 1942, the FBI used several Black officers from the Chicago Police Department and the Metropolitan Police Department of the District of Columbia to infiltrate one of the target groups. Their mission was to report any activities or speeches indicating support for Japan.[1] The Allah Temple of Islam considered itself a "nation," they discovered, and members called it the Nation of Islam (NOI). According to its literature, the NOI considered itself a nation trapped "within a nation," in much the same way that most Palestinians view their predicament in Israel.

Within weeks, informants had enough data to establish that leaders of the group were not opposed to war and that rumors about the organization's philosophy and pro-Japanese stance were true. The NOI's flag consisted of a white star and white crescent moon on a red background. It was similar, agents noted, to the Japanese Army's flag (a red sun with white rays on a red background) and was iconically identical to the flag of Turkey, whose population was more than 90 percent Muslim. In addition, the flag was similar to the Soviet Union's, which was red with a single golden star and golden sickle crossed by a hammer. Wooden rifles were found in the temples. Informants discovered that males practiced with the rifles as part of their self-defense training.[2]

The probe revealed not only that the group strongly endorsed Japan's war effort but also that Japanese individuals with rumored links to the Japanese government were reportedly attending NOI meetings. Moreover, there were reliable intelligence reports that some of these organizations were receiving financial assistance from the Japanese government in violation of the Alien Registration Act (or Smith Act) of 1940. Among these were the Peace Movement of Ethiopia, the Pacific Movement of the Eastern World, and the Society for the Development of Our Own.

After presenting its findings to local courts, the FBI on May 1 obtained blanket search warrants for all locations of the Allah Temple of Islam. Days later, the Criminal Division of the Justice Department advised the U.S. attorney general to prosecute Elijah Muhammad and other leaders of the sect. When he was arrested in the District of Columbia on May 9 for failing to register under the Selective Service Act, Muhammad was questioned extensively about his relationship with W.D. Fard and the latter's whereabouts. Describing Fard as God incarnate, Muhammad stated that he had not seen "Allah" since 1934.[3]

Sultan Mohammed, minister of the Milwaukee temple, was also arrested on May 9 for failing to register, as was Wali Mohammed, head of the Detroit temple and one of Elijah's older brothers. Sultan Mohammed and another regional leader, Linn Karriem, apparently thought they might avoid prosecution by agreeing to go to their local draft board and registering. However, they refused to sign the registration cards. As a result, they served as much time as those who refused to register at all. Pauline Bahar, Karriem's wife, was one of the few women arrested in the sweep.

At the same time as the search warrants were being served, the FBI decided to hone in on the elusive W. D. Fard, who it believed was hiding inside Elijah Muhammad's home at 6026 South Vernon Avenue in Chicago. The bureau ordered the postal carrier for that address to keep tabs on any mail addressed to Fard. Numerous items were addressed to Fard, the mail carrier told agents, but he did not believe that Fard actually lived there. He had been delivering mail for Fard at that address for years, he said, but never saw the man whom agents identified in a photo as Fard.[4] In fact, the agents learned, men were seldom seen at the home. During surveillance, agents saw only oddly dressed women entering and leaving, along with five or six children who lived there. They didn't see a single adult male enter or leave during their stakeout. A neighbor gave agents a glimmer of hope. She said that everyone called one of the boys "W.D." They surmised that the boy probably was Fard's son but soon discovered that he was not. The thirteen-year-old was Wallace Deen Muhammad, Elijah Muhammad's son.

Upon interviewing temple members who had refused to register for the draft, agents collected numerous statements showing that Muhammad had specifically and repeatedly advised members not to register. He had further counseled them to disregard government questionnaires related to the draft. The FBI obtained another strong piece of evidence against the group when Elijah Muhammad confessed to having met with Satohata Takahashi, a suspected agent of the Japanese government who had been a "racial agitator" in the United States since the Great War.[5] Muhammad said that Takahashi attended one of the group's meetings in 1932 or 1933 and later approached him at the headquarters of the Detroit temple at 3408 Hastings Street. He wanted information about the group's philosophy, membership, and purpose.

Muhammad met Takahashi sometime later "at the home of a woman" whose name he had forgotten. He had gone there, he said, to "pick up Brother Abdul Mohammed." Takahashi, who was very ill at the time, remained in Abdul's home for two or three weeks. Muhammad did not mention whether or not Fard was there. They engaged in a general discussion of the plight of African Americans. After reiterating what he had told the elderly Asian about the Nation of Islam, Muhammad said, Takahashi had expressed approval of his teachings. The conversation ended there, Muhammad said. He denied ever having entered into any activities in conjunction with Takahashi and indicated that the meeting was the last time he saw Takahashi. The admission of meetings with Abdul Mohammed and Takahashi was important, as both men had been under surveillance by the Immigration and Naturalization Service for engaging in "unpatriotic" activities.

An illustrated poster drawn by Raymond Sharrieff, a high-level official married to Elijah Muhammad's daughter, was confiscated during a raid of Muhammad's Chicago home in the predawn hours of May 9, 1942. It was nearly an exact copy of a poster FBI agents had seized during a raid on the Detroit headquarters of Takahashi's organization, the Society for the Development of Our Own (SDOO), in the 1930s. Entitled "Calling the Four Winds," Sharrieff's poster contained a map of the United States with Fard in the center. Guns with the word "Asia" written on the barrel were aimed at the United States from all four directions. The only difference between the two posters was that Takahashi was in the center of the SDOO version. Moreover, the title of the poster was from a speech written by Cheaber McIntyre, Takahashi's wife.

In April 1934, Abdul Mohammed wrote a letter to the newly inaugurated U.S. president, Franklin D. Roosevelt, demanding to know whether "Asiatics" are entitled to their "independence or freedom and birthright" under American jurisprudence.[6] INS officials assigned him Case Number 55,850-677 under the category of suspicious "Asiatics" because they did not realize that he was, in fact, African American. In August, he mailed another letter requesting the same information. This one was filed with documents tracking anti-American "Hindu" activity because the INS assumed that he was from South Asia.

Takahashi, also known as Naka Nakane and Taka Ashe, had been on the government's radar for nearly a decade. He was first arrested in Philadelphia in July 1919 as a "racial agitator."[7] The arrest occurred during "Red Summer," the name referring to blood in the streets after race riots in as many as twenty-five American cities. Hundreds were killed and thousands were injured. The riots were triggered in part by the lynching of Black soldiers returning from the Great War. Armed with a new sense of pride after having survived the war, Blacks fought back, resulting in the deaths of dozens of Whites, whose actions triggered almost all of the riots. "There had been no trouble with the Negro before the war," the venerable *New York Times* noted, "when most admitted the superiority of the white race."[8]

On May 11, 1942—two days after Elijah Muhammad's arrest—the FBI's Detroit field office asked the Detroit Police Department for its records on W.D. Fard. Police located two arrest records and mug shots for an individual with a similar name: Wallace Farad. During a file search requested by the FBI, the Chicago Police Department located an arrest record of a "Wallace Ford" for disorderly conduct. According to the documents, he had been arrested in September 1933 while standing on a street corner proselytizing. Someone complained. At the station, Ford gave police a home address in Detroit. FBI agents noted that his height, weight, and physical description were identical to that of W.D. Fard. After reviewing the records, the bureau concluded that Fard, Ford, and Farad were one and the same.

Fard's arrests in Detroit were triggered by the crimes of his followers. The Detroit Police Department files disclosed the arrest of Wallace "Farad" in November 1932 after a member of the Allah Temple of Islam committed a ritualistic homicide. Fard was run out of town and promised never to return. However, he was spotted in Detroit again in May 1932—the temple was only a couple of blocks from a police station—and threatened with indictment if he returned.[9] An FBI agent wrote that Fard was released after serving a short sentence, but that information was inaccurate. He was detained briefly after the homicide incident but not after his second arrest. The bureau also discovered that Ford had an FBI number, 56062, though it had nothing to do with any FBI investigation. Rather, it was the result of Ford having been convicted on federal charges in 1926 and sentenced to San Quentin, as anyone convicted of a federal crime receives an FBI identification number.

Three months after Japan bombed Pearl Harbor, a minister at the Nation of Islam's Washington temple gave a speech in which he specifically described himself as "a man of war." "It will not be long before Japan will be over here in that mothership they have. We know that Allah will protect us. The blueprints for the mothership were made in the holy city of Mecca and sent to the Japanese government." In July 1942, an agent reported that a Japanese male visited the Chicago temple. Introduced as "Muck Muck," he addressed the assembly for more than two hours. Agents keeping tabs on other temples noted that "Mr. Muck Muck" also spoke in Milwaukee, Detroit, and Washington, D.C. Informants told the FBI that Fard had returned to Mecca, but still received mail at Elijah Muhammad's residence in Chicago. When Elijah Muhammad was arrested one month later, it was determined that he was the person agents identified as "Muck Muck." Since they did not have a photograph of him in their field office files, they mistook his ethnicity.[10]

The bureau eventually weeded out all draft-age males in the Nation of Islam and recommended their prosecution, which was carried out. The witch hunt decimated the group and filled prisons in Wisconsin, Michigan, and Illinois with hundreds of African Americans who were simply following the advice of their leader without understanding the likelihood of serious repercussions.[11] By the time federal prosecutors finished their cases against members of the temple, more than 90 percent of the draft-age males were incarcerated, rendering the organization impotent. Muhammad was convicted in 1942 and sent to the Federal Correctional Institution in Milan, Michigan. He was released in 1946. Clara Muhammad tried to keep the NOI together, but it was well nigh impossible to do that while raising so many young children. There were fewer than two hundred members in the whole country, and most of them were the children and wives of men serving time. Consequently, the FBI closed its files on the group.

The respite from federal scrutiny did not last long. By 1956, the Nation of Islam was under intense investigation again. This time, the bureau suspected that it was being manipulated by the Communist Party of the United States of America. President Eisenhower signed the Communist Control Act of 1954, legislation that outlawed the Communist Party, which, until then, had routinely run candidates for political office. While FBI director J. Edgar Hoover had initially opposed the act, fearing that it would lead to heightened subversive activity and make it more difficult to keep tabs on known supporters of communism, he poured resources into enforcement. Facing the 1954 law combined with the Internal Security Act of 1950, socialists, communists, and other radical political parties went underground, as Hoover feared. To penetrate their ranks, the FBI devised a sweeping counterintelligence plan.

In 1952 the FBI placed Elijah Muhammad and his chief minister, Malcolm X Little, on its Security Index. Individuals on the index were subject to warrantless arrest and indefinite detention in the event of any serious threat to national security.[12] Four years later, the bureau developed a national counterintelligence program—COINTELPRO—to keep track of suspected subversives. Following the group's 1957 Saviour's Day convention, which drew thousands of Muslims to Chicago, an agent in the Chicago field office decided to examine the file on the Nation of Islam. He noticed repeated references to "W. D. Fard." Since Fard's name was mentioned often on wiretapped conversations between Muslim officials and in monitored temple sermons, the agent recommended that the FBI make a national effort to locate Fard with the goal of determining whether he was secretly running the group. The agent's recommendation was approved.[13]

The FBI's renewed interest stemmed not only from concerns about the sect's skyrocketing growth but also from the simultaneous rise of Malcolm X as the group's headline-making national representative. Little was listed in the FBI's files of "known Communists," so FBI agents argued that there was a strong likelihood that the Communist Party was aiming to control the "Black Muslims," as the Nation of Islam was labeled by the media. In 1958, FBI director J. Edgar Hoover published the book *Masters of Deceit,* which included a chapter detailing how the Communist Party had burrowed its way into Black America's leadership. In the chapter "Communism and Minorities," the book painted a picture of an ethnic group too gullible to safeguard its own self-interest. Blacks needed government protection from the communists' crafty wiles, he implied.[14] During the first probe of the NOI, the bureau found significant evidence of the group's pro-Japanese sentiments. The new investigation focused on anything the group's leaders said that supported the bureau's contention that it was under the influence of the Communist Party.

Malcolm X's appeal to middle-class Blacks and the skyrocketing development of new temples alarmed FBI agents assigned to "COINTELPRO/Racial Matters," and on New Year's Eve 1956, Hoover requested permission from the Justice Department for increased "technical surveillance" (that is, wiretapping) of the sect. Copies of the request were sent to the State Department and the CIA. In making the request, Hoover wrote: "Members fanatically follow the teachings of Allah as interpreted by Muhammad; they disavow allegiance to the United States; and they are taught they need not obey the laws of the United States. . . . It is believed that a technical surveillance . . . will furnish not only data concerning the fanatical and violent nature of the organization, but also data regarding the current plans of the NOI to expand its activities throughout the United States."[15] Malcolm X was aware of the FBI's unfriendly interest in the Nation of Islam. As early as July 1955, he cautioned new members that the FBI was conducting a harassment campaign against the Nation of Islam, and he urged them not to be intimidated. "Don't talk to government agents about Islam," he advised members of the Philadelphia temple. "Tell them that Islam is a religion of peace," Malcolm X added, but beyond that, "don't discuss the Nation of Islam's business."[16]

Hoover must have known that the "violent nature" of the Nation of Islam was a product of his own imagination, but it helped justify a wiretap. On New Year's Day 1957, U.S. attorney general Herbert Brownell granted Hoover's request. By February 14, Hoover had forwarded copies of the FBI's dossiers on the sect and its leaders to the following divisions of the intelligence community: the State Department's Bureau of Intelligence and Research, the Central Intelligence Agency (CIA), the U.S. Secret Service, the Office of Naval Intelligence (ONI), and the Office of Special Investigations (OSI) of the U.S. Air Force. The Nation of Islam, agents wrote, believed that it would eventually overthrow not only the United States but all governments. Two main NOI tenets were seen as cause for concern. The Nation of Islam still taught that it was necessary for a member to kill at least four "devils" (Caucasians) before he could wear the small metal "button of Islam" on his lapel. The other belief took on an ominous hue in the aftermath of the Holocaust: the earth rightfully belonged to the Black man and all White races must be exterminated.

In August 1957, the Chicago field office received a file from San Quentin State Prison regarding former inmate Wallie D. Ford. "These records reflect that under the name Wallie D. Ford," the agent wrote in his report, "*indicated as the true name of the subject* [W. D. Fard], he was received at San Quentin Penitentiary." This conclusion was derived from photographs, fingerprints, physical features analysis, and biographical similarities.[17] Ford said that he was born in Oregon on February 25, 1891. Prison intake officials listed his parents as Zared and Beatrice Ford of Hawaii. The most significant discovery for the FBI, however, was the name of his former common-law wife, Hazel Barton Ford Osborne Evelsizer. The report noted that Osborne bore Ford's child on September 1, 1920, in Los Angeles and that the child was named Wallace Dodd Ford Jr. Both parents were listed as Caucasian. This was their only child. Lastly, the file detailed Ford's conviction in 1926 on illegal drug and liquor distribution charges.[18]

On October 4, 1957, the bureau received a photograph of Ford taken upon his reception at San Quentin. Two weeks later, the Los Angeles field office obtained Ford's arrest record from the local police department. After digesting the data, agents interviewed Hazel Evelsizer at her home in Los Angeles, where she gave a detailed account of her relationship with

Ford. She had met him in 1919, shortly after relocating from New York with her mother. Ford hired her as a waitress at Wallie's Café, a small restaurant he owned on South Flower Street. They began dating, and she soon moved into his apartment above the restaurant. Their first child was born a year later.

The FBI spent the next two years analyzing thousands of reports on the Nation of Islam to determine how to implement COINTELPRO actions. In February 1959, it leaked sensationalistic material, including phony news stories, to news media in Asia and Africa as part of an effort to prevent foreign government officials from welcoming Malcolm X during his first visit overseas. Later that year, it leaked a dossier and fake news stories on W. D. Fard to domestic media sources. The blitz began on August 11, when *Newsweek* claimed that a congressional probe was about to begin to determine whether the group was subversive. Four days later, the *New Chicago Crusader,* one of the largest and most respected African American newspapers, ran a front-page story based on information in the FBI file. "White Man Is God for Cult of Islam," it read. The writer, Mohd Yakub Khan, claimed that Fard was a Turk who had worked for Germany during World War II and that he had met Elijah Muhammad in prison in 1943. The bureau failed to get any mileage out of the story, however, because it was riddled with errors and because it was clear the information had come from the FBI files.

COINTELPRO actions against the Nation of Islam subsided for two years but reignited in 1962 after a White congressman asked Hoover for the FBI dossier on the group. Lucius Mendel Rivers, a hard-line segregationist representing Charleston, South Carolina, was angered by the NOI's expansive growth. He requested that Francis E. Walter use his influence as chairperson of the House Un-American Activities Committee (HUAC) to launch a probe of the NOI on the grounds that the sect was "subversive."[19] A federal court in the District of Columbia had recently ruled that the Nation of Islam was a legitimate religion and therefore Muslim inmates at a local prison had the right to hold services in the same fashion as Christian inmates. "We must dissect this organization and open up its unsavory history so that the people can see and know it for what it is," Rivers told the HUAC rules committee on August 14. The Rivers proposal came after inmates at Lorton Youth Center had rioted two weeks earlier to protest religious discrimination and the inclusion of pork in some meals.[20]

The resolution had Walter's full support. Like Rivers, Walter was a staunch segregationist. The Democrat from Pennsylvania had supported a race-based immigration quota system since the early 1920s. He was also director of the Pioneer Fund, a group that believed scientific evidence proved "white intellectual superiority" over the darker races. In supporting the probe, Walter told his fellow representative that HUAC had received numerous complaints about the Nation of Islam's un-American activities. A resolution recommending a probe passed on September 6, and subpoenas were issued to Malcolm X, Elijah Muhammad, John Ali, and other high-level Muslim officials in Chicago, Detroit, and New York. Rivers and Walter secretly requested the FBI files on the group, telling Hoover that they needed anything that would "make Elijah Muhammad look ridiculous." The director complied with the request, and the FBI took matters a step further by sending canned news stories to those it considered to be "friendly journalists."

On July 28, 1963, the Hearst-owned *Los Angeles Evening Herald-Examiner* ran a front-page story about W.D. Fard. "Black Muslims Founder Exposed as a White," the headline read. From wiretaps installed inside Muhammad's home, the FBI learned that the ailing leader was furious about the story and planned to file a defamation lawsuit against the newspaper. Advised by his personal attorney William R. Ming Jr. that he had no legitimate grounds to do so, Muhammad reacted by offering a $100,000 reward to anyone who could prove the allegations that appeared in the newspaper.[21]

On August 8, Hazel Evelsizer applied for the reward. She sent Muhammad a detailed letter and other documentation of her relationship with Wallace D. Ford. In rejecting her claim, Muhammad replied that the Los Angeles police files, the San Quentin records, and the photos and fingerprints were fabricated. Letters from believers asking about the accuracy of the story poured into FBI headquarters for the next several months. In every instance, the FBI declined to comment on the particulars. The exposé caused rumblings, but once again Elijah Muhammad was able to contain its impact. To the congregation, which was unaware of Hazel Evelsizer's reply, it appeared that no one came forward to prove the allegations, and they were soon forgotten.

The Nation of Islam was thrust into the national limelight on June 13, 1959, when two young reporters, Mike Wallace and Louis E. Lomax, presented a controversial television series focusing on the sect. Titled *The Hate That Hate Produced,* the series, to the chagrin of Elijah Muhammad, presented news clip after news clip of Malcolm X berating Caucasians as "devils." The show alarmed New Yorkers and was rebroadcast in full or in part in many regions of the country. Instead of having a negative impact, however, it triggered exponential growth for the Nation of Islam and even ignited an interest in the sect on the part of Arab and African nations. Within three weeks of the broadcast, the Los Angeles mosque inducted five hundred new members. Similar figures were reported in other large urban areas.

On July 17, the day the last installment of the series ran, at least thirteen thousand Africans, Arabs, East Indians, and African Americans attended a bazaar in Harlem sponsored by the Nation of Islam and various civic groups. Among the dinner's organizers, who sold tickets bearing the title "United Front of Black Men," were prominent local and state politicians, including Manhattan borough president Hulan E. Jack and state senator James Watson. Among those who attended were Princess Shanyii Zeffii Tau, the executive director of Radio Free Africa, Egyptian embassy attaché A. Z. Borai, and Ishaq Qutub, vice president of the Arab Students Association of the United States.[22] The most important guest that evening, at least in terms of Malcolm X's development as an internationally recognized revolutionary, was Mahmoud Boutiba, a close ally of Ahmed Ben Bella, leader of the Algerian Front of National Liberation (FLN). Boutiba was regarded by the American intelligence community as an expert in propaganda, so he was kept under close surveillance.

While reaction to the Wallace and Lomax series was still reverberating throughout the country, Malcolm X made final preparations for his first trip to Africa and the Middle East. Elijah Muhammad had planned to join him on the trip, but the FBI and the State Department used every legal maneuver imaginable to prevent approval of his passport and the passports of his daughter, Lottie, and three of his sons, Herbert, Wallace, and Akbar. Akbar and Wallace had already been accepted as students at the University of El-Azhar in Cairo. The passport issue remained unresolved for months. William R. Ming Jr., a prominent Chicago lawyer who served as counsel to the Nation of Islam, had to seek help from Illinois senators Paul Douglas and Everett Dirksen before the passports were finally issued.[23]

Malcolm X's trip, which was closely monitored by the intelligence community, began on July 5. During the tour, he visited the United Arab Republic, Saudi Arabia, Sudan, Lebanon, Turkey, Iran, Ghana, and other African and Arab nations. On July 13, Malcolm X's appointment to have lunch with Gamal Abdel Nasser at the Egyptian leader's home was canceled. While the reason for the cancellation remains a mystery, indications are that the intelligence community was again running interference. In addition, Malcolm X did not enter the holy city of

Mecca during his stay in Saudi Arabia. In explaining why he had not made the *hajj,* the pilgrimage made annually by orthodox Muslims, Malcolm X told Black Muslims upon his return to the United States that he had become "very ill" and had been unable to complete the journey. He also said it would have been inappropriate for him to make the *hajj* before the Messenger (that is, Elijah Muhammad), who was still preparing for his trip when Malcolm X returned, had done so.

By 1957, the FBI and local police departments appeared to be carrying out a vendetta against the NOI. On April 14, 1957, Johnson X Hinton and another Black Muslim were minding their own business when they witnessed two White police officers beating Reece V. Poe, a young Black man, with their nightsticks. "You're not in Alabama," Hinton protested, demanding that they stop.[24] The officers complied, but only to change the target of their attack from Poe to Hinton. It took hundreds of stitches to put Hinton's scalp back together, and no area on his body remained unbruised.

News of the attack on Hinton traveled through Harlem fast. Within minutes, more than two thousand Harlemites were in the streets demanding retribution. Panicking, police started placing phone calls to every Black man they could think of who could possibly restore calm. James Hicks, editor of the New York *Amsterdam News,* was summoned as a mediator, but the crowd wanted justice, not mediation. As tempers flared, Inspector William McGowan and several other top police department officials implored Hicks to summon Malcolm X. Hicks found Malcolm X and his new confidante, John Ali, in the crowd—now approaching three thousand people—gathered at Seventh Avenue and 123rd Street. Malcolm X made it clear that there was nothing to negotiate; Johnson had been unjustly brutalized, the police were responsible, and they were denying him medical attention by holding him in the Twenty-Eighth Precinct.

After Hinton arrived at the hospital, Malcolm X sent a photographer to take pictures of his injuries. In the weeks that followed, enlargements of the photographs were shown during temple meetings and were circulated throughout Harlem. The same photographs were later used during the trial that ensued after Elijah Muhammad filed a $1 million lawsuit against New York City and its police department. When the matter was finally resolved, Hinton and his lawyers received $70,000 in compensation. Within months, the Hinton incident was overshadowed by Malcolm X's campaign to spread Islam. He was on the road again by May, opening temples in Pittsburgh, Buffalo, and Richmond, as well as several in California. But the people of Harlem did not forget. Malcolm X had challenged the authority of the New York Police Department and survived without a scratch, and he was now a folk hero.

In July, the owner of a Black newspaper had become sufficiently enamored of the Nation of Islam to grant Malcolm X space for a weekly column. Under the title "God's Angry Men," the first installment ran in the *Los Angeles Herald-Dispatch* on July 18, 1957. For the first time, Malcolm X was able to deliver Elijah Muhammad's message to thousands of readers in the comfort of their homes instead of to thirty or forty people sitting on uncomfortable folding chairs in poorly ventilated and unfamiliar surroundings. Membership in Los Angeles soared after the initiation of the column, and several new temples were opened.

On May 16, two New York City detectives and a federal postal inspector went to Malcolm X's apartment seeking an individual named Margaret Dorsey. The detectives, who had not bothered to get a search warrant, grew hostile when Malcolm X demanded that they present one or leave, and they fired several shots into the apartment. Although no one was injured, the incident rattled Malcolm X. His wife, Betty Shabazz, was four months pregnant with their first child.[25] Word of the attack spread quickly. Within minutes, Black Muslims pounced on the detectives and gave them a severe beating. Malcolm X, John Ali, Minnie Ali, and Betty were taken into custody for resisting arrest and on other charges. They pled not guilty and subsequently filed a $24 million claim (settled out of court in 1958) against the city, its police department, and the U.S. Postal Service.

The FBI launched another counterintelligence campaign, this one to discredit the Nation of Islam among Muslims from Africa and the Middle East. Elijah Muhammad had sent a letter to the Working Muslim Mission in Surrey, England, inviting it to send a delegate to the annual Saviour's Day convention on February 26, 1958. A copy of the letter was reprinted in the February issue of the *Islamic Review,* published by a committee at the Islamic Center, one of the most resplendent buildings in Washington, D.C. Within days of publication, the FBI sent its dossier on Wallace Fard to the publisher, along with detailed information on the criminal records of Fard, Muhammad, and Malcolm X. Copies of *The Supreme Wisdom,* the booklet containing the basic tenets of the Nation of Islam's faith, were also forwarded.

In the March issue of *Islamic Review,* the publisher apologized for printing Elijah Muhammad's letter and denounced the Nation of Islam as a "caricature of Islam."[26] The denunciation had no effect on Muhammad's relationship with prominent Islamic leaders, who recognized that the Nation of Islam was their only link with the American public. When King Ibn Abdullah Saud of Saudi Arabia visited New York in January 1957, he specifically asked Malcolm X to have lunch with him at the Waldorf Astoria Hotel. Since Saud was on the CIA's payroll at the time, it is difficult to say what his motivation might have been.

On July 26, 1958, Malcolm X, Congressman Adam Clayton Powell Jr., and Manhattan borough president Hulan E. Jack were part of a coalition of civic groups that sponsored a reception in honor of Kwame Nkrumah, the prime minister of Ghana. Nkrumah, who was in the United States to seek aid from the Eisenhower administration, was quite familiar with Black nationalist organizations in New York and Pennsylvania. In the early 1930s, when he was a starving student, he had joined the religious sect headed by Father Divine, a controversial leader born into the Gullah tribe off the coast of Georgia who claimed that he was the reincarnation of God. Nkrumah first encountered the Nation of Islam while selling fish in Harlem during the summer of 1936, and he again crossed paths with the NOI in Philadelphia that winter, when he began his graduate studies at Lincoln University (one of his classmates was Thurgood Marshall, who later became the first African American to serve on the U.S. Supreme Court). An early admirer of Marcus Garvey, Nkrumah named Ghana's shipping company after Garvey's Black Star Line shortly after assuming the prime ministership. Nkrumah had visions of a United States of Africa. Toward this end, he formed the Conference of Independent African States in April 1958.

On November 19, 1958, the New York field office noted that surveillance of Malcolm X should be intensified because he "may aspire to replace Elijah Muhammad as NOI leader." In 1963, the FBI finally discovered the Achilles' heel of the Nation of Islam. Elijah Muhammad had fathered a number of children by almost a half dozen of his secretaries. Wiretaps on the leader's home telephone revealed that Malcolm X was unaware of the transgression and might very well quit the group if he found out about it. After igniting a whispering campaign within the NOI about the children (done by sending anonymous letters to Malcolm X, Clara Muhammad, and others), the doubts planted bore fruit. Malcolm X began inquiring about the allegations and soon learned from Wallace Muhammad, Elijah's heir apparent, that they were true. At the same time, the FBI launched another anonymous letter-writing campaign in which Malcolm X was accused of trying to "take over" the NOI.

Through the use of informants within the NOI, the trust between its two national leaders began deteriorating. A March 1964 wiretap revealed that Elijah Muhammad had authorized Muslim enforcers to kill Malcolm X. After several attempts were made on his life, Malcolm X decided to break from the group and form his own organization. A year later, he was dead.

The FBI then turned its attention to Muhammad Ali, the heavyweight boxing champion of the world. Any ground lost by the NOI after the death of Malcolm X was soon recaptured by Ali. While the FBI file on Ali (formerly known as Cassius Clay) is still classified for the most part, the website *Smoking Gun* and scholars have acquired documents showing that the FBI had targeted Ali as early as February 1964 for "neutralization" (a term the bureau used to cover myriad methods of destroying people's lives).[27]

The documents reveal that Angelo Dundee, Ali's trainer, had given agents a list of everyone associated with Ali whom Dundee believed were also members of the NOI. A three-year battle waged by Ali against being inducted into the armed forces ended in 1967 when he was indicted on draft evasion charges and stripped of his heavyweight boxing title. The loss of money from Ali, who was reportedly giving as much as half of his earnings to the NOI, was the beginning of a downward financial spiral for the organization.

COINTELPRO reached new heights following the assassination of Dr. Martin Luther King Jr. in April 1968. By then, the bureau had changed its focus from finding out which way Black organizations were heading to steering the courses of the organizations by placing informants in top-level positions within them.

An ominous directive from Hoover to every FBI field office in the nation outlined goals for undermining the entire civil rights movement under the guise of curbing the Black Power movement. "The purpose of this new counterintelligence endeavor is to expose, disrupt, misdirect, discredit or otherwise neutralize the activities of black-nationalist, hate-type organizations and groupings, their leadership, spokesmen, membership and supporters." The directive continued: "No opportunity should be missed to exploit through counterintelligence techniques the organization and personal conflicts of the leadership of the groups and where possible, efforts should be made to capitalize upon existing conflicts between competitive black nationalist organizations."[28]

While the order specified "black nationalist" organizations, the bureau used the term loosely. Consequently, virtually every Black celeb-

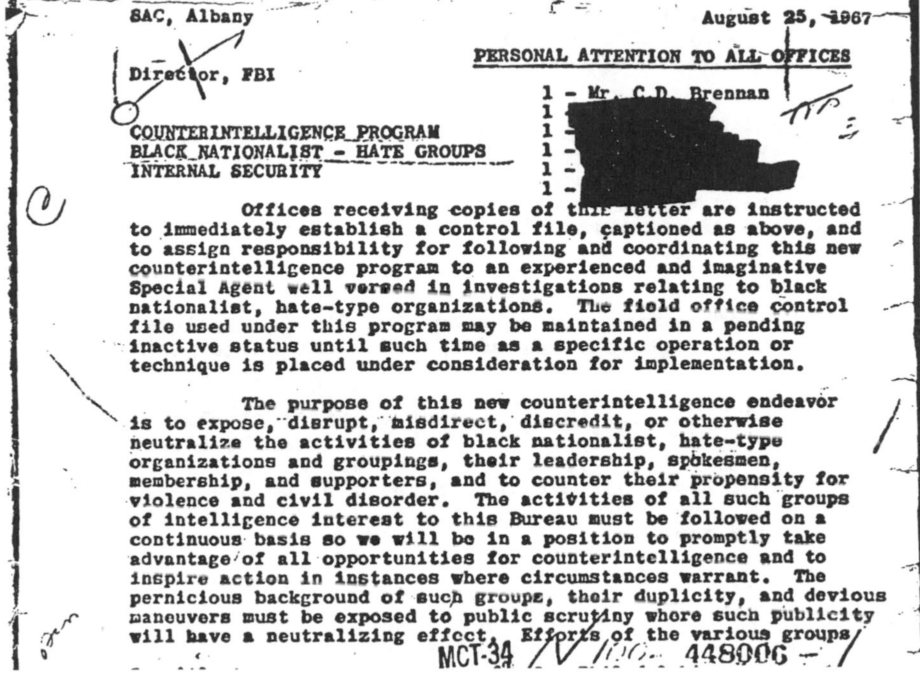

SAC, Albany

August 25, 1967

Director, FBI

PERSONAL ATTENTION TO ALL OFFICES

1 - Mr. C.D. Brennan
1 -
1 -
1 -
1 -
1 -

COUNTERINTELLIGENCE PROGRAM
BLACK NATIONALIST - HATE GROUPS
INTERNAL SECURITY

Offices receiving copies of this letter are instructed to immediately establish a control file, captioned as above, and to assign responsibility for following and coordinating this new counterintelligence program to an experienced and imaginative Special Agent well versed in investigations relating to black nationalist, hate-type organizations. The field office control file used under this program may be maintained in a pending inactive status until such time as a specific operation or technique is placed under consideration for implementation.

The purpose of this new counterintelligence endeavor is to expose, disrupt, misdirect, discredit, or otherwise neutralize the activities of black nationalist, hate-type organizations and groupings, their leadership, spokesmen, membership, and supporters, and to counter their propensity for violence and civil disorder. The activities of all such groups of intelligence interest to this Bureau must be followed on a continuous basis so we will be in a position to promptly take advantage of all opportunities for counterintelligence and to inspire action in instances where circumstances warrant. The pernicious background of such groups, their duplicity, and devious maneuvers must be exposed to public scrutiny where such publicity will have a neutralizing effect. Efforts of the various groups

MCT-34 ... 448006

FIGURE 9.1. First page of an FBI directive dated August 25, 1967, in which Hoover announced plans to, in effect, "neutralize" any group in America advocating black nationalism. From COINTELPRO: Black Nationalist—Hate Groups, Department of Justice, FBI Records: The Vault (vault.fbi.gov).

rity and every civil rights organization in the nation found itself under surveillance. Among the targets were the National Association for the Advancement of Colored People and the Black Panther Party for Self-Defense. Any celebrity who contributed in any way to these organizations was targeted. In fact, choose at random any Black celebrity of the time, from Cleveland Browns football legend Jim Brown to actors Eartha Kitt and Sammy Davis Jr. to musician Jimi Hendrix, and you will find an FBI dossier on them.[29]

The directive of August 25, 1967, was followed by the "Black Messiah Memo" on March 4, 1968—thirty days before Dr. King was assassinated. Contending that the country was in the midst of a racial revolution that threatened to topple the American government, William C. Sullivan, head of the FBI's intelligence-gathering apparatus, wrote that Dr. King was an "integral part" of the revolution and the FBI should use every means available to crush it. The second point of the five-point

Airtel to SAC, Albany
RE: COUNTERINTELLIGENCE PROGRAM
BLACK NATIONALIST-HATE GROUPS

nationalist activity, and interested in counterintelligence, to coordinate this program. This Agent will be responsible for the periodic progress letters being requested, but each Agent working this type of case should participate in the formulation of counterintelligence operations.

GOALS

For maximum effectiveness of the Counterintelligence Program, and to prevent wasted effort, long-range goals are being set.

1. Prevent the coalition of militant black nationalist groups. In unity there is strength; a truism that is no less valid for all its triteness. An effective coalition of black nationalist groups might be the first step toward a real "Mau Mau" in America, the beginning of a true black revolution.

2. Prevent the rise of a "messiah" who could unify, and electrify, the militant black nationalist movement. Malcolm X might have been such a "messiah;" he is the martyr of the movement today. Martin Luther King, Stokely Carmichael and Elijah Muhammed all aspire to this position. Elijah Muhammed is less of a threat because of his age. King could be a very real contender for this position should he abandon his supposed "obedience" to "white, liberal doctrines" (nonviolence) and embrace black nationalism. Carmichael has the necessary charisma to be a real threat in this way.

3. Prevent violence on the part of black nationalist groups. This is of primary importance, and is, of course, a goal of our investigative activity; it should also be a goal of the Counterintelligence Program. Through counterintelligence it should be possible to pinpoint potential troublemakers and neutralize them before they exercise their potential for violence.

4. Prevent militant black nationalist groups and leaders from gaining respectability, by discrediting them to three separate segments of the community. The goal of discrediting black nationalists must be handled tactically in three ways. You must discredit these groups and individuals to, first, the responsible Negro community. Second, they must be discredited to the white community,

- 3 -

FIGURE 9.2. Third page of a March 4, 1968, memo stating that a key goal of the Bureau's COINTELPRO operations was to prevent the rise of a "messiah" with the ability to unify black nationalist organizations. The memo was issued following a massive demonstration to protest the incarceration of Black Panther leaders, during which Stokely Carmichael and H. Rap Brown announced that they were merging SNCC with the Black Panther party. From COINTELPRO: Black Nationalist—Hate Groups, Department of Justice, FBI Records: The Vault (vault.fbi.gov).

CHICAGO DAILY NEWS, Tuesday, Feb. 10, 1976 ☆ 25

Hoover rated Carmichael as 'black messiah'

By Rob Warden

J. Edgar Hoover wrote in a 1968 internal FBI memo just made public that black militant Stokely Carmichael had the "necessary charisma to be a real threat" to the internal security of the United States.

The memo singled out Carmichael as the most likely "messiah" among black leaders at the time to "unify and electrify the black nationalist movement" — more likely than the Rev. Dr. Martin Luther King Jr., Elijah Muhammad or H. Rap Brown.

Hoover said in the memo dated March 4, 1968, that it was important for the FBI to try to prevent the rise of a "messiah" who could put together a coalition of militant black groups.

Carmichael Hoover

FIGURE 9.3. A 1976 news story revealed that Carmichael was a key target of the FBI's secret COINTELPRO operations against black nationalists because Hoover believed he had the potential to become the "black messiah" of the Black Power movement. COINTELPRO was exposed in 1971 following a burglary of the FBI office in Media, Pennsylvania. Clipping from COINTELPRO: Black Nationalist—Hate Groups, Department of Justice, FBI Records: The Vault (vault.fbi.gov).

memo directed agents to prevent the rise of a messiah who could unify and electrify the militant Black nationalist movement. It explains that Malcolm X might have been such a "messiah" and that he was now the movement's martyr. King, Stokely Carmichael, and Elijah Muhammed all aspired to this position, the memo claimed. Elijah Muhammed, however, was less of a threat because of his age. King, Sullivan wrote, could be a very real contender for this position should he abandon his supposed "obedience" to "white, liberal doctrines" (that is, nonviolence) and embrace Black nationalism. "Carmichael has the necessary charisma to be a real threat in this way."[30]

A similar counterintelligence offensive was aimed at right-wing White groups, including the Ku Klux Klan. Informants and agents provocateurs were planted in virtually every Black organization in the country. By the end of the decade, every "radical" organization seemed to be in disarray, much of the turmoil caused by internal dissension created by FBI informants.

By 1970, the Nation of Islam was effectively neutralized. Years of harassment from the Internal Revenue Service (at the behest of the FBI) had led to huge payments to attorneys. Attacks on its livestock in several southern states left the group in a deep financial hole, a predicament exacerbated by irrational spending on the part of both Elijah Muhammad (he purchased a Leer Jet even though he rarely traveled) and his ministers. To make matters worse, gang elements began joining the Nation of Islam and using the group's secrecy to hide illegal drug distribution activities. Facing bankruptcy, Elijah Muhammad did the unthinkable. He requested a meeting with officials of the U.S. government to request money to start a job-training program in Black communities. This, of course, contradicted everything Muhammad had taught for forty years and was a clear signal that the group, like its leader, was gravely ill.

Elijah Muhammad borrowed $3 million from Muammar Gaddafi in 1972, ostensibly to purchase a church to convert into a mosque. He also announced a multimillion-dollar fund-raising drive to build a Black-owned hospital in Chicago. The mosque eventually opened, but the millions raised for the hospital were used to keep the organization financially afloat.[31] When Muhammad died three years later, the NOI was millions of dollars in debt. The group paid $4 million for a church property valued at less than $1.5 million. The few farms it owned owed a half-million dollars. In all, the NOI was drowning in about $10 million of red ink. Following the death of Elijah Muhammad in 1975, the group was forced to sell nearly all of its holdings. The name of the group was changed, but it had been neutralized, just as Hoover had planned.

Elijah Muhammad's son, Wallace, immediately assumed leadership of the sect even though he had defected many times and was a stranger to the majority of NOI members. Most had assumed that Louis Farrakhan, the group's national spokesman, would replace Elijah. The day after Elijah's death, Farrakhan addressed the annual convention of the NOI in Chicago. Through tears, he announced that it had been prophesied by Fard himself that Wallace would succeed Elijah. He noted that Wallace was the founder's namesake.

Wallace renounced his father's teachings within weeks of his ascendancy and announced plans to convert his flock to Sunni Islam. This did not sit well with the rank and file. To make matters worse, Wallace shuffled ministers, including Farrakhan, to different cities as part of his plan to defuse their power bases. He accused them of being in a cabal that was squandering the sect's money. Two years later, Farrakhan defected, taking the majority of NOI followers with him. Today, Farrakhan's sect still practices the race-based theology of Elijah Muhammad.

The defection followed the release of FBI memos from the early 1970s in which agents boasted to Hoover that its informants were in a position to assume leadership of the NOI as soon as Elijah died. Farrakhan suggested publicly that Wallace was one such informant. Similarly, other powerful ministers, including John Muhammad (Elijah's brother) and Silis Muhammad of Atlanta, claimed to possess "evidence" that both Wallace and Farrakhan were informants.

By the mid-1980s, the sect had splintered into more than a dozen cults of personality. Whether this was the result of informants wreaking havoc or the natural reaction of organizations that suddenly lose a beloved leader, or both, is unknown. The mere fact, however, that the FBI devised a plan to manipulate a group whose aims were solely messianic and who openly eschewed politics (NOI members did not vote or participate in the political process in any way) raises disturbing First Amendment issues. While government agents conducted a similar infiltration of the leadership of the Ku Klux Klan, the COINTELPRO activity directed against the NOI was a clear violation of the principles of separation of church and state.

10

Dreams and Shadows

Martin Luther King Jr., the FBI, and the Southern Christian Leadership Conference

SYLVESTER A. JOHNSON

On the Sunday afternoon of October 16, 2011, a buoyant crowd of approximately fifty thousand gathered at the National Mall to join in the celebrative dedication of the national Martin Luther King Jr. Memorial. The event had been several years in the making and was the hard-won result of fund-raising, national organizing, and relentless determination to create a formal site of commemoration to honor the life and legacy the civil rights movement's most iconic activist. The height of the event of was President Barack Obama's address, which urged those gathered to embrace the legacy of King's determination to perfect their nation and to deepen the quest for freedom:

> We forget now, but during his life, Dr. King wasn't always considered a unifying figure. Even after rising to prominence, even after winning the Nobel Peace Prize, Dr. King was vilified by many, denounced as a rabble rouser and an agitator, a communist and a radical. He was even attacked by his own people, by those who felt he was going too fast or those who felt he was going too slow; by those who felt he shouldn't meddle in issues like the Vietnam War or the rights of union workers. We know from his own testimony the doubts and the pain this caused him, and that the controversy that would swirl around his actions would last until the fateful day he died.[1]

Obama urged his audience to contemplate the massive unpopularity and resistance that King encountered, including being branded a communist. Noting that King's "own people" attacked him, the U.S. president clearly meant to mark the stark contrast between King's present-day popularity and the adversity of his own lifetime. The greatest irony, however, is that the MLK Memorial now sits on the Washington Mall, amid other literally monumental icons of the U.S. state. At the height of King's public activism and to the last moments of his life, it was the U.S. government that did by far the most to oppose him. More specifically, the Federal Bureau of Investigation identified King as a national security threat and targeted him for repression as an enemy of the state. By 1967, the FBI would declare King the most dangerous Black person in the United States, and the movement he led would be labeled the nation's single most dangerous internal security threat, exceeding communism as the chief national security concern.

This chapter examines the FBI's engagement with King, a relationship overwhelmingly defined by the bureau's efforts to repress and neutralize King as a potent leader of the civil rights movement. This repression took place within the context of the FBI's role as an integral part of the U.S. security state's intelligence complex. Much has been made of J. Edgar Hoover's personal animus against King, and it is true that Hoover's personal idiosyncrasies substantively shaped the bureau's entire ethos. As I explain, however, the interest that Hoover and the FBI took in King and the Southern Christian Leadership Conference did not arise from Hoover's personal quirks. The bureau's repression of King—and in fact, all of its repression—was thoroughly political and was rooted in the central national security priorities of the FBI and the larger complex of intelligence agencies tasked with securing the nation's prevailing political order against domestic and international threats.[2]

THE FBI, THE SCLC, AND THE SPECTER OF COMMUNISM

The specter of communism constituted the initial premise for investigating SCLC and King. The vigilance against communism had already created special challenges for King, whose mature theology as a Christian minister was rooted in the Social Gospel tradition of interpreting the meaning of Christianity through the imperative of creating worldly justice, and this included critiquing structural poverty and material inequality. One gains some sense of this commitment from one of King's sermons of 1948, at which point he drew on a Marxist critique of capitalism to explain that the United States's unequal economic system was moribund and, given sustained commitments to social reform, would have to give way to a more just system.[3]

King articulated this same theme in 1962 when he delivered a sermon entitled "Can a Christian be a Communist?" He echoed the bromides of mainstream anticommunism by lamenting that communism was commanding a religious type of allegiance from followers around the world. Given communism's association with atheism, it is not surprising that King proclaimed that no Christian could be a communist. It was nevertheless essential, he asserted, for Christians to embrace the "dream" of communism—alleviating inequality and providing for the poor—while rejecting its "creed." Occupying his pivotal role as the face of the civil rights movement, he was purposely succinct about condemning the anti-religious ethos of communism while affirming the importance of Marxist analysis for Social Gospel theology.[4]

When the FBI began to surveil King and SCLC in October 1962, it was not concerned with King's sermons but rather with the larger dynamics of political dissent and grassroots activism. The bureau justified its attention to the organization under a provision in the FBI manual captioned "COMINFIL" (referring to communist infiltration). The bureau would eventually claim that two of King's close associates who worked with SCLC were in fact communist operatives who had gone underground to avoid detection. Most important was Stanley Levison, an attorney in New York who had lent legal support to the boycott against Montgomery's bus system. Levison had handled some financial work for the Communist Party USA (CPUSA) during the 1950s, and he even associated with party members. After the Montgomery boycott, Levison continued his involvement with the civil rights movement throughout the 1960s by providing advisory support to SCLC. He also served as a ghost author for sections of King's monographs, including *Stride toward Freedom*. The second individual whom the FBI identified as a communist was Hunter Pitts "Jack" O'Dell, who had been a member of the CPUSA, though he withdrew his membership before being hired to work for SCLC. King eventually fired O'Dell from SCLC after receiving pressure from President John F. Kennedy's administration. But he continued his friendship and professional relationship with Levison.[5]

At first glance, both Levison and O'Dell might seem the proverbial smoking gun that prompted the FBI's vigilance against communism in SCLC. O'Dell, after all, had at one time been a formal member of the CPUSA. He had also been repeatedly prosecuted by the federal government as a subversive and was forced to testify before the House Un-American Activities Committee and the Senate Internal Security Subcommittee. But O'Dell never attempted to conceal his party membership, and his administrative work with SCLC was in no way an attempt to take over the organization—as the FBI claimed—in order to undermine U.S. society. The bureau's assertions about Levison were even more disingenuous. Despite the reams of FBI claims to the contrary, Levison was never a member of the CPUSA, a fact that seems shocking given the scale of the bureau's characterization of Levison as a party member and underground operative. Not only was he never a communist, but his work with SCLC and his numerous meetings with King concerned organizational strategies to address SCLC's priorities. As has now been acknowledged by experts within and outside the FBI, however, the FBI's focus on Levison was a less-than-honest means to the end of disrupting King and SCLC because of their threat to the racial order of the U.S. state.[6]

In one sense, the FBI's scrutiny of King and SCLC was certainly one more brick in the wall of a broad strategy that employed against domestic citizens the same methods used for engaging foreign subjects. And in that context, communism was easily the most potent public symbol of radical evil that threatened the security of a Christian America. No more urgent imperative could be named for investigating the SCLC.[7]

By portraying communism as the political order of totalitarianism, the FBI, the U.S. State Department, and other high-level government entities achieved multiple, simultaneous effects. They rendered the corporatism of free-market capitalism as auspicious and benevolent. They promoted the noetics of Western colonial rationality by eliding the fundamental problem of colonialism, the murderous system of brutal domination vociferously criticized by non-White activists in South Asia, East Asia, the Middle East, Africa, and the Americas, including the Caribbean. They also augured the appeal of anticommunism as a celebration of Western civilizational superiority.[8]

At the same time, however, the FBI had for decades recognized that Black political organizing and rebellion against America's system of racial hierarchy and White supremacism constituted a formidable threat to U.S. racial hierarchy that required decisive action were they to be quelled. The FBI's repression of the Universal Negro Improvement Association under Marcus Garvey's leadership was the earliest major episode in this history. By the 1960s, however, a plethora of numerically smaller but nonetheless visible movements for Black freedom were inciting the FBI to take measures beyond precedent. As he did with scores of other organizations throughout the United States, Hoover tasked his agents with investigating SCLC to ascertain whether it had come under communist influence. When William Sullivan, who led the Domestic

Intelligence Division, submitted his team's conclusive report to Hoover, Sullivan confidently asserted that there was no credible cause for concern that communism had influenced the civil rights movement. In fact, he emphasized, it seemed a waste of good resources to engage SCLC as a communist front.[9]

The backlash from Hoover was firm and decisive, as he challenged the agents' findings and sternly suggested they reconsider the evidence in order to reach a more reliable conclusion. In a dizzying turn of revision, Sullivan's crew thanked Hoover for the opportunity to review their assessment and, not surprisingly, returned straightaway with a positive finding that SCLC was a valid object of national security concern regarding communism. Sullivan, in fact, now emphasized that the division was in complete agreement with Hoover that communists were influencing King and that, since King was the most prominent of African American leaders, this made King America's "most dangerous and effective Negro leader."[10] In that same year, the FBI placed King's name on Section A of its Reserve Index. This was the bureau's confidential list of individuals deemed to constitute high-level threats to internal security; they were to be captured and detained in the event of any situation judged a national emergency.[11]

During the summer of 1963, as members of Congress responded to activist demands for civil rights legislation, Mississippi governor Ross Barnett and Alabama governor George Wallace appealed to their White colleagues in the Senate to upend civil rights activism, as they claimed SCLC was a communist conspiracy that threatened the nation's integrity. When skeptics challenged assertions about communism, Hoover eventually chimed in, confirming the FBI's official stance that communists were plotting to take over the movement.[12] Such charades enacted by Wallace and Barnett were making waves for federal officials outside Congress and the White House. U.S. attorney general Robert Kennedy was especially compelled to respond to this criticism. Just one day after Wallace accused civil rights supporters of sympathizing with communists, Kennedy called a meeting with his assistant attorney general, Courtney Evans, to propose wiretapping phone calls between King himself and Stanley Levison, the New York attorney with whom King had frequent contact. Evans was taken aback by the suggestion, largely because of the possible repercussions. He foresaw a public relations scandal if the wiretaps were discovered. Evans also doubted the utility of the surveillance. Despite Evans's concerns, Kennedy pressed forward with a request for the FBI to assess the feasibility of the wiretaps. Hoover was only too pleased to indicate that wiretapping the two men would certainly be feasible.

On July 23, just one week later, Attorney General Robert Kennedy sent a communiqué to the Senate Commerce Committee to address members' alarm over the situation. He stressed that "all available evidence from the FBI and other sources" confirmed that civil rights leaders were neither communists nor controlled by communists. Kennedy emphasized that this included King as well as numerous other leaders. Since the attorney general believed that King was being *influenced* by communists, this shrewd phrasing allowed some wiggle room.[13] In light of the injustices suffered by Blacks, he commented, it was notable they had resisted communist efforts to attract followers. In other words, their loyalty to an anticommunist America had been tested and was especially visible.[14]

The surveillance that proved most damaging to King started with a suggestion from William Sullivan in September 1963. To further demonstrate his commitment to intensifying the pressure on SCLC and King, he suggested to Hoover that they install listening devices in King's home and in SCLC offices; this went far beyond merely intercepting King's phone calls. The director was skeptical at first that the attorney general would approve the request, as a similar one had recently been denied. By this time, however, Kennedy was even more determined to get to the bottom of the reported communist activity in the civil rights movement. Thus, he readily approved the request for wiretapping King's home on October 10, 1963, and the New York and Atlanta offices of SCLC on October 21, 1963. Kennedy did caution that the effectiveness of the surveillance be evaluated after one month, but he never specified that any follow-up need occur with his office. The FBI wasted no time implementing the plan and broke into SCLC offices to install the first wiretaps on October 24, just three days later. On November 8, 1963, the FBI installed wiretaps in King's home.

There can be little doubt, in fact, that Kennedy intended to authorize indefinite surveillance. He even included permission to surveil any *future residences* of King. Sullivan's division seized on this provision to surveil King's *hotel rooms,* since he was almost constantly on the road. Not even the FBI could imagine the pay dirt they were about to hit. The first of these hotel bugs was installed in January 1964. Within days, bureau officials found themselves listening to King and his associates engaging in sexual relations with multiple women. Every aspect of these sexual encounters seemed to materialize palpably on the recordings, and King's own vocalized passions were distinct and readily discernible. These sexual encounters were certainly not matters of national security, but the material constituted precisely what the bureau needed—a surefire way to publicly ruin King and turn his most trusted allies against him.[15]

The Domestic Intelligence Division then sprang its next move. On October 15, 1963, Sullivan sent to Alan Belmont, the FBI's assistant director, a monograph that Sullivan's division had prepared to discredit King. The monograph, entitled "Communism and the Negro Movement: A Current Analysis," was arousing, to say the least. Belmont quickly realized that the damning report on King would be nothing short of explosive. It was abundantly clear to the Domestic Intelligence Division and to Belmont that if they were to disseminate this information beyond the bureau, they could generate a backlash against King's movement, which was slowly gaining sympathizers and altering America's legal framework. The report characterized the civil rights movement and King particularly as a destructive threat to the United States that now functioned as a communist plot to take over America from within by controlling the Black rebellion. Its conclusions were so shocking that Robert Kennedy himself would likely be alarmed and furiously resentful, thought Belmont, especially since Kennedy had publicly associated himself with King and the civil rights movement. On this score, Belmont was more perceptive than he realized. This was a golden opportunity for the FBI to strike a blow against King and the larger racial movement that posed a domestic threat of revolution.[16]

A SHIFTING TIDE: INTENSIFYING REPRESSION

In an ironic twist, U.S. counterintelligence operations opposing the civil rights movement were ramping up at the very time the movement seemed to be gaining significant external legitimacy. By the fall of 1964, the nation's most publicly familiar (and, as judged by his opponents, most "notorious") Christian minister had just received the single most important international affirmation of his challenge to American apartheid. More important for King, his receipt of the Nobel Peace Prize was also a major victory for SCLC. It brought a substantial aura of legitimacy to this religious movement's controversial use of civil disobedience and its stridently confrontational methods of challenging legal and cultural pillars of anti-Black racism.

In one sense, the Nobel Prize committee could not have recognized SCLC's work at a more opportune time. The movement was dealing with the difficult challenge of balancing an early history of success against a recent barrage of losses. Activists had been stymied when they tried to force the city of Selma, Alabama, to change its segregation laws. After several weeks of failed efforts, SCLC had to pack up and leave in search of a less formidable opportunity to build momentum and continue tackling the legal and cultural authority of White supremacism in American law.

On December 10, 1964, King traveled to Oslo to receive the Nobel Peace Prize in person. The next day, he delivered his Nobel lecture at the University of Oslo, Norway's most prestigious university. The event marked a major high point of the movement's popularity, second only to the August 1963 March on Washington. Meanwhile, back in Washington, D.C., at FBI headquarters, J. Edgar Hoover could scarcely have been more embittered. Upon hearing the news and seeing the enthusiastic support from governments throughout the world, Hoover directed the FBI to prevent international heads of state and American ambassadors abroad from receiving King. Two weeks before King traveled to Oslo, the FBI's Domestic Intelligence Division issued an updated derogatory report on King's sexual activities to Robert Kennedy and to Bill Moyers, special assistant to the president. With Moyers's permission, 268 copies of the derisive monograph were issued to the nation's federal agencies. Upon learning that UN representatives Adlai Stevenson and Ralph Bunche had been invited to the coming-home celebration to honor King, the FBI issued reports to them as well, certain that the two men would avoid any close association with King after reading the damning document. In addition, U.S. ambassadors in London, Oslo, Stockholm, and Copenhagen were suddenly accosted with the titillating details of King's personal life. And when the FBI learned that King would be publishing an essay in a major national magazine, they called on an inside contact to prevent its publication. To their dismay, they learned the magazine had already entered into a contractual agreement with King to publish the material; they were too late on that front.[17]

The FBI discovered that in King's hometown of Atlanta, a banquet was being planned in his honor. The bureau attempted to chill success of this event as well. As a result of the bureau's efforts, major would-be supporters refused to have anything to do with the event. Both King and the FBI were right in estimating the value of such a prestigious award as the Nobel Prize. It immediately legitimized the racial revolution resulting from this religious rebellion led by African American southerners. This change was marked by the momentous shift among many White individuals and White businesses in the American South that began publicly supporting the Black freedom struggle, a development even more remarkable than the international embrace of SCLC's controversial activism. For every potential White sponsor who staunchly refused to support the banquet (thanks largely to the FBI's intervention), several more popped up ready to associate themselves with the civil rights movement that the Norwegian Parliament had found worthy of honoring. On January 27, 1965, fifteen hundred Black and White residents of the Atlanta area gathered at the Dinkler Plaza Hotel to honor King with a festive dinner that had sold out within a week of tickets going on sale for $6.50 per plate ($45 in today's dollars). Georgia's two African American state senators, Leroy Johnson and Horace T. Ward, the first since Reconstruction, were especially pleased to be in attendance.[18] Atlanta's mayor, Ivan Allen Jr., was on hand to affirm that it was King's devotion to a nonviolent method of social revolution that earned him the Nobel committee's attention.

VIETNAM

For all the contemporary celebrations of King in the twenty-first century that hail him as a lauded figure, the events of 1965 could not have been more different from this rosy portrayal. Hoover's very public antagonism against King deepened into a relentless tangle of pressures extending into the attorney general's office and the administration of President Lyndon Johnson. A growing number of activists within SCLC and the larger civil rights movement considered King a liability and a possible threat to national security. Many hoped he might resign from his leadership of the racial revolution that seemed to be suffering from the rumors about him. Up to that time, King had denied any sexual impropriety, and he feigned bewilderment when asked about the FBI's rumors. His denial was to be short-lived, at least for those in his closest circle.

In January of that same year King's wife, Coretta Scott King, opened a composite tape of King's sexual liaisons secretly sent by William Sullivan. She sat with her husband and their most trusted associates to listen to the tape. Even his dearest friends, such as his wife, Andrew Young, and Ralph Abernathy, were now persuaded that King's denials and bewilderment only thinly veiled an unbearable truth. What is more, the toll his infidelity was taking on his marriage, though well kept from the public, meant that his home offered no respite from strife but was merely another battleground, one of his own making.[19]

Beyond the personal devastation produced by the tapes was the public controversy concerning America's war with the Vietnamese. It demonstrated that critiquing U.S. colonialism was essential to the larger aim of securing social justice. When King first witnessed Ghana's revolutionary rise from a British colony to an independent nation-state in 1957, he had recognized that anticolonialism was not separate from civil rights, and King now applied that awareness to the U.S. context. He resolved to address Vietnam at the SCLC convention in 1965, to be held in Birmingham. Conceding in no uncertain terms that the war was creating destruction and homelessness for most Vietnamese families, King urged that there was "no need to place blame." Instead, energies should be devoted to working for peace. King understood clearly that the United States was the aggressor in Vietnam, but this conciliatory approach was meant to avoid directly critiquing the U.S. military. In exchange for a cessation of U.S. bombing, he proffered, the Viet Cong should cease demands that the United States withdraw from the southern region of Vietnam.[20]

Despite the modest nature of his response, King's speech to SCLC was poorly received and only confirmed for most that he was unfit to continue leading the movement. Meanwhile, the FBI had increasingly characterized the civil rights movement as a racial revolution, one that demanded ultimate vigilance and warranted careful destruction. At the same time, King increasingly viewed revolution as the necessary crux for making the movement meaningful and effective. During the 1950s and early 1960s, he had emphasized that a beloved community of all Americans should unite against what he described as an extremist fringe of southern segregationists. By 1965, however, it had become painfully clear to King that the problem was not extremists but the mainstream. In fact, as early as 1963, King had begun to challenge White American liberals on this very score. He was jailed in Birmingham, Alabama, because he had insisted on demonstrating against U.S. apartheid. Two White Protestant ministers and a Jewish rabbi condemned him as a dangerous extremist. King responded that the fundamental problem was not White extremists but the White moderates who agreed abstractly that Blacks should have equal rights while insisting that the time was not right.

King spent much of 1966 attempting to avoid the issue of Vietnam. He focused instead on building a movement in Chicago, the central site for translating SCLC's strategies in the South to address the challenges of poverty and segregation in the North. But the public dissent against U.S. militarism in Vietnam was growing steadily and commanding increasing attention from multiple constituencies throughout the nation. By early 1967, it was clear that remaining silent on such a looming issue was not a practical option. So King met in the home of Allard K. Lowenstein one Sunday evening for a strategy meeting to discuss possible options for opposing the war in Vietnam. Among those attending were Andrew Young, John Bennett, Norman Thomas, Bayard Rustin, and Harry Wachtel.[21] The meeting lasted well into the night. Even after taking some time to sit alone in one of the rooms of the apartment, King was unable to decide exactly how to proceed. But he was certain that he had to oppose the war publicly somehow—that was already evident to the others gathered. A mass demonstration before the United Nations building in Manhattan was being planned for that spring to express the growing public dissent against U.S. atrocities in Vietnam. Among those most committed to involving King in the Spring Mobilization march was James Bevel, a young Baptist minister from Itta Bena, Mississippi, who chaired the organization. Bevel had successfully united the movement's disparate group. Eventually, King decided to heed Bevel's urging and participate in the Spring Mobilization. He would speak at the rally, he had decided, but he would emphasize that he represented himself only, not SCLC. He would also emphasize that he was not officially sponsoring the march so that he could dissociate himself from the more radical voices of the demonstration.[22]

King's heart sank when he saw the flyers advertising the event. His picture was front and center, and the names of the other speakers were printed in smaller type size at the bottom. Any objective person would naturally assume that King was the central figure of the event. He was among the most publicly familiar Americans, and the Spring Mobilization organizers had obviously realized the value of having the Nobel laureate address the rally. This now created even more pressure on King to communicate his sincere convictions about American empire and avoid being dismissed as eccentric or out of touch. More gut-wrenching than anything else, perhaps, was the fact that members of the CPUSA would be supporting the rally, and King had no doubt that Hoover, Robert Kennedy, and Johnson administration officials would be standing by to issue new condemnations against him.[23]

Meanwhile, the FBI was proving effective in stoking dissent among African Americans over King's growing concern about U.S. militarism. The bureau fed numerous assertions to cooperative newspaper editors who published claims, for instance, that King was seeking to merge the civil rights movement with the peace movement. For this and other reasons, many high-profile Blacks who were staunchly committed to opposing legal segregation vocally opposed King's public dissent against the U.S. war against the Vietnamese. Whitney Young, who headed the Urban League, could not have been more succinct when he publicly condemned King's opposition to U.S. militarism. In the wake of a public argument with King, Young insisted, "The masses of Negro citizens we are committed to serve and who have given Negro leaders the influence they have, have as their first priority the immediate problem of survival in this country." Young was lodged well within the mainstream of U.S. sentiment and thereby enjoyed broad support. Just two decades earlier, at the height of African Americans' anticolonial activism, any claim that the plight of African Americans was unrelated to American imperialism abroad would have met with incredulity and rebuff among mainstream African Americans. But by the 1960s, the U.S. State Department's intensified propaganda overseas (through the United States Information Agency, or USIA), the FBI's infiltration and repression of anticolonial movements, and the U.S. attorney general's prosecution of figures such as Paul Robeson, W. E. B. Du Bois, and Alphaeus Hunton Jr. had proved devastatingly effective. It was now clear that anticolonial movements would receive the wrath of the state. In the Cold War context, anticolonialism was anti-Americanism, and public denunciation of "traitors" was richly rewarded. Whitney Young's position in the spotlight of public praise was both enviable and, in all honesty, difficult to resist.[24]

On the whole, in fact, King's defenders among civil rights leaders were scarce. It was in the radical wing of Black liberation that he was to find support. The Student Nonviolent Coordinating Committee (SNCC), in particular, led the way in critiquing American empire. As the day of the Spring Mobilization rally in New York drew near, public apprehension grew and predictions of violence and conflict abounded. The New York Police Department (NYPD) was assigning thousands of officers to control the event. Organizers had planned to march from Central Park to the United Nations headquarters. In their optimism, they had anticipated a massive display of support for ending the war. They were not disappointed. On April 15, 1967, more than 100,000 activists arrived to voice their dissent against the U.S. bombing of Vietnam. The astounding turnout was at once civil, bold, insurgent, and particularly threatening to federal authorities. One reporter claimed the rally was "unemotional" and insipid, and it was attacked by numerous organizations and newspapers. But the crucial difference between that New York rally and the March on Washington was their object of critique.[25]

Why did the media and many Americans who had lauded King's March on Washington now deprecate the New York rally? The 1963 March on Washington was by no means a critique of Washington. Rather, legislators that very summer were vetting civil rights legislation. The civil rights movement had firmly wedged itself into a posture of alliance with the federal government to oppose a confederation of rogue southern states and local governments that nakedly violated constitutional principles to deny fundamental rights to American citizens. The enemy was the segregation of the recalcitrant South, not America. America proper, by King's own lofty account, was the land of promise, the birthplace of democracy. The April 1967 rally, by contrast, was the notorious love child of anticolonialism and human rights advocacy, and it bore absolutely no loyalties to American nationalism. It was the Vietnam flag, not the U.S. American flag, that adorned the 1967 rally. The speakers, the activists, the entire movement—all worked to subpoena not the American South but rather the U.S. state before the court of international scrutiny and to demand a just halt to the murder of Vietnamese civilians.[26]

As if this were not scandalous enough, several of the Spring Mobilization organizers had floated the idea that King should run for president in the upcoming 1968 election, with Benjamin Spock as a likely running mate. William Pepper, the executive director of the National Conference for New Politics, had already spoken to King about this prospect and had obtained King's permission to introduce King as a possible contender, despite the leader's stated reluctance to become involved in electoral politics. On the same day, in fact, Coretta Scott King was addressing a peace rally in San Francisco, and she was introduced as the possible next First Lady.[27]

After the Spring Mobilization rally, the FBI stepped up its surreptitious journalism to exacerbate conflict within SCLC and among affiliated organizations such as the National Association for the Advancement of Colored People (NAACP). The FBI's news stories, published in cooperative newspapers throughout the country, claimed that King was willingly undermining the potential gains of the civil rights movement by adopting and parroting the political views of the Viet Cong and of the Communist Party. This alliance with the interests of communism, so the reasoning went, was disloyal and promised to tear asunder the ties within the civil rights movement. Like a self-fulfilling prophecy, the propaganda put King on the defensive and forced him to placate SCLC staff members and the NAACP. He explained that at no point had he planned to merge the civil rights movement with the antiwar protest.

Rather, he wished to oppose the war publicly while demonstrating the parallels between the pursuit of civil rights in the United States and the pursuit of human rights in Vietnam. In addition, King officially joined Clergy and Laymen Concerned about Vietnam. This group opposed the war against Vietnam in moderate terms by steering clear of fundamental issues such as the U.S. murder of Vietnamese civilians and the larger context of American imperialism. Its approach was designed to appeal to the sensibilities of America's mainstream—promoting peace as a common ideal and emphasizing the war's impact on U.S. domestic issues.[28]

None of this, however, mollified the rising tide of opposition among African Americans to anticolonialism and antiwar activism. In fact, Roy Wilkins, who had become the executive director of the NAACP in 1964, had been waiting for the opportunity to stage a public denunciation of King's growing radicalism. He had deeply resented King's willingness to accommodate Black Power. In 1966, when King eventually adopted the philosophy of Black Power (after having earlier condemned it) and defended its aims and principles, Wilkins branded it as merely a blackface version of extremist racism—a "reverse Ku Klux Klan"—designed to victimize Whites. More significantly, Wilkins, along with the NAACP's assistant executive director, John Morsell, seized on King's critique of U.S. militarism in Vietnam to condemn King for undermining what Wilkins claimed was the true aim of the civil rights movement: citizenship rights for African Americans. The two NAACP officials also chided King for brushing shoulders with communists by supporting the Spring Mobilization rally. Such condemnation coming from major figures in the civil rights movement was startlingly effective at stoking formerly sympathetic White liberals into a frenzy of angst and resentment against King, as well as against anticolonial activists in SNCC and the Congress of Racial Equality (CORE), such as Floyd McKissick and Kwame Ture.[29]

Meanwhile, the FBI's efforts to destroy King were intensifying. The bureau was incensed over King's unfathomable recalcitrance and audacity. By 1967, King was well aware of the damning evidence of his sexual affairs that the FBI was continuing to leak to journalists, public officials, and foreign states. The FBI continued issuing a steady stream of reports to the White House administration (by that time under Johnson's presidency) asserting that known communists were controlling SCLC and pointing particularly to Stanley Levison. The Kennedy administration had directly insisted to King that he stop associating with Levison lest he be regarded as influenced by communists. But now the bureau was taking an even more aggressive approach. By December 1967, the FBI had once again placed wiretaps on all ten phone lines at the SCLC's Atlanta headquarters. Beyond this, the FBI also pursued another strategy: recruiting a paid informant from the SCLC staff. Hoover had long held an interest in developing an informant from within SCLC but had never been successful (one informant developed in 1964 was by chance fired from SCLC about a month after agreeing to work with the FBI). The Atlanta field office had originally proposed recruiting Andrew Young, but FBI headquarters decided the risk was too great that Young might refuse to cooperate after being approached and then inform King. The FBI hit a rich vein when the Atlanta office suggested approaching Jim Harrison, a young accountant who had begun working with SCLC in 1964. Harrison worked in the finance office of SCLC's Atlanta headquarters. Atlanta agents approached him offering a weekly salary in exchange for information regarding the daily goings-on at SCLC. Harrison promised to consider it carefully and within a few days had signed up. He provided the bureau with extensive information of SCLC's finances, appointments, and strategic plans for mass protests and other sensitive organizational details. In exchange, the bureau compensated him with an annual salary of $10,000 ($74,000 in today's dollars).[30]

Harrison was not the only Black informant. The African American photographer Ernest Withers was also being paid by the FBI to inform on King and SCLC. Withers enjoyed intimate and frequent access to movement leaders. In a larger scope, Harrison and Withers were only two of several thousand African Americans who served as mostly unpaid FBI spies and informants. One of the FBI's signature initiatives was its "Ghetto Informants" program, which at its height employed more than seven thousand African Americans to deliver information to bureau agents by reporting everything from the banal to the spectacular: license plate numbers of acquaintances, new faces who incited Blacks to oppose White supremacism, and those organizing social activism or espousing ideas that might suggest leftist influence. The FBI initiated the Ghetto Informants program in 1967. Those participating were a strategic part of the FBI's arsenal of methods to destroy what was menacingly referred to as an anti-White Negro revolution. But insofar as available historical records indicate, Harrison remained the only paid informant formally within the ranks of SCLC. For this reason, he was the real prize for the FBI. Harrison would resign from SCLC in 1969, but he continued informing on the civil rights movement through the early 1970s.[31]

VIETNAM, MEMPHIS, AND COUNTERINTELLIGENCE

From 1967 until the very moment of King's assassination, according to accounts of bureau officials themselves, the FBI continued to work assiduously to generate chaos within SCLC, to destroy its alliances with other organizations such as the NAACP, to dissuade potential donors and activists nationwide from supporting its planned demonstrations, and to remake the public image of King from that of a devoted, globally admired movement leader to a dangerous and irresponsible demagogue who was out of touch with reality and who was guided by selfishness and corrupt motives. The bureau's unrestrained ambitions against King were particularly shaped by the counterintelligence philosophy that engaged domestic subjects in accordance with the rules for engaging foreign enemies. In his testimony to the U.S. Senate's "Church Committee," tasked with investigating U.S. intelligence agencies, William Sullivan explained: "No holds were barred. We have used [similar] techniques against Soviet agents. [The same methods were] brought home against any organization against which we were targeted. We did not differentiate. This is a rough, tough business."[32]

Among the most important and consequential efforts to portray King as a misguided extremist was the bureau's plan to have him discredited by another African American of national prominence. It found a cooperative figure in Carl Rowan, who had directed the USIA from 1964 to 1965. The USIA was a major element of the U.S. strategy of psychological warfare and devoted resources to propagandizing U.S. militarism and occupation in foreign countries through print and broadcast media. Rowan's appointment in Lyndon B. Johnson's cabinet was part and parcel of a larger strategy whereby White U.S. officials showcased African Americans in prominent positions—as tokens—to demonstrate that the United States was indeed a place where talented, hardworking Blacks could be successful. In his role with USIA, Rowan invested deeply in the expansion of U.S. empire amid the Cold War with the Soviet Union.[33]

Rowan published a six-page essay, entitled "Martin Luther King's Tragic Decision," in the popular magazine *Reader's Digest*. It was a condescending diatribe against King's assessment of U.S. militarism in Vietnam. Rowan began by quoting King's criticism of the war and particularly his assessment that the United States was the "greatest purveyor of violence in the world today." He also listed a roster of other African Americans who had publicly condemned King for opposing U.S. military atrocities in Vietnam—including Roy Wilkins of the

NAACP and Ralph Bunche of the United Nations. Rowan then sketched King's upbringing in Atlanta and narrated his decision to join the struggle against segregation. Rowan claimed that King had begun his career of public activism as humble and sincere, qualities that had earned him the respect of good-willed Whites. However, Rowan explained, King began to boast that his civil disobedience was a forceful tactic exploiting "crisis" to extort concessions from unwilling Whites. Rowan argued in contradistinction that it was the willing support of White liberals and the efficacy of the politics of liberalism generally—not the force of Black civil disobedience—that was the font and hope of racial progress. And he maintained that African Americans had long doubted King's judgment and sincerity on this score. King's public critique of the Vietnam War, Rowan continued, solidly persuaded most African Americans that he was heading down the road to perdition. He suggested two possible explanations for King's public pronouncements. Either King was egotistical, or he was being influenced by communists. Rowan argued that King's antiwar activism was directly destroying the civil rights movement. Rather strikingly, Rowan claimed that White politicians would be vengeful toward King for dissenting against the war and would vindicate themselves by keeping Africans Americans trapped in poverty by refusing to support antipoverty legislation.[34]

Rowan, of course, offered not a single intellectual response to the facts that King presented in his case against U.S. militarism in Vietnam: the United States was killing hundreds of thousands of Vietnamese civilians in addition to the Viet Cong military—all merely to aid the French in perpetuating their colonial rule over the Vietnamese and depriving the mostly peasant population of control over their own lands. Not only did U.S. militarism in Vietnam completely lack humanitarian aims, but it also depended on unconscionable acts of war: carpet bombing and incinerating entire communities of men, women, and children with napalm; permanently contaminating the region's soil and water with radioactive ordnance; and equating the Vietnamese struggle against the racist colonialism of France and the United States with ontological evil. The essay was pure ad hominem invective, and it charged King with fomenting disloyalty, thus associating King with state treason. It is unclear to what extent Rowan's essay was coauthored by bureau officials, but in any case Rowan echoed the same ideological charges against King that the bureau had been circulating for years through its cooperative journalistic allies. By 1967, King and SCLC had become virtually synonymous with "communist influence" or "communist sympathizing."[35]

On August 25, 1967, the bureau headquarters issued a notice to every FBI field office in the country announcing a new initiative under the memorandum heading "COUNTERINTELLIGENCE PROGRAM / BLACK NATIONALIST—HATE GROUPS / INTERNAL SECURITY." As a practical matter, there was nothing new about the bureau's use of "counterintelligence operations." If intelligence can be generalized as the collection of information about targeted subjects, counterintelligence was distinguished by its efforts to disrupt and destroy targets of repression. The FBI had already been using counterintelligence tactics for decades, most notably against U.S. citizens being repressed as suspected communists. More significant, the bureau's own history with King was marked by its efforts to cajole him into committing suicide when William Sullivan's group mailed the composite tape, based on hotel recordings, to King's personal home in 1964, three years earlier. It would be counterfactual to portray COINTELPRO as essentially novel; it was not. The formalization of COINTELPRO against Blacks lay not in its newness, strictly speaking, but in its authorization of a new architecture of national security protocols and policing. By gilding COINTELPRO with formal, explicit authorization, the bureau was instantiating the paradigm of warfare—the overt and covert tactics and strategies typically reserved for military conflict with sovereign entities—as a central element of its engagement with those domestic citizens and organizations deemed enemies of the security state.

As COINTELPRO was expanded to incorporate a wide swath of Black liberation movements, Hoover issued a call for new ideas to be implemented against Black activists. Nothing was to be considered too extreme or inappropriate before at least getting a hearing before the director. Creativity was a must. It was open season on the Black freedom struggle. The predictable result was a frenzy of experimental methods that were often illegal and dangerous. For instance, one tactic was to introduce plants into local chapters of the Black Panther Party; they would then introduce false reports of intrigue from competing groups, seeking to convince legitimate members to retaliate against those groups. The worst of these were designed to incite Blacks to kill other Blacks, and these tactics met with celebrated success.[36]

One important dimension of the bureau's disruption was its duplicity, which functioned both externally and internally. Not surprisingly, the FBI continually projected to the national public the noblest image of itself as the guardian and devoted keeper of liberties and physical security. As the U.S. Senate Select Committee determined unequivocally in the mid-1970s, however, the bureau was actively undermining those very civil liberties that it officially claimed to protect. This is to be expected, in retrospect, given the very nature of counterintelligence. What is more surprising is the duplicity of the agent's activities and discourse within the bureau. For instance, when the bureau issued its official assessment of King in March 1968, just weeks before his assassination, it repeated a common refrain: the threat of violence by activists within the myriad organizations participating in SCLC's organized demonstrations was a high-priority security concern. Bureau officials specifically identified as a "serious danger" the prospect that Black nationalist groups might attempt to "seize the initiative and escalate the non-violent demonstrations into violence." While issuing these siren calls for vigilance in the face of possible violence, however, the bureau continued a long-standing practice of infiltrating Black liberationist organizations and, in close cooperation with municipal police departments, installing agents of provocation within these groups, specifically to unleash violence.[37]

The ascending scale of the bureau's threat assessment of King is also of special significance. When the FBI issued its updated analysis of King on March 12, 1968, it identified him as the "recognized leader of 22 million Negroes" and asserted that he and SCLC "were made to order" in advancing communist control of U.S. policy. Not only were King's assessments of U.S. militarism in Vietnam parroting communist ideology, but King's presence within the peace movement was also an adjunct to the SCLC's voter-registration drives to encourage Black voters to support a communist takeover of the United States. Furthermore, just as U.S. intelligence agencies branded any resistance to colonialism in Africa, Asia, or Latin America as a communist plot, so also did the FBI identify anti-imperialist critiques of U.S. militarism as a communist conspiracy. By naming SCLC as a "tax-dodge," furthermore, the bureau indicated the organization was both a front (for communism) and a fraud. This analysis of King, produced in the midst of his involvement with Memphis and the Poor People's Campaign, advanced the notion that King and the Poor People's Campaign needed to be stopped to preserve the nation's security.[38]

Roughly two weeks after issuing its March 1968 assessment of King, the bureau scored an important victory when the Memphis rally King was leading on March 28, 1968, erupted into a riot, as a consequence of which an African American youth was shot to death by Memphis police, scores of others were injured, and 238 protesters were arrested. The Invaders, a group of roughly one hundred African American activists—mostly younger and more attuned to the criticism of SCLC's nonviolent method of civil disobedience—instigated the violence. But FBI informants and multiple undercover Memphis police agents, one of whom was typically armed with a 7.62 Russian automatic rifle, were among the group's "most active leaders." Under their influence, the Invaders went far beyond publicly challenging the efficacy of nonviolence as a strategy for social change, which was how organizations such as SNCC and the Black Panther Party engaged with SCLC. The Invaders, rather, proved effective in destroying what SCLC had intended to be a nonviolent movement in the city to support striking sanitation workers and to bring national attention to bear on the plight of the massive number of working and unemployed Blacks living in poverty. On the very day of King's assassination, roughly one week after the Memphis riot, the Invaders demanded $750,000 from SCLC and vowed to create more riots if SCLC did not pay up.[39]

Such behavior was bizarre and highly destructive. Reflecting on the situation years later, SCLC organizers such as the Atlanta-based minister Hosea Williams identified the shift that occurred within the Invaders after they were infiltrated by government counterintelligence operatives: "They, like other blacks in the country, were naturally frustrated by the slow pace of change. . . . We usually put them to work as parade marshals or security guards. They would never have hurt Dr. King. But those who infiltrated our groups, and we could never identify them, tried to exploit the youngsters' frustrations and neglect and turn them against us."[40] Such an alliance between the FBI and municipal police was a central element of COINTELPRO's architecture, and the operation made it virtually impossible for SCLC to implement a program of civil disobedience in Memphis. More important, the operation seemed to have destroyed King's own confidence in SCLC's ability to orchestrate a nonviolent march against poverty in the nation's capital, the central aim of the Poor People's Campaign.

At no point in King's career of public activism was he more despondent and disillusioned than in the wake of the Memphis riot. The police killing of a Black youth seemed an insurmountable indictment against SCLC's ability to execute a nonviolent movement to challenge the deep structures of racism and classism. For this reason, King was poised to cancel any further demonstrations in Memphis. And his plan for leading thousands of poor people to occupy the nation's capital—the Washington Spring Project—faced increasingly dim prospects as organizers confronted what seemed an unending series of crises and attacks.

CONCLUSION

The very nature of the FBI's counterintelligence operations against King and SCLC demands a critical accounting. A number of scholars have, in fact, attempted to explain the extreme nature of the bureau's repression of King, the scale of which is especially striking given his iconic status as a champion of nonviolence. The personal dimension of Hoover's use of the bureau to repress King has been the most central element in accounts of this repression. In the words of one scholar, what emerged as a "political and personal struggle" between King and Hoover was rooted in their "philosophical enmity," as evidenced by their indirect exchanges in 1964, when King faulted the bureau for failing to prosecute Whites who committed deadly terror attacks against African Americans and, in return, Hoover emotionally defended the FBI.[41]

There is good reason for this attention to the idiosyncratic dimensions of Hoover's personality. His style of administration was distinctly brutish and unchecked by outside authorities. He directed the bureau for nearly a half century and amassed unparalleled control over the agency. Beyond this, Hoover collected personal information on major government officials (including U.S. presidents), which he repeatedly used to threaten and blackmail those who attempted to oppose him. Hoover's sexuality, furthermore, has been repeatedly examined in a way that diverts critical attention away from his politics: he never married, was not known to cultivate any romantic relations with women, and seems to have developed a lasting romantic relationship with another bureau official, Assistant Director Clyde Tolson. At the same time, Hoover's personal sense of sexual morality has been described as puritanical and is cited as an important factor in his loathing toward King.[42] Hoover's racism, however, is most frequently attended to by scholarly assessments of his personal character. He was southern-born and did not interact with Blacks during his childhood. As FBI director, he required all prospects to be White as a necessary condition for joining the bureau, and he resented and opposed Robert Kennedy's instructions to integrate the bureau. In response to the U.S. attorney general's demands that Hoover hire some token African Americans to desegregate the FBI, Hoover named a few of his African American chauffeurs and his personal butler as "special agents" of the bureau. Their jobs consisted solely of transporting the director and waiting on Hoover and his White guests, but this ploy led many outsiders to perceive the FBI as a progressive, integrated agency.[43]

There can be no question that Hoover's personality significantly influenced the bureau's engagement with King. But this is no less true for other targets of FBI repression—not only King and SCLC but also Huey Newton and the Black Panther Party, Alphaeus Hunton and the Council on African Affairs (CAA), and Assata Shakur. The question, in other words, is not whether Hoover's personality significantly shaped the bureau's engagement with targets for repression; this was patently the case for all targets of FBI repression. Scholars must ask, rather, how to account for the repressive measures as a political formation of events, tactics, and rationalities without reductively attributing the bureau's repression of King to Hoover's personality traits. In other words, just as it would be methodologically flawed to attribute the FBI's repression of W. E. B. Du Bois and his peace movement or of Alphaeus Hunton and the CAA to Hoover's personality, so also would it be erroneous to make Hoover's idiosyncrasies the chief factor in King's repression. Ultimately, the FBI targeted these subjects as a matter of *political,* not personal, intrigue.

Alternatively, one might consider that not only the bureau but also municipal law enforcement entities and state attorneys general throughout the United States targeted King and SCLC with the aim of destroying the organization and rendering it impotent. They did the same to other activist organizations, such as SNCC, the NAACP, and CORE. This occurred both in alliance with the bureau and also through local, autonomous operatives independent of the FBI. If one attributes the FBI repression of King principally to Hoover's personality, how does one account for the repressive regimes of other law enforcement agencies throughout the nation?

Finally, the long-standing pattern of treating anti-Black racism as a uniquely or particularly southern phenomenon must be rejected for what it is—a fundamentally ahistorical account of racism that elides not only the national but also the global formation of racial power and governance. Anti-Black racism (including formal apartheid or segregation laws) has never been simply a regional phenomenon. It was the U.S. Supreme Court, after all, that ruled in *Plessy v. Ferguson* (1896) to affirm anti-Black segregation laws as a constitutional deployment of White racial power. This was not a southern court. It was the highest court of the United States of America. Not only were southern schools and buses segregated, but so were entities like the U.S. Congress, the U.S. Supreme Court, and the U.S. military complex. Unless one cynically regards the Pentagon as a southern institution, the historical account of the FBI's repression of King must render anti-Black racism visible as a national phenomenon, not a southern one.

This means that the FBI's repression of King must be recognized for what it was—one element within a larger superstructure of state-sponsored racism. It is for this reason that scholars of race have developed an account of the racial state in order to explain the political imperatives of racism. Because the United States has been structured since its beginnings as a polity whose privileged body politic has been White, non-Whites have continually been perceived as racial and political outsiders. As a result, their historical efforts to challenge that status quo have repeatedly been engaged by federal authorities as a threat to society (imagined by the FBI as quintessentially White) and national security.[44]

The central motive for the FBI's repression of King is clearly and repeatedly stated throughout the FBI's internal communications: the bureau wanted to prevent African Americans from achieving a united political movement. Whether enacted by unarmed, nonviolent activists or proponents of armed self-defense, Black politics threatened the normative racial structure of the United States. Because the bureau viewed King and the SCLC as the most influential individual and institutional actors at the helm of the civil rights movement, their neutralization became an overriding imperative, particularly after the formalization of COINTELPRO's focus on Black political activism.

11

A Vast Infiltration

Mormonism and the FBI

MATTHEW BOWMAN

On September 29, 1984, Richard Bretzing, the director of the FBI field office in Los Angeles, summoned an agent named Richard Miller to his office. Miller had just failed a polygraph test. This seemed damning evidence that he was guilty of a crime Bretzing had suspected him of for weeks: selling documents to the Soviet Union. Bretzing asked Miller if his suspicions were true, and when the agent demurred, Bretzing made what he called an "appeal to his moral and religious teachings." Bretzing urged Miller to consider the "spiritual ramifications" of the crime and exhorted him to "repent."

This was not standard FBI practice, as Bretzing later acknowledged at Miller's trial, but it drew on the fact that he and Miller shared a particular religious background. Earlier that year, Miller had been excommunicated from the Church of Jesus Christ of Latter-day Saints for adultery—with, it turned out, the Soviet agent to whom he had passed information. He appeared to be penitent and racked with guilt, and Bretzing, as a fellow Mormon—in fact, as a bishop who served as the lay head of a local congregation—was in a unique position of spiritual authority to remind Miller "of his sense of right and wrong" and to urge a confession.[1] Time was of the essence because Miller was involved in a number of critical operations, and Bretzing was desperate to determine what he might have stolen. The appeal worked; Miller broke down in tears and confessed, was arrested October 2, and went to prison.

Bretzing, who had just finished coordinating security for the 1984 Los Angeles Olympics and, two years later, would retire to take a position as head of security for his church, was in many respects the perfectly cast FBI agent. Six foot, four and 220 pounds with silver hair, he certainly looked every bit the part of the government G-man, and he seemed to have the right character as well; his supporters in the agency called him courageous and dignified, with a firm moral compass derived from his faith. On the face of it Bretzing embodied the ideal agent that Hoover and his FBI had worked so hard to cultivate: diligent, noble, and possessed of a faith that imbued him with a strong sense of what a Bretzing supporter called "right and wrong."[2]

And yet the testimony of another agent in the FBI field office gave a very different impression of Bretzing's directorship and of the role of Mormonism in shaping his performance. Bernardo "Matt" Perez served as Bretzing's assistant from 1982 to 1984, until he was replaced by Bryce Christensen, a Mormon like Bretzing. During Miller's trial, Perez testified that Bretzing ignored his recommendation years before that Miller be disciplined or fired, even though Miller, whom Perez called a "bumbler," routinely reported to work grossly overweight. "I believe that happened because they are both Mormons," Perez said. "I saw it happen with other Mormons and only Mormons."[3] Instead of facing discipline, Miller was assigned to report to Christensen, for reasons that also smacked of religious favoritism. "They also indicated they were transferring him to my squad because of our common religious background, thinking I could possibly be a role model," said Christensen at the trial.[4] Perez, a Latino Catholic, sued the FBI for religious discrimination, alleging that in the Los Angeles office, being a Mormon resulted in special treatment, either promotion like Christensen's or lax treatment like Miller's.

The story of Miller and Bretzing impressed itself on the American consciousness at the height of the Reagan-era Cold War and generated intensely contradictory feelings among those Americans who followed the story. In a strange coincidence, another Mormon, the ex–army officer Richard Craig Smith, had been arrested for espionage only that spring, charged with passing the names of American spies to a Soviet agent. Smith claimed that he had been working at the behest of CIA agents who intended to use him as a mole, and he declined to call an attorney in favor of contacting a Mormon bishop.[5] He was eventually acquitted, but in May 1987 the conservative journal *Human Events* drew out the implications for Mormonism in general: over the twentieth century, through diligent effort, Mormons had become respected members of the American establishment—clean-cut, patriotic, indeed symbols of Reagan's America—and yet now Mormons were being exposed for corruption.[6] What had gone wrong?

I argue that what was happening had less to do with Mormons themselves than with the transformation of American culture more generally. When the Mormons were pursuing integration into American society in the mid-twentieth century, an image like Bretzing's, conservative in appearance and firmly patriotic, was useful. Serving the government provided a key way to publicly perform such virtues—this was particularly true in the national security agencies, which consciously sought to project such an image and sought out Mormons for that reason. But by the end of the twentieth century, American culture had shifted. After the cultural crises of the 1960s and 1970s, Americans grew more cynical about their government, a cynicism that extended to the Mormons and their evident patriotism. The result was a revival of a nineteenth-century stereotype of Mormonism as clannish, authoritarian, and untrustworthy.

During the nineteenth century, Mormons regarded the U.S. government with ambivalence, identifying with some of its principles but suspecting the government of corruption. Parley Pratt, for instance, one of Mormonism's most prolific early apologists, wrote that "the American system was indeed glorious in its beginning . . . but it had its weaknesses and imperfections. These were taken advantage of . . . by a loose and corrupt administration, that gradually undermined that beautiful structure." Mormons ascribed their own persecution at the U.S. government's hands to corrupt collusion. They claimed fidelity to the Constitution, which Mormon scripture deems inspired, but just as often they condemned the American government for failing to live up to founding values that happened to be congruent with their own: piety, a commitment to liberty (particularly religious liberty), and economic and political self-sufficiency.[7]

After church leaders officially terminated polygamy in 1890, Mormons began to shift their understanding of what it meant to be a Mormon in order to emphasize those virtues particularly. Through much of the nineteenth century, being Mormon meant immersion in a society constructed by the church: polygamy, economic communalism, congregations made up entirely of one's neighbors. But integration into the United States stripped this form of participatory identity away, and Mormons replaced it with a form of ethicized piety that redefined religious life primarily as a form of self-discipline. In the 1890s, the church began to emphasize the importance of regular payment of tithes. In the 1920s, abstinence from alcohol, tobacco, tea, and coffee, previously encouraged, became a requirement to participate in Mormon temple worship. In 1965, the church put out a pamphlet called "For the Strength of Youth," which advised young people on appropriate dating, dress, and entertainment choices, most of which soon became mandatory at Brigham Young University (BYU).[8] Gradually, Mormons came to see strong self-discipline and conservative cultural values as essential to their faith.

The government career of a figure like Bretzing was, from this perspective, a sign of Mormon success, reflecting the alignment of Mormon self-discipline with participation in American society. In 1981, the Associated Press reported that "the CIA does some of its most successful recruiting in predominantly LDS [Latter-day Saint] Utah."[9] There were reasons both practical and ideological for this practice. On the one hand, as many rumors had it and as the AP confirmed, Mormons' command of foreign languages, usually learned while on the missionary service that Mormon young men came to be expected to provide during the 1950s, made them appealing to national security agencies. On the other, as Gary Williams, a professor of political science at BYU, noted, "our Mormon culture has always been more supportive of the government than American culture as a whole."[10] Williams, and many other Mormons, took allegiance to the national security state to be not merely a sign of Mormon patriotism but also a religious act, one aspect of the Mormon pious ethical ideal that developed in the twentieth century. As the church's official magazine, the *Ensign,* taught in 1976, "We learn to love our country as we learn to love righteousness. A child who has a testimony of Jesus Christ already has a good basis for becoming a patriot," because, as the article explained, patriotism and religious belief were fused in the Mormon conception of the church's relationship to America: "Our feeling for country and Constitution must be based upon an understanding of the special role which the United States was to play as the place in which the gospel could be restored."[11]

From this perspective, service in the government was an opportunity to perform those moral values that had tied Mormons to the nation; indeed, it came to be seen as an exercise of a religious duty particularly incumbent on Mormons. Not only was the federal government premised on virtues congenial to Mormons, but Mormons were thought to have a special appreciation for the value of the Constitution. Rex Lee, the president of BYU who left the university to serve in the Gerald Ford administration, explained, "No group of American citizens has a greater stake in good government and preservation of basic constitutional guarantees than American members of The Church of Jesus Christ of Latter-day Saints."[12] Lee expressed a similar sentiment in a tribute to Ezra Taft Benson, an apostle who served in Dwight Eisenhower's cabinet: "In his service to the nation he has felt he was still laboring for the Lord, for he regards the United States as a nation apart, chosen above all others, chosen for a great destiny." Benson himself fused religion into his description of government service, saying, "Note the qualities that the Lord demands of those who are to represent us. They must be good, wise, and honest."[13]

National security agencies such as the CIA and the FBI were particularly apt venues for the performance of Mormon patriotism because the way these agencies presented themselves to the public seemed so congruent with Mormonism's ethical piety. The image that the FBI sought to project in this period is reflected in a television show broadcast from 1965 to 1974 on ABC. Called *The FBI,* the series was produced with the cooperation of the agency itself. The FBI had veto power over the cast members and provided the show with genuine equipment. That the series was intended as something more than mere fiction is suggested by the way each episode ended: the show's star Efrem Zimbalist Jr. would break character and urge American citizens to aid FBI agents in their pursuit of lawbreakers. The dramas themselves, though broadcast in the age of color television, presented a very black-and-white version of reality: the show ignored hot-button issues like the civil rights movement and the Mafia in favor of stories of honest agents fighting communism and hunting down murderers. The agents depicted in the show, pursuing fictionalized versions of genuine FBI cases, were idealized—upright, rigorously moral, and committed to the nation. Zimbalist himself told the reporter L. Wayne Hicks what was expected of him and the other actors in order to embody that ideal: "From my point of view as an actor, it was interesting because we were denied virtually all of the liberty that most actors are granted. We couldn't have anything to do with women. We couldn't smoke. We couldn't drink. We couldn't put our feet up on the desk. We couldn't take our coat off. We were little good boys. And the fascinating challenge to me was to work within those structures." Hoover, who served as a consultant on the show, thought it a success because of its effort to depict a morally upright vision of the agency to the American public. "Mr. Zimbalist has captured the esprit de corps of the FBI and what it is like to be an FBI agent," the FBI director was quoted in *TV Guide.* ". . . [T]he image he projects is important because it is closely intertwined with the confidence and trust American people have in the FBI."[14]

Depicted in this way, the FBI appeared to be highly congruent with Mormon values, and, in fact, Mormon praise for the virtues of FBI agents reflects a similar adulation. In 1974, the *Ensign,* a Mormon magazine that had begun publication just a few years before, celebrated the life of Samuel Cowley, a Mormon FBI agent who hunted down John Dillinger and was killed in the line of duty. Cowley, the article claimed, embodied the best traits of Mormonism and in fact played a role in helping to secure the agency's moral probity. "The agency at that time did not have the well-known reputation it has today," the magazine instructed readers. "It began with highly idealistic men such as Sam. . . . It is from the efforts of men such as these that the FBI's present-day reputation . . . was derived." The article praised Cowley for being "utterly dependable" and living an "utterly moral life." It suggested that his name should have been Peter because he was "a man who did his best and left the final decision to a Higher Power."[15] The tradition begun with Cowley of equating FBI service and Mormon piety continues into the present. In 2009, Michael McPheters, like Bretzing, an FBI agent and Mormon bishop, published a memoir titled *Agent Bishop,* which draws a connection between government service and religious commitment similar to that drawn in the article about Cowley. "I fought crime and Satan with a pistol in one hand and the scriptures in the other," writes McPheters. Equally telling is his introduction, in which he thanks "my fellow FBI agents for their fidelity, bravery and integrity, and those who exhibited the same characteristics in serving with me in four bishoprics."[16]

In other words, there was a basic congruence between the image that Mormons were presenting to the world through men like Samuel Cowley and the image that agencies like the FBI wanted to project: a clean-cut appearance, moral self-discipline, trustworthiness, unwavering commitment, authoritativeness. As the Cold War and all the social unrest that came with it continued, Mormons (along with other religious conservatives) came to speak of such values with words like "basic" or "old-fashioned"—language that reflects a posture of defensiveness about these values but also suggests their increasing importance for Mormon identity construction. And given that Hoover and other leaders of the national security agencies had worked hard to identify their agencies with these values, Mormon identification with these agencies only intensified as Mormons began moving to the political and social right.[17]

Examples of this growing patriotism and conservatism in the Mormon church are to be found in the *Ensign,* which ran a number of sto-

FIGURE 11.1. Samuel Cowley with his sister, Laura, 1924. Courtesy Special Collections, Merrill-Cazier Library, Utah State University.

ries in the 1970s and 1980s reflecting the growing association between Mormon faith and service in U.S. national security agencies. In one such story, for example, Joseph Clancy, a young Mormon on active duty in Germany in the 1980s, is reported as saying, "I've concentrated on being a missionary wherever I go, and I like being in the military. I guess I'm old-fashioned because I feel that patriotism and honor and duty are important."[18] Lucile Johnson, the wife of a Mormon man in military intelligence, claimed that "men and women and families in uniform are keenly aware of the Church, and they are delighted that we are true to their basic principles of human decency and goodness."[19]

By the time these stories were published in the 1970s, 1980s, and 1990s, however, the very thing the Mormons had come to prize about the culture of the national security state—its congruity with their own ethical piety—were becoming marks of suspicion to other Americans. Suspicion of the federal government is already apparent in a speech delivered on Temple Square in Salt Lake City in 1966 by none other than Ezra Taft Benson under the title "Stand Up for Freedom." While denouncing communism and urging patriotism upon his fellow Mormons, Benson argued that the true assassins of John F. Kennedy, murdered only three years before, in 1963, had been covered up. "When the events surrounding President Kennedy's assassination were remembered last December, practically no mention was made of Oswald's communist affiliations nor the present communist threat to our society," he lamented, but it was communism that "destroyed our President and that communism continually seeks to subvert and destroy our complete way of life."[20] More interesting than Benson's hostility to communism, however, was his suggestion that liberal American political leaders had abetted in the cover-up. "Within an hour after the assassination and before Oswald was captured, Moscow was assuring the world that this crime was a product of the 'rightist' movement on the United States," he said, and he marveled at "the amazing rapidity with which American liberals took up the Moscow line."[21] For Benson, the assassination was the work of communist sympathizers abetted by a coterie of liberal politicians.

The suspicion of the government reflected in Benson's speech would grow over the course of the 1970s and 1980s, with the federal government a particular target, and this trend had a major impact on the public image of the FBI. Losing the heroic luster that it had enjoyed in the 1950s and 1960s, the FBI by the last three decades of the century was seen by many Americans as an untrustworthy institution dedicated not to the public good but to the accumulation of corrupt power, and the Watergate scandal and the fallout from the Vietnam War only exacerbated the distrust.[22] Reflecting the national sentiment, in June 1974 the *Ensign* ran an article pleading with church members not to abandon their trust in the American government even if they felt betrayed by Richard Nixon. "It is the system of government, not the individuals who hold office at any given time, that we are told by the Lord to support and sustain. . . . The United States has one of the most honest, ethical governments on earth."[23] It is not a coincidence that *The FBI* went off the air in 1974 or that by the 1990s the popular image of the FBI was best captured by a very different kind of television drama, *The*

X-Files. What added plausibility to the show's conceit that the federal government was covering up evidence of an alien infiltration was the fact that by the time the show aired, many Americans had come to view the federal government as a shadowy threat and were finding real-life accusations of conspiracy and cover-up within the government to be very credible.

As it happens, many Americans had long been prone to a similar suspicion of Mormons. In the nineteenth century, Mormons had been denounced for their priesthood, their practice of bloc voting (which seemed to violate a republican expectation of individual responsibility in politics and religious faith), and their economic communalism (which seemed at odds with the American ideal of economic individualism).[24] Many Americans were also suspicious of Mormon allegiance to leaders such as Joseph Smith, seeing such devotion as a sign of gullibility and as evidence that Mormons were essentially theocratic. Josiah Strong, a prominent evangelical critic of Mormonism, gave voice to the suspicions of the era: "The Mormon, in his mental make-up, is a distinct type. . . . [T]hey are credulous and superstitious, and are easily led in the direction of their inclinations; they love reasoning but hate reason; they are capable of blind devotion." Mormons as Strong depicted them were incapable of self-government, but they were easily welded into a dangerous undemocratic force: "What is the real strength of Mormonism?" he asked. "It is ecclesiastical despotism."[25]

A century later, in an age when many Americans were highly distrustful of the federal government, the Mormons' close association with the FBI helped revive such conspiracy thinking: Mormons were again understood as a group prone to secrecy, conspiracy, and groupism. It was precisely in this period, in the 1970s and 1980s, that a spate of exposés of Mormonism appeared in periodicals and bookstores across the country, frequently emphasizing what one called "the Mormon corporate empire." In these exposés, the church is presented as a bland bureaucracy, all the more terrifying for the white-shirt-and-tie innocuousness of its members—a stereotype that may be familiar to some readers through the HBO show *Big Love,* which presented its protagonists, the Henricksons, as trapped between a rural polygamous sect on one hand and the institutional LDS church on the other. Tellingly for our purposes, it is not clear who is the more terrifying antagonist in the series—the ragged backwoods prophet or the clean-shaven bureaucrats of Salt Lake City.[26]

In many of these exposés, great weight is placed on the church's financial holdings and complicated, corporation-like hierarchy. Thus, for example, the phrase *LDS Inc.* became popular in the 1980s among evangelical anti-Mormons, some of whom became convinced, as the evangelical Ed Decker put it, that the church has a "Mormon Plan for America, the end times theocracy they will control."[27] Somewhere behind this caricature is a Protestant suspicion of any religious organization with a hierarchy, but that suspicion is mixed with more recent hostility toward anonymous, bureaucratized corporatism. Some of the evangelical critique of Mormonism even has a counterpart in secular descriptions. As the journalist Frances Lang wrote, "Absolute fealty is still the cornerstone of the religion, except that now loyalty to the faith of the Latter Day Saints means unquestioning service not of [Joseph Smith], but of an institution."[28]

Recent examples of the kind of anti-Mormon rhetoric that has taken root in the past few decades are the depictions of Mormonism written by Anson Shupe, a sociologist who conducted research on the "Moonies," televangelists, and other suspect religious groups. The titles of his two works on Mormonism—*The Mormon Corporate Empire* and *The Darker Side of Virtue*—make their perspective clear enough: Mormonism for Shupe "is the story of virtue gone astray, of how admirable traits can turn inward and become obsessions."[29] Shupe's narratives describe how Mormon interest in family history curdled into official suppression of embarrassing facts in the life of Joseph Smith, and how nineteenth-century Mormon economic communalism stultified into twentieth-century officiousness and bureaucratic tyranny. Like Frances Lang, Shupe exemplifies a particular trope in late-twentieth-century critiques of Mormonism: that its all-American, disciplined, and clean image is in fact a façade, and, more than being a façade, such purity is itself a sign of corruption. As was often said about recent presidential candidate Mitt Romney, Mormons are *too* nice. The appearance of virtuousness is a reason to be distrustful of them, as when the syndicated columnist Kathleen Parker observed: "Romney can't earn people's confidence because he's too squeaky clean. Few can identify with a man who never touches coffee or alcohol, whose hair is as precise as the crease in his pants."[30]

In this cultural context the Mormon association with the FBI took on new significance, no longer conveying the close association between Mormon piety and patriotism but now signifying Mormon collusion and corruption. The shift is reflected in the language of Matt Perez, the FBI agent who believed that Richard Bretzing was playing favorites in the FBI. In his lawsuit Perez protested against "the Mormon mafia," a particularly barbed accusation to make against FBI agents given the

Mafia's association with conspiratorial criminality. Earlier anti-Mormon exposés went further in characterizing the relationship between Mormons and the FBI as sinister. In an article published in 1971, "The Mormon Empire," the aforementioned Frances Lang argued that it is not virtue but vice that ties Mormons to the FBI. "It may seem strange" that a religion so persecuted would end up "providing both the CIA and FBI with some of their best men," Lang noted, but their affinity is not so hard to understand: Mormons adhere to "a religion which is stringently hierarchical, profit oriented, racist and never likely to embarrass the foreign interests of the US, or indeed any other capitalist state." All this, Lang contended, made Mormons the perfect servants for a corrupt institution like the Federal Bureau of Investigation.

The connection that has developed between the traditional suspicion of Mormonism and that of post-Watergate American government is nowhere more interestingly developed than in the crime novels of James Ellroy. Ellroy is one of America's most acclaimed writers of crime fiction and modern noir. His work often explores the corruption that lies at the heart of the seemingly pristine, exploding myths about American exceptionalism. His earlier books, for instance, featured a thinly veiled Disney empire that protects murderers and child molesters.[31] In his later work, particularly the *Underworld USA* trilogy (published between 1995 and 2009), Mormon leaders have erected a political machine that controls the state of Nevada. Literalizing the image of the Mormons as a Mafia, Ellroy's Mormons use the façade of religion to quietly engage in organized crime—money laundering, extortion, and occasionally more violent wrongdoing. Yet the appearance of purity and patriotism allows them to penetrate the upper echelons of American government, bringing them into relationship with secretive agencies like the CIA and the FBI that enlist them to pursue their nefarious plots. As one Mormon character muses about his father, "His father was a big Mormon fat cat. Wayne Senior was jungled up all over the nut right. He did Klan ops for Mr. Hoover. . . . He knew about the JFK hit. It was multi-faction, Cuban exiles, CIA, mob."[32] In Ellroy's vision, the Mormons and their conspiratorial association with the CIA and the FBI stand in for what is wrong with the United States: under the guise of pristine virtuousness, they embody the moral decay, hypocrisy, corruption, and violence festering in the underground of American life.

The histories of the FBI and Mormonism are entwined in various ways, each group drawn to the other by a sense of shared values as well as by pragmatic considerations, and that commonality includes a related shift in how they have been perceived by the American public. Since the 1970s, both Mormonism and the FBI have followed a similar arc, at least in the imagination of many Americans, both moving from positions of moral authority to become objects of suspicion and conspiracy thinking. This change does not necessarily reflect how each group sees itself, or sees the other, for that matter. Mormons—like many other conservative Christians in America—continue to tell heroic narratives about the U.S. military and the FBI, just as they did back in the days when *The FBI* was on the air, even as they also now assail the U.S. government more generally as a bastion of corruption. What has changed is the larger context, how the broader American public perceives the two groups: the distrust of the federal government that crystalized after Watergate has converged with newly resurgent anti-Mormon bias. What has long connected the two is the FBI, an institution that allowed Mormons to fuse their particular form of piety with patriotism and that continues to link Mormons with the federal government in an American imagination prone to be highly distrustful of both.

12

The FBI's "Cult War" against the Branch Davidians

CATHERINE WESSINGER

Every incident involving police brutality starts with the suspect not cooperating.

—New Orleans citizen

On February 28, 1993, a shootout resulted from a botched no-knock "dynamic entry" of the Branch Davidians' residence at Mount Carmel, within the rural outskirts of Waco, Texas, by agents with the Bureau of Alcohol, Tobacco, and Firearms (ATF). The violence on this day resulted in the deaths of four ATF agents and six Branch Davidians. FBI agents arrived on March 1 to take charge of what became a fifty-one-day siege. Because federal agents had been killed on February 28, the FBI designated the case with the acronym WACMUR for "Waco Murder."

FBI agents found that David Koresh (1959–1993) and his followers placed greater emphasis on God's authority as revealed by Koresh than on the authority of the FBI. On March 2, Koresh promised FBI negotiators he would come out after an audiotape, on which he explained his theological understanding of the ATF assault and the resulting FBI siege, was played on television and radio. After the tape was played on KRLD Radio in Dallas and the Christian Broadcasting Network, the Branch Davidians picked up a stretcher delivered by the agents to carry out David Koresh, who had suffered a gunshot wound to his side and also his wrist on February 28. When Branch Davidian men attempted to move Koresh onto the stretcher to carry him downstairs and outside the building, they reported that Koresh experienced excruciating pain. The Branch Davidians paused to pray. That is when Koresh received a divine message that they should wait for another word from God for the right time for them to come out and be taken into custody.[1]

Frustrated FBI officials ordered the residence surrounded by tanks to "teach him a lesson."[2] During the siege, FBI agents driving tanks took increasingly aggressive actions against the Branch Davidians and their home. On April 19, 1993, FBI agents implemented a tank and CS gas assault that resulted in the largest number of deaths in a law enforcement action in U.S. history. Seventy-six Branch Davidians of all ages died in a fire that followed the gassing and demolition of their building.

The conflict between federal agents and the Branch Davidians in 1993 occurred after several decades of what new religions scholars have termed the "cult wars." Since the 1970s, secular anticultists had formed organizations to combat religious groups they termed "cults" and had constructed a narrative that promoted what sociologist James T. Richardson terms the "myth of the omnipotent leader" and the corresponding "myth of the passive, brainwashed follower."[3] Anticult activists began promoting coercive "deprogramming" services to concerned family members who were often willing to pay the fees to have their loved ones kidnapped and deprogrammed. Scholars who were pioneers in the study of newly formed religious movements spoke publicly in their publications and in court cases to dispute the anticultists' justification of deprogramming activities, advocating for careful investigation of unconventional religious groups suspected of breaking the law and for the principle of freedom of religion. These scholars were accused of being "cult apologists" by anticultists. The term *cult wars* was coined as a shorthand for the highly contested environment involving members of new religious movements, anticultists and evangelical Christian countercultists,[4] and new religions scholars. Law enforcement was involved in the "cult wars" in various ways, and anticult views sometimes influenced law enforcement officials' approaches to unconventional communities.

The ATF and FBI agents involved in the Branch Davidian case, and the reporters and other media representatives covering the case, were strongly influenced by the "cult" stereotype promoted by anticultists.[5] The "cult" stereotype involves what sociologist John R. Hall calls *cult essentialism,* "whereby the dynamics of religious movements are treated as wholly internal, and unaffected by interaction with the wider social world. Such an analysis would free the cultural opponents and the media from any responsibility for incidents of religious-movement violence."[6] FBI agents articulated this perspective in their descriptions of the Branch Davidians in press briefings held during the siege and in statements and testimonies after the fire. During the siege, the media also promoted a view of the Branch Davidians as "cultists," which dehumanized them and rendered their children invisible.[7] These depictions of the Branch Davidians and cultural assumptions about members of "cults" helped shape public perceptions of the standoff and may well have been a factor leading the majority of Americans to view the FBI's tank and gas assault on April 19, 1993, as reasonable. A CNN/Gallup poll taken after the fire "found that 73 percent of Americans thought the decision to teargas (for seven hours) the men, women, and children (including infants and toddlers) at Mt. Carmel was 'responsible,' and 93 percent believed that Koresh was to blame for their deaths."[8]

The events at Mount Carmel in 1993 were not a metaphorical "cult war," but literal warfare against an unconventional religious group waged by militarized federal law enforcement agents—first by ATF agents on February 28, 1993, and then by FBI agents from March 1 throughout the siege until the April 19, 1993, assault and fire.[9] The concern of FBI officials in the command center in Washington, D.C., and of FBI officials in Waco to defeat an enemy they viewed as responsible for the deaths of federal law enforcement agents overrode the FBI negotiators' concern to get adult Branch Davidians and their children out of the building safely.

This chapter does not attempt to unravel the complex and incomplete evidence concerning precisely how the deadly fire started on April 19. Despite the publication in 2000 of special counsel John C. Danforth's final report, which claims to settle the matter by putting all the blame for the fire on the Branch Davidians, the question of what happened at Mount Carmel is far from clearly determined.[10]

The various analyses, strategies, and goals of different groups of FBI agents can be discerned in internal FBI documents found in the archival collection of Lee Hancock, a reporter for the *Dallas Morning News,* at Texas State University in San Marcos. These documents indicate that FBI agents had gathered relevant "intelligence" about the Branch Davidians and their beliefs, and therefore that FBI officials were well informed about the Branch Davidians' apocalyptic theology of martyrdom when they made decisions to implement "stress escalation" against the Branch Davidians.[11] What amounted to psychological warfare, along with increasing physically destructive actions carried out by agents on the FBI's Hostage Rescue Team (HRT), undermined FBI negotiators' strategies, which were succeeding in persuading Branch Davidian adults to come out and to send their children out.[12] FBI agents in Waco were constantly reporting to FBI officials in the Strategic Information and Operations Center (SIOC) in the Hoover Building in

FIGURE 12.1. "Trophy photo" of FBI Hostage Rescue Team operator taken at the Branch Davidians' Mount Carmel Center, located outside Waco, Texas. Defendant's exhibit in the 1995 criminal trial, courtesy of Clive Doyle.

Washington, D.C. The FBI's internal documents in the Lee Hancock Collection prompt the question of why FBI officials and commanders made decisions about handling the Branch Davidians that contradicted well-known FBI and law enforcement protocols to obtain the safe exit of barricaded subjects.

As a reporter with the *Dallas Morning News,* Lee Hancock covered the 1993 conflict between the Branch Davidians and federal agents. Hancock's investigative reporting on the Branch Davidian case also covered the criminal trial in 1994, congressional hearings in 1995, the wrongful death civil trial in 2000, and the investigation by special counsel John C. Danforth.[13] Someone in the FBI provided Hancock with internal FBI memos, reports, and logs. She used many of them in her important news stories, but she did not utilize all of the information available in these documents. I contacted Hancock for an interview in 2003, which turned out to be when she decided her research on the Branch Davidian case had concluded. She sent boxes of documents to me, and they were placed in the Loyola University New Orleans archive. In 2009 these materials were relocated to the archive of Texas State University, where they are now available to the public.[14]

The internal FBI documents in the Lee Hancock Collection provide a wealth of information on the ways that FBI agents investigated David Koresh and the Branch Davidians, analyzed them for the possibility of mass suicide, and persuaded Attorney General Janet Reno to approve an assault by the FBI's HRT that endangered all the residents of the building, especially the children. These documents indicate that the FBI decision makers were well aware of the apocalyptic theology of martyrdom taught by David Koresh. Consideration of these FBI documents in conjunction with the Branch Davidians' conversations recorded by surveillance devices ("bugs") inside the building prompt the following questions:[15] Given that FBI decision makers were cognizant of the Branch Davidians' apocalyptic martyrdom theology, why was the tank and CS gas assault carried out on April 19, 1993? Since there was a strong likelihood of fire erupting as a result of tanks driving through and dismantling the building—even if the Branch Davidians had not held a theology of martyrdom—why was this particular form of assault carried out? Why did FBI agents fail to inform Attorney General Reno that on April 14 David Koresh had proposed and was implementing an exit plan according to which he would be able to maintain his commitment to God's word and also come out? Why was Reno not informed of the analysis of the FBI's own behavioral scientists indicating the likely violent outcome of an assault carried out by the FBI? Materials held in the Lee Hancock Collection shed new light on these questions.

The collection contains a number of documents of interest in this chapter: (1) two documents summarizing the results of investigations into the probability of the Branch Davidians committing mass suicide, (2) two documents summarizing the results of investigations into the importance that the Branch Davidians attached to Passover, (3) a series of memos written by FBI behavioral scientists ("profilers"), (4) the WACMUR Major Event Log and the WACMUR April 19, 1993, log, and (5) the Reno Briefing File. This chapter reviews this new information in order to show that FBI agents were evaluating the Branch Davidians for the possibility of group suicide up to the day before the FBI's tank and CS gas assault on April 19, and that the information given to Attorney General Reno by FBI officials was slanted to prompt her to approve the ill-conceived assault. The massive fire on April 19 would not have been a surprise to the FBI officials who had seen these reports and the related FBI memos or to those who had either heard or seen the reports of surveillance device monitors regarding Branch Davidians' conversations about prophecies being fulfilled by an assault. Whatever lessons are to be learned from the FBI's conflict with the Branch Davidians must be based on an accurate understanding of what actually happened; what follows, drawing on this new information, is an effort to contribute to that understanding.

BACKGROUND

The Branch Davidians

The General Association of the Branch Davidian Seventh-day Adventists (the Branch Davidians), founded in 1955 by Ben Roden (1902–1978), whose followers regarded him as a prophet divinely inspired to interpret the Bible's apocalyptic prophecies, had split off from an earlier offshoot of the Seventh-day Adventist Church known as the General Association of the Davidian Seventh-day Adventists (the Davidians), which was founded by Victor Houteff (1885–1955) and settled in Waco, Texas, in 1935. Roden acquired the Davidians' second piece of property, known as Mount Carmel, located on the outskirts of Waco, after Houteff's wife, Florence Houteff, had disbanded the General Association of the Davidian Seventh-day Adventists. The failure of her apocalyptic prophecy, based on her deceased husband's biblical interpretations, to materialize on April 22, 1959, prompted the dissolution. Before Roden's death in 1978, his wife, Lois Roden (1905–1986), succeeded him as prophet of the Branch Davidian group, which she called the Living Waters Branch. A number of the Rodens' followers were also former Seventh-day Adventists, a denomination that places special emphasis on the imminent fulfillment of the Christian Bible's apocalyptic prophecies. Seventh-day Adventists believe that in the present time God speaks to prophets, such as Ellen Harmon White (1827–1915), to elucidate God's word in the Bible, and the Davidian and Branch Davidian lineage of prophets continued that belief.[16]

In 1981 twenty-two-year-old Vernon Howell, who had been disfellowshipped from his Seventh-day Adventist church in Tyler, Texas, came to Mount Carmel and began studying under Lois Roden. She began to indicate to the Branch Davidians that Howell would be the prophet to succeed her. This was challenged by her son George Roden (1938–1998), which led Howell and his followers to move away from Mount Carmel in 1984. By that time, the majority of the Branch Davidians had decided that the "Spirit of Prophecy" had left Lois Roden and had been transferred to Howell. In 1985, while visiting Israel, Howell had an experience that indicated that he was called to be the Davidic messiah, Christ, for the Endtime. (According to the theology that he taught, this is not the same thing as being a reincarnation of Jesus Christ.)[17] Upon his return to the United States from Israel, he began traveling, proselytizing, and attracting converts in California, Hawaii, England, and Australia. While in Los Angeles, he also promoted his rock band. In 1986 Howell—who was already married to Rachel Jones Howell—began to take extralegal "wives" with whom to have children. He taught that his children would play a key role in the Lord's Judgment and Kingdom. The Branch Davidians took up residence at Mount Carmel again in 1988. In 1990 Howell changed his name legally to David Koresh as a sign of his messianic status. In 1992 Koresh's Branch Davidians constructed the large residence that figured prominently in the conflict in 1993, and dismantled the small houses that had existed at Mount Carmel until that time.[18]

On the morning of February 28, 1993, when the ATF assault was carried out, there were approximately 124 Branch Davidians at Mount Carmel: eighty-four were Americans, thirty-one were British, five were Australians, two were Canadians, and one was Israeli. Many of these followers were former Seventh-day Adventists. The Branch Davidians were an international and multiracial community reflecting the membership of the Seventh-day Adventist Church. All but two of the Britons were of Afro-Jamaican heritage, one being White and the other of Nigerian heritage. There were eleven African Americans, eight Mexican Americans, and Americans of Japanese, Filipina, Chinese, Samoan, and mixed ethnicities. There were forty-three women (eighteen and older), thirty-seven men (eighteen and older), and forty-four children of all ages. Of the children, thirty were eight years old or younger. Twelve of the children were David Koresh's biological children. Two young women were pregnant with Koresh's babies.[19]

Immediately after the ATF raid, despite being wounded and thinking he was dying, Koresh was active in the negotiations, communicated his theology to the public through calls to CNN and a radio talk show, and

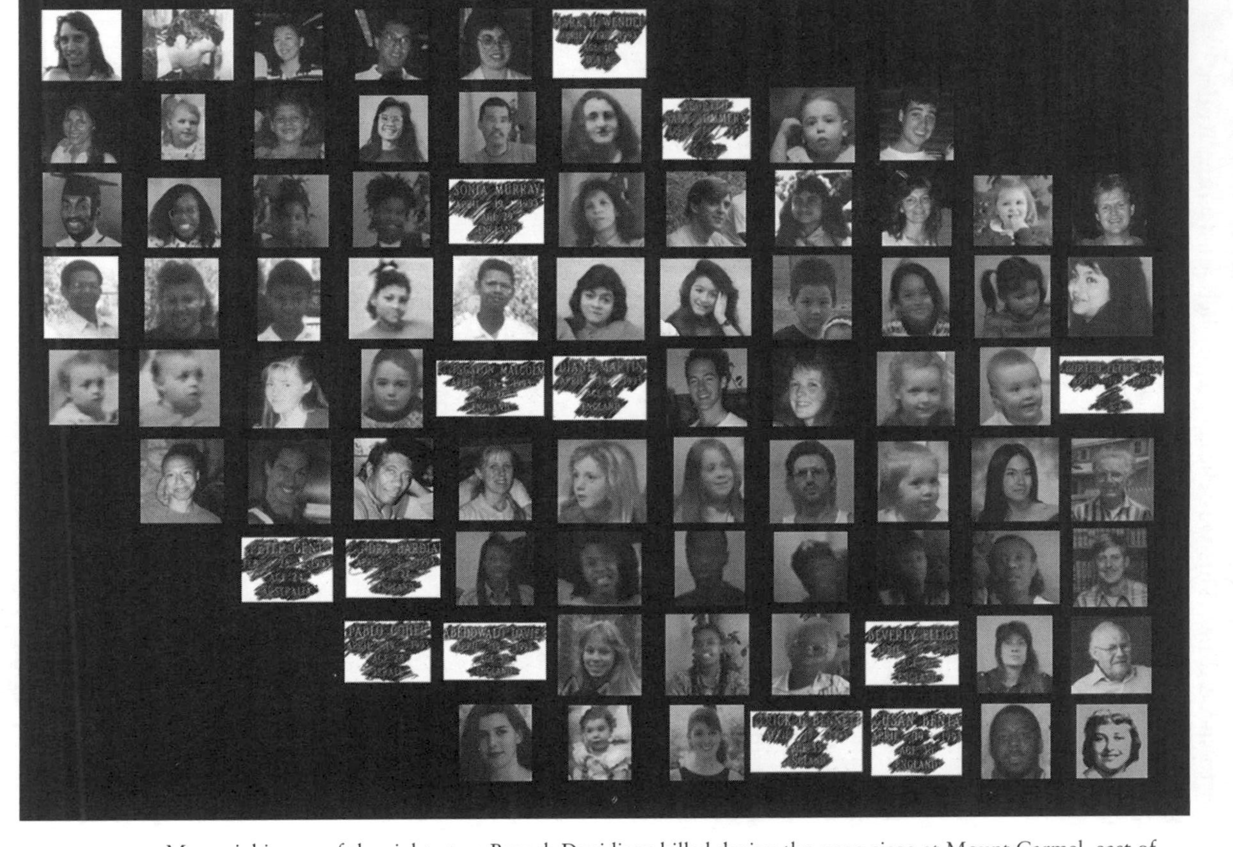

FIGURE 12.2. Memorial image of the eighty-two Branch Davidians killed during the 1993 siege at Mount Carmel, east of Waco, Texas. This composite image was created by Matthew D. Wittmer in 2013 using photographs from the former Visitor's Center at Mount Carmel, which was maintained by survivor Clive Doyle from 1998 until 2006, and from still photographs taken from videotapes filmed by the Branch Davidians during the siege. Rubbings of the memorial name stones at Mount Carmel are inserted for Branch Davidians for whom no photos were available. Courtesy of Matthew D. Wittmer.

recorded an audiotaped sermon. During much of the early siege, however, Koresh was absent from negotiations and was reported to be sleeping. Koresh's right-hand man, Steve Schneider, a former Seventh-day Adventist who had earned a master's degree in religious studies at the University of Hawaii,[20] did most of the negotiating and had a large influence on the outcome of the negotiations. Schneider's wife, Judy Schneider, had become one of Koresh's wives, after which her daughter, Mayanah Schneider, was born; Mayanah was two years old at the time of the raid. The WACMUR Major Event Log indicates that by March 5 (at 9:45 A.M.) Steve Schneider reported to FBI negotiators that Koresh was not well. On March 11 at 11:34 A.M., a negotiator logged a speculation that Koresh might have blood poisoning. At 11:49 A.M. a negotiator discussed septicemia and gangrene with Schneider. By the time Koresh's criminal defense attorney, Dick DeGuerin of Houston, went inside the building on March 29, Koresh had begun to be awake for longer periods and participate more actively in the negotiations; that continued during DeGuerin's visits on March 30, March 31, and April 1 (when he was accompanied by Jack Zimmerman, Schneider's attorney).

David Koresh and the Branch Davidians' interpretations of the Bible's apocalyptic prophecies were not set in stone. They were doing what other believers in an imminent apocalypse do: reading the apocalyptic signs of the Endtime in light of current events, in this case the events that occurred at Mount Carmel on February 28, 1993, and during the siege that followed.[21] They were waiting to see whether it was God's will for them to die at that time to fulfill the Bible's prophecies as interpreted by Koresh. They did not want to die, but as members of the "wave sheaf" (Lev. 23:10–14), the "first of the first fruits" (Lev. 23:20; Rev. 14:4) of those who will be included in the Lord's Kingdom, they would be faithful to God's will.[22]

Participating FBI Agents and Government Officials

Special Agent in Charge (SAC) Jeffrey Jamar of San Antonio, head of the Texas FBI regional office that included McLennan County, in which Waco is located, was put in charge of the WACMUR case. Other special agents in charge (that is, heads of regional offices) arrived to assist Jamar. SAC Bob Ricks of Oklahoma City was frequently the FBI spokesperson at press briefings. On March 17, SAC Dick Schwein of El Paso, Texas, arrived to take charge of the night shift of the siege. Schwein implemented the blasting of high-decibel irritating sounds at the

Branch Davidians through loudspeakers that had been set up outside the building.[23]

When FBI agents took over from ATF agents on March 1, 1993, the FBI's tactical unit, the HRT, which was commanded by Assistant Special Agent in Charge (ASAC) Dick Rogers, surrounded the building with snipers, and the unit brought tanks onto the Mount Carmel property on March 2. The HRT had been founded in 1982 with Danny Coulson as its first commander. The FBI agents who served as HRT "operators" were trained by Delta Force, the U.S. Army's Special Forces counterterrorism unit. As its name suggests, the Hostage Rescue Team's original purpose was to rescue Americans being held in foreign countries by terrorists. They were trained to attack and "neutralize" the terrorists in order to rescue hostages.[24] Dick Rogers was commander of HRT in 1992 when a shootout between federal marshals and Randy Weaver, Kevin Harris, and Weaver's fourteen-year-old son, Sammy, resulted in the deaths of Sammy Weaver and U.S. Marshal William Degan. FBI officials in Washington permitted a change in the HRT's rules of engagement that resulted in the shooting death of Vicki Weaver, the wife of Randy Weaver, as she held her baby daughter in her arms.[25]

Supervisory Agent Gary Noesner arrived in Waco from the FBI's Special Operations and Research Center at Quantico, Virginia, on March 1 to serve as the crisis negotiation team coordinator. Through the efforts of Lieutenant Larry Lynch of the McLennan County Sheriff's Department on February 28 and the later efforts of Noesner and his FBI negotiators, a total of twenty-one children and fourteen adults came out.

Noesner reports that, as early as March 1, he and the other negotiators believed they were dealing with a group that might commit mass suicide. When Koresh offered to come out after he was permitted to broadcast nationally his message about the book of Revelation, Noesner explained, "around the room, we exchanged knowing glances. Fresh on our minds was the 1978 incident in Jonestown, Guyana, when Reverend Jim Jones coerced over 900 of his People's Temple followers to 'drink the Kool-Aid' that led to their deaths. The book of Revelation, with its focus on the apocalypse, could be a dangerous text in the hands of a charismatic and narcissistic leader."[26]

Noesner protested to Jamar about the aggressive actions taken by the HRT—turning the building's electricity off; using tanks to destroy vehicles, fuel tanks, and lumber piles; shining spotlights at the residence all night long; and blasting high-decibel sounds—whenever the Branch Davidians cooperated by sending out children or adults. According to

Noesner, "It seemed that the FBI was deliberately seeking to irritate the [Branch] Davidians. Some of my negotiators began to speculate that this was being done to deliberately undercut the negotiation process."[27] Noesner was removed from the case on March 24. He was informed by his boss that "a high-level official at FBI headquarters wanted Clint Van Zandt . . . to replace me."[28]

Clint Van Zandt served as negotiation coordinator from March 25 to April 19. Van Zandt was given instructions by Jamar, backed up by officials in FBI headquarters, that his negotiators should give Koresh a deadline for ten to twelve people to come out. If Koresh did not meet the deadline, HRT operators in tanks would destroy some of the Branch Davidians' property. Koresh did not respond to this repeated demand from the FBI, and this situation resulted in television footage of the tanks moving and destroying the Branch Davidians' vehicles, including motorcycles and go-carts, and other property. This continued until Dick DeGuerin, Koresh's attorney, went inside the Mount Carmel residence for the first time on March 29.[29]

FBI Supervisory Special Resident Agent Byron Sage was from the FBI's Austin, Texas, office, which is considered a satellite office ("resident agency") of the San Antonio Division.[30] This meant that SAC Jamar was Sage's direct superior in the FBI hierarchy in general and in the operation at Waco in particular. Sage was the first FBI agent to arrive in Waco to assist Lieutenant Larry Lynch in negotiations with the Branch Davidians. He arrived on February 28 and continued to play a key role in the negotiations through April 19. Officially, Sage was not the "chief negotiator," as he is often characterized in news articles, television shows, and documentaries about the case.[31] According to Noesner, after he was removed as negotiation coordinator and replaced by Van Zandt, "Van Zandt did not get along with SAC Jamar, who cut him out of the decision-making process. Byron Sage became the de facto team leader [of the negotiators] and through the remainder of the incident played the key negotiation leadership role in trying to save the lives of those who remained inside the compound."[32]

After the siege at Mount Carmel concluded on April 19, 1993, the FBI compiled the logs of the negotiators, the HRT, the operations center in Waco (located eight miles away from Mount Carmel at the Texas State Technical College), and SIOC into a single log named the WACMUR Major Event Log, which is in the Hancock Collection. The Major Event Log indicates clearly that FBI officials in SIOC were supervising what was happening on the ground at Mount Carmel.

The FBI officials in SIOC to whom agents in Waco most often reported were Larry A. Potts, who was assistant director; Danny Coulson, who was deputy assistant director and former commander of the HRT; and E. Michael Kahoe, who was chief of the Violent Crimes and Major Offenders Section. Both Potts and Kahoe were criticized for their involvement in the process that changed the HRT's rules of engagement in 1992, which contributed directly to the death of Vicki Weaver at Ruby Ridge, Idaho. In 1995 Potts was demoted from his position as deputy director of the FBI, and Kahoe was suspended.[33] In 1997 Kahoe was given an eighteen-month sentence and a fine of $4,000 after he pleaded guilty to obstruction of evidence for destroying an "After Action" report in relation to the Ruby Ridge case; the report showed that "agents complained that headquarters executives like Mr. Potts and his deputy, Danny O. Coulson, had 'micromanaged' the incident from Washington."[34]

Coulson had founded the HRT and was its commander in 1985 when he oversaw the siege of the Covenant, Sword, and Arm of the Lord (CSA), an antigovernment, White-supremacist Christian community in Arkansas that consisted of extreme right-wing men and their wives and children.[35] Van Zandt was the negotiation coordinator at that siege and worked with Coulson to maintain a low-key tactical presence and implement creative negotiation strategies that resulted in the surrender of the men and the safe exit of the women and children.[36]

Coulson's experience in peacefully resolving the CSA siege probably led him to oppose the CS gas and tank assault plan proposed by Rogers and Jamar early in the Branch Davidian siege. At the hearings of the U.S. Senate's Committee on the Judiciary in 1995, Van Zandt and profiler Peter Smerick named Potts and Kahoe as the likely officials in FBI headquarters who directly supervised Jamar and Rogers during the siege of the Branch Davidians.[37]

On the afternoon of March 2, 1993, during the period in which negotiators lost telephone contact with the Branch Davidians while they prayed and waited for Koresh to reveal God's word, someone in SIOC logged a statement indicating that officials in SIOC understood that the FBI was dealing with a religious group with a theology of martyrdom: "One concern that the negotiators have is that Koresh believes in martyrdom and may be preparing his disciples. The children that were sent out were not those of Koresh."[38]

Although on March 19 negotiations had induced two men to come out, the Major Event Log records that on March 20 Coulson gave permission to Jamar to take aggressive actions against the Branch Davidians. While daylong negotiations for the exit of a number of Branch Davidians were occurring, SIOC logged at 9:16 P.M. that Jeffrey Jamar in Waco spoke with Danny Coulson. They "agreed that we seem to get more productive results when we put pressure on the compound ie using CEV's [combat engineering vehicles] to move material from compound area, pushing bus down the road, etc. SAC Jamar is considering more aggressive acts tomorrow." Jamar was thinking of having a CEV strike the corner of the building so the inhabitants could "contemplate the possibilities." The log entry said that Jamar would discuss this strategy with Larry Potts the following morning. The entry records that Coulson and Jamar "both agree that more pressure is needed."[39]

The FBI waited until seven adults came out on March 21 before implementing the increased pressure. After CEVs destroyed and moved some of the Branch Davidians' vehicles on March 21 at 5:54 P.M., additional Branch Davidians who had been planning to come out decided not to. Noesner writes that he confronted Jamar, telling him that tactical actions were not conducive to gaining the Branch Davidians' trust and getting people out. "He appeared unconcerned. I realized then that he had already determined what he was going to do. I met with my team and told them that we were on a crashing airplane. We could parachute to safety or we could try to control the descent and minimize destruction on the ground. Despite their anger and disappointment, and despite the bad decisions coming from our commanders, the entire negotiation team felt we needed to continue our actions."[40]

That evening SAC Richard Schwein began playing irritating, loud sounds all night on loudspeakers to keep the Branch Davidians awake, and at 11:18 P.M. Koresh and Steve Schneider complained to negotiators about the noise. They said the sounds were interfering with their efforts to get people to come out. The Major Event Log records that Koresh said, "Nobody is coming out," and both Koresh and Schneider said that the Branch Davidians would accept whatever was to happen.[41] On the same evening, Noesner learned from his superior that he was going to be taken off the case.

During the Mount Carmel siege, Coulson, Potts, and Kahoe reported to Deputy Director Floyd I. Clarke and Director William S. Sessions, whom they briefed about the situation relative to the Branch Davidians.[42] Clarke served as acting FBI director after President Bill Clinton dismissed Sessions as director in July 1993. Clarke retired from the FBI after Louis Freeh was sworn in as director in September 1993. Sessions was widely regarded as being absent from active management of the

FBI, and he was criticized for misusing FBI funding.[43] During the Branch Davidian incident, Sessions was instrumental in persuading Reno to approve the tank and CS gas assault, as discussed below.

The FBI is an agency within the United States Department of Justice; therefore the attorney general exercises oversight of the bureau. Janet Reno was confirmed as attorney general on March 11, 1993, eleven days after the siege at Mount Carmel began. The Branch Davidian case occurred in the first term of President Bill Clinton, who assumed office on January 20, 1993.

Early in the siege, the WACMUR Major Event Log records calls to SIOC from the president's aides in the White House Situation Room.[44] It was not long thereafter that references to the White House were omitted from the log. In 1999, Lee Hancock and David Jackson of the *Dallas Morning News* reported that, according to newly discovered FBI memos, on March 8, 1993, at the direction of Associate Attorney General Webster Hubbell, a close friend of President Clinton and a former law partner of Hillary Clinton in Little Rock, Arkansas, the FBI faxed to the White House a plan to end the Branch Davidian siege by tear gas assault.[45] It is not known whether this FBI communication with the White House was documented in the 594-page Major Event Log, because the pages of the log in the Hancock Collection jump from page 181 to page 248—the entries for March 8, March 9, and half of March 10 are missing.

A REVISED HISTORY OF THE CONFLICT BETWEEN THE FBI AND THE BRANCH DAVIDIANS

Was Apocalypse Avertible? What Did the FBI Know, or What Could It Have Known, about the Branch Davidians' Beliefs and Psychology?

After the deaths of the Branch Davidians in the disastrous events of April 19, 1993, officials in the Justice Department and the Treasury Department (which oversees the ATF) assembled a team of experts to analyze the case and make recommendations to prevent such tragedies in the future. Sociologist Nancy Ammerman served on this team during the summer of 1993 and subsequently made scholars aware that during the siege, FBI decision makers had not taken into account the analysis and advice of the FBI's own behavioral scientists, or profilers.[46]

During the Mount Carmel siege, profilers Peter A. Smerick and Mark C. Young, in consultation with forensic psychiatrist Park Dietz, wrote a series of memos warning FBI decision makers of a likely disaster if the

Branch Davidians were assaulted again.[47] Their analyses were based on interviews of people acquainted with the Branch Davidians that had been conducted by FBI agents and summarized in memos, which are found in the Hancock Collection. The Smerick-Young memos indicate that the profilers understood the implications of the Branch Davidians' apocalyptic theology of martyrdom, and they attempted to convey this information to their FBI superiors.

In their memo to "SAC's WAC MUR," dated March 5, 1993, Smerick and Young list the goals of the operation:

1. Insure the safety of CHILDREN, who are truly victims in this situation.
2. Facilitate the peaceful surrender of DAVID KORESH and his followers, from Branch Davidians Compound, Mt. Carmel, Waco, Texas.

This memo analyzes Koresh and the Branch Davidians according to the "cult" stereotype, with Koresh termed a manipulative "psychopath" and the followers described as having "low self-esteem" and "unable to act or think for themselves." Smerick and Young considered the Branch Davidians to be "frightened pawns" of Koresh, who taught that the group would be involved in a battle with government agents. "For years he has been brainwashing his followers for this battle, and on February 28, 1993, his prophecy came true." Smerick and Young noted that this was not the typical hostage situation FBI agents handle and that "tactical presence" would not work in this instance. They correctly advised that tactical action, "if carried to excess, could eventually be counter productive and could result in loss of life." They explained, "Every time his followers sense movement of tactical personnel, KORESH validates his prophetic warnings that an attack is forthcoming and they are going to have to defend themselves." Smerick and Young noted that there had been greater success in getting children released when "tactical forces were maintained at a greater distance." They added: "Because of the tremendous fear felt by the majority of DAVID KORESH's followers, it is recommended that there be a de-escalation of the forward movement of tactical personnel." This would create a context in which negotiators could persuade the Branch Davidians that "a battle is not inevitable, and that KORESH's predictions are wrong." This Smerick-Young memo warned that if tactical forces "continue to move closer to the compound, the increased paranoia of these people could result in their firing weapons, thus encouraging retaliation, leading to an escalation of violence."

Two other crucial memos are dated March 7 and 8, 1993. In the March 7 memo, after listing aggressive actions against the Branch Davidians being considered by FBI agents, including shining spotlights at night, blasting irritating noises, flying aircraft over the compound, moving tanks, shutting off electricity, and further tightening the armed perimeter, Smerick and Young concluded, "Many of these options however, would also succeed in shutting down negotiations and convince KORESH and his followers the end is near." They continued:

> If the compound is attacked, in all probability, DAVID KORESH and his followers will fight back to the death, to defend their property and their faith, as they believe they did on February 28, 1993. If that occurs, there will have to be a HRT response and the possibility of a tremendous loss of life, both within the compound, and of Bureau personnel.
>
> Commanders are thus faced with the prospect of defending their actions and justifying the taking of lives of *children,* who are with their families in a "*defensive position,*" defending their religion, regardless of how bizarre and cult-like we believe it is manifested.
>
> If we physically attack the compound, and *children are killed* (even by Davidians), we, in the FBI, will be placed in a difficult position. The news media, Congress, and the American people . . . will ask questions:
>
> Why couldn't you just wait them out?
>
> What threat did they pose to anyone, except themselves?
>
> Why did you cause the children to be killed? [emphasis in original]

The March 7 memo recommended continued negotiations with the assistance of McLennan County Sheriff Jack Harwell, who was respected by the Branch Davidians.

While in Waco, Smerick presented his analysis directly to Jamar. The FBI agent who subsequently interviewed Smerick summarized the situation: "He told Jamar that they could not send in the tanks because if they did so children would die and the FBI would be blamed even if they were not responsible."[48]

Smerick and Young's March 8 memo advised that the Branch Davidians saw Mount Carmel as sacred ground and that Koresh and his followers would die fighting to defend it. The memo acknowledged that FBI officials and tactical personnel were frustrated with Koresh's refusal to exit the residence. Smerick and Young argued, "In this situation, KORESH's arrogant, recalcitrant demeanor may be part of his scheme to manipulate law enforcement commanders, so as to provoke a law enforcement confrontation, in fulfillment of his interpretation of the 7 seals." Smerick and Young inaccurately discussed Koresh's interpretations of the Seven Seals of the book of Revelation, but they correctly grasped that Koresh predicted that some Branch Davidians would die in a conflict with federal agents—as had happened on February 28—and that, after a period, the rest of them would die in an assault. This was Koresh's interpretation of the Fifth Seal (Rev. 6:9–11). Smerick and Young wrote:

> In traditional hostage negotiations with people who are psychopaths, the goal is to wrest control away from the individual and give him a face saving scenario, so he can surrender. With DAVID KORESH, however, perhaps one way to take control away from him is to do the OPPOSITE of what he is expecting. Instead of moving towards him, we consider moving back. This may appear to be appeasement to his wishes, but in reality it is taking power away from him. He has told his followers that an attack is imminent, and this will show them that he was wrong.

The March 8 memo warned that Koresh might order a "mass suicide" if his status as the group's messiah was threatened. The memo strongly advised FBI decision makers to refrain from making the mistake of police officers in Philadelphia who in 1985 dropped a bomb on the residence of an African American group known as MOVE in order to resolve a siege, thereby causing a fire that killed eleven MOVE members, including five children, and destroyed sixty-five houses in the neighborhood.

A confidential FBI memo dated August 24, 1993, reported on a debriefing interview with Smerick in which he stated that the Smerick-Young memo dated March 9 was written under pressure from officials in Washington.[49] The March 9 memo listed hardline measures "to break the spirit of DAVID KORESH and the control he exercises over his followers." It stated that it is "time to consider other measures to wield control of the situation," such as turning the electricity on and off, unpredictably moving tanks and tactical agents, downplaying Koresh's importance in FBI press briefings, controlling the building's television and radio (the FBI had already taken control of the Branch Davidians' telephone lines), and cutting off negotiations until Koresh was willing to discuss what the agents regarded as the real issues. The memo advised that FBI agents should exercise "extreme caution" with Koresh and respond to Branch Davidian aggression only with steps to protect the lives of FBI personnel. "Any loss of life, as a result of hostile action initiated by KORESH would then be his responsibility." Smerick and Young did not advocate an assault on the Branch Davidians.

Smerick left Waco on March 17, 1993, and was not asked by the FBI for any further input on the case. In 2000 Lee Hancock reported on a 1995 FBI memo about an interview in which Smerick stated that he believed that FBI officials, in order to induce Attorney General Reno to approve the April 19 assault, misled her by not including all of the memos written by Smerick and Young in the briefing file shown to her.[50] The FBI's Reno Briefing File is discussed below.

Might the Branch Davidians Have Been Willing to Exit Peacefully?

On April 2, 1993, at 7:52 P.M., Steve Schneider told FBI negotiators the Branch Davidians would come out after the eight days of Passover concluded. At 8:10 P.M., the Major Event Log records that Rick Ross, a "cult de-programmer" who had counseled the ATF agents before the February 28 assault, called the FBI to say that he had received a call from Schneider's sister saying that she had received a cellular call from the Branch Davidian residence. Ross emphasized that Steve and the others badly wanted to come out. Ross said, "Koresh is looking for a way to save face, yet come out peacefully."[51]

David Koresh and the Branch Davidians observed Passover April 5 through 13. The Major Event Log indicates that high-decibel sounds were blasted at the Branch Davidians during this time despite their request for respect during the sacred time. The log reports that Koresh was insulted by the continued noise during Passover, and Schneider complained about FBI agents in tanks "flipping the bird" at the Branch Davidians.[52]

The log further records that at 3:00 P.M. on April 6, SIOC logged a call from the army at Fort Hood, Texas, concerning the FBI's request for forty-eight 40mm illumination rounds and thirty-six 40mm ferret (CS) rounds.[53] Ferret rounds are small, rocket-shaped "plastic projectiles that . . . burst on impact, dispersing their liquid gas load."[54] FBI officials in SIOC were making preparations for the assault. Ferret rounds were used on April 19 to deliver CS gas into the building. Illumination rounds are flares, and their intended use in the assault is unclear.

The Major Event Log indicates that on Good Friday, April 9, between 3:00 and 4:00 P.M., Steve Schneider received permission from the FBI to go outside and light seven smoke canisters (referred to as "incense") to commemorate the death of Christ on the cross. The log records that at 6:30 P.M. an HRT agent reported to SIOC that, per SAC Jamar and HRT commander Dick Rogers, "there would be no plan to fight a fire should one develop in the Davidian compound."[55] There is no indication in the log that SIOC contradicted this decision.

At 7:03 P.M. HRT logged in all capital letters that Steve Schneider came outside unannounced, "approached agents [*sic*] position," and a percussion grenade (flashbang) was thrown at him. Negotiators logged at 7:30 P.M. that Schneider was "absolutely distraught." He screamed at the negotiator that he could come out whenever he wanted. He said he had walked out because he thought an FBI agent in a tank had beckoned to him. (Items were frequently dropped off to the Branch Davidians by agents in the tanks.) Schneider screamed at the negotiator until the call was terminated at 7:40.[56] Also at 7:30 P.M., a Black male in the building's courtyard was flashbanged to force him to go inside.[57]

On April 14, the day after Passover concluded, David Koresh informed his attorney, Dick DeGuerin, who conveyed the information to FBI agents, that he and the Branch Davidians would come out after he wrote a "little book" containing his interpretation of the Seven Seals of Revelation.[58] Since Koresh identified himself with the Seventh Angel holding a small opened scroll in Rev. 10:1–2, by this means Koresh proposed to come out in a manner that conformed to his interpretation of biblical prophecies, thereby maintaining his charismatic authority with his followers. Beginning at 4:25 P.M. that afternoon, banners were hung out of a window: "Read Proverbs 1, 2, 3, 4. We come to love, not war." "Let's have a beer when this is over." "My name is Neil Vaega. I'm from Hawaii." "Media and FBI don't know the truth. You can't accept the truth. We can still have a few beers together." "I'm an American. I love America, but BATF killed my family and friends."[59] Importantly, the Major Event Log reveals that on April 14 Koresh sent out his signed contract to retain DeGuerin as his attorney.[60] In this same packet of materials was a handwritten letter signed by Koresh spelling out his exit plan. This letter was delivered to the FBI by 6:45 P.M.[61]

On April 15 at 2:25 P.M. a negotiator logged that Nicole Gent Little, age twenty-four, was five months pregnant, and that Aisha Gyarfas Summers, age eighteen, was due to give birth in May. At 3:12 P.M. Schneider reported to negotiators that his signed attorney contract was ready to be picked up. At 4:05 P.M. SIOC logged that it received a report from Byron Sage about the two pregnant women and the names and ages of four male children inside the building. At 5:15 P.M. HRT logged that a White male was flashbanged when he came out of the back of the building. When he came out again, he was flashbanged a second time.[62]

The Major Event Log records that Steve Schneider called a negotiator on April 16 at 1:15 A.M. to complain that a Bradley tank had rammed the outside wall of one of the first-floor bedrooms, nearly injuring Graeme Craddock, who was sleeping in a bunkbed with his head to the wall. Nevertheless, Koresh reported at 2:35 A.M. that he had completed his commentary on the First Seal. He reiterated that he was working day and night on the manuscript and that they would come out when it was completed.[63] Branch Davidians began requesting batteries and ribbon cassettes for a battery-operated word processor to facilitate faster production of the manuscript.[64]

The word-processing supplies and milk for the children were delivered to the Branch Davidians at 7:40 P.M. on the evening of April 18, the night before the tank and CS gas assault. Steve Schneider told a negotiator that the First Seal portion of the manuscript could be sent out as soon as it was typed, instead of waiting for Koresh to compose the entire manuscript on the Seven Seals.[65]

The FBI's Plan to End the Standoff and How It Secured Janet Reno's Approval

The Danforth Final Report indicates that a plan for insertion of CS gas was first formulated by the HRT—that is, Dick Rogers with the support of Jeffrey Jamar—early in March. The "Proposed Operations Plan" dated March 10, 1993, was for a rapid insertion of CS gas by CEVs, with "projectible flashbangs" fired into the building as needed. After "discussions within the FBI" of the plan, HRT produced "Proposed Operations Plan–Revision #2," dated March 14, which specified that CEVs would spray tear gas from canisters on their booms and that ferret rounds might be fired inside the building by grenade launchers to release CS gas.[66]

On March 16, Danny Coulson sent an e-mail message to Potts indicating that the Branch Davidians might "engage in mass suicide or start a fire deliberately or by accident" in response to such an assault. Coulson concluded "that personnel safety, among other factors precluded a firefighting response." The Danforth Report indicates that Jamar and Sage did contact the nearby Bellmead Fire Department a few weeks before the April 19 assault so firefighters would be prepared to assist if needed.[67]

The Danforth Report cites a March 22 FBI memo written by "the negotiation team," which said "negotiators were willing to consider the tactical use of tear gas to end the standoff." After the negotiators' memo was received at FBI headquarters, Coulson wrote a March 23 memo critical of Rogers's CS gas and tank assault plan. Citing similar problems with Rogers when he commanded the HRT at Ruby Ridge and formulated a similar proposal to gas the Randy Weaver family, Coulson wrote, "A lot of pressure is coming from Rogers." Coulson argued, "All of their intelligence indicates that David [Koresh] does not intend suicide and that he will come out eventually." Coulson pointed out that negotiations were being hurt by the punitive actions taken against the Branch Davidians by the HRT whenever they cooperated with negotiators.[68] He advised that Potts and Kahoe should go to Waco to assess the situation.[69]

On March 27, Jamar signed off on "Proposed Operations Plan–Revision 3," which outlined the plan implemented on April 18 and 19, 1993. All remaining vehicles and other objects outside the building would be removed the day before the insertion of tear gas by two CEVs and four Bradleys. The CEVs would be driven into the building to spray tear gas from canisters on their booms. The holes in the walls made by the CEVs would be exits for Branch Davidians seeking to escape the gas. Military personnel would be on hand to give medical treatment.[70]

The Danforth Report states that in the FBI discussions of the plan, Coulson advised against it because of the high risk that the Branch Davidians would shoot at the tanks, while Jamar and others wanted an "all-out tear gas assault" involving complete insertion of gas rather than gradual insertion as advocated by Reno and others in the Justice Department.[71]

But how did the tear gas plan receive the necessary approval? The WACMUR Major Event Log, the 1993 Justice Department's *Report to the Deputy Attorney General on the Events at Waco, Texas, February 28 to April 19, 1993*, the Danforth Report, and other sources document how Reno was persuaded to approve the life-threatening tank and CS gas assault. The Reno Briefing File, included in the Hancock Collection, suggests that Reno was not provided all of the available information about Koresh and the Branch Davidians.

On April 7, 1993, Deputy Director Clarke and Assistant Director Potts were in Waco meeting with Jamar and Rogers to determine whether a tactical approach should be taken to resolve the siege. A plan for gradual insertion of CS gas was formulated; it included a contingency plan for rapid insertion of gas in the event the Branch Davidians directed gunfire at the tanks. Clarke and Potts returned to Washington, D.C., and briefed Director Sessions and Associate Deputy Director W. Douglas Gow.[72]

On April 12, Sessions met with Attorney General Reno and Associate Attorney General Hubbell to brief them on the FBI's proposed plan to insert CS gas into the building. A "Briefing Book" was submitted to Reno describing the plan and giving the rationale of "behavioral psychologists" about why it was necessary to gas the Branch Davidians. The Danforth Report indicates that Reno participated in a second meeting in

FBI SIOC on April 12 during which the CS gas and tank plan was described in detail. Reno asked numerous questions about the safety of the plan, possible harm to the children, and why an assault was necessary at that time.[73]

On April 13 Hubbell met with White House officials, including White House counsel Bernard W. Nussbaum, to brief them on the planned changes in the FBI's strategy in dealing with the Branch Davidians. Nussbaum then briefed President Clinton.[74]

A meeting took place in Sessions's office on April 14 with Reno and Hubbell, other officials from the Justice Department, and Clarke, Gow, Potts, Coulson, Rogers, and Anthony Betz, chief of the FBI's Domestic Terrorism unit. "Two military experts provided their assessments of the plan, while a medical doctor summarized the results of studies of the effects of CS gas."[75] One of the military experts was Brigadier General Peter J. Schoomaker of the III Corps of the U.S. Army, based at Fort Hood, Texas, who had formerly served as commander of Delta Force, the army's "tier-one counter-terrorist unit."[76] Schoomaker had met with HRT commander Rogers in Waco on March 1 to discuss the situation. He met with Rogers again in Waco on April 13, and they traveled to Fort Bragg, North Carolina, to pick up Colonel Jerry Boykin, the commander of Delta Force, and then traveled to Washington for the April 14 meeting. Dr. Harry Salem, an army toxicologist, presented purported evidence that CS gas would not cause permanent harm to children, pregnant women, or the elderly.[77] Schoomaker and Boykin suggested that CS gas be inserted into all areas of the building simultaneously. Reno preferred a gradual gassing, which "would best ensure the safety of those inside, especially the children." In her statement in a subsequent congressional hearing, Reno reported: "I directed that if at any point Koresh or his followers threatened to harm the children, the FBI should cease the action immediately. Likewise, if it appeared that, as a result of the initial use of teargas, Koresh was prepared to negotiate in good faith for his ultimate surrender, the FBI should cease the operation." Reno also testified that "experts had advised the Bureau that the chances of suicide were not likely."[78]

On April 14 Schoomaker told Reno that maintaining the HRT personnel on duty for such a long time was causing fatigue, thereby inhibiting their performance, though Rogers disputed this. Reno was told that police SWAT officers were not sufficiently competent to take over while the HRT operators stood down for rest and retraining. The military officers noted there was the possibility of a fire if "pyrotechnic tear gas" devices were fired into the building. Pyrotechnic devices use a spark to release gas and thus can ignite a fire. Reno gave a directive that, were the tear gas operation to be approved, no pyrotechnic devices should be used.[79]

On April 15 Reno tasked Hubbell, other Justice Department officials, and Clarke and Potts of the FBI to determine whether there could be a negotiated end to the standoff. The Justice Department report states that Hubbell and Byron Sage had a two-hour telephone conversation with Clarke and Potts of the FBI and Justice Department personnel listening in. Sage mentioned in his subsequent congressional testimony that FBI personnel in Waco were also included in the telephone call.[80] According to the Justice Department report, Sage indicated to Hubbell that further negotiations with the Branch Davidians would be fruitless. He said that the only people who had been sent out were children who were not fathered by Koresh, the elderly, and adults who were causing trouble. "He was also convinced that the FBI had not succeeded in getting anyone released from the compound through negotiation." Sage said the situation was at a total impasse. According to the Justice Department report, "Hubbell recalls Sage saying he believed there was nothing more he or the negotiators could do to persuade Koresh to release anyone else, or come out himself."[81] This telephone conversation between Sage and Hubbell occurred the day after Koresh promised to come out after completing his manuscript on the Seven Seals and being assured the manuscript had been delivered safely to Bible scholars James Tabor and J. Phillip Arnold. In congressional testimony, Sage stated that he told Hubbell on April 15 about Koresh's plan to come out after he wrote his manuscript, but the negotiators did not see that offer as any different than Koresh's offer on March 2, when he failed to come out. Sage told Congress that the "surrender plan" "had not changed substantially since the understanding that we had with Mr. Koresh allegedly on the 2d of March. The only change that had been inserted was to facilitate the ability to use defense counsel."[82] In congressional testimony, Hubbell confirmed that Sage told him of Koresh's new exit plan, but "he indicated to me that it wouldn't [work], and that the attorneys were being manipulated by Mr. Koresh."[83]

Importantly, there is no evidence in the government documents that Sage told Hubbell that Koresh had signed the contract to retain DeGuerin as his defense attorney, and there is no evidence in these documents that Hubbell reported Koresh's new exit plan to Reno.[84] In congressional testimony, Jamar stated there was not sufficient reason to inform Reno of Koresh's exit plan, because "it was not a serious plan.

It was just another delaying tactic." From Jamar's testimony, it appears he withheld information on Koresh's exit plan from "our channels in the normal discussion"—that is, from the officials in SIOC and FBI Headquarters.[85] On the other hand, the WACMUR Major Event Log indicates that on April 14 at 12:50 P.M. Sage reported to SIOC on Koresh's new exit plan as conveyed orally through DeGuerin to the FBI on that day. The log contains no record that Sage conveyed to SIOC Koresh's written letter detailing the exit plan or his signed attorney contract.

On Friday, April 16, Attorney General Reno met with FBI Director Sessions and "other officials to consider the tear gas plan."[86] She told Hubbell "she had decided not to approve the plan at that time. Ultimately, Director Sessions appealed directly to Attorney General Reno, and requested that she reconsider her decision." After further consideration, Reno "indicated that she was inclined to approve the plan, but wanted to see an even more detailed discussion of the plan and substantial supporting documentation setting out the conditions inside the complex, the status of negotiations, and the reasoning behind the plan."[87] An FBI agent in SIOC logged at 7:58 P.M. that Colonel Michael Sherfield, executive secretary at the Department of Defense, requested reasonable prior notification of an assault so he could notify Secretary of Defense Les Aspin.[88]

On April 17 at 7:30 A.M. the Major Event Log records that FBI officials, including Clarke, Coulson, and Kahoe, were preparing a "paper" to brief Reno about the proposed plan. Later they met with Sessions and Potts. According to the Danforth Final Report, the "materials that they prepared included the written opinion of behavioral psychologist Dr. Park Dietz that negotiations were not likely to resolve the crisis and that Koresh would probably continue to abuse the children."[89] At 5:00 P.M. an agent in SIOC logged that Sessions, Clarke, and Potts briefed Reno on the "proposed operational plan." The large expanding folder of documents in the Hancock Collection labeled "Reno Briefing File" may be the "paper" that was presented to Reno at this meeting, because it prominently displays the memo from Dr. Park Dietz. At 7:00 P.M. SIOC logged that Kahoe had reported that Reno had approved the plan, which would be implemented on April 19.[90]

If the thick Reno Briefing File in the Hancock Collection is an accurate, complete copy, it can be seen how these materials were presented to obtain Attorney General Reno's authorization for the FBI tank and CS gas assault. The first sixty-seven pages of documents in the file relate to allegations of Koresh's abuse of children and include a memo from forensic psychiatrist Park Dietz. The bulk of Dietz's memo details the ways the HRT and the special agents in charge undermined efforts by the FBI negotiation team before concluding, "I do not believe that negotiating in good faith will resolve the situation as it now stands." Concerning the children, Dietz wrote, "Koresh may continue to make sexual use of any female children who remain inside. . . . The possibility of the children who remain inside ever leading a normal life will become increasingly remote."[91] Immediately after the fire, Reno claimed to the media, "We had information that babies were being beaten," an allegation she had to retract as not being supported by evidence.[92]

The Smerick-Young memo of March 5, 1993, recommending de-escalation of tactical force, found on pages 74–76 of the Reno Briefing File, could easily have been overlooked if Reno did not take the time to read all of the documents carefully.

The Reno Briefing File also includes a summary of British studies alleging that CS gas used as a "riot control agent" is not harmful to children and unborn fetuses as long as they are removed quickly from the gassed area.[93] According to attorney David B. Kopel and criminologist Paul H. Blackman in *No More Wacos,* this document omitted information that a baby exposed to CS in a Northern Ireland home spent twenty-eight days in a hospital receiving medical treatment before recovering.[94] Later in 1993, psychiatrist Alan A. Stone was one of a panel of experts asked to review the evidence in the Branch Davidian case and present their reports. Stone wrote, "Based on my own medical knowledge and review of the scientific literature, the information supplied to the [attorney general about CS gas] seems to minimize the potential harmful consequences for infants and children."[95]

The last document in the Reno Briefing File is the proposed operation plan for the assault.[96] Two M-60 CEVs would spray CS gas into the building from canisters mounted on their booms. HRT operators in four Bradley tanks would use M-79 grenade launchers to shoot inside nonpyrotechnic ferret rounds. Plan A approved by Reno allowed for the gradual insertion of CS gas into the building over a forty-eight-hour period in the hope that the parents would bring their children out. It contained a provision that the FBI commanders in Waco could switch to Plan B—the rapid insertion of CS gas—if FBI agents in the tanks received gunfire. Plan B was put into operation within a few minutes after the assault started on the morning of April 19, 1993.

Did the FBI Know the Branch Davidians Might Attempt Group Suicide?

Two documents dated April 18, 1993, in the Hancock Collection—"Passover Analysis Addendum" and "Suicide Addendum"—indicate that as plans were finalized for the tank and CS gas assault on April 19, the FBI behavioral scientists, including negotiators, were continuing to evaluate the Branch Davidians for the possibility of group suicide. These two April 18 documents are follow-up summaries of interviews to two earlier documents—"Suicide References," March 27, 1993, and "Passover Summary," April 1, 1993—also in the Hancock Collection.

The "Passover Analysis Addendum" states that Branch Davidian Janet Kendrick informed the FBI that the group could exercise the biblical option of observing a second Passover (see Num. 9:1–14). Former Branch Davidians were reported as saying that Koresh expected to be killed by authorities and that the followers were expected to die with him. "Passover Analysis Addendum" refers to a "case worker" (probably Joyce Sparks of Texas Child Protective Services) who had visited Mount Carmel as saying that Koresh "often spoke of a fiery and explosive end to judgement day."[97] The document ends with a short report on statements made by Louis Alaniz, a non–Branch Davidian who had entered the residence during the siege and who came out on April 17. He "reported that the occupants were looking at a second Passover." Alaniz said that the dates for the Second Passover were not specific, but they could be from April 14 through April 21. According to the "Passover Analysis Addendum," "It was noted that some or all of Alaniz's information may have been false."[98]

The "Suicide Addendum" reported the opinions of friends, relatives, former Branch Davidians, and current Branch Davidians regarding whether the Branch Davidians were likely to commit suicide or expected to be martyred. Most of the former Branch Davidians emphasized that suicide was not a likely option but said that, in the event of an assault, members of the group were willing to die to fulfill Koresh's prophecies of apocalyptic martyrdom. They tended to stress "suicide by cop" as a possible scenario. The "Suicide Addendum" cited a memo written by psychiatrist Dr. Joseph Krofcheck and negotiation coordinator Clint Van Zandt describing Koresh as "fully capable of creating circumstances that could take the lives of all his followers and as many of the authorities as possible."[99]

Other sources of information, supplemented by evidence from Branch Davidians' discussions recorded on the surveillance audiotapes, indicate that FBI decision makers were aware that a second assault against the Branch Davidians might easily cause a lethal fire. The FBI agents who were making the decisions in SIOC and Waco knew that there was a large propane tank located behind the building's central tower close to the kitchen and that the Branch Davidians had brought kerosene and lanterns into the building from the gymnasium after the FBI turned off the electricity.[100] Anyone could have foreseen that tanks driving through the building would make a fire likely.

Gary Noesner reports that, much to the horror of the negotiators, Jamar expressed excitement as early as March 11 at the prospect of a tank driving through the building. Speaking of the M1 Abrams tanks that had just arrived, Jamar came to the negotiation room; "then, placing his finger on the map of the compound, he pointed out how an M1 was powerful enough to drive from one end of the long compound all the way through and out on the other side without stopping. He seemed excited by the possibility. The negotiators in the room were speechless. Surely he wasn't serious. Had he forgotten about the women and children inside?"[101]

A disturbing entry in the WACMUR April 19 log was made by an agent who recorded receiving a telephone call at 1:25 A.M. from a physician who specialized in pediatric burns at the Galveston Burn Center, offering his assistance if needed.[102] It seems unlikely that a physician in Galveston would have called the FBI in Waco without being called first. This log entry is consistent with reports that about 5:00 A.M. on April 19 an FBI agent contacted the burn unit of the Parkland Memorial Hospital in Dallas to ask how many patients it could treat and whether the hospital could receive patients brought in by helicopter. The FBI had arranged for the army to supply three Boeing CH-47 Chinook helicopters "in the event of a mass casualty."[103] It is evident that FBI agents, including FBI decision makers, were well aware that the assault would be life-threatening to the Branch Davidians.

FBI Efforts to Shape the Public's Perception of the Branch Davidians

After FBI agents took control of Mount Carmel on March 1, 1993, they moved the media and their satellite trucks three miles away to a location that reporters dubbed Satellite City. Reporters had to rely on the FBI's press briefings for information. During the siege, the Branch Davidians sent out three videotapes of the teenagers and adults talking about their views on what was happening and showing the small children, but the FBI did not release these to the press. Had these images had been publicized, the Branch Davidians would have been humanized as intelligent, ordinary people with small children. Without seeing these images, it was easy to forget about the human beings inside the Mount Carmel residence.

FBI agents used the press briefings to disparage David Koresh. Lee Hancock reported that the week before the April 19 assault, the FBI recited "a daily litany of what [SAC Ricks] called the sect's bizarre statements, baseless pledges and outright lies." The press briefing on Saturday, April 17, 1993, was used to disparage Louis Alaniz, who came out that day, as a "religious fanatic." To counter the announcement that had been made the previous Wednesday by attorney Dick DeGuerin that David Koresh would come out after he wrote his little book on the Seven Seals, Ricks stressed that Koresh lied continuously throughout the siege. Ricks said that although Koresh had told negotiators he had completed composing his commentary on the First Seal, the manuscript would be typed by Judy Schneider, which she obviously could not accomplish because her finger was swollen and infected after being wounded by an ATF bullet on February 28. (Clearly someone else would type it.) According to Ricks, the Branch Davidians were asking for word-processing supplies, but "that request isn't likely to be honored . . . because authorities suspect that the Branch Davidians have misused batteries in the past." (Another federal official told Hancock that they did not want the Branch Davidians to use batteries to power cellular phones.) In the April 17 press briefing, Ricks said, "We have never gotten into a quid pro quo situation, where we actually engaged in negotiations." He stated, "There are no indications at all that Mr. Koresh wants any of those people (still inside) to come out. He views those people as necessary for his protection, and we still believe that the final outcome that he wants to take place is a showdown with the government where *massive casualties and deaths will take place*" (emphasis added). The astute Hancock wrote in her article, "Perhaps most notable was what the FBI spokesman left unsaid Saturday, the forty-ninth day of the standoff: If negotiations have failed and Mr. Koresh cannot be trusted, then aggressive tactical moves may be the only way to end the standoff."[104]

The Assault

On Monday, April 19, 1993, at 6:00 A.M. the FBI's Hostage Rescue Team initiated a tank and CS gas assault on the Branch Davidians inside the Mount Carmel residence. CS gas was sprayed into the building through nozzles on the booms of two CEVs, and grenade launchers were used to fire into the building an estimated three hundred ferret rounds that released gas.[105] Although the Chemical Weapons Convention has banned the use of CS gas as a warfare agent, U.S. law enforcement continues to use the gas for police actions. Kopel and Blackman state that the FBI's actions on April 19 constituted "the most massive CS assault against civilians in American history."[106] Furthermore, it was the most massive CS assault against a large number of civilians in *enclosed spaces*.

CS is a powder suspended in a methylene chloride liquid base. It is a tear gas intended for *outdoor use only* as a riot control agent. Both CS and methylene chloride burn the skin and mucous membranes. Methylene chloride is flammable.[107]

Kopel and Blackman point out that high doses of methylene chloride cause effects "cumulative to the carbon dioxide (which reduces oxygen intake) and to CS, which causes fluid to accumulate in the lungs, and which makes breathing difficult, and which is also disorienting and incapacitating."[108] If burning CS comes into contact with water, it can form hydrogen cyanide.[109]

After the FBI assault and resulting fire on April 19, retired army colonel Rex Applegate, an expert on the use and properties of CS gas who invented the ferret round, wrote an unpublished report on the use of CS at Mount Carmel. Applegate indicated that "the total amount of CS gas delivered into the compound from the CEV vehicles is estimated to have been from 8–10 projective loadings," equivalent to "approximately 2,000 grams plus 26,000 grams of methylene chloride."[110]

On the morning of April 19, Reno and other Justice Department and FBI officials were in SIOC as the tank and CS gas assault began. Coulson reports that Reno, Clarke, Potts, and "a few other big shots" sat in the "small command center" in SIOC. Coulson was in SIOC's "big room."[111] When Jamar was queried at subsequent congressional hearings whether he alone directed the April 19 operation at Mount Carmel, he replied that during the assault an open telephone line was maintained with the command post—SIOC—in Washington. When he was asked who was on the other end of the telephone line, Jamar replied, "I believe the Attorney General was there for a period of time. Floyd Clarke, Larry Potts, I think the Director, there was a staff as well."[112]

The WACMUR April 19 log records the HRT notation at 6:04 A.M. that a sniper-observer reported, "Compromise! Compromise!" when he saw gunfire hitting a CEV as it approached the building. At this point Jamar and Ricks shifted from gradual insertion of CS gas (Plan A) to rapid and total insertion (Plan B), which had been initially advocated by Delta Force commanders. Delta Force officers appear to have been present at Mount Carmel on April 19, though the government documents neither indicate in what capacity they were present nor name the Special Forces troops as being Delta Force. Because their military specialties were classified, these troops wore civilian clothes.[113]

The entries recorded in the April 19 log indicate that officials in SIOC were watching and listening to the assault in real time. In 1999, Lee Hancock reported on FBI memos detailing the presence of closed-circuit cameras around the Branch Davidians' residence. She notes that video recordings were made but never released to attorneys for the Branch Davidians (or to other researchers).[114] If FBI officials in SIOC were viewing and listening to the assault in real time, it can be assumed that the FBI special agents in charge and their associates in Waco were doing so as well. It is clear from the April 19 log entries and from my own listening to the audiotapes that officials in SIOC could hear audio captured by surveillance devices (see below).

Reno had instructed the FBI to stop the assault if the Branch Davidians indicated they wanted to negotiate their surrender. The FBI reported that someone threw the telephone out the front door immediately after Sage called into the building at 5:59 A.M. to inform the Branch Davidians that tanks were going to be inserting gas but that "this is not an assault," as agents would not be entering the building. Jamar gave congressional testimony supporting the claim that the telephone was thrown out immediately after Sage spoke with Steve Schneider.[115] The April 19 log does not record that the telephone was thrown out the door. The log indicates that negotiators began calling the Branch Davidians at 6:12 A.M. They continued calling throughout the assault, but no one picked up.

The April 19 log records that at 9:10 A.M. an HRT sniper-observer reported a banner hanging from a window that read, "We want our phone fixed." At 9:11 A.M. Sage said on the loudspeaker that because of gunfire coming from the Branch Davidians, the agents could not fix the phone line. At 9:35 A.M. Sage announced that one unarmed Branch Davidian could go outside to pick up the telephone "you discarded earlier." A bug, apparently located just inside the front door in the foyer, recorded Steve Schneider telling Pablo Cohen to go outside and show the agents that the telephone line was broken. Sage announced that the sole purpose of restoring telephone contact was to arrange for their "orderly exit." At 9:38 A.M. the log records Steve's continued conversation with Pablo in the doorway directing him to show the agents the telephone line was broken. At 9:42 A.M. a bug recorded Sage announcing, "We understand the line is broken." At 9:44 A.M. the bug captured audio of Schneider at the front door telling Graeme Craddock to go outside to see what he could do to get the telephone line fixed. The surveillance device recorded Schneider as saying they wanted to get the phone line repaired so they could tell the agents about Koresh's progress the previous evening on his Seven Seals manuscript.[116] The person monitoring the surveillance device logged that Schneider said, "The manuscript is almost complete" and "I'm going upstairs with David."

At 9:45 A.M. SIOC logged that a man came outside and signaled that the phone line was cut. A sniper-observer reported at 9:47 A.M. that a White male wearing glasses and a T-shirt, nicknamed "phone man," came out of the front door, picked up the phone, and moved toward the south corner of the building. At 9:49 A.M. Sage announced that the agents were trying to obtain another phone to give them. At 9:51 A.M. Sage directed Craddock to pull inside as much of the phone line as he could and indicated that they would bring the Branch Davidians another phone. SIOC logged at 9:51 A.M. that "Graham Summers" (Graeme Craddock) was trying to pull the phone back into the compound. At this time SIOC also logged a statement heard over a bug, "David's transcript is almost complete." A sniper-observer recorded at 9:52 A.M. that "phone man" was back inside.

Graeme Craddock subsequently testified that when he went to the foyer at approximately 9:35 A.M., he saw the phone sitting in its usual location. He said that even if it had been thrown out the front door, they had three other telephones he could have connected. The telephone line set up by the FBI to negotiators ran from the phone in the foyer under the front wall of the building and outside, but a tank had pushed in that wall. Craddock tested the line with a spare phone, but the line still did not work. He conjectured that the line outside was damaged. Upon Steve Schneider's instruction, Craddock walked outside to examine the phone line and to signal that the line was cut.[117]

The telephone line was never fixed. The surveillance device then recorded a man praying in a loud voice, in the style of the Psalms, for courage and God's mercy.[118]

At 11:00 A.M. Eastern Standard Time (10:00 A.M. in Waco), Attorney General Reno departed the Hoover Building to travel to Baltimore to deliver an address, leaving Associate Attorney General Hubbell as the

FIGURE 12.3. An FBI-operated tank drives into the building on April 19, 1993, to gas the children and adults inside the concrete vault, at the base of the central tower, which has an open doorway facing the front of the building. Defendant's exhibit in the 2000 civil trial, in possession of Catherine Wessinger.

highest-ranking Justice Department official in SIOC. Before she left, Reno spoke with President Clinton and, according to the Justice Department report, "told him that everything appeared to be going well at Waco." The Justice Department report stresses that only Reno spoke with President Clinton on April 19; however, Hubbell communicated with White House chief of staff Thomas McLarty.[119]

In 1999 retired army colonel Rodney L. Rawlings, the head military liaison present with FBI agents in Waco during the April 19, 1993, assault, told Lee Hancock that within five minutes of Sage's call into the building, he heard audio from surveillance devices indicating that the mothers and small children took shelter in a concrete room next to the kitchen—a former vault—that the Branch Davidians termed "the cooler."[120] Rawlings reported to Hancock that a surveillance device was in the vicinity of the vault, and women and children could be heard "crying, talking and praying."[121]

At 11:31 A.M., a CEV drove through the front of the building and directed gas toward the open doorway of the vault until 11:55 A.M.[122] At 11:54 A.M. SIOC logged, "Inserting gas in white [front] side and subjects via loudspeakers continue to be advised to surrender." At 11:55 A.M. Rogers advised SAC Bob Ricks "that food stuffs at base of tower gassed—occupants fled moments before—white [front] side." At 11:57 A.M. Ricks advised Rogers "to clear area on white side—to allow occupants to exit quickly—safely." The occupants of the vault had not fled but were in fact choking and suffocating from the CS gas. Attorney David T. Hardy reports that autopsies revealed that nine persons in the vault died of asphyxiation before the fire started, including Mayanah Schneider (two years old), Startle Summers (one year old), and Star Koresh (six years old).[123] At some point, either in reaction to the intense stress of the tank assault, in response to the poisonous gas, or as a result of dying in the fire, Aisha Gyarfas (seventeen years old) and Nicole Gent (twenty-four years old) gave birth to their babies, who died with them.

After the fire, FBI agents said that the children in the vault, which the agents called "the bunker," were gassed to prompt their mothers to pick them up and run out of the building. Retired colonel Applegate wrote in his unpublished report: "It is reasonable to assume that individuals in the Waco building were subjected to such CS gas concentrations, that they were incapacitated to the point where they were physically unable to exit the gassed areas."[124]

At 12:01 P.M. a bug recorded Byron Sage announcing over the loudspeaker: "David, we are facilitating your leaving the compound by enlarging the door. David, you have had your fifteen minutes of fame!" Continuing to announce that people should come out, Sage again addressed David: "You're the person that put those people in that condition. Vernon is no longer the messiah. Leave the building now."

Retired colonel Rawlings told Hancock in 1999 that shortly after the children and mothers were gassed, he heard Koresh say words to the effect, "'OK. Our time is now. It's time to put the children away,' or 'to sleep,' or some such words," and he gave the order to light the fires. Rawlings reported that he heard Koresh say to light the fires, then heard him rescind the order, and then heard him give the order again.[125] This account is similar to that of Branch Davidian survivor Graeme Craddock, but in Craddock's version Koresh was not the one speaking. Craddock said he heard Mark Wendel, who was upstairs, shout, "Light the fire." Pablo Cohen, in the chapel, then shouted, "Wait. Wait. Find out." Craddock reported that a conversation then occurred between Wendel on the second floor and Cohen below on the first floor, during which Craddock heard the command, "Don't light the fire."[126]

After spraying CS gas toward the vault, the CEV moved to the front corner of the south end of the building to drive its boom into the second-floor window and release gas. When the tank backed out of this area, a fire was seen in the window at 12:09 P.M. Within minutes, fires in three other areas of the building were visible to Forward Looking Infrared (FLIR) footage being shot from a Nightstalker aircraft circling over Mount Carmel.

SIOC logged at 12:11 P.M.: "Fire started at compound appears to have been started by them having torched it." At 12:12 P.M. Byron Sage pleaded over the loudspeakers: "David, don't put those people through this. Don't lose control! David, lead those people out. Bring them out. Lead them to safety. David, we need you to bring the people out. David lead those people out. David, bring them out. Exit the building. David, the time is now!"

According to Rawlings's report to Lee Hancock in 1999, a bug picked up gunshots within the burning building and also recorded Koresh's final exchange with Steve Schneider while they were on the second floor. Koresh told Schneider he "was not ready to die, that God wanted him to continue his work." Schneider told him, "You're not going to get away with this. You will go through with this. Look around you. Look around you at all you've caused." Rawlings said he and FBI agents listening to the bugs then heard more gunshots. After the fire burned the building, the bodies of Koresh and Schneider were found near each other where they had fallen from the second floor. Koresh had been shot once in the center of his forehead. Schneider had killed himself by firing an assault rifle in his mouth.[127]

On August 25, 1993, Bob Ricks described to members of the Tulsa, Oklahoma, Rotary Club essentially the same scenario for the last moments of Koresh and Schneider as reported by Rawlings.[128] This surveillance audiotape has never been produced by the FBI, and this description is not the finalized account given by FBI agents.

Fire trucks were called by the FBI at 12:13 P.M. The trucks arrived at 12:34 P.M., but Jamar held the trucks back until 12:41 P.M. By that time the building had burned down completely.[129] Jamar testified at a congressional hearing that he held the fire trucks back so the firefighters would not be injured by gunfire coming from the Branch Davidians.

As the building burned, nine people escaped the fire, some of them badly burned. One of them was Ruth Riddle, who carried in her pocket a computer disk on which was saved the typed version of Koresh's interpretation of the First Seal of Revelation.[130]

At 12:36 P.M. on April 19 someone in SIOC logged: "5 burned and a lot more out. From white side [front] windows observed individuals lighting fires. People clearly seen lighting fires by FBI personnel in Forward TOC [the house across the road]. Seen with binoculars." It was subsequently proved in the criminal trial that no FBI agent who testified actually

FIGURE 12.4. FBI Hostage Rescue Team operators are visible standing outside the tanks as they watch the building burn down. They are standing on the far side of the unfinished storm shelter on the north end of the building. Defendant's exhibit in the 2000 civil trial, in possession of Catherine Wessinger.

saw anyone inside the building light fires. The statements made by agents who claimed they saw this were disproved under cross-examination.[131]

At 12:59 P.M., with the building burned down completely, the Rear Tactical Operations Center radioed: "Children may be in pit area by buried bus." They radioed again at 1:10 P.M.: "Children in underground bunker—We copy." Danny Coulson describes in his book how Dick Rogers climbed out of the Abrams tank he was in and went to the unfinished storm shelter on the north end of the building, part of which had filled with sewage during the siege. A school bus had been buried by the Branch Davidians to make a tunnel leading from the end of the building's first floor, and they had constructed a concrete tunnel leading from the buried school bus to the storm shelter. Coulson states that Rogers put on his gas mask, took his M16 rifle and ballistic shield, and jumped into the storm shelter, which agents termed the "construction pit," with sixteen HRT operators. They waded through waist-deep dirty water with rats, opened the plywood door to the tunnel, went inside, and opened the door to the buried school bus, hoping the children were in there alive. Inside the bus they took off their gas masks. "The air was cool and fresh. It was coming in from the tunnel mouth, which was well away from the fire. If the children had been in here, they would have survived."[132] Coulson writes, "At that moment, Rogers told me later, the enormity of the tragedy hit him, and he felt a wave of nausea sweep over him. The bus/bunker was the last place the children could be. They were lost. They were lost. He and the other men stood silently in the bus; there was nothing to say. The fire was raging, as hot as a refinery blaze."[133] A total of fifty-three Branch Davidian adults and twenty-three children, including two newborn infants, died in the fire.

A local television camera filming from a location north of the building, separate from other television crews at Satellite City, recorded video showing smoke and flames flaring out of the vault for the rest of the afternoon while agents walked to the doorway and looked in. A tank was parked to block the camera's full view of the vault and the agents' activities in front of it. Flames and white smoke can be seen flaring out of the vault's doorway from time to time.[134]

A sniper-observer radioed at 3:10 P.M.: "Unsub came out of bunker." This was Graeme Craddock, who had taken shelter during the fire in a concrete-block utility building next to the old water tower. The log shows that family members began calling the FBI asking for information about their loved ones. Civilians made death threats against Bob Ricks—the face of the FBI at the press briefings—and against ATF agents guarding the outer checkpoint.

The fire burned the Branch Davidians' flag flying on a flagpole in front of the residence's double front doors. "By the time that fire trucks had chilled the building's ashes, a new and victorious banner was flying in its place—someone had raised the flag of the ATF."[135] Photographs show that there were three flags flying in proper order over the smoldering ashes—the American flag on top, followed by the Texas flag, followed by the ATF flag.[136] Presumably, the ATF agents wanted to commemorate the deaths of their comrades who died on February 28, 1993, but the ATF flag flying had the appearance of signaling a victory over enemies.

After the fire, Reno stated to the press that she was the official who had approved the operation. "The buck stops here."[137] This proved to be an effective way to prevent inquiry about the role of the president and the White House in the decision to carry out the tank and CS gas assault against the Branch Davidians.

CONCLUSIONS

Subsequent to the militarized police response to predominantly African American protesters in Ferguson, Missouri, in 2014, after a policeman shot and killed Michael Brown, news stories highlighted the problem of militarization of American law enforcement. However, this militarization did not happen overnight; it was already well under way in 1993 when ATF and FBI agents launched their assaults against the Branch Davidians. The ATF's attempted no-knock dynamic entry on February 28, 1993, was planned "with military assistance by the U.S. Army Special Forces Rapid Support Unit at Fort Hood in three days of training in close quarters combat exercises."[138] The FBI's HRT operators received training from the Army Special Forces unit then called Delta Force, whose officers helped FBI agents plan the CS gas and tank assault and persuade Attorney General Janet Reno to approve its implementation. Members of Delta Force were present during the April 19, 1993, assault in an unrevealed capacity. The Branch Davidian standoff represents a particularly dramatic and tragic example of a law enforcement trend in the United States that began with the Reagan administration's "war on drugs" and continues to shape police behavior.

Sociologist Stuart A. Wright has argued that law enforcement agents trained in military combat techniques approach policing with a warfare mentality. Law enforcement agents' warfare outlook is encouraged by language such as "war on crime" and "war on drugs" and by a sense that law enforcement agents are besieged by criminals. In 1993 the "warfare narrative" held by some FBI agents, especially those associated with the HRT, combined with the popular "cult narrative" to create a context in which some FBI agents likely saw the Branch Davidians as enemies to be defeated rather than as rational persons who could be persuaded to cooperate without having to repudiate their religious worldview and ultimate concerns.[139] Sociologist Jerome H. Skolnick and criminologist James J. Fyfe have pointed out that police and other law enforcement agents constitute a "tribe" with a distinct culture and written and unwritten rules.[140] When members of their tribe are killed, police officers are more likely to respond with violence against those they perceive as perpetrators.[141]

We should not oversimplify the FBI's approach to the Branch Davidians. Two different FBI strategies were being employed simultaneously in 1993. Jeffrey Jamar and Dick Rogers in Waco, their Delta Force advisors, and Michael Kahoe and Larry Potts in SIOC were working with Floyd Clarke and William Sessions to persuade Attorney General Janet Reno to approve the plan for the tank and CS gas assault. At the same time, other FBI agents were collecting intelligence about the Branch Davidians and their theology and producing psychological analysis of David Koresh. This accounts for the difference between the internal FBI documents warning against launching an assault and the actions carried out by the HRT. The FBI logs indicate that the negotiators continued to try to persuade Koresh and the Branch Davidians to come out and that the FBI had intelligence indicating that Koresh had formulated an exit plan, but the intelligence and analysis passed on to FBI commanders in Waco and officials in SIOC were ignored.

In light of the fact that by March 10 (perhaps as early as March 8) a plan for a CS gas and tank assault was being formulated, why did HRT agents, commanded by Rogers, supported by Jamar, and reporting to SIOC officials, seem to go out of their way to undermine negotiation successes through aggressive actions and psychological warfare tactics? Before the siege started, the Branch Davidians held jobs, went to school, and interacted with residents of Waco and elsewhere. During the siege, FBI agents encapsulated the Branch Davidians, limited their access to outside information, prohibited their contacts with loved ones not present at Mount Carmel, prevented them from speaking to intermediaries, and applied psychological warfare and stress escalation tactics that caused sleep deprivation, exhaustion, and fear—not optimum conditions for the Branch Davidians to be making carefully considered decisions.

In the Senate's Committee on the Judiciary hearings on October 31 and November 1, 1995, several law enforcement experts criticized the FBI's handling of the Branch Davidians and indicated that during the siege FBI agents threw out all the law enforcement principles that they knew would likely have worked to get the Branch Davidians to come out without loss of life. FBI Supervisory Special Agent Kenneth V. Lanning demonstrated to the senators that he had read new religions scholarship and was aware that law enforcement agents should not act on cultural prejudices against "cults." He also pointed out that "some normally skeptical law enforcement officers, accept information disseminated about cults without critically evaluating it or questioning the sources." As Lanning saw things: "It is not the role of any law enforcement agency, including the FBI, to determine or maintain lists of which groups are or are not cults. Instead, it is the role of law enforcement to utilize understanding of group or religious motivation to investigate any such group that violates the law."[142]

Although during the siege Lanning was called by an FBI behavioral scientist and a negotiator in Waco, he was not directed by the FBI to go to Waco and offer his advice to the on-site commanders, nor was he consulted by officials in SIOC. Lanning testified that he would "advise any law enforcement agency dealing with such issues to objectively and continuously assess and evaluate their intelligence, to challenge all sources of information, and to try as much as humanly possible to keep their personal emotions under control and out of the case."[143]

Frank A. Bolz, who developed negotiation strategies for the New York Police Department that were adopted by FBI negotiators, testified that the NYPD would have taken a radically different approach to the Branch Davidians. Bolz indicated that the NYPD would never use tear gas against a barricaded group that included children, who have "small lung capacity." He stated that in a barricaded situation "life is the most important consideration," and dangerous tactics should not be used unnecessarily. Bolz stressed the importance of negotiators and tactical operators being trained together and thereby becoming well acquainted so that when a critical incident occurs, they can work together.[144]

In his testimony to the Committee on the Judiciary, criminologist James J. Fyfe, a former NYPD officer, stated, "Waco did not happen because there were no standards to guide authorities on the day of the ATF raid or on the day of the fire. Waco happened because well-known and well-established arrest, hostage, and barricade protocols were ignored." Fyfe told the senators that a police sniper had recently revealed to him that there are two protocols for dealing with barricaded individuals—one written in policies and the other unwritten but known by law enforcement agents.[145] The "Eastern protocol"—the NYPD approach—is "that police officers should take as much time as possible to negotiate people out of situations and should define success in the absence of bloodshed." The unwritten "Western protocol" was that "police officers should regard negotiations as a means of manipulating people into positions where a tactical resolution could be executed." Fyfe stated, "I am very troubled by that. I don't find anything in written standards that conform to it, but I have seen lots of incidents where that [the Western protocol] seems to have been operative."[146] Fyfe subsequently told Stuart Wright that the Western protocol appeared "to derive from the training of SWAT team members of the Los Angeles Police Department (LAPD)."[147]

Members of Congress involved in the 1995 hearings did not pursue lines of inquiry that might have indicated criminal wrongdoing on the part of FBI agents. Instead, Democrats in particular, concerned to defend the administration of President Bill Clinton, promoted the "cult essentialism" narrative that blamed the deaths entirely on David Koresh.[148] The Committee on the Judiciary heard testimony that in 1994 the FBI had formed the Critical Incident Response Group (CIRG) headed by a special agent in charge to whom the HRT commander and the chief negotiator reported during a critical incident, with the aim of putting the negotiation and tactical teams on equal footing. Gary Noesner was the first chief negotiator in the newly created CIRG, and he was able to implement creative negotiation techniques to resolve peacefully the eighty-one-day standoff with the Montana Freemen in 1996.[149]

In this chapter and elsewhere,[150] I have cited statements and testimony that appear to indicate that David Koresh, after the children and mothers were gassed, issued an order to set fires. The evidence, however, is more complicated than that. Stuart Wright notes that items collected from Mount Carmel after the fire and put into a storage locker were discovered in 1999 to include mislabeled devices that could ignite fires, including pyrotechnic percussion grenades and other projectiles.[151] This evidence was not made available for consideration in the criminal trial in 1994, in which the jury exonerated Branch Davidian defendants of conspiracy to murder federal agents but convicted some of them on other charges. Counteracting the jury's verdicts, the judge subsequently pronounced five Branch Davidians guilty of conspiracy to murder federal agents and sentenced each of them to forty years in prison. Four other Branch Davidians were respectively sentenced to twenty years, fifteen years, five years, and three years. As a result of an appeal to the Supreme Court, in 2000 the sentences of six of the convicted Branch Davidians with the lengthiest sentences were reduced to fifteen years each.[152]

On August 24, 1999, Lee Hancock reported in the *Dallas Morning News* that after years of FBI testimony claiming no pyrotechnic ferret rounds had been fired toward the Branch Davidian residence on April 19, 1993, Danny Coulson informed her that pyrotechnic ferret rounds had in fact been used.[153] This news story prompted Attorney General Reno to appoint former senator John C. Danforth to investigate the possibility of FBI wrongdoing in relation to the Branch Davidians. The Danforth Final Report, released in 2000, found that the pyrotechnic ferret rounds fired at the tunnel early in the morning of April 19 could not have caused the fire that erupted by 12:09 P.M. in the building. The Danforth Report found no wrongdoing on the part of FBI agents.

The same FBI personnel were on HRT and in SIOC during both the WACMUR case and the Ruby Ridge, Idaho, debacle, which also began with the shooting death of a law enforcement agent. For the most part, the FBI agents in charge of the assault at Mount Carmel went on to live lives of quiet retirement.

The approach of the year 2000 stirred efforts on the part of FBI agents to prevent anticipated violence from being committed by members of millennialist movements, but all that came and went. On September 11, 2001, the FBI's attention was diverted from "cults" to containing radical Islamist terrorism.

In January 2016, when the FBI received criticism from members of the public for its low-key approach to American antigovernment activists occupying the Malheur Wildlife Reserve in Oregon, retired FBI supervisory special agent Steve Moore told a CNN reporter that the FBI had learned from its mistakes with the Branch Davidians. His statement succinctly pointed to interactive factors that resulted in the deaths of seventy-six Branch Davidians on April 19, 1993: "It was a suicide; however, it was provoked by the FBI intervention."[154]

I thank Lee Hancock for sending her materials to me in 2003. The Hancock Collection in the Wittliff Collections, Texas State University, San Marcos, contains many more documents awaiting analysis.

13

The FBI and American Muslims after September 11

MICHAEL BARKUN

The relationship between American Muslims and the federal government after September 11, 2001, was perhaps the most striking example of tension between the government and a major religious group since that with the Church of Jesus Christ of Latter-day Saints in the late nineteenth century. To be sure, there are significant differences. After 9/11, the Islamic community was never held collectively responsible for the actions of their co-religionists. The president made clear that individual Muslims were blameless. Armed forces were never deployed against Muslims or Islamic institutions, as they were against the Mormons. Nonetheless, the Muslim community felt itself under suspicion and surveillance, especially from FBI personnel.

This FBI stance toward Muslims followed a period during which the bureau had had a very different relationship with religious groups. During the 1980s and 1990s, the Federal Bureau of Investigation, to the extent that it was engaged with religion at all, had been preoccupied with new and alternative religious groups, those tiny organizations that most Americans called cults. The central and most violent of these episodes was the fifty-one-day armed standoff between the bureau and the Branch Davidians outside Waco, Texas, in the early spring of 1993 (see chapter 12). The fire that brought the standoff to an end and cost the lives of more than seventy-five people cast a shadow over the FBI for many years and caused significant internal questioning about how the bureau should deal with nonmainstream religious groups. Indeed, the trauma of Waco caused significant changes to the organization and procedures of the FBI in an effort to avoid repeating those events.[1]

This process of reevaluation was brought up short by the attacks of September 11, 2001, which did not come from the domestic religious groups with which the FBI had previously been concerned. They came, of course, from radical Islamists based outside the United States. That required the bureau to undergo another major reorientation in both religious and cultural terms, and to do so in an extremely short time. In addition, new religious groups—the so-called cults—had usually been small and spatially concentrated, but in this instance there was an already large and geographically dispersed Muslim community in the United States. How should they be dealt with?

The post-9/11 interactions between the FBI and American Muslims cannot be approached, however, without examining two other issues: first, the size, composition, and distribution of the American Muslim community at the time of the attacks and in the years following; and, second, the constraints under which FBI investigations were intended to operate.

THE AMERICAN MUSLIM COMMUNITY ON SEPTEMBER 11 AND AFTERWARD

The 9/11 attacks caught American Muslims at a delicate time, as evidenced by the demographic makeup of the community. Assembling such a demographic picture is not easy. For constitutional reasons, the census cannot ask questions about religious affiliation, so official religious statistics do not exist. However, survey research provides reasonable estimates of size and distribution.

In the absence of official statistics, estimates of the Muslim population have fallen across a broad range, between 3 and 9 million, with many clustering between 5 and 7 million. Although media have tended to place the Muslim population at around 7 million, recent adjusted survey estimates have been far lower, generally between 2 and 3 million.[2] A Pew Research Center estimate made in 2007 placed the size at 2.35 million, the figure most scholars now accept.[3]

More important than numbers for the 9/11 events and their consequences is the community's composition. About two-thirds of the Muslim community at the time of the attacks was foreign-born, a consequence of the liberalization of immigration laws in 1965. The largest segment came from the Arab Middle East and North Africa, which accounted for a quarter of all American Muslims and 41 percent of immigrants. South Asians, of whom Pakistanis constitute the largest bloc, account for 16 percent of all Muslims here and a quarter of the immigrants.[4] An additional 20 to 30 percent of Muslims (estimates vary) are African American, either born into the faith or converts. A frequent path into Islam was the Black Muslim movement of Elijah Muhammad, whose theology departed significantly from the Islamic mainstream. However, after his death in 1975, a successor movement led by his son, Warith Deen Muhammad, moved toward Sunni Islam.[5]

In terms of geographical distribution, American Muslims have been relatively widespread. With the exception of some areas, such as Ann Arbor, Michigan, and Southern California, they have not established points of conspicuous concentration. About one-third live in the East, a quarter each in the South and in the Central Great Lakes regions, and almost one-fifth in the West.[6]

As a result of these demographic forces, at the time of the September 11 attacks the Muslim community, though relatively numerous, was not poised to defend itself effectively against either potential general hostility or government surveillance and penetration. Given their very recent foreign origins, most of its members were just beginning to acculturate to the United States and its norms and practices. Most had not had time to put down substantial roots. They had not yet become politically sophisticated or well organized, and their geographical spread reduced their potential political leverage. While they faced some of the same challenges as earlier minority religious groups, such as Jews, Catholics, and Mormons, the combination of geographical dispersion and the need to acquaint themselves with a new political system meant that when 9/11 occurred, they were in a poor position to defend themselves. Had the attacks occurred, say, twenty years later, or had there been mass Muslim immigration twenty years earlier, the community would have been very differently positioned vis-à-vis law enforcement. As it was, although some Muslim defense organizations existed, historical circumstances placed American Muslims in a relatively passive and vulnerable position.

FBI GUIDELINES

Formal restrictions on the conduct of FBI investigations are an indirect consequence of the scandals that eventually forced Richard Nixon from the presidency in 1974. In addition to earlier inquiries concerning the actions of the president and his aides, the Senate Select Committee to Study Governmental Operations with Respect to Intelligence Operations began in 1975 to investigate the conduct of the FBI. The committee—popularly known as the Church Committee, after its chair, Frank Church—revealed disturbing investigative practices, notably the widespread collection of domestic political intelligence for which there was no law enforcement rationale.[7] These revelations raised questions about how the bureau might be prevented from engaging in such activities in the future.

Richard Nixon's successor, Gerald Ford, appointed as his attorney general Edward Levi, a noted legal scholar and former dean of the University of Chicago Law School. By way of responding to concerns about the FBI's activities, Levi in April 1976 issued "Domestic Security Investigation Guidelines," initially termed the "Levi Guidelines." These were the first in a line of attorney general's guidelines issued over several decades by a number of occupants of the office to spell out the limits on FBI investigative procedures. The documents quickly became both longer and more complex, as well as progressively less restrictive of agents' behaviors. To fully inventory the alterations made subsequently by Benjamin Civiletti, William French Smith, Richard Thornburgh, and Janet Reno would require a substantial chapter in itself.[8] Suffice it to say that, over time, the twin and seemingly opposed forces of bureaucratization and administrative loosening had their effects, though in general the guidelines were only loosened a bit at a time. What matters in the present context are the implications of the September 11 attacks for the guidelines.

On May 30, 2002, a little less than nine months after 9/11, Attorney General John Ashcroft announced a new version of the guidelines. He did so in the context of a reorientation of the FBI's mission. The bureau had traditionally been an organization for the apprehension of criminals and the collection of evidence to assist in their prosecution. From now on, however, Ashcroft asserted, the FBI's mission would be changed: "The prevention of terrorist acts became [after September 11] the central goal of the law enforcement and national security mission of the FBI."[9] The ramifications of this change are twofold. First, counterterrorism moved to the center of the FBI's agenda. Second, and even more significant, the organization for the first time in its history was now to prevent actions from taking place rather than to pursue culprits after actions had occurred. An organization that had never been a crime prevention organization was now to make prevention its primary mission. To advance this objective, Ashcroft altered the guidelines "to free field agents . . . from the bureaucratic, organizational, and operational restrictions and structures that hindered them from doing their jobs effectively."[10] This policy might include waiving the guidelines entirely if the situation warranted, as well as loosening the guidelines so that "FBI field agents may enter public places and attend events open to other citizens, unless they are barred from attending by the Constitution or federal law."[11]

The guidelines were relaxed further during the attorney generalship of Michael Mukasey in 2008. The principal areas of loosening related to the commencement and conduct of inquiries, which could now begin more arbitrarily and unfold with less oversight, and for the most part need not meet some single evidentiary standard.[12] A full investigation could be justified by, among other reasons, "international terrorism or other threat to the national security"; "domestic terrorism"; or "furthering political or social goals wholly or in part through activities that involve force or violence and a violation of federal criminal law."[13]

Measuring the actual impact of the guidelines, in whatever iteration, has been problematic. In September 2005, the FBI's inspector general undertook an elaborate examination of the consequences of revised guidelines—in effect, the Ashcroft guidelines—for the organization. The study's most striking conclusion was how difficult it was to actually determine the effect of the changes. The reason was simple: despite an organizational commitment to elaborate training exercises to acquaint personnel with new guidelines, the altered procedures had clearly not penetrated to every level and branch of the bureau. Three years after the Ashcroft changes, the Office of the Inspector General concluded, "our review . . . showed that the FBI did not provide sufficient training, guidance, administrative support, and oversight to ensure implementation of the revised Guidelines."[14] Thus, the difficulty in dealing with the guidelines, regardless of which version one considers, is the gap between the professed requirements and the actual behavior of agents, since it is unclear whether at any given point in time agents are actually aware of what they are and are not permitted to do.

FBI SURVEILLANCE

Evaluating FBI conduct toward American Muslims is extremely difficult, since the bureau's national security activities are particularly secretive. In addition, many of the Muslim community's concerns appear to be based on perceptions of FBI conduct rather than on clearly identifiable actions. And, as already indicated, the expansion of permissible behavior through the loosening of the attorney general's guidelines has not always been a reliable predictor, since the bureau's ability to clearly communicate the guidelines' content to agents has been spotty. The inspector general's report only sampled FBI offices and did make an effort at systematic study. External evidence concerning bureau behavior, on the other hand, has necessarily been based on anecdotal evidence that has been made public—largely the product of incidents and allegations of infiltration, spying, and other forms of penetration at a few mosques. Nonetheless, these examples are significant enough to warrant examination.

The official position of the FBI has been that such situations have not occurred. Thus, in 2008 the bureau's assistant director, John Miller, issued "FBI Response to Allegations of Mosque Surveillance and Monitoring of the Muslim Community," which included the following statement: "The FBI does not monitor the lawful activities of individuals in the United States, nor does the FBI have a surveillance program to monitor the constitutionally protected activities of houses of worship. We do not target or monitor legal activity of Muslim groups anywhere in the nation."[15]

Some activities have not constituted surveillance per se, but have amounted to forms of intelligence gathering that appear to be precursors thereto. For example, in 2003 FBI field supervisors were instructed to determine the number of Muslims and mosques in their areas. As has already been noted, there is no official religious census, and demographic analyses of Muslims have varied considerably. Although an assistant bureau director claimed that the purpose of the count was to protect mosques, since many have been targets of violence, another official, Wilson Lowery Jr., executive assistant director, offered another purpose to congressional staff: such statistics would provide a productivity baseline for measuring a field office's terrorism investigations and intelligence warrants. Ibrahim Hooper of the Council on American-Islamic Relations responded, "This is obviously an indication to FBI field agents that they have to view every mosque and every Muslim as a potential terrorist."[16]

A covert intelligence-gathering effort occurred between 2001 and 2003 that, again, was not conventional surveillance but was closer to it than the "Muslim census" just described. In this case, the FBI monitored more than one hundred Islamic sites in the Washington, D.C., area for radiation, presumably fearing the presence of nuclear weapons or dirty bombs. However, this surveillance was accomplished without physically entering any structures.[17]

Assistant Director Miller's denial becomes even more difficult to accept in light of events in Orange County, California, in 2006 and 2007, as revealed by an Orange County newspaper and the *Washington Post*. Those journalistic accounts were substantially bolstered by court documents that arose out of the affair. What we know is, however, in part conjectural. What is not conjecture is that an individual named Craig Monteilh went to the Islamic Center of Irvine, a large mosque in an area where Muslims were concentrated, and presented himself as eager to convert to Islam. At the time, he had a clear and documented relationship with the FBI, most probably as an informant. What the FBI did not know was that Monteilh was a convicted forger who, just before his employment by the bureau, had bilked two women out of substantial sums of money, behavior for which he was later convicted.[18]

Monteilh spent ten months at the Islamic Center, as well as at other nearby Muslim sites. He claimed that during this time, at the request of his FBI handlers, he recorded conversations, planted surveillance devices, and noted the religious characteristics of members at several mosques. These activities were in connection with a program dubbed Operation Flex. He was apparently paid $177,000 for his services. In the spring of 2007, he began to talk openly at the Islamic Center about the duty of Muslims to use violence as well as about his own ability to access weapons. Mosque leaders were sufficiently upset by these statements to notify the FBI and to seek and obtain a restraining order barring Monteilh from the center. At this point, in June 2007, his alleged surveillance activities ended.[19]

In 2011, individuals associated with the mosque brought suit against the FBI and a number of its officials, alleging violations of the First, Fourth, and Fifth Amendments and of several federal statutes. Their complaint detailed a number of acts of surveillance that Monteilh allegedly performed on the FBI's behalf. Appended to their complaint was documentary evidence of a nondisclosure form with the FBI that Monteilh had signed. In August 2011, however, Attorney General Eric Holder filed a declaration invoking the state secrets privilege. He claimed that revealing information concerning Operation Flex would damage national security interests.[20] As a result, the district court dismissed claims against the bureau but allowed the suit to go forward against individual FBI personnel.

This was not the end of Craig Monteilh's legal difficulties. In December 2007, at the end of his mosque adventures but before the suit was filed, he was arrested in connection with the con game he had played just before the FBI hired him. That resulted in sixteen months of jail time unconnected with whatever he might have done for the bureau. The unresolved FBI lawsuit resulted in the general belief that Monteilh's account of his surveillance activities were correct, since there was no other explanation for the time he had spent as a "Muslim convert." What remains of the case against FBI agents and their supervisors, *Fazaga v. FBI,* was argued before the Ninth Circuit Court of Appeals on December 7, 2015.[21]

There is no easy way of knowing whether there have been additional instances of similar surveillance or, if so, how many. Assuming there is some truth to Monteilh's account—and Holder's invocation of the state secrets privilege is a strong indication that there is—the incident is unlikely to have been an outlier.

FBI OUTREACH PROGRAMS

As the same time that the FBI was using covert means to secure information from the Muslim community, the bureau embarked on a program of community outreach. The community outreach efforts were intended not only to generate goodwill among Muslims but also to stimulate a flow of intelligence from Muslims about individuals who might pose threats to security and order. Unfortunately, this campaign was destined for significant rough spots, in part because of the difficulties inherent in a government bureaucracy suddenly having to interact with a religious community it knew little about, and in part because of the covert intelligence efforts for which outreach was supposed to provide compensation.

While community outreach efforts faced problems such as underfunding, the major difficulty resulted from the release of documents suggesting that the campaign had ulterior motives. Documents obtained from the FBI by the Asian Law Caucus and the American Civil Liberties Union (ACLU) under the Freedom of Information Act (FOIA) show that the bureau appeared to engage the Muslim community in order to do more than build goodwill and mutual understanding. The documents that have been released cover only Northern California and the period from 2004 to 2008. However, they strongly suggest that at least some of the outreach programs were either intended for or understood to be covers for intelligence gathering.

The information secured at mosque meetings seems to have been entirely innocuous: names, complaints about delays individuals encountered during air travel, ethnicity, purchase of a new mosque, and so on.

Nonetheless, after the events at which agents were present, reports were written up as "positive intelligence" designated "secret." At least some of the reports were sent to other organizations, presumably in law enforcement, notwithstanding the fairly innocent character of the contents. "As a result," the ACLU concluded, "the [FBI] wrongly and unfairly cast a cloud of suspicion over innocent groups and individuals based on their religious beliefs and associations, and placed them at risk of greater law enforcement scrutiny as potential national security threats." When released under FOIA, the outreach reports were heavily redacted.[22]

After the release of the ACLU's report and the accompanying FBI materials, the Muslim community reacted, unsurprisingly, with hostility to further outreach efforts—this despite the plea of FBI assistant director Michael Kortan that "since that time [presumably 2004 to 2008], the FBI has formalized its community relations program to emphasize a greater distinction between outreach and operational activities."[23] The ACLU–Asian Law Caucus materials also cast a shadow over the White House Summit on Countering Violent Extremism in 2014, which advocated the engagement of religious communities to counter radicalization. This initiative rang hollow to many Muslims in light of experiences with the FBI in previous years.[24]

A PAINFUL RELATIONSHIP

As one looks back on the relationship between the FBI and the American Muslim community since September 11, the overwhelming impression is of misunderstanding. In part, this was a function of the cultural gap between the bureau and the community. The bureau's personnel are overwhelmingly Christian and, given the late arrival of most Muslims in the United States, have little depth of experience with Islam, despite the presence of FBI liaison offices in numerous Muslim-majority countries. In addition, the traumatic nature of the 9/11 attacks resulted in major changes in the FBI: the reorientation of resources away from traditional crimes toward counterterrorism, the rapid hiring of many new analysts and others to staff "the war on terror," and the execution of Attorney General Ashcroft's mandate that the bureau now concentrate on prevention. All of these changes made it impossible for FBI personnel to gradually educate themselves about Islam or for the FBI to hire large numbers of people with the requisite knowledge, since the bureau was competing with numerous other federal agencies seeking the same kind of expertise.

FOIA requests have revealed substantial FBI training materials that contained either false statements about Islam or caricatures of its beliefs and practices. At a February 8, 2012, meeting with representatives of Islamic organizations, FBI director Robert Mueller revealed that the bureau had "purged" 876 pages and 392 presentations that were deemed offensive.[25] Although he did not specify the time during which this material was used, the fact that he made the statement at a meeting eleven years after the 9/11 attacks suggests that it was employed for several years after 2001. Speaking to the larger issue, Abed Ayoub, the legal director of the American-Arab Anti-discrimination Committee, has asked, "how did this material get in there in the first place? Do you not have rules or guidelines that will prevent this from happening?"[26] As late as 2014, in response to a question from the *Guardian* newspaper, the White House responded that "it has asked the intelligence community to 'review their training and policy materials for racial and religious bias.'"[27]

In its haste to implement Attorney General Ashcroft's mandates, the FBI needed to rapidly give agents at least a general impression of Islam. That apparently resulted in the production of training materials much of which was biased and inaccurate, based less on a clear understanding of Islam than on popular beliefs about it. As revealed through FOIA requests and the FBI's own admission, some of these materials seem to have been in use at least as late as 2012, if not later. They undoubtedly reinforced those negative stereotypes about Muslims that agents already held, since such stereotypes infused American society in the days after September 11. Given the slight acquaintance most Americans have had with Muslims and Muslim beliefs and practices, their ideas about Islam have in general been based on a combination of half-truths, rumor, and speculation.

The causal relationship between the training materials and FBI behavior is, however, difficult to trace with any assurance. One can at best only speculate. However, it seems reasonable that training materials that portrayed Islam as a religion inherently prone to violence would lead agents to consider mosques legitimate investigative targets, regardless of official statements to the contrary.

THE SAN BERNARDINO ATTACK

The attack at the office Christmas party of the San Bernardino County Department of Public Health on December 2, 2015, killed fourteen people and injured twenty-two. The shooters were a department employee and his wife. Syed Rizwan Farook was a longtime resident of Southern California, born to Pakistani parents and raised in nearby Riverside. The year before the shooting he married Tashfeen Malik, a Pakistani raised in Saudi Arabia and educated in Pakistan. Farook was a highly observant Muslim who originally prayed in the large and moderate Islamic Center of Riverside, but after his marriage he moved to the more obscure Dar Al Uloom Al Islamiyah mosque.[28] As mentioned earlier, Southern California is one of the few places in the country with a concentrated Muslim population, and San Bernardino is an ethnically mixed community, so it is unlikely that the couple would have attracted much attention.

Two aspects of the attack are particularly noteworthy. First, it is clear that it was unplanned. On the one hand, strong circumstantial and other evidence suggest that Farook and Malik were planning some kind of large-scale attack. However, it is unlikely that the attack on the Christmas party was the one they had been planning, since they possessed pipe bombs and substantial amounts of ammunition that they did not use on December 2. They had discussed major targets in the past. But this was neither a symbolic nor an infrastructural target. Instead, they targeted a room full of people who knew Farook, and they had no clear escape plan.[29] Second, their motive for choosing this time and place remains unclear. Had something occurred that set Farook off? Perhaps the presence of Christmas decorations? Or his testy interactions with an end-time believer at work?[30] The event bears the classic stamp of a lone-wolf attack in which accumulated slights, insults, and frustrations suddenly give way to explosive rage.

Necessarily, local law enforcement made the immediate response to the attack. However, two days later FBI director James Comey announced that "this is now a federal terrorism investigation, led by the FBI." He based his decision on "indications of radicalization by the killers and of the potential inspiration by foreign terrorist organizations."[31] This determination involved the FBI in reconstructions of the couple's lives, backgrounds, and associations and necessarily impinged on the local Muslim community. People they spoke with, visited, or met at the mosque were all subject to possible questioning.[32]

The attack was, of course, a traumatic event for the Muslim community, not only because of its severity but because of its rarity. While individuals have been apprehended seeking to join ISIS or preparing to mount an attack, actual attacks by radical Muslims on American soil since September 11 have been exceedingly uncommon. The Southern

California Muslim community responded with a stream of public statements expressing shock and sympathy. Thus, from the Islamic Shura Council of Southern California came a condemnation of "the senseless violence" and an extension of "our sympathies and prayers to those who were senselessly killed." The executive director of the Los Angeles Council on American Islamic Relations asserted, "The Islamic community stands shoulder to shoulder with our fellow Americans in repudiating any twisted mindset that would claim to justify such sickening acts of violence." The Islamic Center of Redlands offered its "deepest condolences to those affected by this tragedy" and said it stood "with our fellow Americans in this difficult time."[33] There was little more that Muslims could do in so painful a situation.

CONCLUSION

The unpleasant and conflictual aspects of the relationship between the Bureau and the Muslim community will, hopefully, diminish with time, particularly in the absence of any further religiously based terrorism on American soil. Time will have an ameliorating effect on both sides: The FBI is, we may hope, in the process of acquiring a more accurate picture of Islam, replacing the cruder ideas that cropped up in prior years. Muslims, for their part, as they become more acculturated, prosperous, and politically sophisticated, will assert their rights more often and more strongly. These predictions, however, must come with an important caveat, and that is that terrorism will gradually recede from American political consciousness as a central problem, a condition as dependent on foreign developments as it is on domestic ones. Any long-term connection between religion and law enforcement would raise troubling and unpleasant implications for the First Amendment, and for that reason a separation between them should be effected at the earliest practical time.

14

Policing Kashmiri Brooklyn

JUNAID RANA

In the early morning hours of July 19, 2011, Syed Ghulam Nabi Fai was arrested by the Federal Bureau of Investigation at his home in Fairfax, Virginia, under the suspicion of having raised funds connected to terrorism and terrorist organizations. The Fai family live in a comfortable suburb of the greater Washington, D.C., metropolitan area, lush with the trees and other greenery that can surprise newcomers. Their home is at the end of a cul-de-sac that rises slightly above the connecting street, making it easy to observe incoming traffic. Fai and his wife took great pride in the carefully manicured garden surrounding their home; the red brick façade would have contrasted sharply with the white flowers typically in bloom at that time of summer. Fai recalled that his children noticed a suspicious sedan parked at the stop sign of the adjoining street the previous day. As they discussed what this could mean, they started to remember the same car parked there throughout the previous week. It was a nondescript car typical of undercover police, though it might also have simply been a new car in the neighborhood. What was unusual was that it was perfectly positioned to monitor their activities. Moreover, what bothered Fai was that the car was parked illegally in the no-parking zone next to the stop sign. Fai resolved not to worry about it and to merely acknowledge that someone might be watching. The night before Fai's arrest, he was out with friends having dinner when one of his family members called the police to report the car. The next morning Fai was arrested.[1]

The FBI searched Fai's home after his arrest. This was not the first time the FBI entered his home. Agents had made numerous visits for interviews. The raid came a month and a half after the targeted assassination of Osama bin Laden in Pakistan and after a series of political and intelligence fiascoes in Pakistan had rattled diplomatic relations with the United States. According to court documents, Fai had been under investigation since 2005 after an informant looking for a reduced jail sentence began detailing connections to the ISI, or Inter-Services Intelligence directorate, the powerful spy agency of the government of Pakistan. Tensions had been high in the on-again, off-again relationship between the United States and Pakistan. Prior to Fai's arrest in 2011, the Obama administration, led by Secretary of State Hillary Clinton, had been threatening to reduce U.S. aid in a standoff over the handling of the frontline of the U.S. War on Terror by the Pakistani military. The Obama administration's goal was to create U.S. governmental oversight for administering U.S. civilian aid and military support in Pakistan, a policy shift from the previous administration's approach, which consisted of flushing dollars into the Pakistani military and intelligence apparatus as a frontline state in the War on Terror.[2] Many in the Obama administration sought to curtail the role of the Pakistani military, which was functioning not only as a U.S. proxy for its terror wars but also as an intelligence apparatus with its own interests in regional affairs. One of those interests—specifically, Kashmir—was at odds with the U.S. war in Afghanistan. In the United States, the Kashmiri struggle for independence has little traction in the public square—in contrast to the issue of Palestine, for example—but the Pakistani government had long used Kashmir as a regional ploy against perennial foe India. Although set in a Brooklyn neighborhood, the Fai case reflected the complex political conflict surrounding Kashmir and the shifting character of the War on Terror.

As the Indian novelist and essayist Pankaj Mishra has written, "Kashmir now hosts the biggest, bloodiest and most obscure military occupation in the world."[3] Often understood in the U.S. media through the lens and language of Palestine, Kashmir has easily been wrapped into the language of the global War on Terror that demonizes Muslims and has created an industry of policing and militarism. In the tale of Pakistani Brooklyn, or more precisely Kashmiri Brooklyn, that I am telling here, the politics of Kashmir and the larger political issues of South Asia that pit India against Pakistan have been caught up in a narrative of preventing terrorism. Kashmiri Brooklyn is a case study in how this narrative can play out at the local level.

Islam has become a convenient excuse for surveillance and secret investigations in the War on Terror that are often far afield from terrorist prevention. In the Fai case, the Kashmiri struggle for self-determination and liberation was a target of law enforcement interest precisely because Kashmir had been rendered part of the "Muslim problem," and hence one that in a post-9/11 context is assumed to have an association with terrorism. There is also an insidious process of racialization at work.[4] Race is often associated with essentializing culture and bodily difference, and Muslims have been subject to that kind of phenotypical essentialization and are often conflated in American imagination with Arabs. The term *terrorist* is often shorthand for the foregone conclusion of the involvement of Muslims or, in the language of U.S. foreign policy analysts, "jihadi culture." What further complicates this process is that Islam, of course, also has a religious dimension. Thus race, religion, and now terrorism have all been conflated in a way that often equates, for example, all Arabs with Muslims and all Muslims with Arabs, despite the fact that a majority of Arabs in the United States are Christian.[5]

Following the arguments of Edward W. Said in order to understand this racism in relationship to imperialism,[6] I argue that the Fai case demonstrates a form of racial statecraft that frames local actors within a racialized-religious schema of international affairs and political détente.[7] In this version of racial statecraft Islam and Muslims have become a primary focus of suspicion, in the way that communism functioned during the Cold War. Such state rhetoric is often based in popular culture and regimes of racialization that have formative implications in social life and the general approach to the legal-juridical framing of Muslims.[8] The case of Kashmiri liberation and the interpretation of terrorism become the pretext for U.S.-based law enforcement policy and policing once the notion of Muslims and Islam enters the narrative. Similarly, such a narrative framing is also attached to the contemporary political understanding of the term *radical,* not as a position of left-wing opposition but as a caricature of terrorist ideology and as an effective shorthand for marking Muslims as terrorists (for example, "radical Islam").[9]

Within this context, the mosque has come to be perceived in the U.S. public sphere as emblematic of the "dangerous" and "threatening" menace of a militant Islam, despite state protections of the freedom of religion. The mosque as imagined in this period is not just a place of worship but a hive for political dissent, militancy, and terrorism.[10] Mosques have subsequently become key points of targeted surveillance and intervention through both formal and informal means such as actual police presence and the widespread use of informants and undercover agents. The depiction of Islam as a threat in need of containment is parallel to the FBI's COINTELPRO (Counterintelligence Program), which targeted radical militants and political dissenters in the 1950s and 1960s, though religion now plays a different role in the way this threat is conceived. Whereas the enemy during the Cold War was the godless communist, government suspicion is now focused on a fanatical Islam. In the example I describe in this essay, the struggle for Kashmiri liberation has been framed within this larger narrative of radical Muslim subversion, a narrative fed by the fact that Fai was often drumming up support for his cause in mosques, among other places, such as restaurants and private homes, where Pakistanis and Kashmiris could be found.

As I discuss later in this essay, much of the investigation against Fai began with the testimony of a confidential witness seeking a reduced sentence for other crimes. Exploiting criminality to produce witnesses in this way is an oft-used tactic in the War on Terror, as is the use of such a tactic to recruit informants, as Trevor Aaronson has documented.[11] From the perspective of U.S. statecraft, Pakistan is a frontline state in the War on Terror that functions as a launching pad for attacks that perpetuate the war in Afghanistan. As a Muslim country, it is conceived as both a problem nuclear state on the verge of failure and a source of potential terrorism. Depicted in this way, Pakistan (like communism) must be contained. Such a logic has been used as a pretext for controlling political debate and dissent, and it lies behind the Fai case. This dynamic focused the FBI's attention on Fai's potential connections to known and unknown terrorist organizations in the Muslim world, ties putatively driven by a dangerous ideology running counter to American interest. Although this rationale imagines Pakistan to be suffused with terrorists and terrorist plots associated with Islam, ironically, Fai adamantly cast the cause of Kashmir as a secular struggle for self-determination.

In the early days of the Obama administration and the stewardship of Hillary Clinton as secretary of state, it became common to see the Pakistani state as divided between a civilian government and the dark intrigues of a rogue intelligence service. Democratic governance in Pakistan has not been stable. Since 1947, and for nearly half of the country's existence, the country has been under direct military dictatorship, and the struggle between democracy and the military is especially complex when it comes to Pakistan's borders and its relationship with its neighbors. The efforts of Ghulam Nabi Fai on behalf of Kashmiri liberation reflected this precarious political terrain. For Fai, the fight for Kashmiri self-determination is a continuation of an unresolved struggle that began with the partition in 1947 that created India and Pakistan. The narrative of colonial and postcolonial occupation is certainly a complex one given that the Indian state denies any culpability in what it considers Pakistani meddling and instigation. In response to this context, Fai began the Kashmiri American Council (KAC), also known as the Kashmir Center, in 1990 as a nonprofit organization to spread information about Kashmiri self-determination and to advocate for Kashmiri independence and self-determination.

A year prior to his arrest, on June, 29, 2010, Fai was pulled over by the New York Police Department (NYPD) for reasons that remain unclear. The NYPD may have been operating on a tip from the FBI and clearly was at least collaborating in this investigation. This was a period of widespread use of the stop-and-frisk policy widely criticized as a way of criminalizing black youth, and the NYPD also used it as a supposed antiterror measure to pull over racially profiled drivers, often cabs and livery vehicles with "Muslim-looking" drivers. The police officers searched Fai's vehicle and discovered $35,000 in cash. When initially questioned, Fai claimed that the money was a donation. By July 8, when he spoke to the FBI, as attested to in an affidavit, he explained the donation in more detail. Fai reported that he had just come from a Brooklyn mosque, the Makki Masjid of Midwood, where he received the money as a cash donation from the imam, Hafiz Mohammad Sabir, to his organization, the Kashmiri American Council. According to FBI phone surveillance, however, Fai had called an unnamed donor, and the two of them, acting on the advice of Zaheer Ahmad, a U.S. citizen who was one of the founders of the KAC and who ran a hospital in Pakistan, decided to claim that the money was from a mosque in Brooklyn headed by Sabir.[12] Confusion over the money's source lay at the heart of the case—pitting Sabir and Fai against each other.

The cash found in the car was pivotal to the material case against Fai, and it provided insight into the level of surveillance and the broad net of activities related to terror prevention that connect law enforcement agencies including the FBI, the NYPD, and the CIA. In this instance, contrary to the oft-repeated claim that U.S. intelligence and law enforcement agencies are unable to work with one another, the case demonstrated an extraordinary level of collaboration and structured coordination between the NYPD and the FBI in the Brooklyn neighborhood of Little Pakistan that must have been in place well before to the Fai case.

The Pakistani community of Brooklyn, while appearing to be a minor character in the Fai case, is notable for its demographic concentration of self-identified Kashmiris and for a politics often perceived as aligned with Pakistan's policy in Kashmir. It was already under surveillance by the NYPD as a "place of interest," a suspected hub of terrorist activity.[13]

In support of the FBI's case, the affidavit contends that the money found in Fai's car in Brooklyn and the constant stream of cash into his organization merely appeared to be from conventional donors but actually originated with operatives of the ISI. In the United States, such donations are considered an illegal transaction if the receiving organization has not properly registered for such donations. The larger and more damning claim, which remained largely unsubstantiated, was that Fai's organization was connected to a known terrorist organization, Lashkar-e-Taiba (LeT), which the ISI putatively uses in its proxy war with India in the Kashmir Valley.[14] Whether there are actually ties between the LeT and ISI is unclear. Some news media sporadically reported such links, as did various Internet sites. Although it did not appear in court documents, the claim linking Fai to the LeT independent of the ISI appeared in occasional news reports. The connection was made largely on Internet media sites in what appears to be some sort of campaign based on reports from supposedly independent security sites whose existence is, incidentally, unproven. Despite the allure of this terrorist intrigue, the media and general public in the United States did not take the bait and remained largely uninterested in this story, perhaps signaling a lack of knowledge about Kashmir altogether.

In a case that involves a maze of other details about an international scandal, the allegation of a connection to the LeT is curious both for its lack of evidence and for the rhetoric it seeks to mobilize. The claim was always circumstantial. Essentially, Fai's connection to the ISI, which is after all a government agency of Pakistan, was supposed to mean that he was connected to a terrorist organization, the LeT, that is sometimes used by this intelligence outfit. As I explain later in this essay, the LeT was somewhat unfamiliar to the U.S. public and was stigmatized by insinuations of a sinister connection to Al-Qaeda and Osama bin Laden. Much of the information on which this suspicion is based is provided by witnesses who seem unreliable and have scores to settle. The facts of the actual connections and the proof of existing illegal activity, however, were secondary in a case in which the specter of terrorism and a money trail were assumed sufficient to render Fai guilty in the U.S. court of public opinion.

Between 2010 and 2011, diplomatic relations between Pakistan and the United States worsened in the face of the Raymond Davis incident, which escalated rapidly. In early 2011, Davis was working as a subcontracted spy for the CIA when he fatally shot two Pakistanis during a gunfight in a crowded thoroughfare of Lahore, one of Pakistan's major cities. At the time, Davis was investigating the activities of the LeT. Soon thereafter, a driver from the U.S. consulate struck and killed a third Pakistani man with his vehicle while attempting to extract Davis from the scene, resulting in a hit-and-run. By March of that same year, Davis returned to the United States after the U.S. government paid an undisclosed amount (in the millions of dollars) in blood money to the bereaved families, as required under Pakistan's use of Islamic law. In May, U.S. military operatives, led by the CIA and the Navy Seals, assassinated Osama bin Laden in the hill town of Abbottabad. The immediate fallout led to allegations of a breach of Pakistani sovereignty and the counter-claims by the United States that the Pakistani military and security apparatus, namely the ISI, had been shielding Osama bin Laden. Two months later, Fai was arrested.

Throughout this period of strained relations between the two countries, the FBI was clearly investigating Fai, and he voluntarily reported to the bureau when summoned for interviews. As his close confidants have reported, and as Fai himself claims, he thought he was under the protection of the CIA, and he continued to raise funds publicly and to lobby for the Kashmir cause.[15] It is not entirely clear why he was subsequently exposed when he continued to run this operation. In this larger context, Fai seems to have been the counterweight to the row created by the Davis and bin Laden affairs in Pakistan. Fai had many important political allies in Washington and an apparently growing influence among a certain sector of the Republican Party. Among his greatest Republican supporters were Representatives Dan Burton of Indiana (now retired) and Joe Pitts of Pennsylvania, who helped Fai start a congressional forum on Kashmir in 2002.

On the day of Fai's arrest, U.S. attorney Neil MacBride of the Eastern District of Virginia was quoted in a *ProPublica* article as saying: "Mr. Fai is accused of a decades-long scheme with one purpose—to hide Pakistan's involvement behind his efforts to influence the U.S. government's position on Kashmir. . . . His handlers in Pakistan allegedly funneled millions through the Kashmir Center to contribute to American elected officials, to fund high-profile conferences, and to pay for other efforts that promoted the Kashmiri cause to decision-makers in

Washington."[16] The same article also refers to Indian news reports from March 2010 that claimed Fai was a "Pakistan Agent." Following these allegations, the U.S. Justice Department asked Fai whether the claim was true and, if so, to register KAC as a foreign agent. Fai denied working on behalf of the Pakistani government, hence his arrest under the single complaint of conspiracy for failing to register as a foreign agent. On the face of it, given the evidence from the FBI affidavit that reported information from electronic and physical surveillance and witness testimony, it appears that Fai was certainly guilty—at least, of having contact with the government of Pakistan and working on its behalf. As the case proceeded, what emerged was a selective process that relied on antiterror enforcement rationales and competing national and personal stakes. The case depended entirely on portraying the ISI as an advocate of terrorism—of course, the rogue kind rather than the explicitly state-sanctioned version in which the government of Pakistan was complicit.

Fai's accomplice in this crime was Zaheer Ahmad, the founder of the Shifa International Hospital in Islamabad. Ahmad was accused of meeting with Osama bin Laden along with a Pakistani nuclear scientist, who died suddenly from a brain hemorrhage a few months after Fai was arrested.[17] This visit implied that he was providing medical services to bin Laden at the behest of the ISI, or at least through some cover provided by the Pakistani military in collaboration with the ISI. Ahmad's sudden death left much of this issue unresolved, and the allegations remained unproven. More to the point, however, is whether Fai was pursued in this case for any reason related, as was claimed, to purported terrorist activities and connections, or whether this case was caught up in the web of the broader diplomatic relations between Pakistan and the United States, as I argue. While all sorts of possibilities can emerge from this question, the Fai case spotlights the systematic use of antiterror policing and the intelligence apparatus at the disposal of U.S. law enforcement and spying agencies.

Despite the intrigue and twisting plot of the Fai case, if one removes the embedded assumptions about the players involved and the various tropes of terrorism employed to make the case, it is not exactly clear that Fai did anything different than what numerous D.C.-based lobbyists do all the time. His simple mistake was that he did not consider registering as a foreign agent—the sole charge to which he eventually pleaded guilty. The bolder implication of this accusation is that Fai and Ahmad were acting on behalf of the Pakistani government to influence the U.S. position on Kashmir—in a word, spying. This is another way of saying that

Fai was a stooge of the ISI who, if he was taking its money, did exactly what the ISI told him to do. There is no evidence of such activity except that money was given to Fai by the government of Pakistan to promote the cause of the Kashmiri struggle.[18] Although he was the fall guy in what seemed a flimsy case, despite the alluring construction of a potential terrorist threat, the real target was the ISI, Pakistan's intelligence service. Often imagined as a rogue proxy that can mobilize militant forces, including portions of the Pakistani army, the ISI as an arm of the Pakistani government represents a larger geopolitical tug of war with the United States. In the case of Fai, the model of FBI entrapment of so-called homegrown terrorists operated in reverse.[19] Rather than using an FBI mole to suggest terrorism, complicity with Pakistani intelligence was implied—where else could this money trail lead, so the thinking went?

The case, however, does not start precisely with a money trail. Rather, it starts with "CW-1," a confidential witness who testified in exchange for reduced jail time. The timing of the fallout with the Pakistani government and the ISI, following the targeted assassination of Osama bin Laden, also influenced the case. That the ISI was a target of the U.S. State Department's opprobrium was no secret. For decades, in fact, the CIA collaborated with the Pakistani military and the ISI, but with the War on Terror taking a different tack, the agency's relationship became complicated. In the initial FBI affidavit, it was Sarah Linden, a member of the counterterrorism division, who reported on the details of the case against Fai. Linden had interviewed Fai on numerous occasions and had been monitoring all of his communications. Hence, the pursuit of Fai was not just a minor infraction or bureaucratic mistake but was instead imagined as a terrorism case that employed counterterrorism tactics and strategies. CW-1 provided corroborating evidence in 2005, 2006, and 2010 (again, in exchange for a reduced sentence) concerning a straw donor scheme. According to this testimony, Fai and Ahmad provided funds to straw donors who in turn financed the KAC's lobbying activity through donations.

Aside from the claim in the initial arrest in 2010 by the NYPD that Hafiz Mohammad Sabir made a donation to the KAC, he is not mentioned in court documents. Longtime friends and well-known political activists in the cause of Kashmiri liberation and self-determination, Sabir and Fai had created a relationship over the previous twenty years. From humble beginnings as a cab driver and self-styled religious leader in Brooklyn's Little Pakistan, Sabir eventually became a significant power broker in community politics. As a founder and de facto imam of the main mosque called Makki Masjid on Coney Island Avenue, Sabir emerged as a major player in the political, social, and economic affairs of the Muslim community. Although his allegiances were to Sunni Islam—particularly to the Sufi brand of Islam practiced by people throughout Pakistan—he made many enemies in the neighborhood by castigating Ahmadi and Shia shop owners, businesspeople, and journalists. With clear commitments to the Kashmir cause, he also dabbled in antiliquor campaigns that blamed Shias for selling alcohol to Sunnis, and he is known to have caused rifts with the Ahmadi community that maintains its own mosques and community centers in a nearby neighborhood. Such old-country divisions are part and parcel of the makeup of social life in Little Pakistan. Indeed, as many in Midwood are fond of saying, it is as if residents never left Pakistan; this is why many stay in the neighborhood and others keep coming back. Sabir is a classic ethnic entrepreneur. Through his social connections and friends, he built a real estate empire not in Brooklyn but in Kansas City, Missouri. As he wielded his influence in Brooklyn over the past several decades, he also followed the movement of many Pakistanis from New York to cities such as Kansas City that have functioned as secondary gateways. Many chose to leave New York to seek opportunities in places that were more affordable and to pursue greater social mobility. For Sabir, this was a gold mine: he acted as a real-estate tycoon and gateway broker for families who had reached a particular class status or had certain educational attainments or other qualifications that would allow them to prosper in middle-class suburbia.

Although Sabir faced constant criticism in the local ethnic Pakistani press in New York, his business dealings and religious attacks became quite serious around the time Fai was receiving heat for his Kashmiri activism. The heightened controversy and the development of legal proceedings against Sabir led him to return to Pakistan for a few years while his friends and family ran his businesses. That Fai and Sabir were involved in the Kashmir struggle is public information, as are most of the details I have recounted here. For Kashmiri activists close to Fai, a different interpretation began to emerge from the events' timing. First was the suspicious shift in Sabir's work with Fai. After Fai's arrest, Sabir reported that he had never exchanged money with Fai as part of his fund-raising for the Kashmiri cause. Although it is clear from his 2010 questioning that Fai had just left Sabir's Makki Masjid when he was picked up by the NYPD, Sabir claims he was out of the country at the time—and subsequently the U.S. attorney general never prosecuted Sabir in relation to this portion of the story. An informant in the mosque was the most likely source of the tip for the stop the NYPD made in 2010 and the subsequent FBI interviews. By this time, Fai was already under investigation for putative ties to a foreign intelligence service that the FBI thought might be connected to terrorist activity. Curiously ignored in the trial was the Indian government's role in claiming through the Indian media that Fai was a "state agent" for Pakistan, which insinuated spying and even working as a double agent. As Fai was making inroads into the Republican Party through high-level contacts, an aspect of his advocacy that would appear as malfeasance in the charge of working for a foreign government, law enforcement was ramping up the number of intelligence-gathering operatives in the mosques of Brooklyn, including informants and handlers divided into what the NYPD called "rakers" and "mosque crawlers" who would later prove pivotal to this case.[20]

Sabir had previously worked with the NYPD and the FBI, and he opened his mosque to the so-called Demographics Unit of the NYPD. As is clear in the FBI affidavit, a second confidential witness who testified to the FBI against Fai connected him to the ISI. The informant clearly had known Fai for a long time and was familiar with intimate details about those he met in the government of Pakistan. It could also be argued, however, that either the FBI or the NYPD gained information about Fai's making a donation in Brooklyn without ever having been in Sabir's mosque. Fai insists that he was there and that someone associated with Sabir gave him the money. Even if this is not the case, numerous incidents associated with the FBI's joint surveillance of this neighborhood with the NYPD have demonstrated that informants within the mosques are providing information. Ultimately, Fai agreed to a plea bargain in which he admitted guilt for failing to register his organization as a recipient of funds from international sources. This infraction, which earned him a jail sentence of thirty months, was a far cry from the terrorism and terrorist connections the FBI had alleged.

Local social relationships within Brooklyn's Little Pakistan were torn asunder, and the antiterror policies of U.S. law enforcement mobilized counterinsurgency tactics that placed CIA consultants in the NYPD. In addition, newly created task forces allowed the FBI, local police, and other law enforcement agencies to police Pakistanis in Brooklyn. Fai's donors were likely from the wealthier classes residing in Long Island and Staten Island. The Little Pakistan of Brooklyn, by contrast, is a working-class neighborhood in which many of the Pakistani residents labor in the lower tiers of the service economy as cabbies, waiters, grocery store clerks, and the like. Despite their economic status, however, many of the working poor who attend Sabir's mosque donate regularly. Makki Masjid has since become more transparent about where donations are going, with regular announcements of the financial affairs of the mosque and an announcement board detailing the expenditures and donations.

The case against Fai can also be read as having been executed prematurely by the FBI. The evidence against Fai contained little beyond hearsay that would directly connect him to "terrorist" activity, unless the U.S. government was contemplating labeling the Kashmiri struggle for self-determination itself as terrorism. The FBI's surveillance and counterinsurgency practices in the Muslim neighborhoods of New York enabled diplomatic and international moves of statecraft between the United States and Pakistan. The case of Syed Ghulam Nabi Fai and his fight for Kashmiri self-determination reveals a system of surveillance and secret intelligence operations pursued by law enforcement agencies that have deep repercussions for the everyday lives and social structures of this Pakistani neighborhood. Despite being well known in the neighborhood of Pakistani Brooklyn, Fai was hardly noticed in the U.S. media, despite the widespread reports that ensued. While Fai is a hero to some and a crook to others, his struggle—the Kashmiri struggle that so many in this neighborhood are committed to—continues. Since his release from prison, Fai has returned to his activities supporting a free Kashmir and continues his work as an activist.

In a May 2013 speech at the National Defense University in Washington, D.C., President Barak Obama announced that the global War on Terror was over, calling on the nation to shift its focus from an endless conflict with a perpetual enemy to more targeted efforts against specific networks. The case of Syed Ghulam Nabi Fai suggests that Muslims will continue as a convenient cover for the persistence of a global War on Terror without the U.S. government's explaining it as such. The rhetoric of terror too easily justifies the investigation and arrest of Muslims with the nebulous idea of "radical Islam," as the Fai case demonstrates. The reasons for pursuing Fai in the first place represent a more troubling tendency of law enforcement and a range of political actors to use the rhetoric of counterterror to stifle activism and legitimate dissent. Largely because of the widespread demonization of Islam and Muslims, it has become commonplace to accept this connection to terrorism as an immediate threat to security. Just as the Cold War had a profound impact on American culture well beyond McCarthyism, so also the ideological battle that constructs Islam as an enemy has exerted influence well beyond the global War on Terror. The likelihood that a basic shift in thinking will ever take place—whether, that is, U.S. governance, policing, and intelligence practices will overcome the religious biases and racial practices that shape the treatment of Muslims—seems dim in light of the historical persistence of the FBI targeting Muslims. Rather, it appears that these forms of scapegoating through religion and racism are in fact the way that organizations such as the FBI operate and that they are deployed with the knowledge of numerous state agencies. Such actions are considered justifiable given specific domestic and foreign-policy objectives attached to the notions of security and counterterror. A more difficult question rarely asked amidst these daunting realizations is: How have political thinking and possibility been curtailed by the wide-ranging repercussions of the Cold War and the War on Terror? How we think of legitimate ideas of dissent and liberatory struggle is now inextricable from suppression itself. The Fai case attests to this.

15

Allies against Armageddon?

The FBI and the Academic Study of Religion

STEVEN WEITZMAN

Both before and after 9/11, as preceding chapters of this book have shown, the FBI conducted surveillance of religious groups thought to endanger public safety. It investigated and arrested individuals thought to be using religion as a cover for criminal behavior, and on occasion it launched assaults against religious communities that led to deaths. Such activity is not inherently wrong given the FBI's responsibilities—which include legally sanctioned use of surveillance and force—but it means that the bureau's relationship to religious communities can be double-edged. It is a protector of religion and an ally, but for some it is also an antagonist and a threat.

Given the FBI's impact on the religious lives of the Americans that it is charged with protecting, it is disturbing that its officials have sometimes brought into the field misunderstandings and prejudices that have colored its interaction with certain religious communities. It cannot be isolated from the rest of American society in this regard: FBI culture is a mirror of the attitudes, misunderstandings, and prejudices within broader American culture. However, with the exception of the Internal Revenue Service, there is probably no other agency of the federal government with more occasions or more power to intrude into religious life, and, for that reason, any bias rooted in its approach to religion can be particularly destructive.

As this book draws to a close, it has come time to think about the future of the FBI's interaction with religious communities. We see evidence that the FBI has become newly sensitive to the diversity of religious perspectives that it encounters in the field—such as community outreach efforts and even an effort to recruit employees who have studied religion—but there have also been news reports of continued problems: cases of misplaced suspicion and possible harassment, embarrassing miscommunication, overly intrusive surveillance decried by civil liberties groups, and religious stereotypes instilled or reinforced through the FBI's training programs. Is there any way to avoid such problems in the future? And should this question be entrusted to the FBI alone to address, or can those outside the bureau be of any help? As the editors of this volume, we are disturbed by the history recounted here, but we also find ourselves struggling with a question that goes beyond our normal role as researchers and teachers: Is this history merely *academic*? Is there anything practical that we can do, as scholars of religion, to help the FBI curtail the effect of bias on its interactions with certain religious groups?

We are not sure we know the answers to these questions, but we need not approach them from scratch. In the years just before 9/11, it so happens, a number of scholars of religion tried to help the FBI gain a deeper understanding of religious mindsets, discourse, and behavior. From 1993 to 2001, this group of scholars experimented in using academic scholarship to influence the FBI's interaction with what some researchers refer to as "new religious movements," newly originating or recently appearing groups deemed outside the mainstream of American religious life and sometimes treated with suspicion (as reflected in another common label for such groups, "cults," which casts them as less authentic than other religious communities and also connotes malevolent motivations). We recount this effort at academic interventionism as a way to explore a larger issue posed by the history detailed in this book: Can academia help the FBI minimize the destructive impact it sometimes has on religious communities?

During the 1990s, both the FBI and the field of religious studies focused on forms of religious violence and conflict rather different from those of the post-9/11 era, not martyrdom and jihad but violent confrontations with secluded religious communities like the Branch Davidians and the threat of apocalyptic violence posed by the turn of the millennium. In the cases with the highest profile, the FBI was drawn into confrontation with religious communities resistant to conventional tactics of deterrence and negotiation, and the FBI sometimes approached these encounters with misinformation or deeply rooted preconceptions.

This is where scholars in this period believed they had something to contribute. They thought their expertise created possibilities for constructive intervention, for analysis, for advice, even for direct mediation. They were outsiders to the FBI, not the social scientists that it normally consulted, and a few behaved in ways the FBI considered annoying. With time, however, they developed a consultative relationship with the bureau.

As it happens, in this period the FBI, or at least part of it, was receptive to such expertise. FBI interest in unconventional religious communities, as this book chronicles, long predates the 1990s, going back to within a decade after the establishment of the original Bureau of Investigation in 1908, when it began surveillance of pacifist religious groups such as the American Friends Service Committee. In the following decades, the Federal Bureau of Investigation monitored and interacted with various religious groups—the Moorish Science Temple of America, the Nation of Islam, Martin Luther King Jr. and the Southern Christian Leadership Conference, and the Catholic Church, among many others—and consulted experts along the way. What distinguished the situation in the late 1990s was the FBI's relative receptivity to scholars of religion, reflecting both the emergence of religious studies as a respected academic field and a shift in how the FBI, or part of the FBI, defined and used scholarly expertise. It is that receptivity that makes this relationship such an interesting chapter in the history of the FBI's interaction with religious communities.

The outcome of this experiment is far from clear. It had been developing only a few years when the events of 9/11 shifted the terrain in dramatic ways. Even at its height, it probably involved no more than a few dozen scholars of religion, with facilitation from the professional staff of the American Academy of Religion (AAR). These scholars were dispersed across multiple institutions, able to gather only for the occasional meeting or conference, and the Internet had just begun taking shape as a medium of communication and organization. Many scholars of religion do not know about their efforts; indeed, I once asked a former president of the AAR from this period about the effort, and even that person did not know very much about it. The FBI's involvement was limited as well, focused through a unit known as the Critical Incident Response Group, which was formed in 1994 to provide field offices and other law enforcement agencies with assistance in responding to crisis situations. Whatever the group learned from scholars could not easily be disseminated to other parts of the FBI; the relationship did not have much time to develop, and whether it had any impact remains an open question.

While this effort might be inconclusive, it nonetheless raises important questions for those hoping that their scholarship can somehow help reduce the amount of violence and conflict in the world. It is one thing to publish analysis and advice; it is another thing to inject that advice in a way that will shape the course of events. A few scholars may be in a position to influence the government's behavior—Michael Barkun, political scientist and author of an essay in this volume, developed a close working relationship with the FBI over the years—but most scholars are not in that position. How does one persuade nonacademics to pay attention to one's scholarship, and how are they to distinguish between good scholarship and bad scholarship when scholars themselves struggle to make that distinction? What are the implications if such expertise does not actually have the impact scholars envision? The scholars who tried to work with the FBI faced such questions, and there is much to learn from their experience, including an understanding of the factors that may make it difficult for a book such as this one to have a lasting effect on the FBI's approach to religious communities.

LEARNING FROM WACO

As a first step, it will help for us to sketch how the FBI and scholars in the field of religious studies first came to engage one another, a development that took place over the 1990s. The following is based on accounts published by scholars involved in this effort, supplemented by brief interviews and e-mail exchanges with some of the participants. It takes the perspective of the scholars involved in this relationship and makes less effort to reconstruct how things may have appeared from the FBI's perspective, partly because the bureau's inner workings are far less accessible and partly because I focus on what scholars hoped to achieve and the challenges they faced.

The FBI's interest in religious communities goes back to its very beginnings as an organization in the early twentieth century, but its efforts to engage the field of religious studies in the past few decades can be traced to a more recent event, its standoff with the Branch Davidians in 1993.

As Catherine Wessinger details in chapter 12, the Branch Davidians originated as an offshoot of the Seventh-day Adventist Church, and their history went back decades, but by the time the FBI encountered them, they were an apocalyptically minded community under the leadership of David Koresh. In February 1993, agents from the Bureau of Alcohol, Tobacco, and Firearms attempted to execute a search of the Branch Davidian ranch at Mount Carmel near Waco, Texas, and that encounter resulted in a gun battle that left four agents and six Branch Davidians dead. The FBI then imposed a siege on the compound that lasted fifty-one days until, on April 19, the bureau launched a second assault. In circumstances that remain somewhat unclear, a fire broke out in which Koresh and more than seventy community members were killed. A government investigation released in 2000 exonerated the FBI of responsibility for starting the fire or improperly using armed force, placing the responsibility on the Branch Davidians, though it also found that the FBI covered up some facts in a way that fed public suspicion.

What is relevant here about this confrontation is a curious episode that occurred in the midst of the siege, an episode that was peripheral to the confrontation itself but would prove catalytic in the later relationship between the FBI and the field of religious studies. As the confrontation was unfolding in March and April 1993, two scholars of religion—Phillip Arnold of the Reunion Institute in Houston and James Tabor, a scholar of the New Testament at the University of North Carolina at Charlotte—sought to help resolve the conflict, hoping to use their understanding of religion to assist in brokering a peaceful resolution. Neither had heard of the Branch Davidians prior to the standoff, but they saw connections to their own research as scholars of apocalypticism and believed their expertise could contribute to the negotiations. Their efforts obviously did not prevent a tragic outcome, but they did influence the course of events after the standoff by establishing a paradigm of intervention that other scholars would learn from and emulate.

Arnold was the prime mover of this intercessory effort. The Reunion Institute, which he directed, was itself an effort at intercession, founded in 1980 in response to the mass killing at Jonestown in Guyana to prevent misunderstanding of what were then known as "cults," marginal or alternative religious groups deemed threatening and coercive. Arnold's aim was to help people to reestablish understanding with family members who had joined such groups, offering an alternative to cult-deprogramming organizations hostile to such groups and known to sometimes use coercion to remove family members from them. When he learned of what was happening at Waco, Arnold's intercessory impulses asserted themselves again. His own research was focused on first-century Jewish Christians, but he saw connections between that community and the scripturally inspired apocalypticism of the Branch Davidians—in his words, "My dissertation suddenly became real."[1] If one tried to understand the apocalyptic narrative that Koresh believed was unfolding, Arnold reasoned, one could avoid saying and doing things that might confirm his and his followers' sense that a violent apocalyptic battle was about to take place. Feeling what he described as "a moral obligation to try to save lives," Arnold decided on March 3 to drive to Waco to share what he knew with the FBI.

The problem that Arnold faced from the onset was how to get the FBI to listen to him. He had not been known to the bureau previously; he was not a social scientist or psychologist, the kind of expert it was accustomed to working with; and he was not the only one offering advice to the FBI—it was inundated with information and offers of help, with agents on the scene complaining about "information overload" and concerned about a "fax meltdown."[2] Arnold was not deterred by agents' initial indifference, however. When he failed to get a hearing with the FBI at a press conference, he drove to the temporary headquarters of the FBI's negotiators and left materials there, which did prompt a follow-up call from an agent. While the agent would not allow Arnold to listen to the negotiation tapes or speak with Koresh, he did eventually reveal that Koresh believed he was in the fifth seal prophesied by the book of Revelation, which meant from Koresh's perspective that the end was near. Since the agent was still declining his offer of help, however, Arnold felt it necessary to attend another press conference, only to find himself thrown out after speaking with a journalist.

Despite these setbacks, Arnold was still determined to help and thus looked for other ways to intervene. In the same period, he was invited for an interview on a radio talk show that Koresh and his followers listened to. In fact, after hearing the interview, the Branch Davidians asked the FBI if they could speak to Arnold directly, a request that was declined. Arnold and Tabor, who had now joined the effort, convinced the talk show host to allow them to make a second appearance in which they would reach out to the Branch Davidians. They had also begun speaking with Livingstone Fagan, who had served as a spokesperson for Koresh before the ATF raid but was now in jail in Waco. They learned from him that Koresh was not certain of his interpretation, and this uncertainty, they came to believe, was an opportunity to influence his thinking.[3] They hoped their radio broadcast would persuade Koresh to rethink his interpretation of Revelation in a way that might lead him to surrender.

As it happens, Koresh did not hear the broadcast himself, because he was meeting with his lawyer at the time, but he was told about it by others and communicated interest in it to the FBI. The FBI agreed to allow a recording to be sent into the compound, and a few days after it was delivered, Koresh released a letter in which he seemed to indicate that he and his followers would come out after he finished a new interpretation of the Seven Seals and was assured of its safe delivery to Arnold and Tabor. The two scholars believed that Koresh would probably surrender within two or three weeks, as soon as he finished his interpretation, but the FBI saw things differently. The bureau had lost patience and believed that Koresh was just stalling for time. The final assault occurred just as Koresh was beginning to compose his interpretation, with a draft preserved on a computer disk that was eventually delivered to Arnold and Tabor.[4]

Here, then, is an instance of scholars "intervening" in violence in a very direct way. Thanks to their understanding of a biblically based apocalyptic worldview, Tabor and Arnold believed they had a chance to influence the thinking of the religious actors in this crisis, to communicate with them in a way that did not require them to abandon their beliefs, and to open new interpretive possibilities in the scriptural texts that might have allowed Koresh to accept surrender. The problem, as they saw it, was that, while the Branch Davidians were open to the scholars' perspective, the FBI was not. The bureau did consult at least thirteen outside experts, but very few of these were from the field of religious studies and, as Tabor recounts things, they did not understand or take seriously the Branch Davidians' religious beliefs or scriptural interpretation, dismissing Koresh's apocalyptic claims as a delusion or a delay tactic. In Arnold and Tabor's view, the crisis need not have ended tragically had the FBI been more open to their expertise.

Whether Arnold and Tabor could have prevented the tragedy at Waco we will never know. Because of what happened at Waco, however, the government became newly receptive to their argument. The FBI had not respected Arnold and Tabor's expertise during the standoff itself, but their involvement garnered attention for their views after the fact, and they used that opportunity to champion their ideas more publicly. Arnold was actually brought in by the FBI in response to a similar crisis in Montana in 1996, and Tabor was asked to testify before Congress as an expert witness.

In addition to Arnold and Tabor themselves, moreover, the aftermath of Waco also gave an opening to other scholars to argue similar views. As part of its effort to understand what went wrong, the Justice Department commissioned reports by sociologists Lawrence Sullivan of Harvard and

Nancy Ammerman of Emory, who reached the same basic conclusion: law enforcement needed to learn more about religion. Ammerman's analysis found that the FBI had been unable to take religion seriously as part of the social world with which its agents had to engage; that it relied too heavily on the advice of a "cult deprogrammer," Rick Ross, who saw it as his mission to rescue people from groups that he identified as cults; and that it ignored its own behavioral scientists and agents, some of whom were also counseling the FBI to take Koresh's religious views seriously. In her view, Arnold and Tabor's approach had been the best hope of resolving the conflict peacefully.[5] Sullivan's analysis was similar, finding that many agents operated with misconceptions about religion, and that religious illiteracy was ingrained in agency culture. He noted, for example, that in the hundreds of interviews investigators conducted with participants in the standoff, they had posed no questions about religion, and he found that religion was absent as a topic from the curricula of the more than seventy enforcement agencies trained by the Justice and Treasury Departments.[6]

Prior to Waco, the FBI had reason to believe it could resolve such standoffs without the benefit of academic expertise. After the post-Waco reassessment, things looked different. The recommendations of Ammerman and Sullivan were endorsed by no less an authority than Deputy Attorney General Philip B. Heyman, who called for federal law enforcement to reach out to a wide range of experts, including scholars of religion.[7] Thus began the period that we are concerned with here, a period of intermittent contact and exchange between the FBI and scholars of religion.

Following up on Ammerman's and Sullivan's recommendations, the Department of Justice contacted the American Academy of Religion in 1994 for help in educating law enforcement officials. The newly created Critical Incident Response Group, formed in response to the Branch Davidian siege to better coordinate tactics, investigation, and expertise, established an advisory committee to recommend ways the FBI could gain access to a wider range of advice in crisis situations. The committee, which met in late 1995 and early 1996, included Michael Barkun, an expert in millenarian movements, and Gregory Saathoff, a psychiatrist who would soon facilitate connections with other religious studies scholars. After a meeting with Barbara DeConcini, the executive director of the American Academy of Religion, and Steve Herrick, its associate director of external relations, Saathoff affirmed the AAR as a forum for future contacts between the FBI and scholars of religion.[8]

That same year, 1996, saw another incident that seemed only to validate the value of such contacts. The incident in question, alluded to earlier, was another standoff, this one in Montana with an armed Christian identity group known as the Justice Freemen. The creation of the Critical Incident Response Group, together with contacts now established between the FBI and academia, seemed to pay off. The FBI this time turned for advice to scholars—Barkun, Jean Rosenfeld, Catherine Wessinger, and even Philip Arnold himself—and the conflict was resolved without a shot fired. At least for the scholars involved, these two facts were connected. Rosenfeld and Wessinger have published accounts of what happened, and both note communication problems with the FBI and a certain level of distrust.[9] (In a personal communication with me, Barkun did not recall any issues of communication.) Despite encountering some of the same resistance from the FBI that had existed at Waco, however, both conclude that scholarly involvement had a positive impact: the FBI's behavior was consistent with the advice they gave. Rosenfeld described the episode as a "landmark success," proof that academia could indeed help resolve potentially violent crises, and its contribution was even recognized by the head of the Crisis Incident Response Group, Robin Montgomery, who reportedly told Arnold, "Your method works."[10]

Building on such progress, contacts became a bit more regularized over the 1990s. At the invitation of the AAR, an agent attended a session about the Oklahoma City bombing at the AAR annual conference in Philadelphia in 1995, and others attended sessions at the conferences in 1996 and 1997. The agents do not seem to have found much value in listening to AAR papers, but they worked with the professional staff of the AAR to develop more informal, by-invitation-only colloquies—fourteen between 1998 and 2000—attended by members of the Crisis Negotiation Unit of the Critical Incident Response Group and of the National Center for the Analysis of Violent Crime, brought together with Barkun and other scholars. Topics included millennialism and violence, violent religious rhetoric on the Internet, and misconceptions about Islam and violence. At least one session was something more than a typical academic panel. At the AAR conference in Nashville in 2000, FBI agents presented a simulated crisis negotiation with a gun-wielding pastor supposed to have taken refuge in a nearby house to escape arrest for refusing to pay taxes. According to an account written by Steve Herrick, the AAR official in charge of government relations, seventy-five scholars were invited and twenty-five attended. During the session itself, the scholars present offered observations and feedback in real time as the negotiators tried to engage the Bible-quoting fugitive, sometimes differing over whether to recommend a particular response.

By this point, however, it was also becoming clear that progress would not be easy to achieve. The Critical Incident Response Group was only one small part of the FBI, and the issues identified in the reports by Ammerman and Sullivan—the institutionalized culture of ignorance about religion, the biases and stereotypes, and the inability to distinguish between authentic expertise and pseudo-expertise—seem to have persisted in other parts of the FBI, as illustrated by an episode that garnered much attention in 1999: the publication of an FBI document known as Project Megiddo.

Made public in October 1999, Project Megiddo was intended to warn law enforcement agencies about the potential for violence by extremist religious groups who believed the world was destined to end in the year 2000. Much of the document is a survey of religious groups deemed dangerous, from Christian identity groups to the Black Hebrew Israelites, and it includes a list of characteristics that make some "cults" more prone to violence than others, including a sequestered communal life, the use of violent language, and the inclusion in the group's inner circle of people familiar with weapons or with military training. The report had been produced by an FBI division neither involved in Waco nor connected to the Critical Incident Response Group.

At first, the production of such a report suggests that the FBI had come to recognize religion as an important motivator rather than as just a pretext for criminal activity. To the religious studies scholars who had been working with the FBI, however, the document was disappointing, revealing an FBI operating with questionable ideas about how new religious movements function and oblivious to the recommendations made in the reports by Ammerman and Sullivan.[11] The report makes little or no use of the scholarship of Barkun, Wessinger, Rosenfeld, or others who had been working with the FBI—to Barkun, in fact, it is not clear that the authors consulted anyone outside the bureau.[12]

As Gregory Saathoff was keen to point out, to understand the significance of Project Megiddo's publication, one has to note what happened afterward: a follow-up discussion between the authors of the report and scholars arranged a month or so later in the context of the 1999 annual meeting of the AAR in Boston. Three analysts from the Counterterrorism Unit who had participated in drafting Project Megiddo agreed to attend, and they engaged in a conversation with Barkun and other invited scholars who were critical of the report's tone and conclusions.[13] Saathoff cited that exchange as a sign of progress in its own right. The relationship between the FBI and scholars of religion was only then beginning to develop, he explained, and the FBI is such a large organization that it can be difficult for one part to know what other parts have learned. In such a context, it is not surprising that what one unit was in the midst of learning from scholars of religion had not yet been disseminated throughout the FBI. In addition, Saathoff noted, one should also take into consideration that the authors of the report itself were willing to engage scholars, hear their criticisms, and share their perspective. Project Megiddo itself was flawed, but the candid follow-up exchange was a sign that the relationship between the FBI and those in the field of religious studies was maturing.

Even as scholars and FBI agents were building bridges, however, the fact that some within the bureau could think Project Megiddo a good idea suggested that the institutional ignorance about religion that Ammerman and Sullivan observed in the FBI in 1993 had not been overcome—not just because of ignorance or bias among individual agents but also because of deeper institutional issues. The FBI experiences much more rapid turnover than the academic world: new attorneys general and FBI directors get appointed frequently (there have been eight regular or acting attorneys general since Janet Reno left office in 2001), and agents are frequently reassigned, promoted, or retire. Such rapid change alters priorities and complicates the development of personal relationships, trust, and institutional memory. Scholars also soon recognized the tension between academia's ethos of open criticism and deliberate reflection and the FBI's need for discretion and for clear-cut, easily accessed information.[14] The cultural and institutional differences between the FBI and academia went well beyond the subject of religion itself, and made it difficult for scholars to have a deep or lasting impact on the bureau's practices.

One might have expected 9/11 to galvanize the development of a working relationship between the FBI and scholars of religion, but, if anything, that event presented new complications. For one thing, 9/11 introduced changes in the institutional culture of the FBI that eclipsed some of the relationships and institutional experience developed in the 1990s. As the FBI's focus shifted from negotiating for hostages, managing crises, and solving crimes to preventing terrorist attacks, and from focusing on new domestic religious movements to tracking a globalized Islam, scholars of religion found themselves facing new counterparts in the FBI who had not always been privy to whatever insight had been gleaned before 9/11.

Michael Barkun's experience may be illustrative in this regard. In the 1990s, he emerged as a mutually trusted intermediary between the FBI and academia, playing an important role in the Critical Incident Response Group, in the Justice Freemen incident, and in the scholarly exchange with the FBI that followed Project Megiddo. In 2006, at the annual meeting of the AAR in Washington, D.C., he and three other scholars were invited to FBI headquarters to meet with a group of FBI terrorism analysts—a significant step in that all his previous meetings had been with the Critical Incident Response Group. What is striking about this episode is that five years had passed since 9/11 and a decade had elapsed since the initial contact between the FBI and the AAR, and yet, according to Barkun, this may well have been the first contact between the FBI's counterterrorism unit and the AAR.[15]

Barkun suggests that part of the reason for this delay is structural: the highly compartmentalized nature of the FBI makes it difficult for one unit to communicate with or learn from the experience of others. It seems possible that the reorganization prompted by 9/11 has made this problem worse—that is at least the implication of news reports suggesting that anti-Muslim bias crept into FBI training as a result of the counterterrorism unit's relative autonomy, which exempted it from some of the oversight applied to other units. As the journalist Dina Temple-Raston explained in a National Public Radio report from 2011: "It [the counterterrorism unit] is essentially in charge of putting together its own training module and then is supposed to find a way to fit that training into a broader curriculum for agents at Quantico. Because of the way it is structured, the vetting process for the counterterrorism curriculum was minimal." Although the issues might have been specific to the counterterrorism unit, FBI officials acknowledged the problem might be more widespread by noting at the time that they planned to review every training module in the curriculum for inaccuracies and bias.[16]

In the wake of 9/11, the mindset of many academics also changed, and the idea of cooperating with federal law enforcement became less appealing for many. Two events had a particular impact on the ways scholars of Islam thought about the government in this period. First, proposed legislation known as the International Studies in Higher Education Act, which included a provision for monitoring academic work in Middle Eastern studies programs that received federal funding, was passed by the U.S. House of Representatives in 2003 (though never made law).[17] Second, the controversial scholar Tariq Ramadan was barred from the United States by the Department of Homeland Security for undisclosed reasons—an event directly relevant to the AAR, which became party to a lawsuit against the Department of Homeland Security for having prevented Ramadan from speaking at the AAR conference that year.[18] Some argue that academia's fears in this period were overblown, but such incidents reinforced the concern among academics that a "new McCarthyism" was setting in, an era of surveillance and meddling in academia similar to what happened during the Cold War.[19]

All of this brings us to the present moment and to a series of questions that the field of religious studies might well ask of itself twenty years after Waco. The FBI and those in the field of religious studies have had a number of intellectual exchanges—the FBI has even consulted with scholars during actual crises—but the results of their efforts are equivocal at best. Observer-participants in the Justice Freemen standoff such as Wessinger and Rosenfeld understood their impact to be have been a positive one, but even they do not really know whether the FBI heeded their counsel. More than fifteen years later, media reports reveal that the FBI is still beset with some of the same problems: insufficient or misguided training procedures that perpetuate outmoded or biased information and a relationship with religious studies scholars that remains sporadic, unstructured, and without clear guidelines or measures of success. Is there something that scholars could have done to make more progress in the past decade? And what should they be doing now—engaging the FBI more deeply, or differently, or not at all?

Looking back at its history two decades after it began, the interaction between those in the field of religious studies and the FBI arguably exposes a mismatch between scholarly aspirations and reality. Arnold and other scholars involved in the initial stages of the relationship felt a sense of urgency and importance—they were trying to save lives—but, in retrospect, the impact of their efforts seems comparatively modest. Beyond the Critical Incident Response Group, the FBI has not fully absorbed the recommendations that Ammerman and Sullivan proposed in the aftermath of Waco: the same lack of understanding and bias evident in Project Megiddo surfaced in the anti-Islamic training materials that the FBI now needs to purge. A few success stories may have been achieved in the late 1990s, notably the peaceful resolution of the Justice Freemen standoff, but even that case does not necessarily demonstrate what scholars at the time believed it did. When one scrutinizes later accounts of the standoff, it becomes clear that scholars were never quite certain whether their advice was actually heard or truly helped. Wessinger notes that some in the FBI found their involvement beside the point and even a distraction because of their incessant demands for more data. Moreover, it is plausible that the FBI could have achieved a peaceful resolution without the assistance of scholars, as it did in 1985, before Waco, when it negotiated the surrender of an armed Christian identity group known as the Covenant, the Sword, and the Arm of the Lord.

Looking at the underlying theory at work can help to better understand why this effort by scholars of religion to engage the FBI has not lived up to its potential. In cases like the Waco standoff, scholars were grappling with the challenge of negotiation—how to find common ground between the FBI and the religious communities it faced—and they believed their expertise gave them the power to bridge these perspectives, a kind of mediation they came to refer to as *worldview translation.* In the section that follows, drawing on the history that we have recounted here, we reexamine worldview translation as a model of scholarly intervention. How was this kind of "translation" supposed to help resolve a conflict between law enforcement and a religious community, and why did it not work in the way its practitioners hoped it would?

SCHOLARSHIP, TRANSLATION, ADVOCACY

Like other kinds of experts, scholars of religious studies can provide reliable information that may be helpful for understanding a particular religious actor or community. Scholars like Eileen Barker have recognized the public's need for reliable information and have worked hard to make it accessible, creating resources like *Inform*, a publicly funded organization located within the London School of Economics and established to provide up-to-date information about new and nonconventional religions.[20] In this role, the scholar functions in the background of the crisis as an informant. The scholars discussed earlier envisioned a more interventionist role. During the Waco standoff, Arnold and Tabor tried to interpose themselves between the FBI and the Branch Davidians as mediators, seeking ways to communicate with Koresh and to explain his perspective to the FBI. Their efforts did not avoid a tragedy, but they did establish a model for how scholars might meaningfully and productively intervene in a conflict.

The need for such an intermediary was premised on the idea that the conflict between law enforcement and a religious community like the Branch Davidians was one not only of clashing interests but also of different conceptions of reality. On the one hand, the FBI operated within a secularized worldview that inclined it to interpret Koresh's religious claims as an indication of mental illness or as a cover for criminal behavior. On the other hand, Koresh and the Branch Davidians interpreted reality from within a religious orientation, understanding their encounter with the FBI in light of scriptural prophecy. Their differing worldviews led the two sides to interpret and talk about reality in different ways—to the FBI, Koresh's scriptural references seemed like "Bible babble," while to Koresh, the FBI's behavior seemed a fulfillment of prophecy—and the result was misunderstanding and distrust. Thus, a third party was needed, a mediator not identified with either side, someone who could offer the evidence-driven, rational expertise the FBI valued but could also understand, empathize with, and communicate with those coming from a religious perspective.

What qualifies a scholar to play such a role? The FBI's negotiators were perfectly aware of the group's religious orientation and sought to accommodate it, but they simply did not know enough about religion to communicate effectively with the Branch Davidians or to see all the negotiating options that existed within their understanding of scripture. This, at least, was how scholars saw things after the fact. Trained as biblical scholars and having some understanding of religious psychology, Arnold and Tabor believed they could understood Koresh's perspective in a way the FBI could not—and this was proven by Koresh's responsiveness to their claims, his request to meet with them, and his effort to produce a new interpretation of Revelation that might have provided scriptural justification for surrender, had the FBI allowed him to complete it. A scholar specializing in the Branch Davidians might have more pertinent expertise than did two biblical scholars, but more important than the focus of a scholar's research was his or her abilities as a worldview translator, as a mediator between religious and secular mindsets.

The role of the religious studies scholar as a worldview translator did not emerge out of nowhere. It drew on the earlier conception of the anthropologist as a cultural translator, a self-conception bequeathed to the field of religious studies and one that was becoming widespread by the 1980s. It is reflected, for example, in the writing of one of the leading scholars of the field, J.Z. Smith, who argued in his now-classic *Imagining Religion* that such translation was possible even for a religious community as seemingly irrational as the group that committed mass suicide at Jonestown.[21] As incomprehensible as the Jonestown residents' behavior might seem, Smith contended, it reflects beliefs and behavior that have parallels in the histories of other religious communities, and one can seize on those similarities to make it understandable. The intellectual effort was not essentially different from that involved in making a text written in one language comprehensible to people using another language. Indeed, were such translation not possible, "the academy, the enterprise of understanding, the human sciences themselves become, likewise, impossible in principle since they are fundamentally translation enterprises."[22] The concept of the worldview translator emerged from such arguments; what seems to have been new in the 1990s was the effort to put it into practice in real-world conflicts.

Once scholars began to deploy the concept in this way, however, they soon realized that worldview translation was not in fact the same as translating a literary text. With a literary translation, the object of the translation is fairly stable, a text more or less fixed in content. Not so with the object of worldview translation—namely, a religious mindset or the collective mentality of a group—which can be unstable, inconsistent, and unpredictable.

A further complication emerged when scholars came to realize the gap between their worldview and the FBI's. As observed by Jayne Seminare Docherty, a scholar of conflict studies, FBI agents and religious studies scholars are separated not only by different professional and ethical responsibilities but also by different conceptions of reality that incline each group toward different explanations for human behavior and different ideas about how to respond to it. One can see this difference reflected in Tabor's accounts of the Waco standoff, in which, as noted above, he has a harder time understanding the perspective of the FBI than he does that of the Branch Davidians. It takes more than goodwill to overcome these differences, Docherty argued; it takes a process of worldview translation *between* scholars and the FBI. She suggests ways that scholars and the FBI might overcome this difference—reading each other's work, cross-training, joint research projects—but the process she describes requires time and commitment, and it is not clear that it could actually work given high turnover rates in the FBI and a limited budget that makes it difficult for the FBI to consistently send even a few agents to academic conferences.[23]

It did not take long for scholars to realize complications like these. What is not noted in any of the pertinent scholarship from the 1990s that I have read is a more fundamental problem with worldview translation, a problem that can be traced back to the anthropology from which the concept was inherited. In 1986, Talal Asad published a critique of

British anthropology and its use of translation as a model for scholars' interaction with the cultures they study.[24] The focus of Asad's critique was the anthropologist who understood his or her role as a cultural translator able to render the mindset of "primitive" or "alien" cultures comprehensible to a modern Western mindset. The cultural translation performed by such figures casts itself as neutral and empathetic, but that posture masks an underlying reality. "The process of 'cultural translation' is inevitably enmeshed in conditions of power—professional, national, international," Asad argued, "and among these conditions is the authority of ethnographers to uncover the implicit meanings of subordinate societies."[25] Advantaged by his political position relative to the people he is representing, the anthropologist claims the power to identify the implicit meaning of their behavior whether or not that meaning is acknowledged by the people themselves. By constructing this meaning, he does more than translate culture; he invents thoughts and intentions.

No one at the time thought to apply this critique to the concept of the worldview translator, but it does have potential implications for our understanding of this role. Consider the case of James Tabor, Arnold's partner in the effort to broker a peaceful resolution to the Waco standoff. Tabor is certainly a very different kind of scholar than those whom Asad focused on, but his role as a worldview translator lends itself to a similar kind of critique inasmuch as it depends on a similar ability to determine implicit meanings. In his published accounts, Tabor is critical of the psychologists whom the FBI relied on for their understanding of Koresh's mental state, arguing that they had no real evidence for their conclusions given their lack of direct access to Koresh.[26] For his own conclusions about Koresh's intentions, however, what evidence did Tabor have? One of his key contentions is that at the end of the siege, when the FBI launched its assault, Koresh, largely under the influence of Arnold and Tabor themselves, had rethought his understanding of the apocalyptic script he believed was unfolding and was in all likelihood willing to surrender. The basis for this claim was a partially completed manuscript that Koresh was working on at the time of the assault, and especially the final concluding statement: "Should we not eagerly ourselves be ready to accept this truth and come out of our closet and be revealed to the world as those who love Christ in truth and in righteousness."[27] Tabor and Gallagher cite this line as "the best evidence of what [Koresh] had in mind that last evening before the fire," taking the phrase "come out of our closet" to mean that Koresh intended to leave the compound. This interpretation is consistent with an earlier letter that

Koresh dispatched from the compound in which he also indicated his willingness to "come out," but it is, in the end, an inference. Like the rest of the commentary, Koresh's statement here is written in evasive apocalyptic code, its exact interpretation is uncertain, and what it reveals about Koresh's intentions is an open question. Given the apocalyptic context, it seems equally possible that he was referring to eschatological self-disclosure, as if he were a hidden messiah thinking about when to disclose himself to the world. Nothing in the evidence resolves the ambiguity, and it is even conceivable that Koresh was deliberately vague in order to keep his options open.

Whatever conclusions one draws on the basis of this document are actually beside the point, however, for Arnold and Tabor had no access to this document at the time that they were trying to intervene: it was preserved on a computer disk that survived the fire and was later passed on to Arnold and Tabor through Koresh's lawyer. Arnold and Tabor's understanding of Koresh's intentions was based on inferences from his public statements and what they learned from others about him; they had no direct access to the man himself, much less a way into his inner thoughts. This is where their role as worldview translators resembles that of the cultural translators critiqued by Asad: their authority as mediators depends entirely on whether or not one accepts that their expertise gives them a special ability to understand unexpressed thoughts and intentions.

Tabor differs from the British anthropologists of Oxford that Asad was talking about in that he could not simply assume such authority for himself. To the contrary, as we have noted, the FBI was very reluctant to give him a hearing during the standoff. Tabor would eventually have considerable success in establishing his authority with the public as an expert, often appearing in the media and even testifying in congressional hearings, but that did not happen until later, and it took rhetorical effort on Tabor's part to secure that status, as Christopher Eisenhart shows in a recent analysis of Tabor's performance as a public expert.[28] In fact, Eisenhart's analysis suggests that Tabor's representation of what happened at Waco was part of this effort. In publications such as *Why Waco?* Tabor shapes his representation of the Waco standoff in ways that stress the contrast between his special grasp of the Branch Davidians' perspective and the lack of understanding that marred the response of law enforcement. In Eisenhart's reading, Tabor's narrative amounts to advocacy for the legitimacy of his expertise, using the Waco experience to illustrate a problem—the threat to religion caused by the government's lack of understanding—that only he as a scholar was able to solve.

Even if Tabor derived professional benefit from his role as a worldview translator, that does not necessarily refute his understanding of the situation or discredit the role he tried to play in it. Later scholars agreed that Tabor and Arnold's approach was the most likely to yield a nonviolent outcome. What one learns from Asad and Eisenhart, however, is that the role of the worldview translator may not be as disinterested as it appears. As Darryl G. Hart notes, academic religious studies has been struggling to find a rationale for itself ever since detaching itself from its origins in seminary education and beginning the quest for legitimacy as part of secular academia.[29] Worldview translation would seem to provide a rationale for religious studies, and that itself is a reason to be suspicious of its neutrality. I do not question the sincerity of the scholars who seek to operate in this way, but the fact remains that they stand to gain real benefits from playing the role of worldview translator whether they acknowledge those benefits or not: a sense of legitimacy as a public expert and the feeling of doing something useful for the world.

One of the potential problems with worldview translation, in other words, is that it casts the scholar in the role of advocate, an advocate not only for whatever religious community the scholar may be studying but also for the value of worldview translation itself as a form of public expertise. There are scholars in the field of religious studies who feel it is their obligation to advocate on behalf of the religious communities they work with, either to defend them against persecution or to help them gain understanding within the larger society.[30] Sometimes there are important principles or existential issues at stake—human rights or religious liberty—but other times the communities in question can ask for specific favors, such as testimony in a court case or participation in protests, that can create professional and ethical dilemmas for scholars committed to an ethos of neutrality.

Some scholars of religion nonetheless argue that such advocacy is perfectly legitimate, rejecting the idea of the scholar as impartial and disengaged.[31] The very existence of religious communities can be at stake, and scholars of those communities may be among their only advocates in the outside world. On the other hand, such advocacy can come at the expense of the field's public legitimacy. In 1995, a religious group known as Aum Shinrikyo came to the world's attention when it launched a poison gas attack against the Tokyo subway system that killed thirteen people. Shimada Hiromi, a scholar who had earlier published sympathetic accounts of the group, lost his job as a professor as a result of his advocacy, and according to Ian Reader, the reputation of academic religious studies suffered in Japanese society because of its perceived naivete.[32]

The line between worldview translation and advocacy is hard to draw. If Tabor's accounts of the Waco standoff are any indication, much of his activity as a would-be intermediary amounted to trying to foster empathy for the Branch Davidians, and as we have noted, he was also advocating for the field of religious studies as a socially useful form of expertise. Scholars who advocate for a particular community or for their own professional interests, even if they profess the benign and neutral goal of translation or mediation, can risk their reputation with peers who do not recognize such advocacy as a legitimate scholarly endeavor. Functioning as an advocate can also undercut the legitimacy of one's expertise in the eyes of a nonacademic actor like the FBI, which has its own professional obligations, if it is perceived as serving a group's interests at the expense of law enforcement and public safety.

That there may have been something self-serving about Tabor and Arnold's attempted intervention does not by itself negate the value of such intervention. After all, their argument that the FBI should look for negotiating opportunities within the Branch Davidians' belief system was the same recommendation that some of the FBI's own in-house experts were making.[33] If there is a chance that religious studies scholars can help to clarify that worldview, some would argue pursuing that opportunity is worth whatever risk comes from mistranslation. What is in question here is not the utility of religious studies as a reference source, but its power to intervene in conflict, a power it has claimed for itself both before and after 9/11. When a scholar proposes to know things about the mindset of a jihadist that should have an impact on law enforcement, he or she is endorsing the view of religious studies that has now been tested by the relationship between the FBI and religious studies scholars since the Waco standoff, and the results of that test reinforce doubts about the efficacy of the scholar as a helpful intermediary between the state's security apparatus and the religious communities that it regards as a threat to the public.

CONCLUSION

The kind of scholarly interventionism that we have described here may rest on debatable intellectual premises, pose significant ethical risks for academics, and seem frustrating or utterly useless to members of the FBI, but there is one counterconsideration that needs to be factored in as well: a refusal to intervene can create an expertise vacuum that other kinds of experts are all too willing to fill—and in ways that can be very harmful.

Concern about the influence of self-declared experts or pseudo-experts was part of what motivated the original efforts to connect religious studies scholars and the FBI after Waco. In addition to the FBI's own lack of understanding about religion, another issue that concerned scholars like Arnold, Tabor, Ammerman, and others was the bureau's inability to decide what counted as relevant expertise and to distinguish between reliable and unreliable expertise. The FBI may have had a hard time taking scholars like Arnold seriously, but it did sometimes listen to self-styled experts, figures like the cult-buster Rick Ross, whose approach to the Branch Davidians was colored by ideas such as brainwashing (that is, that charismatic cult leaders like David Koresh used mind-control techniques to maintain control over their members) that have been repudiated by scholars of religion and by the American Psychological Association.[34] In the post-9/11 age, a new kind of expert has emerged, the counterterrorism expert who claims to understand the mindset of Muslim terrorists, and such figures pose a similar problem. In fact, according to journalistic reports, reliance on this kind of expertise seems to have contributed to the anti-Muslim bias that has emerged in FBI counterterrorism training.[35]

Such developments suggest another reason for the FBI to continue to engage the academic study of religion. Twenty years after Waco persuaded the FBI that there is value in understanding more about religion, parts of the FBI still struggle with some of the same biases and blind spots detected by Sullivan and Ammerman in the 1990s. If scholars opt not to interact with the FBI because of the many quandaries such a relationship raises, they are leaving an opening for less vetted and less professionally accountable experts to step in. For its part, even if the FBI has gotten little from engaging the academic study of religion as practiced at the American Academy of Religion, it might protect itself and the public by learning how to avoid the wrong kind of teachers.

This essay—indeed, this entire volume—was born from the hope that the FBI can overcome the problems that have beset its relationship with religious communities in the past, with benefits for both religious liberty and law enforcement. In recent years, the web page listing career opportunities in the FBI's Counterterrorism Division has recommended an undergraduate degree in religion, "especially Islam," as a useful educational background for intelligence analysts. The current director of the FBI, James Comey, was a religious studies major himself and has publicly embraced partnership with educational institutions such as the U.S. Holocaust Memorial Museum, requiring every new special agent and intelligence analyst to visit the museum and learn its lessons.[36] We take these developments as a sign that the FBI remains open to engaging religious studies, and while there may be persistent organizational and cultural issues at work on both sides that make such engagement extremely difficult, we also believe, for reasons that have been laid out in the various chapters of this book, that the issues at stake are simply too important for either side to give up. Such issues include upholding the First Amendment (part of the Constitution that FBI agents are sworn to defend), how law enforcement responds to the threat of religious violence, and the future welfare of religiously motivated dissent in American democracy.

For this reason, we end this volume by calling on our fellow scholars of religion and the FBI to continue to engage each other, albeit with a greater awareness of all the problems and pitfalls posed by such an endeavor. Scholars may have been deluding themselves when they thought they could function as worldview translators and conflict resolution specialists, and perhaps FBI leaders and agents will continue to feel they have little to learn from them in a practical sense about how to interact with religious communities. But scholars do have something to contribute. At their best, they know how to hold reasoning to account and are often very good at being skeptical of pseudo-experts, skills that could have proven helpful in some of the episodes that earlier chapters describe. Our own experience in the classroom has also taught us that whatever lessons are to be learned from the academic study of religion are best learned in the right kind of environment, in a context where there is sufficient time to overcome misunderstandings and build mutual trust, time for reflection, and time for open-ended dialogue, not in the midst of a conflict, in an atmosphere of tension, pressure, and crisis. This book is offered as a contribution to that kind of learning, and whatever lessons it may contain, we hope the right people have an opportunity to learn them well before the next Waco or 9/11.

Notes

INTRODUCTION

1. "F.B.I. Chided for Training That Was Critical of Islam," *New York Times,* September 16, 2011; Spencer Ackerman, "FBI Teaches Agents: 'Mainstream' Muslims Are 'Violent, Radical,'" *Wired,* September 14, 2011, http://www.wired.com/dangerroom/2011/09/fbi-muslims-radical/all/1 (accessed October 14, 2015); Mosque Study Project, *The Mosque in America: A National Portrait* (Washington, DC: Council on American-Islamic Relations, 2001).

2. On the connection between the Oklahoma bombing and Waco, see Michael Barkun, *Religion and the Racist Right: The Origins of the Christian Identity Movement* (Chapel Hill: University of North Carolina Press, 1997).

3. Sharia Mayfield has recently published an account of her experience in *Improbable Cause: The War on Terror's Assault on the Bill of Rights* (Salem, NH: Divertir, 2015).

4. Britney J. McMahan, "Mayfield, Brandon," in *Encyclopedia of Muslim-American History,* ed. Edward E. Curtis IV (New York: Facts on File, 2010), 1:363–64. Geert-Jan G. J. Knoops, *Redressing Miscarriages of Justice: Practice and Procedure in (International) Criminal Cases* (Leiden, Germany: Martinus Nijhoff, 2013).

5. For the inspector general's report, see Office of the Inspector General, Oversight and Review Division, "A Review of the FBI's Handling of the Brandon Mayfield Case," March 2006, https://oig.justice.gov/special/s0601/final.pdf (accessed October 28, 2015).

6. Laurie Goldstein, "FBI Tool to Identity Extremists Is Criticized," *New York Times,* November 1, 2015, A10, http://www.nytimes.com/2015/11/02/us/fbi-tool-to-identify-extremists-is-criticized.html?_r=0 (accessed November 2, 2015).

7. 9/11 Review Commission, *The FBI: Protecting the Homeland in the 21st Century* (March 2015), 96, https://www.fbi.gov/stats-services/publications/protecting-the-homeland-in-the-21st-century.

8. Talal Asad, *Formations of the Secular: Christianity, Islam, Modernity* (Stanford, CA: Stanford University Press, 2003); John Lardas Modern, *Secularism in Antebellum America: With Reference to Ghosts, Protestant Subcultures, Machines, and Their Metaphors; Featuring Discussions of Mass Media, Moby-Dick, Spirituality, Phrenology, Anthropology, Sing Sing State Penitentiary, and Sex with the New Motive Power* (Chicago: University of Chicago Press, 2011); Kathryn Lofton, *Oprah: The Gospel of an Icon* (Berkeley: University of California Press, 2011); Tracy Fessenden, *Culture and Redemption: Religion, the Secular, and American Literature* (Princeton, NJ: Princeton University Press, 2007); Janet R. Jakobsen and Ann Pellegrini, eds., *Secularisms* (Durham, NC: Duke University Press, 2008).

9. For a condensation of scholarship on the FBI, see Athan Theoharis, ed., *The FBI: A Comprehensive Reference Guide* (Phoenix: Oryx, 1999); and William Vizzard, "The FBI: A Hundred Year Retrospective," *Public Administration Review* 68 (2008): 1079–86, which notes the methodological challenges of understanding the FBI from the outside and of maintaining a balanced perspective on its actions. The two histories mentioned here are Rhodri Jeffreys-Jones, *The FBI: A History* (New Haven: Yale University Press, 2008); and Timothy Weiner, *Enemies: A History of the FBI* (New York: Random House, 2012). Much additional bibliography appears below.

10. See, for example, Dianne Kirby, ed., *Religion and the Cold War* (Basingstoke, UK: Palgrave, 2003); and Jonathan Herzog, *The Spiritual-Industrial Complex: America's Religious Battle against Communism in the Early Cold War* (Oxford: Oxford University Press, 2011).

11. We are intensely conscious of the many religious groups that we were not able to encompass in this volume. One topic not addressed, for example, is the history of the FBI's interaction with American Indians, a history that goes back to 1923 when the Bureau of Investigation was called to investigate the murder of several Osage Indians. (Hoover, then assistant to the director, responded with one of his first undercover operations, sending four undercover agents into Osage territory, including one disguised as a "medicine man.") The history includes episodes such as the 1973 Wounded Knee standoff between followers of the American Indian Movement and federal officials, including FBI agents, and the 1975 shootout at Jumping Bunch Ranch, in which two FBI agents were killed. It was not for lack of trying, but we were simply unable to recruit a scholar to address possible religious dimensions of the interaction, and the subject remains a desideratum for future research. In the meantime, for a journalistic treatment of the FBI's efforts against the American Indian Movement, see Steve Hendricks, *The Unquiet Grave: The FBI and the Struggle for the Soul of Indian Country* (New York: Thunder's Mouth, 2006).

We hoped to include other religious groups as well. The antagonistic relationship between Scientologists and the FBI is a fascinating subject. See Hugh Urban, "Fair Game: Secrecy, Security, and the Church of Scientology in Cold War America," *Journal of the American Academy of Religion* 74 (2006):

356–89. So too is the FBI's more recent interaction with the Westboro Baptist Church, infamous for its homophobia and its role in picketing military funerals. (In one strange episode, the FBI invited members of the church to the marine base in Quantico, Virginia, as part of a counterterrorism training program, an initiative that was canceled after criticism from within the bureau.) See Dina Temple-Raston, "FBI Invited Controversial Church to Talk to Agents," *National Public Radio,* June 29, 2011, http://www.npr.org/2011/06/29/137454497/fbi-invited-controversial-church-to-talk-to-agents (accessed May 18, 2016).

Even Buddhists were once treated as an object of suspicion by the FBI. During World War II, the FBI compiled a list of suspected collaborators that included the leaders of Buddhist temples investigated and detained in internment campus out of a fear that they were colluding with the Japanese. See Duncan Williams, "Camp Dharma: Japanese-American Buddhist Identity and the Internment Experience of World War II," in *Westward Dharma: Buddhism beyond Asia,* ed. Charles Prebish and Martin Baumann (Berkeley: University of California Press, 2002), 191–200. Our failure to include such communities was due either to our not successfully recruiting a scholar to write on the topic or to the community having escaped our notice until it was too late in the editorial process. That is not to defend their exclusion, and we hope this volume encourages research that goes deeper and broader than we were able to go.

CHAPTER 1. AMERICAN RELIGION AND THE RISE OF INTERNAL SECURITY: A PROLOGUE

1. Federal Bureau of Investigation, United States Department of Justice, and Office of Public and Congressional Affairs, *Abridged History of the Federal Bureau of Investigation* (Washington, DC: U.S. Dept. of Justice, 1994), 1.

2. Ibid., 2; Athan G. Theoharis, *The FBI and American Democracy : A Brief Critical History* (Lawrence: University Press of Kansas, 2004), 15.

3. Theoharis, *The FBI and American Democracy,* 16; Federal Bureau of Investigation, United States Department of Justice, and Office of Public and Congressional Affairs, *Abridged History of the Federal Bureau of Investigation,* 2.

4. *Hearings Before the Subcommittee of the House Committee on Appropriations . . . in Charge of Deficiency Appropriations for 1908 and Prior Years on Urgent Deficiency Bill,* 202–3.

5. Federal Bureau of Investigation, United States Department of Justice, and Office of Public and Congressional Affairs, *Abridged History of the Federal Bureau of Investigation,* 2; Theoharis, *The FBI and American Democracy,* 16

6. Federal Bureau of Investigation, United States Department of Justice, and Office of Public and Congressional Affairs, *Abridged History of the Federal Bureau of Investigation,* 2; Theoharis, *The FBI and American Democracy,* 16–17.

7. Harry S. Stout, *Upon the Altar of the Nation: A Moral History of the Civil War* (New York: Viking, 2006), xxi.

8. Charles Reagan Wilson, *Baptized in Blood: The Religion of the Lost Cause* (Athens: University of Georgia Press, 1980), 75.

9. Linda Frost, *Never One Nation: Freaks, Savages, and Whiteness in U.S. Popular Culture, 1850–1877* (Minneapolis: University of Minnesota Press, 2005), 115; see also Edward J. Blum, "'The First Secessionist Was Satan': Secession and the Religious Politics of Evil in Civil War America," *Civil War History* 60, no. 3 (September 2014): 234–69.

10. Kelly J. Baker, *Gospel According to the Klan: The KKK's Appeal to Protestant America, 1915–1930* (Lawrence: University Press of Kansas, 2011), 7.

11. Ibid.

12. Rhodri Jeffreys-Jones, *The FBI: A History* (New Haven: Yale University Press, 2007), 22.

13. See ibid., ch. 2.

14. See Shawn Alexander, *Reconstruction Violence and the Ku Klux Klan Hearings: A Brief History with Documents* (Boston: Bedford/St. Martin's, 2015); Jeffreys-Jones, *FBI*, ch. 2. See also Eric Foner, *Reconstruction: America's Unfinished Revolution, 1863–1877*, New American Nation Series (New York: Harper & Row, 1988); W.E.B. Du Bois, *Black Reconstruction: An Essay toward a History of the Part Which Black Folk Played in the Attempt to Reconstruct Democracy in America, 1860–1880*, 1st ed. (New York: Harcourt, Brace and Company, 1935).

15. W.E.B. Du Bois, "The Conservation of Races," *American Negro Academy Occasional Papers*, no. 2, ed. Jim Manis (1897; reprinted, Pennsylvania State University Electronic Classics Series, 2006).

16. Earl Lewis, *In Their Own Interests: Race, Class, and Power in Twentieth-Century Norfolk, Virginia* (Berkeley: University of California Press, 1991), 90–92.

17. C. Eric Lincoln and Lawrence H. Mamiya, *The Black Church in the African-American Experience* (Durham, NC: Duke University Press, 1990), 21–39, 47–91; Albert J. Raboteau, *Canaan Land: A Religious History of African Americans* (Oxford: Oxford University Press, 2001), 61–81.

18. Raboteau, *Canaan Land*, 79.

19. Lerone A. Martin, *Preaching on Wax: The Phonograph and the Shaping of Modern African American Religion* (New York: New York University Press, 2014), 129.

20. Ibid., 33.

21. Jacob Riis, *How the Other Half Lives: Studies among the Tenements of New York, with Illustrations Chiefly from Photographs Taken by the Author* (New York: C. Scribner's Sons, 1890).

22. See Heath W. Carter, *Union Made: Working People and the Rise of Social Christianity in Chicago*, 1st ed. (New York: Oxford University Press, 2015). See also Ralph Luker, *The Social Gospel in Black and White: American Racial Reform, 1885–1912* (Chapel Hill: University of North Carolina Press, 1991); Terrell Dale Goddard, "The Black Social Gospel in Chicago, 1896–1906: The Ministries of Reverdy C. Ransom and Richard R. Wright, Jr.," *Journal of Negro History* 84, no. 3 (summer 1999): 227–46; Richard J. Callahan Jr., *Work and Faith in the Kentucky Coal Fields: Subject to Dust* (Bloomington: Indiana University Press, 2008); Matthew Pehl, "'Apostles of Fascism,' 'Communist Clergy,' and the UAW: Political Ideology and Working-Class Religion in Detroit,

1919–1945," *Journal of American History* 99, no. 2 (September 2012): 440–65; Jarod Roll, *Spirit of Rebellion: Labor and Religion in the New Cotton South* (Urbana: University of Illinois Press, 2010); and Wallace D. Best, *Passionately Human, No Less Divine: Religion and Culture in Black Chicago, 1915–1952* (Princeton, NJ: Princeton University Press, 2005).

23. Josiah Strong, *Our Country: Its Possible Future and Its Present Crisis* (New York: Baker & Tyler, for the American Home Missionary Society, 1891), 59.

24. Ibid., 209–10.

25. Ibid., 227 (emphasis in original).

26. See Michael P. Young, *Bearing Witness against Sin: The Evangelical Birth of the American Social Movement* (Chicago: University of Chicago Press, 2006); David Sehat, *The Myth of American Religious Freedom* (New York: Oxford University Press, 2011); Amanda Porterfield, *Conceived in Doubt: Religion and Politics in the New American Nation* (Chicago: University of Chicago Press, 2012); and James Morone, *Hellfire Nation: The Politics of Sin in American History* (New Haven: Yale University Press, 2003).

27. Kathryn Gin Lum, *Damned Nation: Hell in America from the Revolution to Reconstruction* (New York: Oxford University Press, 2014), ch. 6; and Morone, *Hellfire Nation*, 228.

28. Catharine Beecher, *A Treatise on Domestic Economy for the Use of Young Ladies at Home, and at School,* rev. ed. (Boston: Thomas H. Webb, 1843); John Todd, *The Student's Manual: Designed, by Specific Directions, to Aid in Forming and Strengthening the Intellectual and Moral Character and Habits of the Student,* 4th ed. (Northampton, MA: J.H. Butler; Boston: Crocker & Brewster and William Pierce; New York: Leavitt, Lord; Philadelphia: Wm. Marshall; Buffalo: T. & M. Butler, 1835); see Lum, *Damned Nation,* ch. 3.

29. Morone, *Hellfire Nation,* 228–29.

30. Ibid., 242.

31. Jane Addams, *Twenty Years at Hull-House: With Autobiographical Notes* (New York: Macmillan, 1912), 125.

32. Ibid., 120.

33. See Gail Bederman, *Manliness and Civilization: A Cultural History of Gender and Race in the United States, 1880–1917* (Chicago: University of Chicago Press, 1995), esp. ch. 5, "Theodore Roosevelt: Manhood, Nation, and 'Civilization.'"

34. Attorney General Charles Bonaparte to President Theodore Roosevelt, The White House, January 14, 1909, Department of Justice File, 44-3-11-Sub 3, 12/5/08–4/6/09, FBI, https://www.fbi.gov/about-us/history/brief-history/docs_lette1909 (accessed August 11, 2015).

35. Ibid.

36. Jeffreys-Jones, *FBI,* 6–7 and ch. 4, "Loss of Mission." For more on the Mann Act as a continuation of Progressive reform, see David Langum, *Crossing over the Line: Legislating Morality and the Mann Act* (Chicago: University of Chicago Press, 2007). On the role of this law in the creation of the FBI, see Jessica Pliley, *Policing Sexuality: The Mann Act and the Making of the FBI* (Cambridge, MA: Harvard University Press, 2014).

37. Online/Print Media Unit, Office of Public Affairs, Federal Bureau of Investigation, *The FBI: A Centennial History, 1908–2008* (U.S. Department of Justice, Federal Bureau of Investigation, August 2008), 1.

CHAPTER 2. "IF GOD BE FOR YOU, WHO CAN BE AGAINST YOU?" PERSECUTION AND VINDICATION OF THE CHURCH OF GOD IN CHRIST DURING WORLD WAR I

1. An earlier version of this essay appeared as chapter 6 of Theodore Kornweibel Jr., *"Investigate Everything": Federal Efforts to Compel Black Loyalty during World War I* (Bloomington: Indiana University Press, 2002).

2. "The Founder and Church History," Church of God in Christ, Inc., n.d., http://www.cogic.org/our-foundation/the-founder-church-history (accessed April 14, 2015).

3. German R. Ross, *History and Formative Years of the Church of God in Christ* (Memphis: Church of God in Christ, 1969), 14–16; Lucille J. Cornelius, *The Pioneer: History of the Church of God in Christ* (N.p.: privately printed, 1975), 9–12; I.C. Clemmons, "Mason, Charles Harrison," in *Dictionary of Pentecostal and Charismatic Movements,* ed. Stanley M. Burgess and Gary B. McGee (Grand Rapids, MI: Zondervan, 1988), 585–88.

4. "The Founder and Church History."

5. Cornelius, *Pioneer,* 3–5, 11–13; Ross, *History and Formative Years,* 17–18; David M. Tucker, *Black Pastors and Leaders: Memphis, 1819–1972* (Memphis: Memphis State University Press, 1975), 88–90.

6. Tucker, *Black Pastors,* 91. The Church of God in Christ was the first Black Pentecostal denomination, and it remains the largest. S.C. Stanley, "Churches of God," in *Dictionary of Christianity in America,* ed. Daniel G. Reid (Downers Grove, IL: InterVarsity, 1990), 279; Lawrence Neale Jones, "The Black Pentecostals," in *The Charismatic Movement,* ed. Michael P. Hamilton (Grand Rapids, MI: Eerdmans, 1975), 150.

7. Vinson Synan, *The Holiness-Pentecostal Movement in the United States* (Grand Rapids, MI: Eerdmans, 1971), 177; C.E. Jones, "Church of God in Christ," in Burgess and Moore, *Dictionary of Pentecostal and Charismatic Movements,* 204–5.

8. Tucker, *Black Pastors,* 95–96. By 1926 there were seven hundred congregations and thirty thousand members, two-thirds residing in the South, with more congregations in urban areas than in rural districts; see Charles E. Hall, *Negroes in the United States, 1920–1932* (Washington, DC: U.S. Government Printing Office, 1935), 532, 538–50.

9. Stephen M. Kohn, *Jailed for Peace: The History of American Draft Law Violators, 1658–1985* (Westport, CT: Greenwood Press, 1986), 29.

10. A good survey of this intolerance is H.C. Peterson and Gilbert C. Fite, *Opponents of War, 1917–1918* (Seattle: University of Washington Press, 1968). Other useful sources are Zechariah Chafee Jr., *Free Speech in the United States* (Cambridge, MA: Harvard University Press, 1941); Donald Johnson, *The Challenge to American Freedom: World War I and the Rise of the American Civil*

Liberties Union (Lexington: University of Kentucky Press, 1963); Harry N. Scheiber, *The Wilson Administration and Civil Liberties, 1917–1921* (Ithaca, NY: Cornell University Press, 1960); William Preston, *Aliens and Dissenters: Federal Suppression of Radicals, 1903–1933* (Cambridge, MA: Harvard University Press, 1963); Julian F. Jaffe, *Crusade against Radicalism: New York during the Red Scare, 1914–1924* (Port Washington, NY: Kennikat, 1972); Paul L. Murphy, *The Meaning of Freedom of Speech: First Amendment Freedoms from Wilson to FDR* (Westport, CT: Greenwood, 1972); and Murphy, *World War I and the Origin of Civil Liberties in the United States* (New York: W. W. Norton, 1979). For details on treatment of Black conscientious objectors, see Theodore Kornweibel Jr., "Apathy and Dissent: Black America's Negative Responses to WWI," *South Atlantic Quarterly* 80 (summer 1981): 331.

11. Paul Murphy, *World War I and the Origin of Civil Liberties* (New York: W. W Norton, 1979), 15.

12. The Black Tom explosion was an act of sabotage by German agents in midsummer 1916, destroying a large munitions depot in Jersey City from which arms and ammunition for the Allies were shipped.

13. The growing Black militancy to which the federal government took such strong objection is analyzed in depth in Kornweibel, *"Investigate Everything"*; and Kornweibel, *"Seeing Red": Federal Campaigns against Black Militancy, 1919–1925* (Bloomington: Indiana University Press, 1998).

14. Peterson and Fite, *Opponents of War,* 121–25.

15. U.S. War Department, *Statement concerning the Treatment of Conscientious Objectors in the Army* (Washington, DC: U.S. Government Printing Office 1919), 7–9, 14–19.

16. Arthur E. Barbeau and Florette Henri, *The Unknown Soldiers: Black American Troops in World War I* (Philadelphia: Temple University Press, 1974), 35–37; U.S. Provost Marshal General's Office, *Second Report of the Provost Marshal General to the Secretary of War on the Operation of the Selective Service System to December 30, 1918* (Washington, DC: U.S. Government Printing Office, 1919), 459, 461.

17. Cornelius, *Pioneer,* 68; Ross, *History and Formative Years,* 25–28.

18. "Chancery Courts have jurisdiction over disputes in matters involving equity; domestic matters including adoptions, custody disputes and divorces; guardianships; sanity hearings; wills, and challenges to constitutionality of state laws. Land records are filed in Chancery Court." "Chancery Court: About the Court," State of Mississippi Judiciary, Administrative Office of Courts, https://courts.ms.gov/aboutcourts/chancerycourt_about.html (accessed May 10, 2015). Quote from Agent M. M. Schaumburger to Bureau of Investigation, September 24, 1917, "Old German" case file 144128, Record Group 65, Investigation Case Files of the Bureau of Investigation, National Archives and Records Administration (hereafter OG[case file no.], RG65, BI, NARA).

19. Agent Schaumburger to Bureau of Investigation, September 24, 1917.

20. Schaumburger to Bureau, September 26, 1917, OG172841, and September 27, 1917, OG64788, RG65, BI, NARA.

21. Agent G. T. Holman to Bureau, February 27, 1918, OG64788, RG65, BI, NARA.

22. "Draft Evasion in Holmes County Due to Pro-German Teachings among Blacks," *Vicksburg Post,* April 1, 1918; "Negro Admits Preaching Objection to Draft," *New York Globe,* April 2, 1918; "German Money Fights Draft," *New York Sun,* April 2, 1918; "German Money," *New York Age,* April 6, 1918.

23. H. Leider, field representative, U.S. Food Administration, to Col. Ralph H. Van Deman, April 2, 1918, case file PF1811-2; Van Deman to Maj. Walter H. Loving, April 12, 1918, case file PF1811-3, both in Record Group 165, War Department, Military Intelligence Division, National Archives (hereafter RG165, MID, NARA).

24. Agent Harry T. Gulley to Bureau, April 2, 1918, OG64788, RG65, BI, NARA.

25. Ibid. The church's antiwar doctrine is printed in Cornelius, *Pioneer,* 68.

26. Gulley to Bureau, April 2, 1918, OG64788, RG65, BI, NARA.

27. "Negro Preacher Tarred," *Memphis Commercial Appeal,* April 18, 1918, p. 11.

28. Agent W.E. McElveen to Bureau, May 2, 1918, OG64788, RG65, BI, NARA.

29. Agent V.W. Killick to Bureau, June 3, 1918, OG64788, RG65, BI, NARA. The presence of Whites in the church was not unusual, for, following the interracial Azusa Street revival, there were many mixed Pentecostal congregations in the early twentieth century. Jones, "Black Pentecostals," 148; Jay Beaman, "Pacifism among the Early Pentecostals," in *Proclaim Peace: Christian Pacifism from Unexpected Quarters,* ed. Theron F. Schlabach and Richard T. Hughes (Urbana: University of Illinois Press, 1997), 89.

30. Chief A. Bruce Bielaski to Agent J.P. Finlay, May 17, 1918; Bielaski to Division Superintendent Forrest C. Pendleton, May 17, 1918, both in OG644128, RG65, BI, NARA.

31. Agent E. Palmer to Bureau, June 20, 1918, OG227347, RG65, BI, NARA; "Lexington Negro Pastor Held under New U.S. Espionage Law," *Jackson Daily News,* June 19, 1918; "Jail Pastor for Obstructing Draft," *Chicago Defender,* June 29, 1918. No record has been found to identify the men sent into the military or to determine whether they persisted in claiming to be conscientious objectors. Such summary "justice" obviously narrowed their options.

32. Palmer to Bureau, June 20, 1918, OG227347, RG65, BI, NARA; "Lexington Negro Pastor Held."

33. Col. Marlborough Churchill to F. Sullens, editor, *Jackson Daily News,* June 25, 1918; Sullens to Churchill, June 29, 1918, case file 99-7, RG165, MID, NARA; Churchill to Bielaski, July 13, 1918 (quotation), ibid.; Churchill to Intelligence Officer, Los Angeles, June 19, 1918, ibid.; and Churchill to IO, St. Louis, July 13, 1918, ibid.

34. Agent DeWitt S. Winn to Bureau, July 16, 1918, OG64788, RG65, BI, NARA.

35. Agent Claude McCaleb to Bureau, July 15, 1918, OG245662, RG65, BI, NARA.

36. Winn to Bureau, July 16, 17, 19, 1918, OG64788; McCaleb to Bureau, July 15, 16, 1918, OG245662, both in RG65, BI, NARA; "The Founder &

Church History"; McCaleb to Bureau, July 1, 16, 1918, OG245662, RG65, BI, NARA.

37. "Charged with Working Holy Roller Negroes," *Paris Morning News*, July 17, 1918; Winn to Bureau, July 19, 20, 1918, OG64788, RG65, BI, NARA; McCaleb to Bureau, July 16, 18, 1918, OG245662, RG65, BI, NARA. The trio was charged with violating sections 32 and 37 of the U.S. Penal Code.

38. "Brief History of the MSNG," Mississippi National Guard, http://ms.ng.mil/history/Pages/Brief-History-of-the-MSNG.aspx (accessed May 11, 2015).

39. Killick to Bureau, July 19, 23, 25, 1918, OG64788, RG65, BI, NARA.

40. Killick to Bureau, August 6, 1918, OG64788, RG65, BI, NARA.

41. Alfred Bettman to Lt. Van Dusen, August 8,1918, OG64788, RG65, BI, NARA; Carlton J.H. Hayes, MIS, to Special Assistant to the Attorney General John Lord O'Brian, September 4, 1918 (quotation), case file 195341, Record Group 60, Department of Justice, National Archives and Records Administration; U.S. attorney Clarence Merritt to Attorney General Thomas W. Gregory, September 21, 1918, ibid.; Churchill to Bielaski, July 26, 1918, case file 99-7, RG165, MID, NARA; Walter J. Hollenweger, "A Black Pentecostal Concept," *Concept* 30 (June 1970): 61–63; Kornweibel, "Apathy and Dissent," 330–31. Information on the other dissenting churches is in case files 99-7 and 99-68, RG165, MID, NARA, and case file OG27320, RG65, BI, NARA.

42. Division superintendent Charles E. Breniman to division superintendent Hinton G. Clabaugh, August 31, 1918; Agent R.G. Habda to Bureau, September 10, 1918; Agent W. Neunhoffer to Winn, September 16, 1918; Neunhoffer to Merritt, September 16, 1918, all in OG64788, RG65, BI, NARA.

43. Winn's death was mourned by his bureau colleagues, who testified to his dedication and professionalism. Tragically, his daughter also succumbed to influenza on the same day. Personnel file of DeWitt S. Winn, obtained from the Federal Bureau of Investigation through the Freedom of Information Act. Through the remainder of the war the flu epidemic would claim more German and Allied troops' lives than bullets.

44. Agent Lewie H. Henry to Bureau, October 27, 1918, OG64788, RG65, BI, NARA; Capt. Moss, Los Angeles, to Department Intelligence Officer, San Francisco, October 18, 1918, case file 99-7, RG 165, MID, NARA.

45. Henry to Bureau, November 2, 1918, OG64788, RG65, BI, NARA; "Local News" columns, *Paris Morning News*, October 30 and November 2, 1918 (quotation).

46. "A Complaint against Holy Roller Negroes," *Paris Morning News*, November 2, 1918; "Local News," ibid., November 3 and November 5, 1918; quotation from November 5 edition.

47. "A Complaint against Holy Roller Negroes"; "Local News," *Paris Morning News*, November 3 and November 5, 1918; quotation from November 5 edition.

48. Theodore Kornweibel Jr., *No Crystal Stair: Black Life and the* Messenger, *1917–1928* (Westport, CT: Greenwood, 1975), ch. 1; Kornweibel, "Apathy and Dissent."

49. Neither Jones's and Cornelius's authorized histories of the denomination nor Mason's own accounts provide any details on the assessment.

50. Mason quoted in Ross, *History and Formative Years,* 23–24.

51. Letter to author, August 3, 1982, National Archives and Records Administration, Southeast Region, Atlanta (East Point), Georgia. I am indebted to my late colleague Richard Steele for pointing out the differing expectations of federal grand juries and federal attorneys.

52. Beaman, "Pacifism among the Early Pentecostals," 88, 92n13, 92n14. One list of absolutist resisters is "Religious C.O.s Imprisoned at the U.S. Disciplinary Barracks, Ft. Leavenworth, Kansas," published by Mennonite minister J.D. Mininger, March 10, 1919, at Kansas City. Mininger visited prisoners at Fort Leavenworth prison and various military camps during and after the war. Michael Casey, professor of communication at Pepperdine University, has a copy of this list.

53. Beaman, "Pacifism among the Early Pentecostals," 90.

54. David Daniels, McCormick Theological Seminary, Chicago, telephone conversation with the author, October 15, 1992; Bishop George D. McKinney, St. Stephens Church of God in Christ, San Diego, to the author, August 31, 1992. Regarding COGIC men in CPS camps, see Melvin Gingerich, *Service for Peace* (Akron, PA: Mennonite Central Committee, 1949).

CHAPTER 3. THE FBI AND THE MOORISH SCIENCE TEMPLE OF AMERICA, 1926–1960

1. Muhammad Sani Umar, *Islam and Colonialism: Intellectual Responses of Muslims of Northern Nigeria to British Colonial Rule* (Boston: Brill, 2006); David Motadel, *Islam and the European Empires* (Oxford: Oxford University Press, 2014).

2. Richard Turner, *Islam in the African American Experience,* 2nd ed. (Bloomington: Indiana University Press, 2003).

3. Michael Angelo Gomez, *Black Crescent: The Experience and Legacy of African Muslims in the Americas* (Cambridge: Cambridge University Press, 2005), 203–10.

4. Incorporation papers, box 1, folder 2, MSTA Collection, New York Public Library. Gomez, *Black Crescent,* 215.

5. Gomez, *Black Crescent,* 212–13.

6. James Lorand Matory, *Black Atlantic Religion: Tradition, Transnationalism, and Matriarchy in the Afro-Brazilian Candomblé* (Princeton, NJ: Princeton University Press, 2005).

7. Rhea Whitley to Director of FBI [J. Edgar Hoover], Internal Memorandum, September 12, 1931, p. 3, FBI file 62-25889, "Moorish Science Temple of America," Part 1, U.S. Department of Justice, FBI Records: The Vault, https://vault.fbi.gov/Moorish%20Science%20Temple%20of%20America (accessed July 9, 2016). (Hereafter, all references to this online collection of FBI documents are rendered as FBI-MSTA files, FOIA Vault.) Matory, *Black Atlantic Religion,* 535. Sylvester A. Johnson, "Religion Proper and Proper Religion: Arthur Fauset and the Study of African American Religions," in *The New Black*

Gods: Arthur Fauset and the Study of African American Religions, ed. Edward E. Curtis IV and Danielle Brune Sigler (Bloomington: Indiana University Press, 2009), 153–56.

8. Rhea Whitley to Director of FBI [J. Edgar Hoover], memorandum, September 12, 1931, p. 3, Part 1, FBI-MSTA files, FOIA Vault.

9. Ibid., 2.

10. Report made at Springfield, Illinois, January 28, 1942, file no. 100-3095, unnumbered page, in Part 1, FBI-MSTA files, FOIA Vault.

11. Richmond (Virginia) FBI field office report, file no. 100-5698, December 15, 1942, in Part 1, FBI-MSTA files, FOIA Vault.

12. Ibid.

13. "Charles Kirkman Bey," Richmond (Virginia) FBI field office report, file no. 100-5698, December 15, 1942, 5, Parts 3 and 4, FBI-MSTA files, FOIA Vault.

14. "St. Mary's Church and Power Center of Applied Christianity, St. Mary's Spiritual Church: Moorish Science Temple of America," file no. 100-2273, December 8, 1942, in Part 3, FBI-MSTA files, FOIA Vault.

15. Ibid.

16. Memorandum, J. T. Pissell, War Department, Military Intelligence Service, to J. Edgar Hoover, Federal Bureau of Investigation, Department of Justice, December 18, 1942, Part 4, FBI-MSTA files, FOIA Vault.

17. Newark (New Jersey) FBI field office report, "Moorish Science Temple of America," December 15, 1942, p. 1; Indianapolis (Indiana) FBI field office report, "Colonel C. Kirkman Bey, with aliases, et al.; Moorish Science Temple of America," December 22, 1942, p. 1; and Louisville (Kentucky) FBI field office report, "Colonel C. Kirkman Bey, With aliases: William Kirkman Bey, Bill Kirkland, 'Frog Eyes' . . . ," December 26, 1942, 1, Part 4, FBI-MSTA files, FOIA Vault.

18. Jackson (Mississippi) field office report, Part 1, FBI-MSTA files, FOIA Vault.

19. Indianapolis (Indiana) field office report, Part 4, FBI-MSTA files, FOIA Vault.

20. Memorandum, Assistant Attorney General William F. Tompkins to J. Edgar Hoover, May 21, 1956, Part 20, FBI-MSTA files, FOIA Vault.

21. Ibid.

CHAPTER 4. J. EDGAR HOOVER, THE FBI, AND THE RELIGIOUS COLD WAR

1. In one decade, the religious dimension moved from being a neglected aspect to a subgenre of Cold War studies. See Dianne Kirby, *Religion and the Cold War* (Basingstoke, UK: Palgrave Macmillan, 2002); Philip Muehlenbeck, ed., *Religion and the Cold War: A Global Perspective* (Nashville: Vanderbilt University Press, 2012); and Julius Filo, ed., *Christian World Community and the Cold War* (Bratislava, Slovakia: Comenius University Press, 2012).

2. Fred Halliday, *The Making of the Second Cold War* (London: Verso, 1983), 8.

3. Reg Whitaker, "Fighting the Cold War on the Home Front: American, Britain, Australia and Canada,'" *Socialist Register* 21 (1984): 23–67.

4. Anthony Summers, *The Secret Life of J. Edgar Hoover* (London: Ebury, 1993), 54–55.

5. For a diverse range of articles addressing anticommunism, see volume 21 (1984), "The Uses of Anticommunism," of *Socialist Register.* The volume was edited by Ralph Miliband, John Saville, and Marcel Liebman.

6. Donald Crosby, *God, Church, and Flag: Senator Joseph R. McCarthy and the Catholic Church, 1950–57* (Chapel Hill: University of North Carolina Press, 1978); Steve Rosswurm, *The FBI and the Catholic Church, 1935–62* (Amherst: University of Massachusetts Press, 2009).

7. Dianne Kirby, "From Bridge to Divide: East–West Relations and Christianity during the Second World War and Early Cold War," *International History Review* 36, no. 4 (2014): 721–44. See also S. M. Miner, *Stalin's Holy War: Religion, Nationalism, and Alliance Politics, 1941–1945* (Chapel Hill: University of North Carolina Press, 2003).

8. Walter Russell Mead, *Special Providence: American Foreign Policy and How It Changed the World* (New York: Routledge, 2002).

9. Conrad Cherry, ed., *God's New Israel: Religious Interpretations of American Destiny* (Englewood Cliffs, NJ: Prentice Hall, 1971).

10. David Caute, *The Great Fear: The Anti-Communist Purge under Truman and Eisenhower* (London: Secker & Warburg, 1978), 30.

11. Douglas T. Miller and Marion Nowak, *The Fifties: The Way We Really Were* (New York: Doubleday, 1977), 38, 91.

12. Jonathan Herzog, *The Spiritual-Industrial Complex: America's Religious Battle against Communism in the Early Cold War* (Oxford: Oxford University Press, 2011), 6.

13. Ibid., 84.

14. Ibid., 84–85.

15. Robert Lamphere to Ronald Kessler, June 15, 2001, cited in Ronald Kessler, *The Bureau: The Secret History of the FBI* (New York: St Martin's Press, 2002), 103.

16. Athan Theoharis, *Spying on Americans: Political Surveillance from Hoover to the Huston Plan* (Philadelphia: Temple University Press, 1978), 160–63.

17. Frank McNaughton and Walter Heymeyer, *This Man Truman* (New York: McGraw Hill, 1945), 179.

18. Dianne Kirby, "Truman's Holy Alliance: The President, the Pope, and the Origins of the Cold War," *Borderlines: Studies in American Culture* 4, no. 1 (1997): 1–17.

19. John Cooney, *The American Pope: The Life and Times of Francis Spellman* (New York: Times Books, 1984), 146–48.

20. Kirby, "Truman's Holy Alliance."

21. Martin Eve, "Anti-Communism and American Intervention in Greece," *Socialist Register* 21 (1984): 101–13.

22. Summers, *Secret Life,* 185–86; Herzog, *Spiritual-Industrial Complex,* 85–86.

23. Testimony of J. Edgar Hoover, March 26, 1947, *Hearings before the Committee on Un-American Activities, House of Representatives, 80th Congress, 1st Session* (Washington, D.C.: U.S. Government Printing Office, 1947).

24. Hoover, "How to Fight Communism," *Newsweek* 9 (June 1947): 32.

25. Philip Brenner, "Waging Ideological War: Anti-Communism and US Foreign Policy in Central America," *Socialist Register* 21 (1984): 230–60.

26. Summers, *Secret Life*, 218.

27. Francois Houtart, "Religion and Anti-Communism: The Case of the Catholic Church," *Socialist Register* 21 (1984): 349–63.

28. *New York Herald Tribune*, February 21, 1955, cited in Dianne Kirby, "The Cold War, the Hegemony of the United States and the Golden Age of Christian Democracy,' in *World Christianities, c. 1914–c. 2000*, Vol. 9 of *The Cambridge History of Christianity*, ed. Hugh McLeod (Cambridge: Cambridge University Press, 2006), 285–303.

29. Michele Rosenthal, *American Protestants and TV in the 1950s: Responses to a New Medium* (New York: Palgrave Macmillan, 2007), 39.

30. J. Edgar Hoover, "Communism: A False Religion," in *Masters of Deceit: The Story of Communism in America* (London: Dent & Sons, 1958), 319–30.

31. Ibid.

32. Dianne Kirby, "John Foster Dulles: Moralism and Anti-Communism," *Journal of Transatlantic Studies* 6, no. 3 (2009): 279–89.

33. Hoover, "Communism," 330.

34. Kirby, "The Religious Cold War," in *The Oxford Handbook of the Cold War*, ed. Richard H. Immerman and Petra Goedde (New York: Oxford University Press, 2013), 491–530.

35. Theoharis, *Spying on Americans*, 166.

36. Robert Moats Miller, *Bishop G. Bromley Oxnam: Paladin of Liberal Protestantism* (Nashville: Abingdon, 1990), 524.

37. Veronica A. Wilson, "Anticommunism, Millennialism, and the Challenge of Cold War Patriarchy: The Many Lives of FBI Informant Herbert Philbrick," *American Communist History* 8, no. 1 (2009): 73–102.

38. Herbert Philbrick, "The Communists Are After Your Church," *Christian Herald* 76 (April 1953): 18–20, 92–95.

39. Raymond A. Schroth, *Bob Drinan: The Controversial Life of the First Catholic Priest Elected to Congress* (New York: Fordham University Press, 2011), 183, 216, 318–19.

40. Robert Wall, "Special Agent for the FBI," *New York Review of Books*, January 27, 1972, pp. 12, 14–18.

41. Adam Fairclough, "Was Martin Luther King a Marxist?" *History Workshop* 15 (1983): 117–25.

42. Hoover, "Communism."

43. Ibid.

44. Subcommittee to Investigate the Administration of the Internal Security Act and Other Internal Security Laws of the Committee on the Judiciary, United States Senate, 84th Congress, *The Communist Party of the United States: What It Is, How It Works; A Handbook for Americans* (Washington, DC: U.S. Government Printing Office, 1956), 94–95.

45. Benjamin Gitlow, *I Confess: The Truth about American Communism* (New York: E.P. Dutton, 1940). "Refusal to Speak May Send Dr. Uphaus to Jail," *Sunday Herald*, December 13, 1959, https://news.google.com/newspaper

s?nid=2229&dat=19591206&id=_OAyAAAAIBAJ&sjid=cQAGAAAAIBAJ&pg=5187,1422648&hl=en (accessed July 29, 2015).

46. Willard Uphaus, Appellant, v. Louis C. Wyman, Attorney General, State of New Hampshire, decided June 8, 1959, https://www.law.cornell.edu/supremecourt/text/360/72 (accessed 30 July 2015).

47. "Refusal to Speak."

48. All the information on Ward comes from David Nelson Duke, *In the Trenches with Jesus and Marx: Harry F. Ward and the Struggle for Social Justice* (Tuscaloosa: University of Alabama Press, 2003).

49. Ibid., 227.

50. Miller, *Bishop G. Bromley Oxnam,* 87.

51. Ibid., 531.

52. Testimony of Bishop G. Bromley Oxnam, *Hearing before the Committee on Un-American Activities, House of Representatives,* 83rd Congress, 1st sess., July 21, 1959, Internet Archive, https://archive.org/stream/testimonyofbishooounit/testimonyofbishooounit_djvu.txt (accessed May 29, 2016).

53. As recounted by Oxnam in *I Protest* (New York: Harper, 1954).

54. Hoover, "Communism."

55. Ibid.

56. Ibid.

57. Mark Silk, *Spiritual Politics: Religion and America since World War II* (New York: Simon & Schuster, 1988), 107.

58. Leo P. Ribuffo, "Moral Judgments and the Cold War: Reflections on Reinhold Niebuhr, William Appleman Williams, and John Lewis Gaddis," in *Cold War Triumphalism: The Misuse of History after the Fall of Communism,* ed. Ellen Schrecker (New York: New Press, 2004), 35.

59. Ibid., 38.

60. "Defend Right of Dissent," *Christian Century,* November 10, 1965, p. 1373, cited in Mark G. Toulouse, *Religion and Culture Web Forum,* June 2007, p. 3, http://divinity.uchicago.edu/religion-and-culture-web-forum-o.

61. Shawn Francis Peters, *The Catonsville Nine: A Story of Faith and Resistance in the Vietnam Era* (Oxford: Oxford University Press, 2012), 283. The information on the Berrigans comes from this source.

62. Heather A. Warren, *Theologians of a New World Order: Reinhold Niebuhr and the Christian Realists, 1920–1948* (New York: Oxford University Press, 1997), 128.

63. "Notes on the WCC as Between East and West," Papers of the Archbishop of Canterbury, Geoffrey Fisher, vol. 66, page 200, Lambeth Palace, London (the administrative center of the Church of England).

CHAPTER 5. APOSTLES OF DECEIT: ECUMENISM, FUNDAMENTALISM, SURVEILLANCE, AND THE CONTESTED LOYALTIES OF PROTESTANT CLERGY DURING THE COLD WAR

1. Walter Goodman, *The Committee: The Extraordinary Career of the House Committee on Un-American Activities* (New York: Farrar, Straus & Giroux, 1968), 196.

2. On Hoover's flair for the religious, see Stephen J. Whitfield, *The Culture of the Cold War,* 2nd ed. (Baltimore: Johns Hopkins University Press, 1996).

3. *Investigation of Un-American Propaganda Activities in the United States, Part 2: Testimony of J. Edgar Hoover, Director of the Federal Bureau of Investigation,* 80th Congress, 1st sess. (Washington, DC: U.S. Government Printing Office, 1947), 44.

4. Ibid., 43.

5. Ibid., 35, 44, 43.

6. Hoover preferred the formulation "Judaic-Christianity" over the more common contemporary hyphenated term "Judeo-Christianity." The phrase appears in many of his writings. See, for example, J. Edgar Hoover, *Masters of Deceit: The Story of Communism in America and How to Fight It* (New York: Henry Holt, 1958), 107; Hoover, "The Communist Menace: Red Goals and Christian Ideals," *Christianity Today,* October 10, 1960, pp. 3–4; and Hoover, "Let's Fight Communism Sanely!" *Christian Herald,* January 1962, p. 63.

7. Among historians, the notable exception to this trend has been Finnish church historian Markku Ruotsila. This chapter is especially indebted to his essays "Carl McIntire and the Fundamentalist Origins of the Christian Right," *Church History* 81, no. 2 (June 2012): 378–407; and, "'Russia's Most Effective Fifth Column': Cold War Perceptions of Un-Americanism in US Churches," *Journal of American Studies* 47, no. 4 (November 2013): 1019–41.

8. "Membership of Constituent Communions National Council Of Churches, 1960," in . . . *The Truth* (New York: National Council of the Churches of Christ in the USA, n.d. [c. 1960]), box 72, folder 5, Billy James Hargis Papers (MC 1412), Special Collections of the University of Arkansas Libraries, Fayetteville (hereafter cited as BJH).

9. Tony G. Poveda, "Controversies and Issues," in *The FBI: A Comprehensive Reference Guide,* ed. Athan G. Theoharis (Phoenix, AZ: Greenwood, 1998), 118.

10. On the wider context of state investigative committees, see Don E. Carleton, "'McCarthyism Was More Than McCarthy': Documenting the Red Scare at the State and Local Level," *Midwestern Archivist* 12, no. 1 (January 1987): 13–19.

11. Hoover rarely invoked Islam, but when he did, he hoped to call attention to the general commitment to a deity shared by all major world religions. His invocation of "Mohammedans" alongside Jews and Christians echoed President Eisenhower's contemporary rhetoric of the civic necessity of a generic commitment to religion, especially Judeo-Christianity, as a foundation for battling communism. On the cultural significance of this appeal to Judeo-Christianity and generic religious commitment, see Patrick Henry, "'And I Don't Care What It Is': The Tradition-History of a Civil Religion Proof-Text," *Journal of the American Academy of Religion* 49, no. 1 (1981): 35–49; Mark Silk, "Notes on the Judeo-Christian Tradition in America," *American Quarterly* 36, no. 1 (spring 1984): 65–85; and Kevin M. Schultz, *Tri-faith America: How Catholics and Jews Held Postwar America to Its Protestant Promise* (New York: Oxford University Press, 2013).

12. Richard Gid Powers, *G-Men: Hoover's FBI in American Popular Culture* (Carbondale: Southern Illinois University Press, 1983), 229–54; Powers, *Secrecy and Power: The Life of J. Edgar Hoover* (New York: Free Press, 1987), 346.

13. On the ideal nuclear family in the 1950s, see Elaine Tyler May, *Homeward Bound: American Families in the Cold War Era* (New York: Basic Books, 1988). For concerns about the family's breakdown and the rise in crime rates from the late 1950s through the 1970s, see Michael W. Flamm, *Law and Order: Street Crime, Civil Unrest, and the Crisis of Liberalism in the 1960s* (New York: Columbia University Press, 2005); and Robert O. Self, *All in the Family: The Realignment of American Democracy since the 1960s* (New York: Hill & Wang, 2012).

14. Powers, *G-Men,* 232, 230.

15. Hoover, *Masters of Deceit,* 106.

16. Ibid.

17. J. Edgar Hoover, "Secularism—Breeder of Crime," in *The Christian Faith and Secularism,* ed. J. Richard Spann (New York: Abingdon-Cokesbury, 1948), 180–89.

18. Ibid., 182. Hoover developed a similar argument regarding secularism, communism, and crime in "What Does the Future Hold?" *Christianity Today,* June 19, 1961.

19. Hoover, "Secularism," 187 (emphasis in the original).

20. J. Edgar Hoover, "Spiritual Priorities: Guidelines for a Civilization in Peril," *Christianity Today,* June 22, 1962, p. 3.

21. Jason W. Stevens, *God-Fearing and Free: A Spiritual History of America's Cold War* (Cambridge, MA: Harvard University Press, 2010), 25.

22. On the significance of the theological concepts of sin and salvation to mid-century U.S. culture, see Andrew S. Finstuen, *Original Sin and Everyday Protestants: The Theology of Reinhold Niebuhr, Billy Graham, and Paul Tillich in an Age of Anxiety* (Chapel Hill: University of North Carolina Press, 2009); and Stevens, *God-Fearing and Free,* 25.

23. William C. Sullivan, "How to Fight Communism," *Christian Herald,* January 1962, p. 63.

24. J. Edgar Hoover, "Faith of Our Fathers," *Christianity Today,* September 11, 1961, p. 6.

25. Ibid., 7.

26. On Graham and Hoover's relationship, see Steven P. Miller, *Billy Graham and the Rise of the Republican South* (Philadelphia: University of Pennsylvania Press, 2009); and Grant Wacker, *America's Pastor: Billy Graham and the Shaping of a Nation* (Cambridge, MA: Belknap Press of Harvard University Press, 2014).

27. William C. Martin, in *With God on Our Side: The Rise of the Religious Right in America* (New York: Broadway Books, 1996), 42, discusses the "flagship" status of *Christianity Today.*

28. J. Edgar Hoover, "Communist Propaganda and the Christian Pulpit," *Christianity Today,* October 24, 1960, p. 5.

29. Ibid.

30. Ibid.

31. Ibid., 6.

32. Ibid.

33. Internal Federal Bureau of Investigation memo, "Brief on 'Communism and Religion,'" vol. 1, March 1960, p. iii, 100-403, 529-112, Internet Archive, https://archive.org/details/foia_Communism-Religion_HQ_serial_112 (accessed April 4, 2016). This memorandum and many of the other FBI files cited in this chapter are available in the "Ernie Lazar FOIA Collection," available online through the Internet Archive, https://archive.org/details/lazarfoia.

34. "Brief on 'Communism and Religion,'" ii.

35. Ibid., iii.

36. Rhodri Jeffreys-Jones, *Cloak and Dollar: A History of American Secret Intelligence,* 2nd ed. (New Haven: Yale University Press, 2002), 92.

37. Hoover, "Spiritual Priorities," 3.

38. For further details regarding the receptiveness of evangelicals and fundamentalists to Hoover's anticommunist vision, see M.J. Heale, *American Anticommunism: Combating the Enemy Within, 1830–1970* (Baltimore: Johns Hopkins University Press, 1990), 168–77; and Jonathan P. Herzog, *The Spiritual-Industrial Complex: America's Religious Battle against Communism in the Early Cold War* (New York: Oxford University Press, 2011), 205–11. Hoover's themes also resonated with Catholics; see Philip Jenkins, *The Cold War at Home: The Red Scare in Pennsylvania, 1945–1960* (Chapel Hill: University of North Carolina Press, 1999), 166–83; and Steve Rosswurm, *The FBI and the Catholic Church, 1935–1962* (Amherst: University of Massachusetts Press, 2010).

39. On Hoover's association of Christianity with traditional Americanism, see Powers, *Secrecy and Power,* 13–20; and Whitfield, *The Culture of the Cold War,* 64–69.

40. George M. Marsden, *Fundamentalism and American Culture,* 2nd ed. (New York: Oxford University Press, 2006), 91–93.

41. Just as the NCC's activism would draw FBI interest at mid-century, in the 1910s and 1920s the FCC had similarly attracted the investigative attention of the Bureau of Investigation (BI), the precursor of the modern FBI. During World War I the BI monitored pacifist FCC clergy. The BI paid even closer attention to the FCC in the aftermath of the extralegal Palmer Raids (1919–20), which rounded up and deported communists and foreign nationals. BI agents investigated FCC clergy who drafted a resolution calling for "legislation by Congress to protect aliens in the United States," and another resolution alleging "illegal acts by Department of Justice Agents—in connection with the apprehension and detention of alien Communists" during the Palmer Raids. See, respectively, Department of Justice Memorandum "In re: the Federal Council of Churches of the Churches of Christ in the USA," December 2, 1920, 204048-P; and Department of Justice Memorandum "Re: Complaint of Federal Council of Churches of the Churches of Christ in America on Treatment of Arrested COMMUNISTS," December 24, 1920, 204048-20, both in Bureau Section Files, 1909–21, roll 943, Microfilm Publication of the Investigative Reports of the Bureau of Investigation, 1908–1922.

42. *What about the National Council of Churches?* (Denver: Colorado Council of Churches, n.d.), box 72, folder 5, BJH.

43. Jonathan J. Edwards, *Superchurch: The Rhetoric and Politics of American Fundamentalism* (East Lansing: Michigan State University Press, 2015).

44. Markku Ruotsila, *Fighting Fundamentalist: Carl McIntire and the Politicization of American Fundamentalism* (New York: Oxford University Press, 2015), offers the most comprehensive overview of the life and controversial ministry of Carl McIntire.

45. Carl McIntire, *National Council of Churches, 1963* (Collingwood, NJ: 20th Century Reformation Hour, n.d.), 8, box 34, folder 2, Radical Right Collection (90012), Hoover Institution Archives, Stanford University, Stanford, CA.

46. Matthew Avery Sutton, *American Apocalypse: A History of Modern Evangelicalism* (Cambridge, MA: Belknap Press of Harvard University Press, 2014), 285.

47. The most famous example of laypeople attempting to restrain liberal clergy was J. Howard Pew's National Lay Committee of the National Council of Churches. Pew, the president of Sun Oil Company, formed the National Lay Committee in an effort to check the social activism of clergy and discourage their participation in economic and political controversies. After clergy stymied Pew's committee, he issued a scathing report about the NCC and declared that the council and its various organs "constitute the most powerful subversive force in the United States." J. Howard Pew to B. E. Hutchinson, quoted in Allan J. Lichtman, *White Protestant Nation: The Rise of the American Conservative Movement* (New York: Atlantic Monthly Press, 2008), 194. See also Eckard V. Toy, "The National Lay Committee and the National Council of Churches: A Case Study of Protestants in Conflict," *American Quarterly* 21, no. 2 (summer 1969): 190–209.

48. [Redacted] to J. Edgar Hoover, December 7, 1954, 100-403529-37, Internet Archive, https://archive.org/details/foia_Communism-Religion-2 (accessed April 4, 2016).

49. On the sales numbers of the RSV, see Whitfield, *Culture of the Cold War,* 84. Chapter 4 in Peter J. Thuesen, *In Discordance with the Scriptures: American Protestant Battles over Translating the Bible* (New York: Oxford University Press, 2002), outlines the controversy related to RSV translators.

50. [Redacted] to J. Edgar Hoover, December 7, 1954.

51. [Redacted] to J. Edgar Hoover, November 19, 1956, 100-403529-69 (emphasis in the original), Internet Archive, https://archive.org/details/foia_Communism-Religion-3 (accessed April 4, 2016).

52. [Redacted] to J. Edgar Hoover, November 30, 1954, 100-50869-249, Internet Archive, https://archive.org/details/foia_National_Council_of_Churches-HQ-7 (accessed April 4, 2016).

53. [Redacted] to J. Edgar Hoover, May 9, 1955, 100-50869-275, Internet Archive, https://archive.org/details/foia_National_Council_of_Churches-HQ-7 (accessed April 4, 2016). In this case, the bureau replied to the correspondent to deny that it had ever classified the FCC or the NCC as subversive.

54. William C. Sullivan and Bill Brown, in *The Bureau: My Thirty Years in Hoover's FBI* (New York: W. W. Norton, 1979), 85–87, discuss Hoover's disdain for form letters.

55. J. Edgar Hoover to [redacted], June 10, 1960, 100-50869-459, Internet Archive, https://archive.org/details/foia_National_Council_of_Churches-HQ-10 (accessed April 4, 2016).

56. Sullivan and Brown, *The Bureau,* 86.

57. J. Edgar Hoover to [redacted], June 17, 1960, 100-50869-459, Internet Archive, https://archive.org/details/foia_National_Council_of_Churches-HQ-10 (accessed April 4, 2016).

58. *Testimony of J. Edgar Hoover,* 33.

59. Reprint of J. Edgar Hoover, "How to Fight Communism," *Newsweek,* June 9, 1947, 3, box 688, J. Edgar Hoover folder, J.B. Matthews Papers (RL.00857), David M. Rubenstein Rare Book and Manuscript Library, Duke University, Durham, NC.

60. The best introduction to the circuits of information exchange between the FBI and private groups is Frank J. Donner, *Age of Surveillance: The Aims and Methods of America's Political Intelligence System* (New York: Vintage, 1981).

61. Frank Hughes, *The Church League of America Story* (Wheaton, IL: Church League of America, n.d.), box 90, folder C-1970, J. Howard Pew Personal Papers (Accession 1634), Hagley Museum and Library, Wilmington, DE. See also Lichtman, *White Protestant Nation,* 96–97.

62. These details of Bundy's biography are from "Baptist Minister and Author," *New York Times,* November 13, 1966, p. 6; "Edgar C. Bundy, II," *Wheaton History A to Z,* http://a2z.my.wheaton.edu/alumni/edgar-bundy (accessed April 4, 2016); and "Edgar C. Bundy," *ReCollections: Re-telling Stories of Gems from the Wheaton College Archives and Special Collections,* December 12, 2011, http://recollections.wheaton.edu/?p=4177 (accessed April 4, 2016).

63. Edgar C. Bundy, *Apostles of Deceit* (Wheaton, IL: Church League of America, 1966), xi, 12–21. See also Edgar C. Bundy, *Collectivism in the Churches: A Documented Account of the Political Activities of the Federal, National, and World Council of Churches* (Wheaton, IL: Church League of America, 1958), 135.

64. *What Is the Church League of America?* (Wheaton, IL: Church League of America, n.d), 2; Church League of America contribution and petition form, 62-104576-195, Internet Archive, https://archive.org/details/foia_Bundy_Edgar_C.-Church_League_America-HQ-5 (accessed April 4, 2016).

65. Edgar C. Bundy, "A Special Report to All Church League of America Friends and Supporters," January 1968, p. 14, box 75, folder 26, BJH.

66. Church League promotional letter to potential supporters, n.d. (c. 1967); "The Three Services of the Church League of America," n.d. (c. 1967), both in box 75, folder 26, BJH.

67. *What Is the Church League of America?* 2.

68. Ibid., 2–3.

69. Ibid., 3.

70. "Detective Firm Says It Uses Right-Wing Group's Data," *Washington Post,* January, 27, 1977, A3.

71. See, for example, Billy James Hargis, *The National Council of Churches Indicts Itself on 50 Counts of Treason to God and Country,* 8th ed. (Tulsa, OK:

Christian Crusade, n.d.); and, David A. Noebel, *"Religion in Red": Does the National Council of Churches in the U.S.A. Speak for You??* (Tulsa, OK: Christian Crusade, n.d.), both in box 2, folder 30, BJH.

72. For an extensive discussion of Bundy's collaboration with McIntire, see Ruotsila, *Fighting Fundamentalist,* 113–40. Ruotsila documents Bundy's important role in stoking controversies over the RSV and exposing the alleged communist sympathies of Methodist bishop and former FCC president G. Bromley Oxnam.

73. Note attached to a letter from J. Edgar Hoover to [redacted], May 17, 1955, 100-50869-275, Internet Archive, https://archive.org/details/foia_National_Council_of_Churches-HQ-7 (accessed April 4, 2016).

74. J. Edgar Hoover, "Wholly Loyal," *Crusader: The American Baptist Magazine,* June 1961, p. 15, box 19, folder 17, Americans United Subject Files (MS 1555), Rare Book and Manuscript Library Collections, Columbia University, New York.

75. Ibid.

76. William C. Sullivan, "Communism and Religion in the United States," an address at Highland Park Methodist Church, Dallas, Texas, October 19, 1961, 15, box 17, folder 34, BJH.

77. "F.B.I. Aide Equates 'Far Right Aid Left,'" *New York Times,* December 1, 1962.

CHAPTER 6. THE FBI AND THE CATHOLIC CHURCH

1. John F. Cronin to Howard J. Carroll, October 7, 1945, box 24, National Catholic Welfare Conference Papers, Department of Manuscripts and Archives, Catholic University of America, Washington, DC (hereafter NCWC Papers, CUA).

2. Steve Rosswurm, *The FBI and the Catholic Church, 1935–1962* (Amherst: University of Massachusetts Press, 2009).

3. Regin Schmidt, *Red Scare: FBI and the Origins of Anticommunism in the United States, 1919–1943* (Copenhagen: Museum Tusculanum Press, 2000).

4. Richard Gid Powers, *Secrecy and Power: The Life of J. Edgar Hoover* (New York: Free Press, 1987), 144–227; Rhodri Jeffreys-Jones, *The FBI: A History* (New Haven: Yale University Press, 2007), 81–99.

5. Athan Theoharis, ed., *From the Secret Files of J. Edgar Hoover* (Chicago: Ivan R. Dee, 1991), 179–94.

6. Matthew Cecil, *Hoover's FBI and the Fourth Estate: The Campaign to Control the Press and the Bureau's Image* (Lawrence: University Press of Kansas, 2014).

7. Aaron I. Abell, *American Catholicism and Social Action: A Search for Social Justice, 1865–1950* (Garden City, NY: Hanover House, 1960), 88–89, 172–73, 185–86, 189–99, 207–28.

8. R.A. McGowan, *Bolshevism in Russia and America* (New York: Paulist, 1920), in box 25, NCWC Papers, CUA.

9. George Q. Flynn, *American Catholics and the Roosevelt Presidency, 1932–1936* (Lexington: University Press of Kentucky, 1968), xi, 36–121;

George Q. Flynn, *Roosevelt and Romanism* (Westport, CT: Praeger, 1976), xvi, 126; Abell, *American Catholicism and Social Action,* 248–56.

10. John J. Burke to Charles R. Crane, June 14, 1923; Archbishop Edward J. Hanna to M. Tchitcherin (telegram), March 28, 1923, both in box 26, NCWC Papers, CUA.

11. Michael J. Ready, memorandum, July 7, 1933; James J. Burke to the Honorable William Phillips, Undersecretary of State, September 30, 1933; William F. Montavan, Memorandum to Father Burke, Subject: Recognition of Russia, December 1933, all in box 25, NCWC Papers, CUA.

12. *NCWC News Service,* 1938–40, box 51, NCWC Papers, CUA; letter to George Leech, December 3, 1937, with attached draft response, box 23, NCWC Papers, CUA; Office Memorandum, February 10, 1938, box 51, NCWC Papers, CUA.

13. Archbishop Edward J. Mooney et al. to Hon. Franklin D. Roosevelt, December 13, 1944, box 25, NCWC Papers, CUA.

14. Powers, *Secrecy and Power,* 209–14.

15. Rosswurm, *The FBI and the Catholic Church,* 53–96.

16. Francis Joseph Cardinal Spellman, undated memorandum stamped April 19, 1955, 94-4-5826-40; SAC New York to Director FBI, Subject: Cardinal Francis Spellman, February 28, 1961, 94-4-5826-?, both at U.S. Department of Justice, FBI Records: The Vault, https://vault.fbi.gov/.

17. J. Edgar Hoover to Francis J. Spellman, November 18, 1942, 94–4-5826, U.S. Department of Justice, FBI Records: The Vault, https://vault.fbi.gov/.

18. Memorandum, SAC New York to Director FBI, February 28, 1961, 94–4-5826-?; Spellman to Hoover, June 3, 1963, 94-4-5826-59, both at U.S. Department of Justice, FBI Records: The Vault, https://vault.fbi.gov.

19. Hoover to E.E. Conroy, July 20, 1944, 62-26225-35-394; Conroy to Hoover, August 2, 1944, 62-26225-35-420; Hoover to Spellman, May 23, 1946, 94-4-5826-10; Hoover to Spellman, November 29, 1954, 94-4-5826-?; James J. Kelly to Hoover, December 28, 1954, 94-4-5826-34; copy of letter, undated, 94-4-5826-35; William G. Simon to Hoover, January 3, 1955, 94-4-5826-36; memorandum to Mr. Nichols, January 5, 1955, 94-4-5826-?; SAC New York to Director FBI, January 12, 1955, 94-4-5826-39, all at U.S. Department of Justice, FBI Records: The Vault, https://vault.fbi.gov/.

20. SAC New York to Director FBI, June 2, 1944, 94-4-5826-9; Conroy to Hoover, November 24, 1944, 94-4-5826-?; SAC New York to Director FBI, December 20, 1954, 94-4-5826-?; memorandum, April 30, 1955, 94-4-5826-[unrec.]; SAC New York to Director FBI, February 28, 1961, 94-4-5826-?; D.C. Morrell to Mr. DeLoach (memorandum), June 3, 1963, 94-1-32011-83X; SAC New York to Director FBI, May 2, 1961, 94-55315-1, all at U.S. Department of Justice, FBI Records: The Vault, https://vault.fbi.gov/.

21. Thomas C. Reeves, *America's Bishop: The Life and Times of Fulton J. Sheen* (San Francisco: Encounter Books, 2001).

22. Fulton J. Sheen to Hoover, April 21, 1944, 94-4-6389-7; Sheen to Hoover, February 19, 1958, 94-4-6389-50, both at U.S. Department of Justice, FBI Records: The Vault, https://vault.fbi.gov/.

23. Executive Conference to Mr. Tolson (memorandum), Subject: FBI National Academy Graduation Speaker, May 4, 1959, 94-4-6389-20; Hoover to Sheen, May 5, 1953, 94-4-6389-22; Hoover to Sheen, June 12, 1953, 94-4-6389-28; SAC New York to Director FBI, January 20, 1954, 94-4-6389-38; L.B. Nichols to Mr. Tolson, March 9, 1956, 94-4-6389-[unrec.], all at U.S. Department of Justice, FBI Records: The Vault, https://vault.fbi.gov/.

24. SAC New York to Director FBI (memorandum), January 9, 1967, 94-4-6389-[unrec.], U.S. Department of Justice, FBI Records: The Vault, https://vault.fbi.gov.

25. D.M. Ladd to the Director (memorandum), October 29, 1948, 94-4-6389-14; "Bishop Fulton J. Sheen," undated memorandum (May 1953), 94-4-6389-21, both at U.S. Department of Justice, FBI Records: The Vault, https://vault.fbi.gov/.

26. Joshua B. Freeman and Steve Rosswurm, "The Education of an Anticommunist: Father John F. Cronin and the Baltimore Labor Movement," *Labor History* 33 (1992): 217–47; John T. Donovan, *Crusader in the Cold War: A Biography of Fr. John F. Cronin, S.S. (1908–1994)* (New York: Peter Lang, 2005), 3–27.

27. John F. Cronin to Most Reverend Edward Mooney, October 27, 1942, box 23, NCWC Papers, CUA.

28. Ibid.

29. Cronin to Rev. Magr. Michael J. Ready, November 5, 1942, box 23, NCWC Papers, CUA.

30. John F. Cronin, "Communist Activities," n.d., attached to November 5, 1942, letter, box 23, NCWC Papers, CUA.

31. For a somewhat different interpretation, see Rosswurm, *FBI and the Catholic Church,* 147–48, which describes Cronin already at this stage as a "negative," or conservative, anticommunist.

32. Cronin to Ready, November 17, 1944, box 24, NCWC Papers, CUA.

33. Ibid.

34. John F. Cronin, "Report on the Investigation of Communism, November 13–December 31, 1944," n.d., box 24, NCWC Papers, CUA.

35. Donovan, *Crusader in the Cold War,* 165–67; Rosswurm, *FBI and the Catholic Church,* 150–54, 159–60, 162–67.

36. Rosswurm, *FBI and the Catholic Church,* 150–51, 153–54, 156, 159–60, 162–64, 166–67.

37. John F. Cronin to Howard J. Carroll, October 7, 1945, box 24, NCWC Papers, CUA.

38. Allen Weinstein, *Perjury: The Hiss-Chambers Case* (New York: Vintage Books, 1979); Ronald Radosh and Joyce Milton, *The Rosenberg File: A Search for the Truth* (London: Weidenfeld & Nicolson, 1983).

39. John Earl Haynes, Harvey Klehr, and Alexander Vassiliev, *Spies: The Rise and Fall of the KGB in America* (New Haven: Yale University Press 2009), 1–143.

40. Karl J. Alter to Your Excellency, December 4, 1945, box 24, NCWC Papers, CUA; Cronin to Carroll, October 7, 1945, box 24, NCWC Papers, CUA.

41. A copy of the report was found in the papers of Karl Baarslag, the anticommunist expert of the American Legion (box 5, Karl Baarslag Papers, Hoover Institution Archives, Stanford University, Stanford, CA).

42. John F. Cronin, *The Problem of American Communism in 1945: Facts and Recommendations; A Confidential Study for Private Circulation* (Baltimore: St. Mary's Seminary, October 29, 1945), in box 24, NCWC Papers, CUA.

43. Ibid., 1, 4–6; Cronin, "Addenda to November Report," ibid., 146a.

44. Cronin, *Problem of American Communism in 1945*, 3, 6–15, 61.

45. Ibid., 16–44a.

46. Ibid, iii.

47. Ibid., 49; also 51.

48. Ibid., 47–52, 146a.

49. Ibid., 62.

50. Ibid., 64–80.

51. Rosswurm, *FBI and the Catholic Church*, 174.

52. Charles E. Curran, *American Catholic Social Ethics: Twentieth-Century Approaches* (Notre Dame, IN: University of Notre Dame Press, 1982), 173–75; Charles E. Curran and Richard A. McCormick, *Official Catholic Social Teaching* (New York: Paulist, 1986), 69–76.

53. Donovan, *Crusader in the Cold War*, 55–69.

54. Ibid., 52; Weinstein, *Perjury*, 7–8.

55. Donovan, *Crusader in the Cold War*, 42–45.

56. Ibid., 143–88.

57. Marie Gayte, "The Vatican and the Reagan Administration: A Cold War Alliance?" *Catholic Historical Review* 97 (2011): 713–36.

58. Theoharis, *From the Secret Files of J. Edgar Hoover*, 317–23; Athan Theoharis and John Stuart Cox, *The Boss: J. Edgar Hoover and the Great American Inquisition* (New York: Bantam Books, 1990), 307–31.

59. Robert Ellsberg, "Five Years with Dorothy Day," *America*, November 21, 2005, http://americamagazine.org/print/147492 (accessed June 16, 2015); Robert Ellsberg, "Dorothy Day: Unapologetic Radical, but No Marxist," *Sojourners*, March 29, 2010, http://sojo.net/print/blogs/2010/03/29/dorothy-day-unapologetic-radical-no-marxist (accessed June 16, 2015).

60. Richard Steven Street, "The FBI's Secret File on César Chávez," *Southern California Quarterly* 78 (1996): 347–84.

CHAPTER 7. HOOVER'S JUDEO-CHRISTIANS: JEWS, RELIGION, AND COMMUNISM IN THE COLD WAR

1. J. Edgar Hoover to [redacted], January 25, 1960, "Zionist Organization of America" FBI files (hereafter, ZOA files), 7 of 10, p. 13.

2. "Testimony of J. Edgar Hoover, Director of Federal Bureau of Investigation," *Investigation of Un-American Propaganda Activities in the United States: Hearing before the Committee on Un-American Activities, House of Representatives, Eightieth Congress, First Session, on March 26, 1947* (Washington, DC: Government Printing Office, 1947), 44.

3. Patrick Henry, "And I Don't Care What It Is: The Tradition-History of a Civil Religion Proof-Text," *Journal of the American Academy of Religion* 49 (1981): 41.

4. Nathan Glazer, *The Social Basis of American Communism* (New York: Harcourt Brace, 1961), 130.

5. Stuart Svonkin, *Jews against Prejudice: American Jews and the Fight for Civil Liberties* (New York: Columbia University Press, 1999), 114–16; Larry Ceplair, *Anticommunism in Twentieth-Century America: A Critical History* (Santa Barbara, CA: ABC-CLIO, 2011), 119–20.

6. Svonkin, *Jews against Prejudice,* 159–72; Marc Dollinger, *Quest for Inclusion: Jews and Liberalism in Modern America* (Princeton, NJ: Princeton University Press, 2000), 133–37.

7. "Saboteurs Avoid Atom Bomb Plant," *New York Times,* December 26, 1951, p. 26.

8. For an in-depth story, see Eric Schlosser, "Break-In at Y-12," *New Yorker,* March 9, 2015, pp. 46–69.

9. Aviva Weingarten, *Jewish Organizations' Responses to Communism and Joseph McCarthy* (London: Valentine & Mitchell, 2008), 33–34.

10. Charles Herbert Stember, *Jews in the Mind of America* (New York: Basic Books, 1966).

11. "FBI Is Main Target at Rights Conference," *New York Times,* July 17, 1949, p. 10.

12. Peter Novick, *The Holocaust in American Life* (New York: Houghton Mifflin, 1999), 93.

13. FBI "Surreptitious Entries" File, 62-117-166, Part 14 of 23, Department of Justice, FBI Records: The Vault (vault.fbi.gov). On the Emma Lazarus Federation, see Joyce Antler, "Between Culture and Politics: The Emma Lazarus Federation of Jewish Women's Clubs and the Promulgation of Women's History, 1944–1989," in *U.S. History as Women's History: New Feminist Essays,* ed. Linda K. Kerber, Alice Kessler-Harris, and Kathryn Kish Sklar (Chapel Hill: University of North Carolina Press, 1995).

14. Committee on the Study of Teaching Materials in Intergroup Relations, *Intergroup Relations in Teaching Materials: A Survey and Appraisal* (Washington, DC: American Council on Education, 1949), 105.

15. FBI "Charlie Chaplain," April 5, 1951, File 100-15641, Part 8 of 10, p. 80, Department of Justice, FBI Records: The Vault (vault.fbi.gov).

16. Walter Roth, *Looking Back: Stories from Chicago's Jewish Past* (Chicago: Academy Chicago, 2002), 243–45.

17. Tony Poveda, "The Traditions and Cultures of the FBI," in *The FBI: A Comprehensive Reference Guide,* ed. Athan H. Theoharis, ed. (Phoenix, AZ: Oryx Press, 1999), 196.

18. David Caute, *The Great Fear: The Anti-Communist Purge under Truman and Eisenhower* (New York: Simon & Schuster, 1978), 115.

19. "Summary of the Communist Infiltration into the Motion Picture Industry," July 15, 1949, reprinted in Daniel Leab, "Communist Activity in the Entertainment Industry: FBI Surveillance Files on Hollywood, 1942–1958" (reel 13, frame 167, Microfilm Collection, University Publications of America, 1991). See

also John Noakes, "Racializing Subversion: The FBI and the Depiction of Race in Cold War Movies," *Racial and Ethnic Studies* 26, no. 4 (2003): 728–49.

20. Jewish Telegraph Agency, "J. Edgar Hoover Differentiates FBI from St. Louis Classification System," October 20, 1949.

21. Aaron Beim and Gary Allen Fine, "Cultural Frameworks of Prejudice: Reputational Images and the Postwar Disjuncture of Jews and Communism," *Sociological Quarterly* 48 (2007): 388.

22. Weingarten, *Jewish Organizations' Responses,* 68.

23. Curt Gentry, *J. Edgar Hoover: The Man and the Secrets* (New York: W.W. Norton, 1991), 354–58. For more of the details of this complex and ongoing relationship, see the essays in *Beyond the Hiss Case,* ed. Athan Theoharis (Philadelphia: Temple University Press, 1992).

24. Howard Suber, "Politics and Popular Culture: Hollywood at Bay, 1933–1953," *American Jewish History* (June 1979): 517–33.

25. Joseph Litvak, *The Un-Americans: Jews, the Blacklist, and Stoolpigeon Culture* (Durham, NC: Duke University Press, 2009), 14.

26. *Red Channels: The Report of Communist Influence in Radio and Television* (New York: Counterattack, 1950).

27. Nancy E. Bernhard, *U.S. Television News and Cold War Propaganda, 1947–1960* (Cambridge: Cambridge University Press, 2003), 56.

28. Glenn D. Smith Jr., "'The Guiding Spirit': Philip Loeb, the Battle for Television Jurisdiction, and the Broadcasting Industry Blacklist," *American Journalism* 29, no. 3 (2009): 93–126.

29. Theoharis, *Beyond the Hiss Case,* 64–66.

30. For one recent example, see Marjorie Garber and Rebecca Walkowitz, eds., *Secret Agents: The Rosenberg Case, McCarthyism, and the Fifties* (New York: Routledge, 1995).

31. ZOA file, 10 of 10.

32. [Redacted] to Hoover, January 8, 1948, ZOA file, 1 of 10, p. 25.

33. Hoover to [redacted], April 20, 1961, ZOA file, 7 of 10.

34. J. Edgar Hoover, *Masters of Deceit: The Story of Communism and How to Fight It* (New York: Henry Holt, 1958), 266.

35. File 9-15269, Department of Justice, FBI Records: The Vault (vault.fbi.gov). The file contains mainly missing page reports, entirely blacked-out pages, and some newspaper clippings. Hoover's name is signed on the bottom of several otherwise all-blacked-out documents.

36. Raphael Medoff, *Militant Zionism in America: The Rise and Impact of the Jabotinsky Movement in the United States, 1926–1948* (Tuscaloosa: University of Alabama Press, 2002), 191.

37. Henry, "And I Don't Care What It Is," 41.

38. On the history of the term "Judeo-Christian," see Mark Silk, "Notes on the Judeo-Christian Tradition in America," *American Quarterly* 36 (spring 1984): 65–85.

39. Jonathan Herzog, *The Spiritual Industrial Complex* (Oxford: Oxford University Press, 2011), 69.

40. Historian Kevin Schultz has called the late 1940s and 1950s the "triumphant years" of the American trifaith image; *Tri-Faith America: How Catholics*

and Jews Held Postwar America to Its Protestant Promise (New York: Oxford University Press, 2011), 7.

41. *Congressional Record, Proceedings and Debates of the 80th Congress,* March, 26, 1947 (Washington, DC: U.S. Government Printing Office, 1947), 43.

42. Cheryl Greenberg, *Troubling the Waters: Black-Jewish Relations in the American Century* (Princeton, NJ: Princeton University Press, 2006), 175.

43. Arnold Shankman, "A Temple Is Bombed—Atlanta, 1958," *American Jewish Archives* 23, no. 3 (1971): 131.

44. "Statement of Rabbi Rothschild and William Schwartz, Jr." *Southern Israelite,* October 17, 1959, 1.

45. Committee on the Study of Teaching Materials in Intergroup Relations, *Intergroup Relations,* 171.

46. Hoover, *Masters of Deceit,* 223.

47. Ibid.

48. Ibid.

CHAPTER 8. POLICING PUBLIC MORALITY: HOOVER'S FBI, OBSCENITY, AND HOMOSEXUALITY

1. On the FBI and its public image, see Matthew Cecil, *Hoover's FBI and the Fourth Estate: The Campaign to Control the Press and the Bureau's Image* (Lawrence: University Press of Kansas, 2014). Cecil is also working on a book examining the Crime Records Division. Examples of Hoover's anticommunist educational campaign include the following: "FBI Head Sees Red Attacking Religion," *New York Times,* May 6, 1954; J. Edgar Hoover, "An Open Letter to College Students," September 21, 1970, Richard Nixon Presidential Library, http://www.nixonlibrary.gov/virtuallibrary/documents/jul10/58.pdf (accessed June 22, 2016).

2. Trude B. Feldman, "J. Edgar Hoover Discusses His Religious and Ethical Values," *Chicago Tribune,* December 26, 1971.

3. Ibid.

4. Ibid.

5. Richard Gid Powers, *Secrecy and Power: The Life of J. Edgar Hoover* (New York: Free Press, 1987), 12–18.

6. On Hoover's lack of church attendance in adulthood, see Anthony Summers, *Official and Confidential: The Secret Life of J. Edgar Hoover* (New York: Putnam, 1993).

7. See Douglas M. Charles, *Hoover's War on Gays: Exposing the FBI's "Sex Deviates" Program* (Lawrence: University Press of Kansas, 2015), 10–21, 29–32.

8. For a detailed examination of the Mattson case and the FBI's systematic collection of information about gays, see Charles, *Hoover's War on Gays,* ch. 2.

9. J. Edgar Hoover, "War on the Sex Criminal," *New York Herald Tribune,* September 26, 1937, p. 2; Hoover, "War on the Sex Criminal!" *Los Angeles Times,* September 26, 1937, K2; Ralph H. Major Jr., "New Moral Menace to Our Youth," *Coronet,* September 1950, p. 11.

10. Hoover, "War on the Sex Criminal," 2.

11. Ibid.

12. Ibid., 2, 23.

13. J. Edgar Hoover, "How Safe Is Your Daughter?" *American Magazine* 144 (July 1947): 32.

14. Ibid.

15. J. Edgar Hoover, "Needed: A Quarantine to Prevent Crime," *Milwaukee Journal,* March 10, 1957, p. 8.

16. Ibid., 9–10; *Mattachine Newsletter,* April 1957, in FBI 100-45888-1A59, U.S. Department of Justice, FBI Records: FOIA request.

17. See Douglas M. Charles, *The FBI's Obscene File: J. Edgar Hoover and the Bureau's Crusade against Smut* (Lawrence: University Press of Kansas, 2012), 20–31.

18. [Redacted] to Cartha DeLoach, July 7, 1959, FBI 80-662-NR, U.S. Department of Justice, FBI Records: FOIA request.

19. Ibid.

20. For a discussion of the FBI and *Our Sunday Visitor,* see Steve Rosswurm, *The FBI and the Catholic Church, 1935–1962* (Boston: University of Massachusetts Press, 2009), 70–80.

21. J. Edgar Hoover, "Combating Merchants of Filth: The Role of the FBI," *University of Pittsburgh Law Review* 25, no. 3 (March 1964): 469.

22. Ibid., 469–70.

23. Ibid., 470–71.

24. Ibid., 471.

25. Ibid., 474.

26. J. Edgar Hoover, "Poison for Our Youth: FBI Chief Calls for Nationwide Effort to Curb Obscenity," *Our Sunday Visitor,* December 27, 1964, p. 1 (page numbers reflect the FBI's FOIA-released master copy).

27. Ibid., 2.

28. Charles, *FBI's Obscene File,* 31–32; Hoover, "Poison for Our Youth," 2.

29. Hoover, "Poison for Our Youth," 2.

30. Ibid., 3.

31. See Charles, *The FBI's Obscene File,* 86.

CHAPTER 9. THE FBI AND THE NATION OF ISLAM

1. Memo, Washington, D.C., Field Office to Chicago Field Office, June 13, 1942, pp. 1–5, FBI HQ File on Wallace D. Fard.

2. In a lengthy statement to the FBI made on September 20, 1942, Elijah Muhammad conceded that the Nation of Islam taught self-defense to its male members by using wooden rifles. Memo, Chicago Field Office to FBI HQ, September 30, 1942, p. 37, FBI HQ File on Wallace F. Fard.

3. Ibid.

4. Ibid. Reference Report dated April 2, 1942, FBI HQ File on Wallace F. Fard.

5. Memo, Chicago Field Office to FBI HQ, September 30, 1942, p. 37, FBI HQ File on Wallace F. Fard.

6. Immigration and Naturalization Service (INS) Record 55,850–677, on "Abdul Mohammed," April 18, 1934, in *U.S. Subject Index to Correspondence and Case Files of the Immigration and Naturalization Service, 1903–1959,* online database, Ancestry.com (accessed May 12, 2013, 8:04 P.M.).

7. INS Record 55,818–465 on "Taka Ashe," July 15, 1919, in *U.S. Subject Index to Correspondence and Case Files of the Immigration and Naturalization Service, 1903–1959,* Ancestry.com (accessed April 30, 2013, 12:33 P.M.).

8. "For Action on Race Riot Peril," *New York Times,* October 5, 1919, A1.

9. "Voodoo's Reign Here Is Broken: Slayer Held Insane; Fard Quits City," *Detroit Free Press,* December 7, 1932, A7.

10. Memo, Chicago Field Office to HQ, September 11, 1942, p. 2, FBI HQ File on Wallace D. Fard.

11. "Another Negro Fanatic Seized as Plot, Leader; U.S. Continues Probe of Jap Influence," *Chicago Daily Tribune,* September 23, 1942, A8.

12. See, in general, the FBI HQ file on Elijah Muhammad and the FBI HQ file on Malcolm X Little.

13. Memo, Chicago Field Office to HQ, May 16, 1957, pp. 1–2, FBI HQ File on Wallace D. Fard.

14. See J. Edgar Hoover, *Masters of Deceit* (New York: Henry Holt, 1958), 243–54.

15. "June File" Memo to U.S. Attorney General, December 31, 1956, FBI HQ File on Elijah Muhammad.

16. Malcolm X knew that he was under surveillance even earlier. See Karl Evanzz, *The Messenger: The Rise and Fall of Elijah Muhammad* (New York: Pantheon, 1999), 166.

17. CX: "Background Information on Wallace Dodd (alias Fard, Farrad, etc.)" FBI memo dated March 8, 1965, Section 1, pp. 6–8, FBI HQ File on Wallace D. Fard.

18. Ibid.

19. "House to Probe Black Muslims," *Miami News,* August 14, 1962, p. 10.

20. "Check Black Muslims," *Owosso (Michigan) Argus-Press*, August 22, 1962, p. 3.

21. "Nation of Islam Offers Hearst $100,000 to Prove Charge," *Muhammad Speaks,* August 14, 1963, African-American newspaper archives, Moorland-Spingarn Research Center, Howard University; see also Section 3, pp. 339–41, FBI HQ File on Wallace D. Fard (reproduction).

22. Karl Evanzz, *The Judas Factor: The Plot to Kill Malcolm X* (New York: Thunder's Mouth, 1992), 76–78.

23. Ibid.

24. Evanzz, *Messenger,* 171–72.

25. Evanzz, *Judas Factor,* 73.

26. Ibid., 74.

27. "Ali's Trainer Told FBI of Boxer's Islam Ties: Angelo Dundee Met with Agents before 1964 Title Bout," *The Smoking Gun,* February 1, 2013, http://www.thesmokinggun.com/documents/angelo-dundee-fbi-487613 (accessed June 24, 2016).

28. Memo, Hoover to all FBI field offices, August 25, 1967, COINTELPRO: Black Nationalist—Hate Groups, Department of Justice, FBI Records: The Vault (vault.fbi.gov).

29. Some of the files are available in the FBI's electronic "Reading Room" at https://vault.fbi.gov/reading-room-index; see, for example, "James Marshall 'Jimi' Hendrix," https://vault.fbi.gov/james-marshall-jimi-hendrix/james-marshall-jimi-hendrix/view (accessed June 24, 2016).

30. Memo, Assistant FBI Director William C. Sullivan to all FBI field offices. See also Rob Warden, "Hoover Rated Carmichael as 'Black Messiah,'" *Chicago Daily News,* February 10, 1976, p. 10; and general news reports about the memo at https://vault.fbi.gov/cointel-pro/new-left/cointel-pro-new-left-hq-part-05-of-05 (accessed June 24, 2016).

31. "Libya Makes $3 Million Loan to Black Muslims," *Jet,* May 25, 1972, p. 44.

CHAPTER 10. DREAMS AND SHADOWS: MARTIN LUTHER KING JR., THE FBI, AND THE SOUTHERN CHRISTIAN LEADERSHIP CONFERENCE

1. Barack Obama, "Remarks by the President at the Martin Luther King, Jr. Memorial Dedication," The White House, October 16, 2011, http://www.whitehouse.gov/the-press-office/2011/10/16/remarks-president-martin-luther-king-jr-memorial-dedication (accessed April 25, 2015).

2. Senate Report No. 94–755 (1976), *Final Report of the Select Committee to Study Governmental Operations with Respect to Intelligence Activities: United States Senate Supplementary Detailed Staff Reports on Intelligence Activities and the Rights of Americans, Book III: Dr. Martin Luther King Jr., a Case Study* (Washington, DC: U.S. Government Printing Office, 1976), 82–97.

3. Martin Luther King, Jr., "Will Capitalism Survive?" in *The Papers of Martin Luther King, Jr., Volume VI: Advocate of the Social Gospel, September 1948–March 1963,* ed. Clayborne Carson (Berkeley: University of California Press, 2007), 104–5.

4. Martin Luther King, Jr., "Can a Christian Be a Communist?" in *Papers of Martin Luther King, Jr.,* 4:446–54.

5. Senate Report No. 94-755 (1976), *Final Report of the Select Committee,* 93–95.

6. Michael Friedly and David Gallen, eds., *Martin Luther King, Jr.: The FBI File,* 1st ed. (New York: Carroll & Graf, 1993), 23–25; Gerald McKnight, *The Last Crusade: Martin Luther King, Jr., the FBI, and the Poor People's Campaign* (Boulder, CO: Westview Press, 1998), 8.

7. Senate Report No. 94-755 (1976), *Final Report of the Select Committee,* 93–95.

8. George Kennan, "The Sources of Soviet Conduct," *Foreign Affairs* (July 1947): 566–82. William Pietz, "The Post-Colonialism of Cold War Discourse," *Social Text* 19–20 (autumn 1988): 63–65.

9. Senate Report No. 94-755 (1976), *Final Report of the Select Committee,* 107.

10. Ibid., 113.

11. Ibid., 87.

12. Ibid., 11–12; "Ga. KKK Asks Probe of Liberal School Ousted from Tennessee," *Chicago Defender,* July 25, 1963; Jeff Woods, *Black Struggle, Red Scare: Segregation and Anti-Communism in the South, 1948–1968* (Baton Rouge: Louisiana State University Press, 2004), 12–15.

13. David J. Garrow, *The FBI and Martin Luther King, Jr.: From "Solo" to Memphis,* 1st ed. (New York: W.W. Norton, 1981), 25–50.

14. Senate Report No. 94-755 (1976), *Final Report of the Select Committee,* 100.

15. Ibid., 133–59.

16. Ibid., 131–32.

17. Ibid., 139–142.

18. Lillian S. Calhoun, "Confetti," *Chicago Daily Defender,* January 28, 1965; "Raise Voices on Race Issue, Dr. King Urges: Feted in Home Town as Nobel Winner," *Chicago Tribune,* January 28, 1965; "Atlanta Praises Dr. King at Fete: Integration Leader Honored for Winning Nobel Prize," *New York Times,* January 28, 1965.

19. Senate Report No. 94-755 (1976), *Final Report of the Select Committee,* 158–60.

20. Martin Luther King Jr., Statement to SCLC Convention, Birmingham, Alabama, August 12, 1965, Martin Luther King Jr. Research and Education Institute, Stanford University, http://mlk-kpp01.stanford.edu/index.php/encyclopedia/documentsentry/statement_by_king_at_the_sclc_convention/ (accessed April 10, 2014).

21. David S. Broder and William Chapman, "Secret Struggle over King: Story behind King's New Role," *Washington Post and Times-Herald,* April 16, 1967, A1.

22. Paul Good, "The Rev. Mr. Bevel Makes His Protest in a Yarmulke: Reinforcing the Rhetoric," *Washington Post,* April 30, 1967; James E. Westheider, *The African American Experience in Vietnam: Brothers in Arms* (Lanham, MD: Rowman & Littlefield, 2008), 64.

23. Broder and Chapman, "Secret Struggle over King," A1.

24. Penny M. Von Eschen, *Race against Empire: Black Americans and Anticolonialism, 1937–1957* (Ithaca, NY: Cornell University Press, 1997). Sylvester A. Johnson, *African American Religions, 1500–2000: Colonialism, Democracy, and Freedom* (New York: Cambridge University Press, 2015), 358–62.

25. Richard Dougherty, "Thousands March in War Protests: 100,000 Take Demands to U.N. as Others Rally across Nation; Thousands in Marches Protesting Viet War," *Los Angeles Times,* April 16, 1967; Good, "Rev. Mr. Bevel Makes His Protest"; Paul Hofmann, "Dr. King Is Backed for Peace Ticket," *New York Times,* April 22, 1967.

26. Good, "Rev. Mr. Bevel Makes His Protest"; Dougherty, "Thousands March in War Protests"; Hofmann, "Dr. King Is Backed for Peace Ticket."

27. Dougherty, "Thousands March in War Protests"; Good, "Rev. Mr. Bevel Makes His Protest"; Hofmann, "Dr. King Is Backed for Peace Ticket."

28. Harvard Sitkoff, *King: Pilgrimage to the Mountaintop* (New York: Macmillan, 2009), 217–18.

29. Peter B. Levy, "Blacks and the Vietnam War," in *The African American Voice in U.S. Foreign Policy since World War II*, ed. Michael L. Krenn (New York: Garland, 1998), 178–79; Fairclough, *To Redeem the Soul of America*, 507; and Simon Hall, *Peace and Freedom: The Civil Rights and Antiwar Movements of the 1960s* (Philadelphia: University of Pennsylvania Press, 2005), 82–87.

30. Garrow, *FBI and Martin Luther King, Jr.*, 180–90; McKnight, *Last Crusade*, 23.

31. U.S. Senate, "The Use of Informants in FBI Intelligence Investigations," in *Final Report of the Select Committee to Study Governmental Operations with Respect to Intelligence Activities: Book III, Supplementary Detailed Staff Reports on Intelligence Activities and the Rights of Americans*, 228.

32. Senate Report No. 94-755 (1976), *Final Report of the Select Committee*, 81, 82–83.

33. Von Eschen, *Race against Empire*, 177–80.

34. Carl Rowan, "Martin Luther King's Tragic Decision," *Reader's Digest* (September 1967): 37–42.

35. Ibid., 38, 41–42. As USIA director, Rowan had received a copy of the FBI's derisive "King monograph," which asserted that both King and SCLC were controlled by communists and were a veritable national security threat. Writing one year after King's assassination, Rowan claimed the monograph was mostly "barnyard gossip" and contained little related to matters of national security. See Senate Report No. 94-755 (1976), *Final Report of the Select Committee*, 133n220.

36. "Counterintelligence Program Black Nationalist—Hate Groups Internal Security," memorandum, FBI Director [J. Edgar Hoover] to FBI field offices, August 25, 1967, FBI file no. 100-448006, COINTELPRO Black Extremist, part 1 of 23, U.S. Department of Justice, FBI Records: The Vault, https://vault.fbi.gov/cointel-pro/cointel-pro-black-extremists (accessed April 13, 2015).

37. Federal Bureau of Investigation, "Martin Luther King, Jr.: A Current Analysis," March 12, 1968, in Friedly and Gallen, *Martin Luther King, Jr.*, 557.

38. Ibid., 555–70.

39. Les Payne, "FBI Tied to King's Return to Memphis," *Newsday*, February 1, 1976, in Friedly and Gallen, *Martin Luther King, Jr.*, 663–64; McKnight, *Last Crusade*, 46–48; David Levering Lewis, *King: A Biography*, 3rd ed. (Urbana: University of Illinois Press, 2013), 380–81, 384.

40. Payne, "FBI Tied to King's Return to Memphis," 663–64.

41. Friedly and Gallen, *Martin Luther King, Jr.*, 18; Garrow, *The FBI and Martin Luther King, Jr.*; McKnight, *Last Crusade*. Despite his substantial attention to the personality of Hoover, McKnight does, nevertheless, identify the primary factor in King's repression as the FBI's interest in preserving the racial politics of the United States.

42. Friedly and Gallen, *Martin Luther King, Jr.*, 66–67.

43. Ibid., 61.

44. Michael Omi, *Racial Formation in the United States: From the 1960s to the 1990s*, 2nd ed. (New York: Routledge, 1994); David Theo Goldberg, *The Racial State* (Malden, MA: Blackwell, 2002).

CHAPTER 11. A VAST INFILTRATION: MORMONISM AND THE FBI

1. The Bretzing-Miller story is told in William Overend, "Richard T. Bretzing: FBI's LA Boss Passes Hardest Test," *Los Angeles Times,* January 11, 1987, p. 1; Overend, "Mormon Issue Raised in Miller Spy Trial," *Los Angeles Times,* August, 29, 1985, C1; Overend, "Showdown over Miller Mormon Issue Fizzles," *Los Angeles Times,* October, 4, 1985, B1.

2. Overend, "Richard T. Bretzing"; idem, "Mormon Issue Raised." For the image of the "G-man" in mid-twentieth-century America, see Claire Potter, *War on Crime: Bandits, G-men, and the Politics of Mass Culture* (New Brunswick, NJ: Rutgers University Press, 1998); and Richard Gid Powers, *G-Men: Hoover's FBI in American Popular Culture* (Carbondale: Southern Illinois University Press, 1998).

3. William Overend, "FBI Official Says Mormon Bias Prevented Firing of Spy Suspect," *Los Angeles Times,* October 3, 1985, A3.

4. Catherine Gewertz, "Spy Suspect Held Coveted Office Job," United Press International, October 5, 1985.

5. "Spy Suspect Is Released on $500,000 Bond," *Washington Post,* May 9, 1984, A3.

6. Francis McNamara, "William Webster and the Future of US Intelligence," *Human Events,* May 23, 1987, p. 10.

7. Parley Parker Pratt, *The Angel of the Prairies; Or, a Dream of the Future* (Salt Lake City: A. Pratt, 1850), 17. For Mormon protests that Latter-day Saints possessed true Americanism, see R. Laurence Moore, *Religious Outsiders and the Making of Americans* (New York: Oxford University Press, 1986), 45–46.

8. Jan Shipps, *Mormonism: The Story of a New Religious Tradition* (Urbana: University of Illinois Press, 1987), 131–51; Katie Clark Blakesley, "A Style of Our Own: Modesty and Mormon Women, 1951–2008," *Dialogue: A Journal of Mormon Thought* 42, no. 2 (summer 2009): 20–53. On the "Word of Wisdom," Mormonism's dietary code, see Thomas G. Alexander, *Mormonism in Transition: A History of the Latter-day Saints, 1890–1930* (Urbana: University of Illinois Press, 1986), 258–72.

9. Donna Anderson, "Mormon Missionaries Mistaken for CIA Agents Abroad," *Salt Lake Tribune,* October 1, 1981.

10. Anderson, "Mormon Missionaries Mistaken for CIA Agents Abroad." On the disciplining of young Mormons for missionary service, see Gregory Prince and William Robert Wright, *David O. McKay and the Rise of Modern Mormonism* (Salt Lake City: University of Utah Press, 2005), 227–56; and Tania Rands Lyon and Mary Ann Shumway McFarland, "Not Invited but Welcome: The History and Impact of Church Policy on Sister Missionaries," *Dialogue: A Journal of Mormon Thought* 36, no. 3 (fall 2003): 71–101.

11. Robert K. Thomas, "Declaration of Dependence," *Ensign* (June 1976).

12. Rex Lee, "A Lawyer Whose Client Is the United States," *Ensign* (June 1976).

13. Mark Petersen, "Ezra Taft Benson: A Habit of Integrity," *Ensign* (October 1974); Ezra Taft Benson, "Our Divine Constitution," *Ensign* (September 1987).

14. "How J. Edgar Hoover Felt about TV's *The FBI*," *TV Guide*, May 20–26, 1972, pp. 28–30. On *The FBI* and the agency's performance of liberal democratic patriotism in the 1960s and 1970s, see William Keller, *The Liberals and J. Edgar Hoover: Rise and Fall of a Domestic Intelligence State* (Princeton, NJ: Princeton University Press, 1989), 72–111.

15. "Samuel P. Cowley: Unflinching Courage," *Ensign* (February 1974).

16. Michael McPheters, *Agent Bishop* (Provo, UT: Cedar Fort, 2009), x–xi.

17. On the relationship between the religious right more generally and the national security state, see Linda Klintz, "Culture and the Religious Right," in *Media, Culture, and the Religious Right*, ed. Linda Klintz (Minneapolis: University of Minnesota Press, 1998), 2–31; and Lisa McGirr, *Suburban Warriors: The Origins of the New American Right* (Princeton, NJ: Princeton University Press, 2003), 217–24. On the overwhelming political and social conservatism of twentieth-century Mormonism, see David E. Campbell, John C. Green, and Quin Monson, *Seeking the Promised Land: Mormons and American Politics* (New York: Cambridge University Press, 2015), 77–103; and Armand Mauss, *The Angel and the Beehive: The Mormon Struggle with Assimilation* (Urbana: University of Illinois Press, 1994), 46–60.

18. "Standing Guard," *Ensign* (July 1981).

19. "Saints in the Military," *Ensign* (February 1982).

20. Ezra Taft Benson, *Stand Up for Freedom* (Belmont, MA: American Opinion, 1966), n.p.

21. Ibid.

22. Robert Alan Goldberg, *Enemies Within: The Culture of Conspiracy in Modern America* (New Haven: Yale University Press, 2001), 1–22; Garry Wills, *A Necessary Evil: A History of American Distrust of Government* (New York: Touchstone, 1999), 15–23.

23. "I Have a Question," *Ensign* (June 1974).

24. For more on the critique of Mormons from outside the church, see Richard Bushman, *Joseph Smith: Rough Stone Rolling* (New York: Knopf, 2005), 350–60, which documents the Mormon confrontation with non-Mormon settlers in Missouri; Sarah Barringer Gordon, *The Mormon Question: Polygamy and Constitutional Conflict in Nineteenth-Century America* (Chapel Hill: University of North Carolina Press, 2001), 55–85; and Kathleen Flake, *The Politics of American Religious Identity: The Seating of Senator Reed Smoot, Mormon Apostle* (Chapel Hill: University of North Carolina Press, 2004), 34–46.

25. Josiah Strong, *Our Country* (New York: Baker & Taylor, 1891), 116, 112. For a discussion of these attacks, see Spencer Fluhman, *A Peculiar People: Mormonism and the Making of Religion in Nineteenth-Century America* (Chapel Hill: University of North Carolina Press, 2012), 79–103.

26. A useful discussion of *Big Love* can be found in John-Charles Duffy, "Mormonism and American Television," in *Mormons and Popular Culture: The Global Influence of an American Phenomenon*, ed. James Michael Hunter (Westport, CT: Praeger, 2013), 91–121.

27. See, for example, Ed Decker, *My Kingdom Come* (Issaquah, WA: Xulon Press, 2007), 363; Tricia Erickson, *Can Mitt Romney Serve Two Masters?* (Bloomington, IN: Thomas Nelson Press, 2011), 101; and Marcia van Outen,

The Mormon Contradiction (London: Author House, 2011), 317. For earlier examples of such exposés, see Jon Krakauer, *Under the Banner of Heaven: A Story of Violent Faith* (New York: Random House, 1999); Jerald and Sandra Tanner, *Mormonism: Shadow or Reality?* (Salt Lake City: Lighthouse, 1972); and Walter Martin, *The Maze of Mormonism* (Minneapolis: Bethany House, 1992). Discussion of such critiques may be found in J.B. Haws, *The Mormon Image in the American Mind: Fifty Years of Public Perception* (New York: Oxford University Press, 2013), 110–12.

28. Frances Lang, "The Mormon Empire," *Ramparts* (September 1971).

29. Anson Shupe, *The Darker Side of Virtue: Corruption, Scandal, and the Mormon Empire* (Buffalo, NY: Prometheus, 1991), 13.

30. Kathleen Parker, "A Nice Guy in a Season of Nastiness," *Washington Post,* November 10, 2011.

31. See, for instance, James Ellroy, *LA Confidential* (New York: Mysterious Press, 1991); and Peter Schmidt-Nowara, "Finding God in a World of Leg-Breakers and Racist Shitbirds: James Ellroy and the Contemporary LA Crime Novel," *Western American Literature* 36, no. 1 (2001): 117–31.

32. James Ellroy, *Blood's a Rover* (New York: Knopf, 2005), 16.

CHAPTER 12. THE FBI'S "CULT WAR" AGAINST THE BRANCH DAVIDIANS

Epigraph: Quoted in Jarvis DeBerry, "Police Should Expect Unruly Suspects—and Not Abuse Them," *New Orleans Times Picayune,* July 4, 2015, www.nola.com/crime/index.ssf/2015/07/video_nopd_brutality.html.

1. WACMUR Major Event Log, March 2, 1993, Lee Hancock Collection, Wittliff Collections, Texas State University, San Marcos (hereafter Lee Hancock Collection). See "A Guide to the Lee Hancock Collection," www.thewittliffcollections.txstate.edu/research/a-z/hancock.html (accessed August 4, 2015).

2. Gary Noesner, *Stalling for Time: My Life as an FBI Hostage Negotiator* (New York: Random House, 2010), 110.

3. Quoted in Catherine Wessinger, *How the Millennium Comes Violently: From Jonestown to Heaven's Gate* (New York: Seven Bridges, 2000), 273–74.

4. Douglas E. Cowan, "Constructing the New Religious Threat: Anticult and Countercult Movements," in *New Religious Movements: A Documentary Reader,* ed. Dereck Daschke and W. Michael Ashcraft (New York: New York University Press, 2005), 317–30.

5. James D. Tabor and Eugene V. Gallagher, *Why Waco? Cults and the Battle for Religious Freedom in America* (Berkeley: University of California Press, 1995).

6. John R. Hall, with Philip D. Schuyler and Sylvaine Trinh, *Apocalypse Observed: Religious Movements and Violence in North America, Europe, and Japan* (New York: Routledge, 2000), 16.

7. James T. Richardson, "Manufacturing Consent about Koresh: A Structural Analysis of the Role of the Media in the Waco Tragedy," in *Armageddon in Waco: Critical Perspectives on the Branch Davidian Conflict,* ed. Stuart A. Wright (Chicago: University of Chicago Press, 1995), 153–76; Catherine Wess-

inger, "The Branch Davidians and Religion Reporting: A Ten-Year Retrospective," in *Expecting the End: Millennialism in Social and Historical Perspective,* ed. Kenneth G.C. Newport and Crawford Gribben (Waco, TX: Baylor University Press, 2006), 147–72.

8. Stuart A. Wright, "Introduction: Another View of the Mount Carmel Standoff," in *Armageddon in Waco,* xiii–xxvi (quote on xv).

9. Stuart A. Wright, "Explaining Militarization at Waco: The Construction and Convergence of the Warfare Narrative," in *Controversial New Religions,* ed. James R. Lewis and Jesper Aagaard Petersen (New York: Oxford University Press, 2005), 79–97.

10. John C. Danforth, Special Counsel, "Final Report to the Deputy Attorney General, Concerning the 1993 Confrontation at the Mt. Carmel Complex, Waco, Texas," November 8, 2000, https://en.wikisource.org/wiki/Final_report_to_the_Deputy_Attorney_General_concerning_the_1993_confrontation_at_the_Mt._Carmel_Complex,_Waco_Texas (accessed July 19, 2016 hereafter cited as Danforth Final Report. For a critical analysis of the Danforth Final Report, see Jean E. Rosenfeld, "The Use of the Military at Waco: The Danforth Report in Context," *Nova Religio* 5, no. 1 (2001): 171–85. Kenneth G.C. Newport replicates the findings of the Danforth Final Report in *The Branch Davidians of Waco: The History and Beliefs of an Apocalyptic Sect* (Oxford: Oxford University Press, 2006). See the debate about the responsibility for the fire between Newport, Stuart A. Wright, and Catherine Wessinger in *Nova Religio* 13, no. 2 (2009).

11. United States Department of Justice, *Report to the Deputy Attorney General on the Events at Waco, Texas, February 28 to April 19, 1993,* Redacted Version, October 8 (Washington, DC: U.S. Government Printing Office, 1993), 138.

12. Ibid., 139–40; Stuart A. Wright, "Anatomy of a Government Massacre: Abuses of Hostage-Barricade Protocols during the Waco Standoff," *Terrorism and Political Violence* 11, no. 2 (1999): 39–68; Noesner, *Stalling for Time,* 94–132.

13. Wessinger, "Branch Davidians and Religion Reporting," 159–62.

14. "Guide to the Lee Hancock Collection."

15. See Catherine Wessinger, "Deaths in the Fire at the Branch Davidians' Mount Carmel: Who Bears Responsibility?" *Nova Religio* 13, no. 2 (November 2009): 25–60.

16. Eugene V. Gallagher, "The Davidian and Branch Davidian Seventh-day Adventists (1929–1981)," 2013, World Religions and Spirituality Project, http://wrldrels.org/profiles/BranchDavidians1.htm (accessed June 26, 2016); Tabor and Gallagher, *Why Waco?* 33–40.

17. For Branch Davidian theology, see Clive Doyle, with Catherine Wessinger and Matthew D. Wittmer, *A Journey to Waco: Autobiography of a Branch Davidian* (Lanham, MD: Rowman & Littlefield, 2012), 75–98.

18. Catherine Wessinger, "Branch Davidians (1981–2006)," World Religions and Spirituality Project, 2013, http://wrldrels.org/profiles/BranchDavidians.htm (accessed June 26, 2016); Bonnie Haldeman, *Memories of the Branch Davidians: The Autobiography of David Koresh's Mother,* ed. Catherine Wessinger (Waco: Baylor University Press, 2007).

19. With input from Clive Doyle, I have revised the list of residents published in Newport, *Branch Davidians of Waco,* 359–64.

20. Ibid., 193.

21. Eugene V. Gallagher, "'Theology Is Life and Death': David Koresh on Violence, Persecution, and the Millennium," in *Millennialism, Persecution, and Violence: Historical Cases,* ed. Catherine Wessinger (Syracuse: Syracuse University Press, 2000), 82–100.

22. See Doyle, with Wessinger and Wittmer, *Journey to Waco,* 83–91, 93–94, 95, 109.

23. Noesner, *Stalling for Time,* 122–24.

24. David B. Kopel and Paul H. Blackman, *No More Wacos: What's Wrong with Federal Law Enforcement and How to Fix It* (Amherst, NY: Prometheus Books, 1997), 131.

25. See Jess Walter, *Every Knee Shall Bow: The Truth and Tragedy of Ruby Ridge and the Randy Weaver Family* (New York: Harper, 1995).

26. Noesner, *Stalling for Time,* 106.

27. Ibid., 124.

28. Ibid., 127.

29. WACMUR Major Event Log, March 25–29, 1993.

30. Map of territory/jurisdiction, San Antonio Division, FBI, www.fbi.gov/sanantonio/contact-us/territory-jurisdiction (accessed August 8, 2015).

31. Sara Rimer, "From Hope to Ashes: F.B.I. Negotiator Looks Back," *New York Times,* April 29, 1993, www.nytimes.com/1993/04/29/us/from-hope-to-ashes-fbi-negotiator-looks-back.html (accessed June 28, 2016).

32. Noesner, *Stalling for Time,* 128.

33. David Johnston, "Director of F.B.I. Demotes Deputy," *New York Times,* July 15, 1995, www.nytimes.com/1995/07/15/us/director-of-fbi-demotes-deputy.html (accessed June 28, 2016).

34. "National News Briefs: Ex-F.B.I. Man Sentenced in Ruby Ridge Case," *New York Times,* October 11, 1997, www.nytimes.com/1997/10/11/us/national-news-briefs-ex-fbi-man-sentenced-in-ruby-ridge-case.html (accessed June 28, 2016).

35. Danny O. Coulson and Elaine Shannon, *No Heroes: Inside the FBI's Secret Counter-terror Force* (New York: Pocket Books, 1999); Kerry Noble, *Tabernacle of Hate: Why They Bombed Oklahoma City* (Prescott, Ontario: Voyageur, 1998).

36. Clint Van Zandt, with Daniel Paisner, *Facing Down Evil: Life on the Edge as an FBI Hostage Negotiator* (New York: G. P. Putnam's Sons, 2006), 73–129.

37. Committee of the Judiciary, United States Senate, *The Aftermath of Waco: Changes in Federal Law Enforcement,* October 31–November 1, 1995, Serial No. J-104-51 (Washington, DC: U.S. Government Printing Office, 1997), 176.

38. WACMUR Major Event Log, March 2, 1993, 17:22.

39. Ibid., March 20, 1993, 21:16.

40. Noesner, *Stalling for Time,* 126.

41. WACMUR Major Event Log, March 21, 1993, 23:18, 23:32, 23:33, 23:35, 23:36.

42. U.S. Department of Justice, *Report to the Deputy Attorney General,* 121.

43. David Johnston, "Defiant F.B.I. Chief Removed from Job by President," *New York Times,* July 20, 1993, www.nytimes.com/1993/07/20/us/defiant-fbi-chief-removed-from-job-by-the-president.html (accessed June 28, 2016); Ronald Kessler, *The Secrets of the FBI* (New York: Crown Archetype, 2011).

44. WACMUR Major Event Log, March 2, 1993, 5:25.

45. Lee Hancock and David Jackson, "Siege Plans Weighed by FBI Detailed," *Dallas Morning News,* October 9, 1999, available at Center for Studies on New Religions, www.cesnur.org/testi/waco35.htm (accessed June 28, 2016).

46. Nancy T. Ammerman, "Waco, Federal Law Enforcement, and Scholars of Religion," in *Armageddon in Waco,* 282–96; Ammerman, "Report to the Justice and Treasury Departments Regarding Law Enforcement Interaction with the Branch Davidians in Waco, Texas, September 3, 1993," available at Hartford Institute for Religion Research, http://hirr.hartsem.edu/bookshelf/ammerman_article1.html (accessed June 28, 2016).

47. See Smerick's bio at Academy Group, Inc., www.academy-group.com/smerick.html (accessed August 3, 2015); Peter Smerick testimony, in Committee of the Judiciary, *Aftermath of Waco,* 163.

48. Suzan E. DeBusk, "Interview of SSA Peter A. Smerick," August 24, 1993, memo marked CONFIDENTIAL, Lee Hancock Collection.

49. Ibid.

50. Lee Hancock, "FBI Misled Reno to Get Tear-Gas OK, Ex-agent Alleged," *Dallas Morning News,* March 6, 2000, available at Center for Studies on New Religions, www.cesnur.org/testi/waco59.htm (accessed June 28, 2016).

51. WACMUR Major Event Log, April 2, 1993, 19:52, 20:10.

52. Ibid., April 6, 1993, 18:02, 20:00; April 7, 1993, 2:00, 20:20.

53. Ibid., April 6, 1993, 15:30.

54. Danforth Final Report, 154.

55. WACMUR Major Event Log, April 9, 1993, 15:00, 15:05, 18:30.

56. Ibid., April 9, 1993, 19:03, 19:30.

57. Ibid., April 9, 1993, 19:30.

58. Ibid., April 14, 1993, 11:45, 12:50.

59. Ibid., April 14, 1993, 16:25, 17:15.

60. Ibid., April 14, 1993, 18:19, 18:45, 18:51, 18:52, 18:54.

61. Ibid., April 14, 1993, 18:45. See Letter of David Koresh, April 14, 1993, available at Letters of Note, www.lettersofnote.com/2011/04/we-are-standing-on-threshold-of-great.html (accessed June 28, 2016).

62. WACMUR Major Event Log, April 15, 1993, 14:25, 15:12, 16:05, 17:15.

63. Ibid., April 16, 1:15, 2:35, 3:00, 3:05, 3:07, 3:11, 14:00, 14:46. See my partial transcription of this conversation in Wessinger, *How the Millennium Comes Violently,* 105.

64. WACMUR Major Event Log, April 16, 2015, 14:59, 15:01, 15:04.

65. Ibid., April 18, 2015, 17:32, 18:15, 19:20, 19:28, 19:40.

66. Danforth Final Report, 143–44.

67. Ibid., 144–45.

68. Lee Hancock, "Memo Reveals FBI's Debate on Waco Plan," *Dallas Morning News,* February 28, 2000, available at Center for Studies on New Religions, www.cesnur.org/testi/waco57.htm.

69. Danforth Final Report, 145.

70. Ibid., 145–46.

71. Ibid., 146.

72. U.S. Department of Justice, *Report to the Deputy Attorney General,* 104, 256–59; Danforth Final Report, 146.

73. Danforth Final Report, 147–48.

74. Ibid., 148.

75. U.S. Department of Justice, *Report to the Deputy Attorney General,* 105–6.

76. "Delta Force: Missions and History," Military.com, www.military.com /special-operations/delta-force.html (accessed September 28, 2015).

77. See Salem's bio at BELLE: Biological Effects of Low Level Exposures, www.belleonline.com/bios/salem.htm (accessed August 9, 2015). Testimony of Janet Reno, in Joint Hearings before the Subcommittee on Crime of the Committee on the Judiciary, House of Representatives, and the Subcommittee on National Security, International Affairs, and Criminal Justice of the Committee on Government Reform and Oversight, *Activities of Federal Law Enforcement Agencies toward the Branch Davidians,* Parts 1–3 (Washington, DC: U.S. Government Printing Office, 1996), 3:354.

78. "Statement of Attorney General Janet Reno before the Committee on the Judiciary, House of Representatives," April 28, 1993, Department of Justice, www.justice.gov/archive/ag/speeches/1993/04-28-1993b.pdf (accessed June 28, 2016).

79. Department of Justice, *Report to the Deputy Attorney General,* 266–68; Danforth Final Report, 149–50; Rosenfeld, "Use of the Military at Waco," 180–81.

80. Testimony of Byron Sage, in Joint Hearings, *Activities of Federal Law Enforcement Agencies,* 3:345.

81. U.S. Department of Justice, *Report to the Deputy Attorney General,* 270–71; testimony of Byron Sage, 2:345.

In Sage's congressional testimony in 1995 he stated that the Justice Department report's account of his statements to Hubbell was overstated and that he "never abandoned the concept or the hope that negotiations could successfully and peacefully resolve this matter. . . . I felt that we were at an impasse, that we had not gotten a single child out, which again was our first priority, since the 5th of March." As far as Koresh's plan to exit after he composed his "little book," Sage said it was his recollection that Koresh proposed that plan after Sage spoke with Hubbell. Further, since Koresh had not demonstrated any progress in writing his little book, it was not a plan to be taken seriously.

82. Ibid., 2:507–8 (quotation on 508).

83. Testimony of Webster Hubbell, in Joint Hearings, *Activities of Federal Law Enforcement Agencies,* 3:39–40 (quotation on 39).

84. Kopel and Blackman, *No More Wacos,* 154.

85. Testimony of Jeffrey Jamar, in Joint Hearings, *Activities of Federal Law Enforcement Agencies,* 2:305–6.

86. U.S. Department of Justice, *Report to the Deputy Attorney General,* 107.

87. Danforth Final Report, 151.

88. WACMUR Major Event Log, April 16, 1993, 19:58.

89. Danforth Final Report, 152.

90. WACMUR Major Event Log, April 17, 1993, 7:30, 10:00, 12:00, 17:00, 19:00.

91. Park Dietz, M.D., Ph.D., to Jim Wright, re David Koresh/Waco Situation, Reno Briefing File, April 17, 1993 (p. 55 of the PDF in author's possession), Lee Hancock Collection (hereafter cited as Reno Briefing File).

92. Sam Howe Verhovek, "Death in Waco: The Overview," *New York Times,* April 20, 1993.

93. Reno Briefing File, 163–68.

94. Kopel and Blackman, *No More Wacos,* 156, 160.

95. Alan A. Stone, "Report and Recommendations concerning Handling of Incidents Such as the Branch Davidian Standoff in Waco, Texas," November 10, 1993, FindLaw, http://news.findlaw.com/cnn/docs/waco/stone_rpt.html (accessed June 28, 2016).

96. Reno Briefing File, 169–77.

97. [FBI], "Passover Analysis Addendum," April 18, 1993, p. 5, Lee Hancock Collection. Compare with Testimony of Joyce Sparks, in Joint Hearings, *Activities of Federal Law Enforcement Agencies,* 1:575–78.

98. [FBI], "Passover Analysis Addendum," 7.

99. [FBI], "Suicide Addendum," April 18, 1993, p. 3, Lee Hancock Collection.

100. Doyle, with Wessinger and Wittmer, *A Journey to Waco,* 140.

101. Noesner, *Stalling for Time,* 119–20.

102. Major Case 80, WACMUR, Updated Event Log, April 19, 1993, printed May 24, 1993, 1:25, Lee Hancock Collection.

103. Kopel and Blackman, *No More Wacos,* 194–95, 216n79.

104. Lee Hancock, "Man Who Sneaked into Compound Leaves," *Dallas Morning News,* April 18, 1993.

105. Kopel and Blackman, *No More Wacos,* 180n236.

106. Ibid., 155.

107. "Methylene Chloride," Canadian Centre for Occupational Health and Safety, www.ccohs.ca/oshanswers/chemicals/chem_profiles/methylene.html (accessed June 28, 2016).

108. Kopel and Blackman, *No More Wacos,* 158.

109. Ibid., 159.

110. Rex Applegate, "Unpublished Report on FBI Planning and Operations Relating to the CS Gas Assault at Waco, Texas, February 28 to April 19, 1993," Scottsburg, Oregon, 1995, 27, quoted in Kopel and Blackman, *No More Wacos,* 157.

111. Coulson and Shannon, *No Heroes,* 453.

112. Testimony of Jeffrey Jamar, 3:277.

113. Rosenfeld, "Use of the Military at Waco," 178

114. Lee Hancock, "FBI Cameras Encircled Compound, Files Show," *Dallas Morning News,* October 14, 1999. On the status of videos and audiotapes recorded in relation to the WACMUR case, see Matthew D. Wittmer, "Traces of the Mount Carmel Community: Documentation and Access," *Nova Religio* 13, no. 2 (November 2009): 95–113.

115. Testimony of Jeffrey Jamar, 3:277.

116. Wessinger, "Deaths in the Fire," 39–40; SA 73, no. 4, April 19, 1993, in Mark Swett Collection, Texas Collection, Baylor University, Waco, TX.

117. Graeme Craddock testimony, in Committee of the Judiciary, *Aftermath of Waco,* 171–72.

118. SA 73, no. 4, April 19, 1993, Wessinger, "Deaths in the Fire," 39–40.

119. U.S. Department of Justice, *Report to the Deputy Attorney General,* 245; Carol Moore, *The Davidian Massacre: Disturbing Questions about Waco Which Must Be Answered* (Franklin, TN, and Springfield, VA: Legacy Communications and Gun Owners Foundation, 1995), 343–45.

120. Hancock, "Ex-colonel Says FBI Heard Sect's Fire Plans," *Dallas Morning News,* October 8, 1999, available at Center for Studies on New Religions, www.cesnur.org/testi/waco34.htm.

121. Ibid. This audiotape is not in the Mark Swett Collection of FBI negotiation and surveillance device audiotapes.

122. David T. Hardy, with Rex Kimball, *This Is Not an Assault: Penetrating the Web of Official Lies Regarding the Waco Incident* (N.p.: Xlibris, 2001), 275–76, 285.

123. Ibid., 276.

124. Applegate, "Unpublished Report," 23, quoted in Kopel and Blackman, *No More Wacos,* 157.

125. Hancock, "Ex-colonel Says FBI Heard Sect's Fire Plans."

126. Wessinger, "Deaths in the Fire," 43; Oral and Videotaped Deposition of Graeme Craddock, October 28, 1999, *Isabel G. Andrade et al. v. Phillip J. Cojnacki et al.,* United States District Court for the Western District of Texas, Waco Division, No. W-96-CA-139, 201–5; Oral and Videotaped Deposition of Graeme Craddock, October 29, 1999, ibid., 254, 259–64, 405.

127. Hancock, "Ex-colonel Says FBI Heard Sect's Fire Plans."

128. Bob Ricks, Rotary Club Speech, August 25, 1993, transcript, lines 209–19, 269–73, Lee Hancock Collection.

129. Hardy, with Kimball, *This Is Not an Assault,* 321–22. Jamar testified at a congressional hearing that he held the trucks back so the firefighters would not be injured by gunfire coming from the Branch Davidians. Hardy points out that photographs and FLIR videotapes show that FBI agents were standing outside the tanks about ten yards away from the burning building with no apparent fear of being hit by gunfire.

130. David Koresh, "The Seven Seals of the Book of Revelation," reprinted in Tabor and Gallagher, *Why Waco?* 191–203.

131. Doyle, with Wessinger and Wittmer, *Journey to Waco,* 168–69; Jack DeVault, *The Waco Whitewash: The Mt. Carmel Episode Told by an Eyewitness to the Trial* (San Antonio: Rescue, 1994), 109–10.

132. Coulson and Shannon, *No Heroes,* 451–52 (quote on 452).

133. Ibid., 452.

134. Video footage shot by Channel 25 and captured as live satellite feed by Ken Fawcett, and kindly provided to the author by Ken Fawcett.

135. Dick J. Reavis, *The Ashes of Waco: An Investigation* (New York: Simon & Schuster, 1995), 277.

136. Photographs of the flags were displayed by Clive Doyle in the Visitor's Center at Mount Carmel Center from 2000 to 2006. Photographs can also be located on the Internet.

137. Marshall Ingwerson and Scott Pendleton, "Clinton Team Scrutinized after the Waco Tragedy," *Christian Science Monitor,* April 21, 1993, www.csmonitor.com/1993/0421/21011.html (accessed June 28, 2016).

138. Wright, "Explaining Militarization at Waco," 80.

139. Ibid. See Tabor and Gallagher, *Why Waco?*; and Phillip Lucas, "How Future Wacos Might Be Avoided: Two Proposals," in *From the Ashes: Making Sense of Waco,* ed. James R. Lewis (Lanham, MD: Rowman & Littlefield, 1994), 209–12.

140. Jerome H. Skolnick and James J. Fyfe, *Above the Law: Police and the Excessive Use of Force* (New York: Free Press, 1993), 90.

141. Wright, "Anatomy of a Government Massacre," 59.

142. Testimony of Richard V. Lanning, in Committee of the Judiciary, *Aftermath of Waco,* 120. See Lanning's bio at Academy Group, Inc., www.academy-group.com/lanning.html (accessed March 25, 2016).

143. Testimony of Richard V. Lanning, 120–21.

144. Testimony of Frank A. Bolz, in Committee of the Judiciary, *Aftermath of Waco,* 118, 122–23, 132, 134, 135.

145. Testimony of James J. Fyfe, in Committee of the Judiciary, *Aftermath of Waco,* 9, 13, 18.

146. Ibid., 18.

147. Wright, "Anatomy of a Government Massacre," 62.

148. See Dan Gifford, William Gazecki, and Michael McNulty, producers, *Waco: The Rules of Engagement* (Los Angeles: Fifth Estate Productions, 1997).

149. Noesner, *Stalling for Time,* 148–76; Wessinger, *How the Millennium Comes Violently,* 158–217.

150. Wessinger, "Deaths in the Fire."

151. Stuart A. Wright, "Revisiting the Branch Davidian Mass Suicide Debate," *Nova Religio* 13, no. 2 (November 2009): 15, 21n6.

152. Doyle, with Wessinger and Wittmer, *Journey to Waco,* 169–73.

153. Lee Hancock, "2 Pyrotechnic Devices Fired at Davidians, Ex-Official Says," *Dallas Morning News,* August 24, 1999.

154. Ralph Ellis, Holly Yan, and Sara Sidner, "Leader of Armed Protesters in Oregon Took Out $530,000 Federal Loan, *CNN,* January 6, 2016, www.cnn.com/2016/01/05/us/oregon-wildlife-refuge-armed-protest (accessed June 28, 2016).

CHAPTER 13. THE FBI AND AMERICAN MUSLIMS AFTER SEPTEMBER 11

1. Michael Barkun, "*Project Megiddo,* the FBI and the Academic Community," in *Millennial Violence: Past, Present and Future,* ed. Jeffrey Kaplan (Portland, OR: Frank Cass, 2002), 97–108.

2. Tom W. Smith, "Estimating the Muslim Population in the United States," American Jewish Committee, 2001, http://www.ajc.org/site/apps/nlnet/content3.aspx?c=70JILSPwFfJSG&b=8451903&ct=12481869 (accessed July 2, 2016). Ghulam M. Haniff, "The Muslim Community in America: A Brief Profile," *Journal of Muslim Minority Affairs* 23 (June 2010): 303–11.

3. Pew Research Center, "Muslim Americans: No Signs of Growth in Alienation or Support for Extremism," August 30, 2011, http://www.people-press.org/2011/08/30/section-1-a-demographic-portrait-of-muslim-americans (accessed December 5, 2014).

4. Haniff, "Muslim Community"; Pew Research Center, "Muslim Americans."

5. Haniff, "Muslim Community."

6. Ibid.

7. Office of the Inspector General, U.S. Department of Justice, "The Federal Bureau of Investigation's Compliance with the Attorney General's Investigative Guidelines," September 2005, pp. 32–34, https://oig.justice.gov/special/0509/final.pdf (accessed July 2, 2016).

8. Ibid., ch. 2.

9. John Ashcroft, "Remarks of Attorney General John Ashcroft: Attorney General Guidelines," U.S. Department of Justice, May 30, 2002, http://www.justice.gov/archive/ag/speeches/2002/53002agpreparedremarks.htm (accessed December 5, 2014).

10. Ibid.

11. Ibid.

12. Allison Jones, "The 2008 FBI Guidelines: Contradiction of Original Purpose," *Public Interest Law Journal* 19 (2009): 137–74.

13. "The Attorney General's Guidelines for Domestic FBI Operations," II.C., p. 23 (October 15, 2011), http://www.justice.gov/sites/default/files/ag/legacy/2008/10/03/guidelines.pdf (accessed July 2, 2016).

14. Office of the Inspector General, "Federal Bureau of Investigation's Compliance," 292.

15. Federal Bureau of Investigation, "FBI Response to Allegations of Mosque Surveillance and Monitoring of the Muslim Community," May 30, 2008, https://www.fbi.gov/news/pressrel/press-releases/fbi-response-to-allegations-of-mosque-surveillance-and-monitoring-of-the-muslim-community (accessed February 4, 2015).

16. Eric Lichtblau, "F.B.I. Tells Offices to Count Local Muslims and Mosques," *New York Times,* January 28, 2003, http://www.nytimes.com/2003/01/28/politics/28MOSQ.html (accessed February 4, 2015).

17. Mary Beth Sheridan, "U.S. Says It Didn't Target Muslims," *Washington Post,* December 29, 2005, B01.

18. Jerry Markon, "Tension Grows between Calif. Muslims, FBI after Informant Infiltrates Mosque," *Washington Post,* December 5, 2010, http://www.washingtonpost.com/wp-dyn/content/article/2010/12/04/AR2010120403710.html (accessed April 9, 2015); Nick Schou, "The FBI, the Islamic Center of Irvine and Craig Monteilh: Who Was Conning Whom?" *Orange County Weekly,* April 30, 2009, http://www.ocweekly.com/content/printVersion/411452/ (accessed February 11, 2015).

19. The narrative of the incident appears in documents connected with the case of *Yassir Fazaga et al., Plaintiffs v. Federal Bureau of Investigation et al., Defendants* in the United States District Court for the Central District of California, Case No. SA CV 11-0030-CJC (VBKx). Of particular interest are "Declarations of Craig Monteilh Submitted by Plaintiffs in Support of Their Oppositions to Motions to Dismiss" and the First Amended Complaint Class Action. The latter is dated September 13, 2011, the former January 30, 2012.

20. "Declaration of Eric H. Holder Attorney General of the United States," in *Fazaga v. Federal Bureau of Investigation,* July 29, 2011.

21. http://www.youtube.com/watch?v=P_4C9REWXbg (accessed December 10, 2015). Case no. 12-56867.

22. "ACLU Eye on the FBI," March 27, 2012, American Civil Liberties Union, https//www.aclu.org/files/assets/aclu_eye_on_the_-_mosque_outreach_03272012_0_0.pdf (accessed July 2, 2016); "FOIA Documents," Asian Law Caucus, http://asianlawcaucus.org/foia-documents (accessed April 1, 2015).

23. Azmat Khan, "Docs Reveal FBI Used Muslim Outreach as Guise to Collect Intel," *Frontline,* March 28, 2012, http://www.pbs.org/wgbh/pages/frontline/foreign-affairs-defense/are-we-safer/docs-reveal-fbi-used-muslim-outreach-as-guise-to-collect-intel (accessed April 28, 2015).

24. Juliet Eilperin, "Trying to Counter Extremism at Home, U.S. Faces a Risk: Sowing More Mistrust," *Washington Post,* February 16, 2014, https://www.washingtonpost.com/politics/trying-to-counter-extremism-at-home-us-faces-a-risk-sowing-more-mistrust/2015/02/16/43f742d8-b58b-11e4-aa05-1ce812b3fdd2_story.html (accessed February 17, 2015); Tamara Audi, "U.S. Muslim Community Divided over White House Outreach Plan," *Wall Street Journal,* April 20, 2015, http://www.wsj.com/articles/u-s-muslim-community-divided-over-white-house-outreach-plan (accessed April 28, 2015).

25. "Documents Obtained by Judicial Watch Reveal FBI Training Curricula Purged of Material Deemed 'Offensive' to Muslims," Judicial Watch, June 3, 2013, http://www.judicialwatch.org/press-room/press-releases/documents-obtained-by-judicial-watch-reveal-fbi-training-curricula-purged-of-material-deemed-offensive-to-muslims (accessed June 1, 2015).

26. Erica Goode, "F.B.I. Chided for Training That Was Critical of Islam," *New York Times,* September 16, 2011, http://www.nytimes.com/2011/09/17/us/fbi-chided-for-training-that-was-critical-of-islam.html (accessed June 1, 2015).

27. John Cook, "Civil Rights Organizations Demand Answers from White House on Surveillance of Muslim Leaders," *The Intercept,* July 9, 2014, http://firstlook.org/theintercept/2014/07/09/civil-rights-organizations-demand-answers-white-house-surveillance-muslim-leaders (accessed July 10, 2014).

28. William Finnegan, "Last Days: Preparing for the Apocalypse in San Bernardino," *New Yorker* (February 22, 2016), 50–59.

29. "Everything We Know about the San Bernardino Terror Attack Investigation So Far," *Los Angeles Times,* December 14, 2015, http://www.latimes.com/local/california/la-me-san-bernardino-shooting-terror-attack-investigation-htmlstory.html (accessed March 3, 2016); Finnegan, "Last Days."

30. Finnegan, "Last Days."

31. "FBI Will Investigate San Bernardino Shootings as Terrorist Act," Federal Bureau of Investigation, https://www.fbi.gov/news/news_blog/fbi-will-investigate-san-bernardino-shootings-as-terrorist-act (accessed March 8, 2016).

32. Doug Smith, "Federal Agents Investigating Possible Terrorism Link in San Bernardino Mass Shooting," *Los Angeles Times,* December 3, 2015, http://www.latimes.com/local/lanow/la-me-ln-fbi-probe-terror-link-san-bernardino-shooting (accessed March 8, 2016).

33. "American Muslims on San Bernardino Attack," December 11, 2015, Wilson Center, https://www.wilsoncenter.org/article/american-muslims-san-bernardino-attack (accessed March 3, 2016).

CHAPTER 14. POLICING KASHMIRI BROOKLYN

1. Ghulam Nabi Fai, interview with the author, Fairfax, VA, June 28, 2014.

2. See Junaid Rana, "The Desperate U.S.-Pakistan Alliance," in *Dispatches from Pakistan,* ed. Qalandar Memon, Vijay Prashad, and Madiha Tahir (New Delhi: LeftWord Books, 2012; reprinted, Minneapolis: University of Minnesota Press, 2014).

3. Panjak Mishra, "Introduction," in *Kashmir: The Case for Freedom,* ed. Tariq Ali (New York: Verso Books, 2011), 1.

4. See the related argument I make in Junaid Rana, *Terrifying Muslims: Race and Labor in the South Asian Diaspora* (Durham, NC: Duke University Press, 2011).

5. Steven Salaita, *Anti-Arab Racism in the USA: Where It Comes From and What It Means for Politics Today* (London: Pluto, 2006).

6. See, in particular, Edward W. Said's two classics—*Orientalism* (New York: Vintage, 1978) and *Culture and Imperialism* (New York: Vintage, 1993)—but also his dated yet entirely relevant *Covering Islam: How the Media and the Experts Determine How We See the Rest of the World* (New York: Pantheon, 1981).

7. For the policy implications, see Stephen Sheehi, *Islamophobia: The Ideological Campaign against Muslims* (Atlanta, GA: Clarity, 2011); and Nathan Chapman Lean, *The Islamophobia Industry: How the Right Manufactures Fear of Muslims* (New York: Pluto, 2012).

8. Sherene Razack, *Casting Out: The Eviction of Muslims from Western Law and Politics* (Toronto: University of Toronto Press, 2007); Moustafa Bayoumi, *This Muslim American Life: Dispatches from the War on Terror* (New York: New York University Press, 2015).

9. I elaborate this point in my short essay "Terror," in *Keywords for American Cultural Studies,* ed. Bruce Burgett and Glenn Hendler (New York: New York University Press, 2014).

10. Ibid.

11. Trevor Aaronson, *The Terror Factory: Inside the FBI's Manufactured War on Terrorism* (Brooklyn: Ig, 2013).

12. FBI Affidavit, Agent Sarah Linden, July 18, 2011, pp. 37–39, *ProPublica*, https://www.propublica.org/documents/item/253434-kac-affidavit#document/p38/a33909 (accessed July 4, 2016).

13. For example, see the Demographics Unit of the NYPD files collected by the Associated Press, in "Highlights of AP's Pulitzer Prize–Winning Probe into NYPD Intelligence Operations," *AP*, http://www.ap.org/media-center/nypd/investigation (accessed July 4, 2016).

14. Jerry Seper, "FBI Arrest Points to Pakistan Influence-Peddling Scheme," *Washington Times*, July 19, 2011, http://www.washingtontimes.com/news/2011/jul/19/fbi-arrests-man-as-agent-of-pakistan/ (accessed July 4, 2016). Seper writes: "Some of the charges of Pakistani support for terrorism center on the ISI and Lashkar-e-Taiba, an officially banned jihad group that launches terrorist attacks against India over the Kashmir dispute. The terrorist group planned and executed from Pakistan, reportedly with aid from the ISI, the 2008 Mumbai attacks that killed more than 160 people." Ibid.

15. "'The ISI probably told him: "Don't worry, you're taken care of, you're part of the tacit agreement we have with the CIA,"' said Vijay Sazawal, who is from the Indian side of Kashmir and started a rival Kashmiri group in the United States. 'He's not stupid. I have to believe he was confident he was shielded.'" Kim Barker, Habiba Nosheen, and Raheel Khursheed, "The Man behind Pakistan Spy Agency's Plot to Influence Washington," *ProPublica*, October 3, 2011, http://www.propublica.org/article/the-man-behind-pakistani-spy-agencys-plot-to-influence-washington (accessed July 4, 2016).

16. Kim Barker, Sebastian Rotella, and Marian Wang, "In an Unusual Criminal Case, the U.S. Points the Finger at Pakistan's Top Spy Agency Again," *ProPublica*, July 19, 2011, http://www.propublica.org/article/in-an-unusual-criminal-case-the-u.s.-points-the-finger-at-pakistans-top-spy (accessed July 4, 2016).

17. Habiba Nosheen and Kim Barker, "Man Accused in Pakistani Spy Plot Dies," *ProPublica*, October 7, 2011, http://www.propublica.org/article/man-accused-in-pakistani-spy-plot-dies (accessed July 4, 2016).

18. For the Statement of Facts document to which Fai pled guilty, see "FAI's Statement of Facts," *ProPublica*, https://www.propublica.org/documents/item/fais-statement-of-facts (accessed July 4, 2016).

19. On this FBI model, see Aaronson, *Terror Factory*.

20. On the broad reach of the NYPD Demographics Unit, see Matt Apuzzo and Adam Goldman, *Enemies Within: Inside the NYPD's Secret Spying Unit and Bin Laden's Final Plot against America* (New York: Simon & Schuster, 2013).

CHAPTER 15. ALLIES AGAINST ARMAGEDDON? THE FBI AND THE ACADEMIC STUDY OF RELIGION

1. My information about Phillip Arnold's experiences comes from Nike Carstarphan, "Third Party Efforts at Waco: Phillip Arnold and James Tabor"

(1995), an unpublished manuscript that draws on interviews with Arnold. I thank Dr. Carstarphan for sharing her work with me.

2. Nancy Ammerman, "Report to the Justice and Treasury Departments Regarding Law Enforcement Interaction with the Branch Davidians in Waco, Texas," in *Recommendations for Improvements in Federal Law Enforcement after Waco* (Washington, DC: U.S. Government Printing Office, 1993), 288.

3. Castarphan, "Third Party Efforts at Waco," 18.

4. James Tabor and Eugene Gallagher, *Why Waco? Cults and the Battle for Religious Freedom in America* (Berkeley: University of California Press, 1995), 191–203.

5. Ammerman, "Report to the Justice and Treasury Departments"; see also Ammerman, "Waco, Federal Law Enforcement, and Scholars of Religion," in *Armageddon in Waco: Critical Perspectives on the Branch Davidian Conflict,* ed. Stuart A. Wright (Chicago: University of Chicago Press, 1995), 282–98.

6. Lawrence Sullivan, *Recommendations to the US Departments of Justice and the Treasury Concerning Incidents Such as the Branch Davidian Standoff in Waco, Texas* (Washington, DC: U.S. Department of Justice, 1993).

7. Philip Heyman, *Lessons of Waco: Proposed Changes in Federal Law Enforcement* (Washington, DC: U.S. Department of Justice, 1993), 11.

8. Michael Barkun, "Project Megiddo, the FBI, and the Academic Community," in *Millennial Violence: Past, Present, and Future,* ed. Jeffrey Kaplan (London: Taylor & Francis, 2002), 102.

9. Jean Rosenfeld, "The Importance of the Analyses of Religion in Avoiding Violent Outcomes: The Justus Freeman Crisis," *Nova Religio* 1 (1997): 72–95, reprinted in revised form in *Millennialism, Persecution, and Violence: Historical Cases,* ed. Catherine Wessinger (Syracuse, NY: Syracuse University Press, 2000), 323–44; Catherine Wessinger, "Religious Studies Scholars, FBI Agents, and the Montana Freemen Standoff," *Nova Religio* 3 (1999): 36–44.

10. Rosenfeld, "Importance of the Analyses of Religion," 85; Wessinger, "Religious Studies Scholars," 41.

11. Barkun, "Project Megiddo"; Eugene Gallagher, "Questioning the Frame: The Canadian, Israeli, and U.S. Reports," in *Millennial Violence,* 109–22.

12. Barkun, "Project Megiddo," 104.

13. Ibid., 103. Herrick attended this conference, held under the auspices of the Center for Millennial Studies at Boston University, and remembers the scholarly response to have been a mixture of appreciation and critique. In a personal communication, Barkun recalls that the conversation was "spirited" and that they raked their FBI interlocutors over the coals.

14. Jayne Seminare Docherty, "Bridging the Gap between Scholars of Religion and Law Enforcement Negotiators," *Nova Religio* 3 (1999): 8–26; Docherty, *Learning Lessons from Waco: When the Parties Bring Their Gods to the Table* (Syracuse, NY: Syracuse University Press, 2001); Barkun, "Project Megiddo."

15. Michael Barkun, e-mail correspondence with the author, March 23, 2011.

16. Dina Temple-Raston, "How Did Anti-Muslim Bias Seep into FBI Training?" *Morning Edition,* National Public Radio, September 29, 2011, www.npr

.org/2011/09/29/140902739/units-autonomy-may-be-why-fbi-missed-bias (accessed July 4, 2016).

17. Amir Hussain exemplifies the concern this caused scholars of Islam in "Thoughts on Being a Scholar of Islam and a Muslim in America Post-9/11," in *Religion, Terror, and Violence: Religious Studies Perspectives,* ed. Bryan Rennie and Philip Tite (New York: Routledge, 2008), 227–42.

18. For more on the AAR's lawsuit against the Department of Homeland Security, see court documents at IPT: The Investigative Project on Terrorism, http://www.investigativeproject.org/documents/case_docs/246.pdf (accessed July 11, 2011).

19. Joel Beinen, "The New McCarthyism: Policing Thought about the Middle East," in *Academic Freedom after September 11,* ed. Beshara Doumani (New York: Zone, 2006), 237–66; cf. Mike Keen, *Stalking Sociologists: J. Edgar Hoover's FBI Surveillance of American Sociology* (Westport, CT: Greenwood, 1999); and David Price, *Threatening Anthropology: McCarthyism and the FBI's Surveillance of Activist Anthropologists* (Durham, NC: Duke University Press, 2004).

20. See Inform's website at www.inform.ac.

21. Jonathan Z. Smith, "The Devil in Mr. Jones," in *Imagining Religion: From Babylon to Jonestown* (Chicago: Chicago University Press, 1982), 102–20.

22. Ibid., 105.

23. Docherty, "Bridging the Gap."

24. Talal Asad, "The Concept of Cultural Translation in British Social Anthropology," in *Writing Culture: The Poetics and Politics of Ethnography,* ed. James Clifford and George Marcus (Berkeley: University of California Press, 1986), 141–64.

25. Ibid., 163.

26. Tabor and Gallagher, *Why Waco?* 168–69.

27. Ibid., 203.

28. Christopher Eisenhart, "The Humanist as Public Expert," *Written Communication* 23 (2006): 150–72.

29. Darryl G. Hart, *The University Gets Religion: Religious Studies in American Higher Education* (Baltimore: Johns Hopkins University Press, 1999).

30. Michael Stausberg, "Advocacy in the Study of Religion/s," *Religion* 44 (2014): 220–32.

31. For examples of religious studies scholars promoting advocacy, see "Advocacy in the Study of Religion," special issue, *Religion* 44, no. 2 (2014).

32. Ian Reader, "Scholarship, Aum Shinrikyo, and Integrity," *Novo Religio* 3 (2000): 368–82.

33. Lawrence Sullivan, "'No Longer the Messiah': US Federal Law Enforcement Views of Religion in Connection with the 1993 Siege of Mount Carmel near Waco, Texas," *Numen* 43 (1996): 219–20.

34. Stuart Wright, "Reframing Religious Violence after 9/11: The ACM Campaign to Exploit the Threat of Terrorism," *Nova Religio* 12 (2009): 5–27.

35. Spencer Ackerman and Noah Shachtman, "Video: FBI Trainer Says Forget 'Irrelevant' Al-Qaida; Target Islam," *Wired,* September 20, 2011, http://

www.wired.com/dangerroom/2011/09/fbi-islam-qaida-irrelevant (accessed July 5, 2016).

36. This information comes from Director Comey's remarks at the U.S. Holocaust Memorial Museum's national tribute dinner on April 15, 2015. For a video of his address, see "FBI Director James Comey's Remarks at 2015 National Tribute Dinner," YouTube, posted by the United States Holocaust Memorial Museum, April 22, 2015, https://www.youtube.com/watch?v=wfCQvPoszKk (accessed May 14, 2015).

Contributors

MICHAEL BARKUN is Professor Emeritus of Political Science in the Maxwell School of Syracuse University and the author of *A Culture of Conspiracy: Apocalyptic Visions in Contemporary America* (2003).

MATTHEW BOWMAN is Associate Professor of History at Henderson State University, Arkadelphia, Arkansas, and the author, most recently, of *The Urban Pulpit: New York City and the Fate of Liberal Evangelicalism* (2014).

DOUGLAS M. CHARLES is Associate Professor of History at Penn State University's Greater Allegheny campus near Pittsburgh and has most recently authored *Hoover's War on Gays: Exposing the FBI's "Sex Deviates" Program* (2015).

KARL EVANZZ is the author of five books, including the highly acclaimed *The Judas Factor: The Plot to Kill Malcolm X* (1992) and *The Messenger: The Rise and Fall of Elijah Muhammad* (1999).

KATHRYN GIN LUM, Assistant Professor of Religious Studies at Stanford University, is the author of *Damned Nation: Hell in America from the Revolution to Reconstruction* (2014) and coeditor of the forthcoming *Oxford Handbook of Religion and Race in American History.*

SARAH IMHOFF is Assistant Professor in the Religious Studies Department and the Robert S. Borns Jewish Studies program at Indiana University, Bloomington, and is completing a book manuscript titled "Masculinity and the Making of American Judaism."

SYLVESTER A. JOHNSON is Associate Professor of African American Studies and Religious Studies at Northwestern University, author of *African American Religions, 1500–2000: Colonialism, Democracy, and Freedom* (2015), and coeditor of the *Journal of Africana Religions.*

DIANNE KIRBY is Research Fellow at Queen's University Belfast and a pioneering scholar in the religious dimension of the Cold War.

THEODORE KORNWEIBEL JR. is Professor Emeritus of Africana Studies at San Diego State University and has authored a memoir and five volumes of African American history, including the prize-winning *Railroads in the African American Experience* (2011).

LERONE A. MARTIN is Assistant Professor of Religion and Politics at the John C. Danforth Center on Religion and Politics at Washington University in St. Louis and author of *Preaching on Wax: The Phonograph and the Shaping of Modern African American Religion* (2014).

MICHAEL J. McVICAR is Assistant Professor in the Department of Religion at Florida State University, Tallahassee, and is writing a book on the subject of the FBI's engagement with conservative evangelical groups.

JUNAID RANA is Associate Professor of Asian American Studies at the University of Illinois at Urbana-Champaign and author of the award-winning *Terrifying Muslims: Race and Labor in the South Asian Diaspora* (2011).

REGIN SCHMIDT is Associate Professor in American history at the University of Copenhagen, Denmark, and is the author of *Red Scare: FBI and the Origins of Anticommunism in the United States, 1919–1943* (2000).

STEVEN WEITZMAN serves as the Abraham M. Ellis Professor of Hebrew and Semitic Languages and Literature in the Department of Religious Studies at the University of Pennsylvania and as the Ella Darivoff Director of the Herbert D. Katz Center for Advanced Judaic Studies.

CATHERINE WESSINGER is the Rev. H. James Yamauchi, S.J., Professor of the History of Religions at Loyola University-New Orleans, author of *How the Millennium Comes Violently: From Jonestown to Heaven's Gate* (2000), and coeditor of *Nova Religio: The Journal of Alternative and Emergent Religions.*

Index

Note: Italic page numbers indicate illustrations.